SPRINGER SERIES
IN PERCEPTION ENGINEERING

Series Editor: Ramesh Jain

Springer Series
in Perception Engineering

Ramesh C. Jain   Anil K. Jain
Editors

Analysis and Interpretation of Range Images

With 161 Illustrations

Springer-Verlag
New York Berlin Heidelberg
London Paris Tokyo Hong Kong

Ramesh C. Jain
Electrical Engineering and
    Computer Science Department
University of Michigan
Ann Arbor, MI 48109
USA

Anil K. Jain
Department of Computer Science
Michigan State University
East Lansing, MI 48824
USA

Series Editor

Ramesh C. Jain
Electrical Engineering and
    Computer Science Department
University of Michigan
Ann Arbor, MI 48109
USA

Printed on acid-free paper.

Camera-ready copy provided by the authors using LaTeX.

9 8 7 6 5 4 3 2 1
ISBN-13: 978-1-4612-7980-8   e-ISBN-13: 978-1-4612-3360-2
DOI: 10.1007/978-1-4612-3360-2

Preface

Most of the machine perception research has concentrated on using digitized intensity images as sensor data. Automatic analysis and interpretation of intensity images for complex tasks, such as navigation and 3D object recognition has proven to be extraordinarily difficult. One important problem is that digitized intensity images, which are rectangular arrays of numbers which indicate the *brightness* at individual points on a regularly spaced grid, contain no *explicit* information that is directly usable in *depth perception*. In recent years digitized range data has become available from both active and passive sensors, and the quality of this data has been steadily improving. Many tasks for machine vision systems will be significantly simplified by the use of range images. The last few years have seen growing interest in the application of range images in industrial applications. It is expected that the vision systems based on range images will be very useful in autonomous navigation systems also.

Considering the growing interest in range image understanding, a Workshop on this topic was held on the campus of Michigan State University, East Lansing, March 21-23, 1989, supported by the National Science Foundation under the grant number IRI-8713775. The aim of this Workshop was to bring together a small number of active researchers in range image understanding to discuss emerging themes in this field which may play a key role in automation. The participants were selected from academic institutions, research centers, and industry.

This book is the result of that workshop. It includes coverage of major topics related to the theme of the Workshop and the final report of the Workshop submitted to the NSF. The overview chapters are written by well-known researchers and give a good idea of the current state-of-the-art in acquisition, processing, interpretation, and application of range imagery. The Workshop report is the result of intensive group discussions and represents the consensus among the participants.

We believe that this book will be of interest to computer vision researchers and practitioners who are interested in the use of range data to solve inspection, object recognition, or navigation problems.

We are thankful to the participants of the Workshop. They contributed their valuable time and expertise to make the Workshop lively and successful. The authors of the chapters in this book and leaders of the discussion groups at the Workshop have spent considerable amount of time to complete their contributions. They had to revise their contributions to satisfy our reviewers who carefully read each contribution for exposition and clarity. Alice Furomoto-Dawson and Cathy Davison helped in the organization of the workshop. National Science Foundation provided funds to support the Workshop. Their support and the encouragement of Dr. Y.T. Chien is gratefully acknowledged. Finally, Kurt Skifstad spent long hours to type and retype the chapters to bring them to a uniform style and format. His contribution is a major factor in the timely completion of this book. Thanks, Kurt.

Ann Arbor, Michigan

Ramesh Jain
Anil K. Jain

Contributors

J. K. Aggarwal The University of Texas at Austin.

Ruzena Bajcsy University of Pennsylvania.

Paul J. Besl General Motors Research Laboratory.

N. R. Corby General Electric Company.

Alok Gupta University of Pennsylvania.

Martial Hebert Carnegie Mellon University.

Anil K. Jain Michigan State University.

Ramesh Jain The University of Michigan.

A. C. Kak Purdue University.

Takeo Kanade Carnegie Mellon University.

InSo Kweon Carnegie Mellon University.

J. L. Mundy General Electric Company.

N. Nandhakumar The University of Texas at Austin.

Franc Solina University of Pennsylvania.

George Stockman Michigan State University.

S. Tanaka Purdue University.

Contents

1

Report: 1988 NSF Range Image Understanding Workshop

Ramesh Jain[1]
Anil K. Jain[2]

1.1 Introduction

Most computer vision research has concentrated on using digitized gray-scale intensity images as sensor data. It has proven to be extraordinarily difficult to program computers to understand and describe these images in a *general purpose* way. One important problem is that digitized intensity images are rectangular arrays of numbers which indicate the *brightness* at individual points on a regularly spaced rectangular grid and contain no *explicit* information that is directly usable in *depth perception*. Yet human beings are able to correctly infer depth relationships quickly and easily among intensity image regions whereas automatic inference of such depth relationships has proven to be remarkably complex. In fact, many famous visual illusions, such as Kanizsa's triangle, vividly demonstrate that humans impose 3-D surface structure on images to interpret them. Computer vision researchers recognized the importance of surfaces in the understanding of images. The popularity of *shape from ...* approaches in the last decade is the result of this recognition.

In recent years digitized range data has become available from both active and passive sensors, and the quality of this data has been steadily improving. Range data is usually produced in the form of a rectangular array of numbers, referred to as a *depth map or range image*, where the numbers quantify the distances from the sensor plane to the surfaces within the field of view along the rays emanating from a regularly spaced rectangular grid. Not only are depth relationships between depth map regions explicit, but the three-dimensional *shape* of depth map regions approximates the

[1] Artificial Intelligence Laboratory, Electrical Engineering and Computer Science Department,The University of Michigan, Ann Arbor, Michigan 48109-2122. NSF Grant No. IRI-8713775

[2] Computer Science Department,Michigan State University, East Lansing, Michigan

three-dimensional shape of the corresponding object *surfaces* in the field of view. Therefore, the process of recognizing objects by their shape *should* be less difficult in depth maps than in intensity images due to the explicitness of the information. For example, since correct depth map information depends only on geometry and is independent of illumination and reflectivity, intensity image problems with shadows and surface markings do not occur. Nonetheless, it seems that existing vision techniques have influenced many investigators and this has led to restricted approaches to processing range data. The range image understanding problem is a well-posed problem as contrasted with the ill-posed intensity image understanding problem.

Many tasks for machine vision systems will be significantly simplified by range images. The last few years have seen growing interest in the application of the range images in industrial applications. It is expected that the vision systems based on range images will be very useful in autonomous navigation systems also.

Considering the growing interest in range image understanding, NSF funded our proposal to organize a workshop on this topic. The aim of the workshop was to bring together active researchers in range image understanding to discuss emerging themes in this field that may play a key role in automation. In addition to the researchers in range image understanding, we invited a few researchers interested in designing range sensors also. The participants were drawn from academic institutions, research centers, and industry. The aim of the workshop was to identify major research areas that should be addressed by researchers for making range image understanding systems useful in industrial and other applications.

Format of the Workshop

The workshop was for 2.5 days. The emphasis in this workshop was on group discussions. The workshop began with seven overview talks, one on general range image understanding by Ruzena Bajcsy and one on each of six major areas in range image understanding and its applications that are active:

- Early processing (Paul Besl)

- Object recognition (Robert Bolles)

- Sensor integration (Jake Aggarwal)

- Navigation (Takeo Kanade)

- Inspection (Joe Mundy)

- Range sensors (Avi Kak)

These talks were expected to set the tone for the discussions at the workshop.

The second day of the workshop was devoted to group meetings. The research issues were divided into three classes:

- Short term research and development work that may result in applications in the next 3-5 years.

- Long term research issues that may result in applications in 5-10 years.

- High risk areas.

The purpose of the group discussions was to make recommendations for the research in the specific areas.

The recommendations were presented by group leaders on the third day in the general meeting. Consensus recommendations were formed during that discussion. These recommendations are presented in the following sections.

The list of participants of the workshops, different groups, overview speakers, and group leaders is given in the Appendix.

1.2 Issues in Sensing and Sensors

Nelson Corby, GE
Kevin Harding, ITI
Avi Kak, Purdue
Robert Sampson, ERIM
George Stockman (Chair), MSU

1.2.1 GENERAL BACKGROUND

Sensors connect intelligent processes, whether in man or machine, to the external 3D world. Engineering approaches have separated sensor design from the design of the overall intelligent system. In some well-specified applications such design has led to successful systems. Techniques are getting better and cheaper, and there seems to be good potential for many future industrial applications.

For some very difficult problems, such as autonomous navigation or object detection in significant clutter, higher level processes have not yet been proved successful. Therefore, it is not clear exactly what kind of data is necessary and what top-down information must be employed. Uncertainty in the overall system design is thus problematical for specification of the sensing module. A related problem is that of *multisensor fusion*:

data from different sensors must be integrated in such a way as to maintain a continuous/cohesive representation of the real world. Fusion may be done at a low level, for instance at the (x, y, z) *point level*, or at a higher *structural/symbolic level*. A final notion to mention is that of *active versus passive sensing*. A common definition of active sensing would apply to any sensor that provided and controlled its own illumination – such as triangulating with structured light or timing a laser pulse. At a higher level we may define active sensing to mean that the sensing is *goal-directed*; that is, the intelligent consumer of the data is gathering that data for hypothesis testing.

Having made the given caveats, the report proceeds, concentrating on the sensor as a separate system. Top-down control of the sensor via the interface to higher level modules is sometimes addressed, but only to a modest degree.

1.2.2   POPULAR 3D RANGE SENSORS

According to Kak, the three most popular 3D sensing techniques are:

1. stereo,

2. structured light, and

3. time-of-flight (sensors which measure phase change, rather than time, as a function of distance traveled are lumped into this category).

The most important characteristics of these techniques are as follows.

Stereo

The chief advantage is that it is passive. The main disadvantage is that it apparently cannot produce dense range measurements over uniform regions due to lack of features or presence of too many features for correspondence. The cost of two intensity sensors (cameras) is low, but hardware needed to produce the correspondences add significantly to the cost of a system. There has been a great deal of R&D on stereo sensing, and the technique is of common use in making maps from aerial imagery. Progress in robotics has been disappointingly slow, but researchers seem to agree that there is more potential to tap. In certain industrial environments, it is easy to use active illumination to aid in solving the correspondence problem.

Structured light

The main advantages are simplicity and the resulting low costs, making this the most common technique in industry. Various forms of structured light may be projected onto a scene, such as a ray, a sheet, a grid, or even cylinders, etc. Measurements may be dense or sparse depending upon the light pattern and on whether or not it is scanned over the scene. The active illumination can be a disadvantage in natural or hostile environments and even in industrial environments where specular reflections can be a problem. There is also the problem of lack of data due to one object shadowing another from the projected light.

Time-of-flight

The main advantage is that a dense and (almost) complete range image is output and that little or no image processing is required to get range. There is also the growing capability of obtaining several bits of registered reflectance data, thus allowing simple sensing of most of the so-called *intrinsic image*. The chief disadvantage is cost. Most sensors developed so far have been *one-of-a-kind* and have six-figure price tags. Lower prices are expected as successful applications increase the market, but chances for low prices are dim because of the costly optical and mechanical parts used in current designs. More details are described in the sections below.

1.2.3   OTHER 3D SENSING TECHNIQUES

There are other 3D sensing techniques which are likely to find increasing application. These include:

(a) depth-from-focus,

(b) Moire fringe pattern interpretation, and

(c) the use of acoustic or radar signals to measure distances via timing of returned signals.

1.2.4   NEEDS OF FIVE MAJOR APPLICATION AREAS

Different application problems place different requirements on the sensor system. Requirements can be defined in terms of many parameters; such as working volume, materials in the scene, object placement, precision of measurements and measurement rate. A summary of application areas and the spatial resolution and data rates required was done by Nelson Corby and Joe Mundy of General Electric and is given below:

1.2.5   EXAMPLE: ERIM RANGE SENSOR SPECS

There are several companies that have manufactured time-of-flight range sensors. Most of these have been designed with a specific application in mind. However, the technology is likely to be applied in other cases which were not considered during design. For the purpose of informing readers of current capabilities, the following data are given for the most recent sensor designed at ERIM.

TABLE 1.1. Sensing Requirements for Various Applications

Application Area		Spatial Resolution	Data Rate
Integrity and Placement	Detect missing of mis-aligned components in product assemblies; emphasis is on assembly and configuration control.	0.01 to 0.1 inches	100K to 1M range points per sec.
Metrology	Provides precision measurements of machine parts and electronic patterns.	1 to 100 microinches	10 to 100K range points per sec.
Surface Inspection	Exhausitvely scan part and assembly surfaces to detect surface flaws and component defects.	0.1 to 10 mils	10K to 1M range points per sec.
Modeling	Extract a 3D solid model from multiple range views; model supports design and engineering simulation.	0.1 to 10 mils	10K to 1M range points per sec.
Navigation	Provide scene data for mobile robot or autonomous vehicle.	perhaps 1 inch to 1 foot	perhaps 10K to 1M range points per sec.

- 16 inch x 16 inch x 16 inch envelope

- 12 bit range values of 0.004 inch (0.1 mm) resolution

- data rate of 0.25M rangels per second

- reflectance data as well as range

1.2.6   STATUS OF MOIRE TECHNOLOGY

Moire technology shows good promise for inspection of smooth surfaces. For purposes of information, some of the characteristics of a Moire sensor are outlined.

- advantages

    - uses white light image

    - low cost

    - gives *snapshot* data; i.e., no scanning needed

- resolution

  - 12 bits of depth obtainable, e.g., 0.0004 inch steps over 2 inches
  - x,y resolution depends on camera used

- data rate

  - 100K range points per second can be obtained

- limitations

  - maximum surface slope about 30-60 degrees
  - surface steps must be below 0.06 inches ambiguity interval
  - shadows created due to different projection and viewing angles
  - limited by dynamic range of reflectance

1.2.7 COMMONLY CITED PROBLEMS IN RANGE SENSING

A diversity of problems and limitations can be cited. These can be related
to the components of the equipment, the physical phenomena used, the
overall system, or even the environment of the application. A few problems
are worthy of special note. First, is the problem of dynamic range. For solder joint inspection the dynamic range in surface reflection can approach
100,000 to 1, thus placing severe constraints on the detector design. A second important problem is that of resolution and work volume requirements
– sensors typically can achieve a good resolution over a limited work volume. For instance, if a sensor can deliver only a 12 bit value for range,
this allows a resolution of 0.004 inches over 16 inches. If a dimension of 32
inches is required, then the sensor must be moved (or reset in some other
way). If such scanning must be done to enlarge the work envelope, then
the sensor design is complicated and both data rates and overall system
precision may be decreased. A related problem is that of providing variable
work envelopes in order to allow smarter sensing of larger scenes without
excess data or scanning times.

- Component limitations

  - dynamic range of light intensity can be 100,000 to 1
  - drift due to changes of environment, such as temperature
  - stuck bits or loss of sync often observed

- Design limits

  - multiple reflections
  - shadows

- ambiguity interval
- motion of sensor or objects being sensed
- resolution versus duration of sensing
- spatial resolution and mixed pixels
- missing data or artifact
- power consumption

- System limits

  - sensor to application match
  - cost of sensor
  - representation gap between sensed data and application process
  - fusion of range data with other sensor data
  - need for variable sampling in same scan

1.2.8 FUTURE EFFORTS

Previous sections identified some state-of-the-art technology and some of the problems yet existing in that technology. This section identifies a few lines of attack where new work or continued development effort is needed.

- Breakthroughs needed

  - sensors are needed which give *snapshot* range images, e.g., without scanning. These would be immune to motion problems and the high cost components used in current sensors.
  - sensors should work in a closed loop with the higher level processes of image and scene understanding.

- Engineering for breakthroughs

  - continued progress on the development of sensors that deliver registered range and reflectance is needed.
  - sensors are needed which directly deliver higher level primitives such as edges or surface patterns.
  - sensors are needed which provide variable speed, resolution, and work envelope.

- Miscellaneous

  - more experience is needed in the use of range sensors in applications
  - documentation, in the form of texts or handbooks, is needed to educate users in the capabilities of 3D range sensors and how to fit them to specific application problems.

1.3   Early Processing

The early range image processing (EP) discussion group consisted of:

Gerard Medioni, USC (Chair)
Paul Besl, General Motors
Patrick Flynn, MSU
Richard Hoffman, Northrop
Gerhard Roth, NRC-Canada and McGill
Ishwar Sethi, Wayne State

1.3.1   ISSUES IN EARLY PROCESSING OF RANGE IMAGES

In a general machine perception system structure, a range imaging sensor is recognized as a single contributor of sensory information within a suite of other possible sensors. Early processing of range image data may take place in isolation from other sensor data, but it is also possible and sometimes desirable to process imaging sensor data from multiple sensors at the pixel level, usually under the constraint that all simultaneously processed pixels come from registered images. Since processing data from multiple sensors falls in the domain of sensor integration algorithms and strategies, the EP group discussed early range image processing in isolation from other types of sensor information.

One "fact" that was painfully apparent in many of the discussions and presentations is that no single range imaging sensor, no single early processing strategy, no single object recognition scheme or navigation technique or inspection algorithm, and no single sensor integration approach will be adequate in the near term for the wide variety of practical applications that would benefit from range sensing technology. As a result, range imaging system design tends to be application driven and will probably remain so until a significant number of successful range imaging systems are being used. In other words, the application requirements will generally specify the type of range imaging sensor that will be used. For example, specifications for range accuracy, depth of field, field of view, image acquisition time, standoff distance, lateral sampling intervals, optical properties of scene materials, and other application specifications can severely constrain the choice of range sensing technology. The range imaging sensor and the image features needed by higher-level application-specific processes then place fundamental constraints on the choice of early processing algorithms. The EP group attempted to address many of the common issues involved in potential applications.

1.3.2 DEFINITION OF "EARLY" PROCESSING

A definition of early range image processing was needed since the interface between early processing and sensing can be muddled with emergence of smarter sensors. In addition, the distinction between early range image processing and later processing can also be difficult to make. An early range image processing algorithm is any geometric signal processing algorithm that organizes (abstracts) discrete range sensor data into a more convenient form for application-specific (task-oriented) reasoning. Early processing algorithms do not directly address range estimation nor do they infer the existence of objects in the image data. The goal of an early processing algorithm is to accept input from a range imaging sensor and to extract geometric primitives or features relevant to higher level application-dependent processes. Ideally, early processing completely partitions, or segments, the range data into geometric primitives so that almost all image data points are grouped with some geometric representation.

1.3.3 SURFACE GEOMETRY

It is common in early processing to assume that most visible surfaces of interest are piecewise smooth and more specifically, C^2 almost everywhere (first and second derivatives exist except on sets of zero area: points or curves). This assumption arises from the fact that matter is cohesive. Although visual texture due to surface reflectance variations are common in the everyday world, significant physical surface texture, such as the texture present in trees, mountain ranges, and clouds, is not as common in many potential range imaging application environments. When physical surface texture is important, fractal or Markov random field (MRF) models have been explored and will require further investigation with respect to application requirements.

Assuming an underlying piecewise smooth surface geometry exists that approximates the range image data well, how is it recovered, estimated, or analyzed? Many researchers agree that knowledge of the differential properties of a range image is useful for many purposes. For example, edge detection requires estimation of at least the first partial derivatives and estimation of second partial derivatives and mixed partials is commonly done. The majority of early processing algorithms seem to lie somewhere between (1) first partial derivative estimation at the simple end of the EP spectrum (e.g. a Sobel operator) and (2) computation of a complete principal (Darboux) frame field for the entire range image at the complex end of the EP spectrum. Knowledge of the principal frame field of a range image implies that one knows the surface normal and principal directions at each point in the image and possesses a line of curvature surface parameterization that approximates the data well. If this information is known, then any other surface information, such as surface curvatures, can be easily computed. The goals of many early processing approaches are summarized as the (1) detection of C^0 (jump), C^1 (crease), and C^2 (curvature) discontinuities and their junctions and (2) the approximation or characterization of the smooth C^2 surface patches whose boundaries are the aforementioned discontinuities. There are many methods to create approximate surface patches without using differential properties of the pixel data. These methods rely mostly on surface fitting.

Differential properties are most often estimated either explicitly or implicitly via local window surface fits (a.k.a. local facet model). Such methods yield adequate results quickly, but the depth, or range, direction is a preferred direction in space. For isotropic computation, surface normals can also be estimated by diagonalizing the covariance matrix of points in a neighborhood and selecting the eigenvector associated with the minimum eigenvalue. Curvature can then be computed from surface normal estimates. The consensus seemed to be that surface normals and curvature can be computed fairly reliably at the majority of points in a range image by either method, but that there are no existing reliable low-level methods that work everywhere, especially near crease edges or curvature edges.

In order to estimate differential properties of range image data, it is common to use non-adaptive Gaussian or binomial weighted pre-smoothing operators (low pass FIR filters) to filter out unwanted noise. Linear filters unavoidably round sharp edges, so it is also common to use non-linear filters that tend to (1) preserve edges and (2) smooth non-edge image regions. The K-nearest-neighbor smoothing approach with K=5 is a good inexpensive adaptive alternative to constant coefficient 3x3 smoothing operators. Other methods exist in the literature, but none have proven to be the unique best solution for all applications.

1.3.4 EARLY PROCESSING ALGORITHMS

The goal of any preliminary filtering operator in range image processing is to preserve geometry while attenuating noise. Whereas no combination of smoothing and derivative estimation have proven themselves superior to other techniques, there is a serious lack of an optimality criterion. It was suggested in the early processing group discussions that surface curvature types from synthetic range images might allow a testing criterion. For example, if the ideal surface curvature types are known at every pixel in a range image, any scheme for estimating partial derivatives might be evaluated using the percentage of misclassified pixels. A "perfect" algorithm would have a zero misclassification rate for a series of preselected test images with different types of surface geometry and different levels of noise. In general, standardized segmentation error metrics are needed to help advance the state-of-the-art. No quantitative metrics are measured on standard test images in most of today's research environments.

The output from an early processing algorithm should be representations of geometric primitives: points, curves, surfaces, and/or volumes. If symmetry is present in the data, an early processing algorithm should recognize the symmetry and encode it in the extracted geometric primitive. For example, lines (dihedral crease edges), circles, planes, spheres, cylinders, cones, and undeformed superquadrics can be recognized directly by low-level processes and used to limit the possible degrees of freedom of the objects. Feature points, such as polyhedral vertices, cone tips, and isolated umbilic points, also provide powerful constraints for higher-level processes when available. Other types of more general shape primitives might also be extracted, such as B-spline space curves and tensor-product surfaces. Other shape description representations, such as Extended Gaussian Images (EGI's) and 4-vector EGI's, are also useful for describing elliptic and hyperbolic surfaces. Geometric representations are critical concerns for higher level processes and the selection of particular representations will dictate requirements to early processing algorithms.

Multi-resolution methods were discussed and it was decided by the group that a multi-resolution paradigm is probably not relevant to early range image processing unless it provides computational advantages. That is, the best, finest resolution results should be returned by early range image processing algorithms. If multi-resolution concepts are useful for later matching representations, then later processes can coarsen the models for the given algorithm or application.

As far as general purpose system integration issues are concerned, a range imaging sensor should return a model of its processes and a model of possible noise sources to an early processing algorithm when queried. For example, range image noise is typically non-normal and is definitely non-stationary and might usually consist of random measurement noise, quantization noise, and systematic sensor noise (e.g., a small amount of ripple) as well as "outlier" noise, which causes bad range readings due to depth discontinuities and finite laser beam width, steep relative surface slopes, specular reflection, absorption, multiple reflections, etc. Similarly, the sensor/noise model and a model of the early processing algorithms and their possible errors should be passed on to higher level processes. A general-purpose early processing algorithm will need to adapt itself to situations that depend on which sensor is used and which application is seeking geometric features from the image data. Although such issues may not impact today's planned practical systems, we must begin thinking along these lines to move toward general purpose systems.

Range images can be represented in (raster) $r(i,j)$ form (range as a function of two integer indices) or in (scattered) 3-D (x, y, z) form. Several comments indicated that all early processing should be performed in the $r(i,j)$ image form since the uncertainty in range r is much larger than the uncertainty in the actual 3-D ray corresponding to the (i,j) indices. There may be a global uncertainty about where the range imaging sensor is pointing, but the point-to-point uncertainty is minimal. Hence, all probabilistic

2nd moment information can be well-approximated by a $\sigma_r(i,j)$ range variance image and a 2x2 Σ_{ij} covariance matrix for the overall sensor direction. That is, one number per point plus four numbers per image. In contrast, the (x, y, z) form of a range image would require a 3x3 covariance matrix (nine numbers) for each point. As Kalman filtering algorithms become more common for integrating estimates of point positions from multiple views acquired at different times, these memory and efficiency concerns may be critical. As a general guideline, range image data should be processed in the sensor coordinate frame. Geometric primitives extracted from the image will need to be transformed to the relevant global coordinates with their related uncertainty information.

Is multiple view integration an early process or a later process? It appears to depend on the application. For instance, in ALV range images, each scan line (and possibly each point) may be coming from a different viewpoint during image acquisition. In such applications, image data must be corrected before other early processing algorithms can begin. Hence, such viewpoint corrections are a key feature of early processing stages of the system. In contrast, an automated geometric modeling system may perform integration of extracted geometric primitives from different views after all the early processing is done. In general, if multiple view integration is required for geometric primitive extraction, then it is early processing; otherwise, it is not. High-level multiple view integration algorithms should tie into sensor integration algorithms in a natural unified manner.

A never ending source of difficulty (and often confusion) is the set of early processing algorithm parameters (window sizes, thresholds, tolerances, etc.). It is often difficult to verify the results of others without knowing the algorithm parameters they used. As a general rule of thumb, the number of parameters should be minimized. For each parameter used, the range of values tested and the effects should be clearly documented by those describing the algorithm for others. Besides edge detection thresholds, a classic case is fitting unconstrained quadrics to range data from cylinders. Sometimes a long, but enclosed, ellipsoid is generated; other times, a long non-closed hyperboloid is generated. A threshold is needed to decide when the surface is a cylinder and when it is something else. In addition to parameter set listings, the EP group agreed that all journals in the field should insist on explicit concise pseudo-code listings or flow-charts as algorithm documentation in papers describing algorithms or the results of algorithms.

1.3.5 SUMMARY

In order to make progress as an engineering and scientific discipline, the computer vision community, and the range imaging understanding interest group in particular, should begin to share software and image data in a more open manner. We need to avoid duplication of effort and to enable quantitative comparisons of different approaches. It was suggested that journals require that new algorithms be run on at least one standardized image and compared to at least one other well-accepted algorithm. As examples, the Alvey consortium of universities and industry in England standardized on C and Sun workstations making it possible for a large group to share results and source code. In the numerical analysis community, people can send CSNet messages to netlib at Argonne National Labs and receive numerical software back in Fortran. The workshop group agreed that an image database should be setup to allow easy access to range imagery given the scarcity of good sensors. For software, it is suggested that standard algorithm libraries be begun in (ANSI) C and (Common) Lisp languages. Candidates for standard software libraries include the following: adaptive/non-adaptive smoothing and derivative estimation functions; jump/crease/curvature discontinuity edge detection/tracking/linking; region growing based on various uniformity predicates; regression code for curve and surface fitting of various types of geometric entities (e.g., B-splines); standardized rotation matrix manipulation codes (e.g., quaternions, etc.); device independent 3-D display algorithms for points, curves, surfaces, and volumes (Silicon Graphics interfaces); device independent range image generation algorithms from polyhedra, superquadrics, Bezier patches, or B-splines (NURBS) for different types of scanner configurations; and geometric operations such as free-form surface-surface intersections and Boolean operations.

Early processing of time-varying range imagery is an area that requires more research. A complicating feature of most range imaging sensors is long image acquisition times (greater than 0.25 seconds). This is a general feature of most range imaging sensors that will not be alleviated in the near term except at great expense in sensor technology. Dynamic algorithms must be able to handle this artifact of range imaging sensors.

1.4   Object Recognition

Object Recognition Group Discussion Summary

> Thomas O. Binford (Chair)
> Robert Bolles
> Francis Quek
> Richard Weiss

Recognition and interpretation integrate vision system functions. Recognition must account for results from preceding analysis, i.e. sensing, early analysis, and any multi-sensor integration. Figure 1.1 shows a convenient hierarchy in model-based vision. It shows dimension of representation, not control. On the left side is modeling, on the right is observation, while matching connects models with observations. Application scenarios provide a background for requirements which depend on the task:

RECOGNITION LEVELS

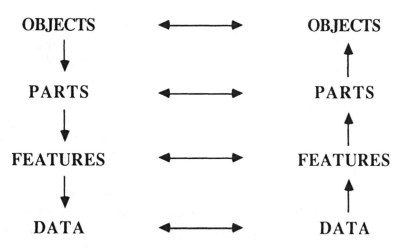

FIGURE 1.1. Model-Based Vision

1. The ALV (Autonomous Land Vehicle) scenario involves cross country navigation outdoors. Objects vary greatly within object classes, terrain, vegetation, and structures. This is an extreme of the generic object class requirement.

2. Industrial robot vision tasks require handling one or a few objects at any time. However, large companies have many parts in production, e.g., 150,000. Programming many objects provides some motivation for generic object class capabilities.

3. Industrial inspection requires finding a wide variety of flaws, some of which occur infrequently, in the face of cosmetic marks which do not affect function. The number of different inspection tasks may be large. Inspection motivates generic object class treatment.

4. Space applications may not require generic models. The environment on-board will be heavily documented. Planetary exploration does encounter terrain which makes generic methods valuable.

5. Home and service robots work in complex environments with complex objects. Generic methods appear valuable.

6. The attraction of robots in warehousing is flexibility of routes and stacks. Automatic retrieval of objects from storage may be very com-

plex, verifying correct placement in bins. Navigation is of intermediate difficulty, i.e., there may be obstacles which come and go.

These scenarios motivate criteria for system design.

1. Number of object models: from one to many, e.g., one million.

2. Variability of models: from classes of identical objects, from a "cookie cutter", to object classes with variability such as humans, who vary greatly one from another, and each of whom varies greatly over time, changing clothes, growing old, etc.

3. Complexity of Background: simple or uniform on one hand to "any"

4. Computational Complexity: one model per object, i.e., order n complexity for n objects, at the brute force extreme, to log n complexity with indexing.

Much range image analysis and other vision is aimed toward recognition of few, identical objects. These application scenarios put value on recognition algorithms for many objects, object classes, complex backgrounds, with low complexity.

1.4.1 MATCHING

We summarize briefly a selected set of issues from group discussion. Among three components of recognition, modeling, observation, and matching, there was consensus that matching is a weak link, has highest priority and is most neglected. Issues relate to performance in time and performance in quality of recognition or interpretation.

We discuss recognition within this interpretation paradigm: hypothesis generation, hypothesis management, hypothesis verification, and refinement. Performance in time motivates study of the following issues:

1. Structural indexing for hypothesis generation is a part of efficient recognition.

2. Control of the recognition process involves a group of issues: execution strategy, e.g., resource allocation; structuring recognition for parallel and distributed computation; data structures for matching; and algorithm synthesis based on detailed model-based complexity.

3. Currently, the key to successful system building is using special case simplifications. A step toward this is study of general methods to use domain-specific information.

Quality of performance further motivates other important issues. One key is refinement of pose and parameters. A second is accurate implementation of geometric and probabilistic constraints in solution.

$$s_1 \quad \begin{array}{c} (X1,C1)\ (t) \\ - - - - - - > \end{array} \quad f_1 \ -- > \quad |$$

$$s_2 \quad \begin{array}{c} (X2,C2)\ (t) \\ - - - - - - > \end{array} \quad f_2 \ -- > \quad |$$

$$\cdot$$

$$\cdot \qquad\qquad\qquad\qquad\qquad | \ -- > R < - - - > K$$

integration

$$(X_n, C_n)(t)$$

$$\cdot$$

$$s_n \quad - - - - -- > \quad f_n \ -- > \quad |$$

FIGURE 1.2. Sensor Integration.

1.4.2 MODELING

The power and generality of recognition depends on accurate modeling overall. First is the modeling of objects and scene. A new issue is generic modeling of object class. Another issue is building models and knowledge base. Second is modeling of observables, i.e., generating models for sensors and operators.

1.5 Sensor Integration

Tom Henderson (Chair)
Ramesh Jain
Y.T. Chien
Jake Aggarwal
Ruzena Bajcsy

Multisensor integration is the combination of evidence or sensed data from several sensors. Most aspects of the sensor integration problem can be characterized in terms of Figure 1.2:

where

s_i is the ith sensor,

X_i is the ith sensor data,

C_i is a measure of the uncertainty of X_i,

f_i is the ith parameter produced,

t is the time parameter,

R is the composite model or representation,

K is the knowledge used in the problem.

Sensors deliver:

1. position and properties, and

2. absence of objects.

Integration techniques and the level of integration are functions of:

- the physical relation (or coupling) of the sensors, and

- the physical properties which characterize the object.

Major issues:

1. The representation of the composite model: This representation should be such that information acquired from disparate sensors can be integrated and assimilated. This representation should capture details and should represent symbolic information, also. One area of study is the use of explicit 3D connectivity data structures as opposed to image data structures and the determination of appropriate applications for such techniques.

2. The combination of measurements is an estimation technique and well-understood; however, inference techniques which operate on derived features need study. There are many approaches to uncertainty management. It is not clear which one performs better under given real world conditions. We require a good scientific study to determine the scope and limitations of uncertainty management techniques.

3. It is important to determine how the nature of the properties of problems influences the techniques selected or the parameters. This requires the study of requirements models and the related physical sensor models. It is essential to get at the cost of obtaining information with sensors and the development of an information-based complexity model for sensing systems. This is particularly urgent for multisensor systems.

4. It is necessary to define the time-varying requirements of multisensor systems. This includes defining strategies for the sequence of application of sensors which complement each other, as well as the sequence of motions required for individual sensors.

5. In many cases, it is possible to obtain similar information using two different types of sensors. It is not clear that we understand the scope and limitations of sensors well enough to determine which sensor should be used in a given situation (this includes masking off parts of the sensed data).

1.6 Range Sensing for Navigation

C.M. Brown (Chair)
T. Kanade
W.E.L. Grimson
U.K. Sharma

1.6.1 SYSTEM PARAMETERS, AND NAVIGATIONAL TASKS, AND REPRESENTATION

The concept of navigation is ill-specified and potentially extremely broad, encompassing tasks like finding space in a robotic environment, following an underwater course while maintaining a known pose and accounting for known and unknown currents, driving at speed over urban or open terrain with or without accurate or inaccurate maps. Thus, *the role of, the requirements for, and the necessary future research and development on range sensors for navigation all depend on the navigational task at issue.*

In order to keep this truism from being our last word on the subject, we decided to try to identify important and representative navigational tasks and system parameters that could affect choices, and to consider two case studies that illustrated various issues and answers. We also tried to address the topics of other groups and make explicit what capabilities in those areas we would like to see. In particular, we outlined what we should like to see in the areas of sensors, early processing, object recognition, and sensor fusion.

Autonomous navigation is not usually called for unless there are considerable practical problems involved, and so often the constraints that make it necessary also make it harder. The system or mission assumptions that seemed most crucial were the following.

1. Autonomy time – how long the navigator runs open loop. We considered times from hours (land vehicle reconnaissance mission) to weeks (undersea monitoring).

2. Weight and power restrictions. These can vary from loose (for a land vehicle) to stringent (for a Mars rover).

3. Task specifications.

The navigational tasks we considered in some detail were the following.

1. Finding navigable space.

2. Recognizing landmarks.

3. Localizing self in relation to an environment.

4. Servoing motion and detecting obstacles.

The sensor technologies we considered were the following.

1. Laser ranging.

2. Passive stereo or structured light triangulation.

3. Active camera tracking and focusing, including low-level reflexes.

4. Sonar.

An important question is the representations to be used for navigation. Perhaps one of the more surprising outcome of this group's discussions was the agreement that a small set of representations would probably suffice. There are interesting issues involving the algorithms that manipulate them, but the basic data structures we thought necessary are the following.

1. Occupancy maps or elevation maps – discrete, iconic representations of local topography, possibly *annotated* with symbolic information or labels.

2. Planar-faced and planar-polyhedral representations of geometry, perhaps labeled. More complex shapes can be approximated by these representations.

3. Materials should be represented explicitly when known or discovered. This information can be represented as labels on geometric elevation representations.

4. Topological connectivity ("has been navigated" or "can be navigated" connectivity) between areas represented as occupancy or elevation maps.

5. Coordinate systems are basic.

1.6.2   CASE 1: AN UNDERWATER SURVEYOR

A small underwater robot is to construct an elevation map of an area, annotating it with results of other sensors (where a chemical level exceeds a threshold, where a certain material is found, etc.). The robot has a range sensor that returns ranges R_{ij} for a local area (perhaps the output is a one-dimensional scan line). The robot has an orientation and orientation-derivative detector, and a velocity detector. This is a minimal scenario in several senses. The weight and power restrictions mean that "smart" sensing technology can be traded for processing, which is weight- and space-efficient. There are no real-time constraints, so processing can be complex. The sensor technology itself can be relatively primitive. We noted that the underwater robot technology has grown quite sophisticated and that more cooperation between land and sea robotics workers would be a good idea.

The following paragraphs relate this case to the requirements for the subtasks mentioned above and for the subjects addressed by other working groups.

Sensors

The basic system is a sonar ranger. If close-up work, such as oil rig inspection, is called for, then there exist underwater laser systems that could be used for the requisite high resolution sensing. This sub-scenario calls for different mobility requirements and generally more sophistication. Ambiguity intervals could become an issue, for instance. There may be millimeter-wave radar for underwater use. Materials analysis from the sensor is a desideratum. High resolution and speed are not issues, since in this case we are not time-limited.

Representation

The desired output is an annotated elevation map.

Spurious output detection is necessary. Registration of the results is a primary problem, but this is covered under Self-localization below. Averaging or combining multiple readings from one location may be called for. Nothing in the way of segmentation, surface-fitting, dealing with occlusion, etc. is needed.

Sensor Fusion, Object (Landmark) Recognition, Finding Navigable Space

Not needed.

Self-Localization

This issue is quite important, since unknown currents may affect the robot's location, and the output is a quantitative map of the area. There are engineering solutions (a buoy with a transponder that uses an outside reference source, like a navigation satellite). Failing that, the issue would come down to matching currently-available sensing data to match against the map derived so far, which could be rather difficult.

Obstacle Detection

Not needed in the simple scenario, and relatively easy to do using another echolocation sensor, except insofar as avoidance maneuvers could make self-localization more an issue.

Map Creation

This is not difficult if the self-localization issue can be solved and if the sensors return the requisite data. The basic technique is temporal fusion of data, done in software.

1.6.3   CASE 2: SURVEYING AN URBAN ENVIRONMENT

Here we assumed a large autonomous vehicle carrying several depth and imaging sensors, whose job it was to investigate a small deserted area of urban terrain and record differences between the current situation and the situation expected from an onboard map. The task could include checking if buildings still existed, if their identifications on the map were correct, if roads are still open, etc.

Sensors

The assumptions here invite more sophistication to be built into the sensors, in order to relieve the higher level processing. The following desiderata all raise considerable research and technological issues. This case may call for the following capabilities.

1. Stability for the sensor platform is necessary, to provide something like a Vestibulo-Ocular Reflex (VOR) to keep the sensor fixated on a spot or to isolate it from vehicle motions.

2. A laser ranger should provide five times the speed, five times the distance, and five times the depth resolution of current sensors. It should have a vertical angular extent of 60 degrees.

3. Effective techniques based on traditional image sensing might be possible. The technology to provide structured (or "unstructured") light for triangulation or stereo ranging over a wide area does not seem as daunting as laser-ranging technology. Multi-spectral scanners (or "pokers") for material identification are useful but a different issue. Recent work in active vision, such as "depth from parallax" or kinetic depth determination, (related to depth from flow), is aimed at duplicating the (very effective) processing performed by humans. Fixation and object tracking reflexes can simplify object recognition and also depth and egomotion calculations. Stereo is still a hot topic and could yield at any time. Our group felt that the potential power of techniques based on high-resolution optical images should not be overlooked.

4. Auto-registration of input through time would be an interesting option. This capability would compensate for vehicle motion as it happened. The goal would be to have the sensor emit true (x, y, z, t)

information (point locations in a global fixed coordinate system) instead of $R(i, j, t)$ information (range from the sensor in direction (i, j) at time t). At present, the hardware does not exist to do automatic motion compensation. Further, it is important not to throw away covariance information (error ellipsoids are oriented toward the ranger, whereever it is). However, the hardware situation may be changing, and taking account of the effect of errors is not a particularly difficult problem). The desired effect is the "stable world" we perceive when we move our eyes.

5. Many times it is desirable to work on $R(i, j, t)$ data, rather than on (x, y, z, t) data, because the latter involves more parameters and therefore more computational time. Also, most of the time low-level processing is done in the local coordinate system, and only important features are converted into the global coordinates. Usually, such features contain only 5% of the image points. Therefore, we save about 95% of the coordinate translation time by not converting (or not demanding the sensor to convert) the entire image into the global coordinate system.

If we expect the sensor to give (x, y, z, t) information in the global coordinate system, the sensor can perform "translation" based on inertial navigation system (INS) data to get the global value at each pixel. Therefore, the image acquisition time in global (x, y, z, t) will be more than that in local (x, y, z, t), and much more than $R(i, j, t)$. Most of the time, $R(i, j, t)$ suffices (e.g. obstacle detection, surface normal computation) but, some times (x, y, z, t) global or local is needed (e.g. for motion analysis, etc.).

In summary, there are 3 formats:

(a) $R(i, j, t)$ data

(b) (x, y, z) local data

(c) (x, y, z) global data

Depending upon the task and the penalty paid in time to the sensor for (2) and (3), one can determine which format is best.

Representation

Annotated, planar polyhedral representations for objects and annotated elevation maps for topography, linked topologically to indicate navigability (perhaps by simple "stay on the road" servoing), seem to be all that is required.

Early Processing

Segmentation into regions of spatial or material homogeneity is the primary desideratum here. Simple planar regions with dihedrals labelled as to convex, concave, or obscuring type would be adequate. Reflexes, such as obstacle avoidance, can operate before segmentation. Multi-resolution methods may well be useful.

Sensor Fusion

The usefulness of combining depth and intensity data for more reliable segmentation has been demonstrated in several contexts. The primary reason for sensor fusion is to do more reliable segmentation. Insufficient information from a single sensor, e.g. only TV camera or only range sensor may lead to incomplete or incorrect object recognition. For example, range data obtained from a laser scanner, and intensity data obtained from a TV camera provide complementary information. Range data provides important clues on the geometry of an observed scene. However, it does not provide any information about the physical properties of the scene objects such as color or intensity. On the other hand, it is extremely difficult to extract geometrical information from TV data. Therefore, both types of data need to be analyzed. Doing this correctly involves understanding the physics of the problem, and thus how one sensor's output is related to another's. However, the existence of multiple sensors also raises the possibility of switching modes as called for by the task, so flexibility in sensor choice is a desideratum. Fusion can be done with help from the structural level, not just at the iconic level. That is, semantic labels or segments can be useful to constrain matches between sensor outputs. Last, temporal fusion is important in this scenario, as in almost all navigational tasks. Using a pre-existing map can help, but sophisticated techniques like Kalman filtering can be swamped by the registration problems that are inherent in real-world multi-frame data. Thus, robust temporal combination techniques are another important research area.

Object (Landmark) Recognition

Landmark Recognition (or self localization) is helpful so that the vehicle (or robot) can use triangulation to one or more landmarks to correct position errors caused by drift in the vehicle's inertial navigation system. Recognition of specific objects from a small catalog is not considered to be a problem these days. Much more relevant in any real-world situation, including this scenario, is the ability to recognize a "generic object." That is, to recognize to which class (e.g., "gas station," "vehicle") a particular instance belongs. Rule-based techniques may be applicable here, but construed broadly, this is almost *The Vision Problem.*

Self-Localization

This is "The Matching Problem," in a particular context, with particular
representations. The knowledge or context provided by previous movements
and known landmarks may make this problem slightly easier.

Servoing, Obstacle Detection, and Navigable Space

Servoing to guide motion with respect to road-width constraints and to
sense obstacles ahead (at slow speeds) can be provided by a skirt sonar
sensor. Stationary obstacles ahead can show up with minimal processing
as "tombstones", whose material properties it may be important to know.
This problem is currently under study in a number of places, and most
autonomous robots have reasonable obstacle avoidance and servoing capabilities today. As motion speeds get faster, there are increasing demands
on the sensor speeds and distances.

There seems to be no agreement today on how best to attack the navigable space problem. Whether space should be represented explicitly or
implicitly (absence of known masses) is a basic question. Our assumptions
here are consistent with either representation, but also make our problem
easier, since the map would presumably yield a potential navigable space
to be verified.

Map Creation

The main goal in this case is no more difficult than any other computer
vision undertaking, given the capabilities outlined above. That is, it is a
big problem presenting many difficult intellectual and technical problems.
Depending on the semantic content of the desired map, its component of
geometric representation, and the disparity between the reality and the expectations, the task will be more or less reasonable given today's knowledge.
The contribution of range information to the job is to provide information
about the three-dimensional world, largely in service of navigation itself.
However, an un-annotated, iconic elevation map could perhaps be produced
by ranging alone. Further, the fusion of depth and image data can yield
more reliable segmentation and thus improve navigation, recognition, and
mapping.

1.7   Applications Group Report

Anil Jain, Michigan State University
Martin Levine, McGill University
C.W. "Ron" Swonger, ERIM (Chair)

The Applications Group of the Range Image Understanding Workshop
focused upon examination of issues affecting the current and near-future

routine "production" use of range image-based machine vision for substantially unconstrained applications (i.e., applications where "image understanding" is a non-trivial undertaking). This focus inherently led to
dismissal from serious consideration of passive stereo techniques and some
other methods such as shape-from-shading methods. The group therefore
intentionally considered uses beyond the research, development, test, and
evaluation (RDT&E) phase of the classical high-technology system life cycle. Uses in industry, aerospace/defense and civil government were considered, but the intent of the group was to offer an integrative or "big picture"
assessment of application issues across these communities.

First, (Table 1.2) a number of application areas were characterized as
being "present" or "future" with respect to routine production use *with
range image data*. Counter examples were later solicited from all workshop
attendees, but none were volunteered.

Next, (Table 1.3) several broad generalizations were offered concerning
the application needs and benefits of range image data for image understanding problems. One observation in Table 1.3 was an assessment of the
approximate performance level of range image *sensors*, stated in terms of
five cost/performance parameters, required in order for a significant increase to occur in the industrial/commercial/government use of range image understanding systems. These performance/cost levels should again be
taken as the rough "knees of the curves" of the number of sensors which
might be sold nationally versus the indicated parameter values. No sensor is currently known to be available which is close to meeting all of the
cost/performance values indicated.

The value of range image data in achieving integrated iconic (i.e., pixel-
domain) and symbolic processing was also noted in Table 1.3. It should
also be noted that active "laser radar" or LIDAR sensor designs are currently evolving which offer significant potential for multimodal sensing and
associated information fusion at the image (pixel) level. Specifically, image sensors can be built to provide fully registered images of scenes which
directly encode range, panchromatic reflectance, multispectral reflectance
(material properties), surface roughness, radial velocity, vibration, polarization, temperature, and/or other properties for each pixel in the scene.

Thirdly (see Table 1.4), the group undertook to prioritize the few most
significant obstacles currently limiting the practical "production use" of
range image understanding systems. Cost, algorithmic concepts, data availability, and processing hardware issues each enter into that list.

Finally, a brief list was compiled (Table 1.5), from the knowledge of
the group members and immediately available references, of organizations
known to currently build range image sensors (including point, contour or
profile, and array or whole image sensors). No attempt was made to characterize or compare these sensors other than the indicated categorization.
No endorsement is implied and no completeness or accuracy is guaranteed
for this listing. It is quite unclear whether the list provided will grow or

shrink over the next few years given the technological issues, compelling needs, and economic difficulties within the machine vision supplier and user communities worldwide.

TABLE 1.2. Production Applications of Range Imagery

Present

- Assembly Control and Verification

- Weld Seam Tracking

- Sheet Metal Part/Assembly Metrology

- Electronics Inspection – Leads, SMD's, etc.

Future

- Contoured Object Inspection/Verification – e.g., Turbine Blades

- Unconstrained Material Handling

- Wheel Alignment

- General Geometric Flaw Inspection

- Automated Geometric Modeling of Prototype Parts

- Electronics Inspection – Solder, Wirebonds, etc.

- Food Processing – Quality Control, Sorting, Grading

- Vehicle Guidance

- Automatic Target Recognition (ATR)

1.8 Appendix

1.8.1 OVERVIEW SPEAKERS

Avi Kak (Purdue Univ.): Sensing
Paul Besl (General Motors Reseach): Early Processing
Robert Bolles (Stanford Research Institute): Object Recognition
Jake Aggarwal (Univ. Texas): Sensor Integration

TABLE 1.3. Range Image Understanding Application Observations

1. The density of range data required depends upon:

   • The richness and lack of constraint of scenes to be observed.

   • The required variety and selectivity/accuracy of output decisions or actions.

2. Improvements most needed for practical application of range image sensors

	Cost	< $25 K
	Frame Rate	< 1 second
are:	Tolerance of Reflectance Variations	> 10^4 : 1
	Size (Scanning Head)	< 1/4ft^3
	Range Noise	standard deviation < 0.1% of work envelope

3. Range images offer significantly greater opportunity for achieving the long-sought and critical integration of iconic and symbolic processing for 3D scene interpretation.

Takeo Kanade (Carnegie Mellon Univ.): Navigation
Joe Mundy (General Electric): Application
Ruzena Bajcsy (Univ. Pennsylvania): 3-D Vision

1.8.2   LIST OF PARTICIPANTS

This list of participants gives affiliation of people and groups (identified by letter codes: SI - sensor integration, EP - early processing, OR - object recognition, RS - range sensing, N - navigation, APP - applications) in which they participated.

1. Jake Aggarwal (U. Texas) (SI)

2. Ruzena Bajcsy(U. Penn) (SI)

3. Paul Besl (GMR) (EP)

4. Tom Binford (Stanford) (OR)

5. Robert Bolles (SRI) (OR)

6. Chris Brown (Rochester) (N)

TABLE 1.4. Prioritized Obstacles to Application of Range Imagery

1. Sensor cost for required resolutions and data rates.

2. Difficulty of interpreting substantially unconstrained scenes.

   (a) Segmentation

   (b) Object Recognition

3. Inadequate availability to researchers of multimodal registered image data.

4. Inadequate availability of special-purpose hardware for real-time geometric feature computation (e.g. Gaussian curvature).

7. Y.T. Chien (NSF) (SI)

8. Nelson Corby (GE) (RS)

9. Patrick Flynn (MSU) (EP)

10. Eric Grimson (MIT) (N)

11. Kevin Harding (ITI) (RS)

12. Tom Henderson (Utah) (SI)

13. Richard Hoffman (Northrop) (EP)

14. Anil Jain (MSU) (APP)

15. Ramesh Jain (U. Michigan) (SI)

16. Avi Kak (Purdue) (RS)

17. Takeo Kanade (CMU) (N)

18. Martin Levine (McGill) (APP)

19. Gerardo Medioni (USC) (EP)

20. Joe Mundy (GE) (APP)

21. Francis Quek (U. Michigan) (OR)

22. Gerhard Roth (NRC-Canada) (EP)

TABLE 1.5. Known Builders of Range Image Sensors

Organization	(Current, Industry-Applicable) Spatial Resolution	Data Rate
Boulder Electro-Optics[1]		•
Chesapeake Laser		•
Cyberoptics	•	
Diffracto	•	
Digital Signal		•
ERIM	•	•
G.E.		•
Hymark (Canada)	•	•[2]
Industrial Technology Institute		•
Keyence (Japan)	•	
NRC		•
Odetics		•
Oldelft (Netherlands)	•	
Perceptron	•	•
Photonic Automation		•
RVSI	•	
Servo-Robot (Canada)	•	•[2]
Selcom	•	
Siemens (W. Germany)		•
Synthetic Vision Systems	•	
Technical Arts	•	•[2]

[1] Acquired by Melles Griot.
  Machine no longer available.

[2] Nodding mirror option

Caveats
  Undoubtedly Incomplete
  Accuracy Not Guaranteed

23. Robert Simpson (ERIM) (RS)

24. Ishwar Sethi (Wayne State) (EP)

25. Uma Kant Sharma (FMC) (N)

26. George Stockman (MSU) (RS)

27. Ron Swonger (ERIM) (APP)

28. Richard Weiss (U Mass) (OR)

1.8.3   WORKSHOP GROUPS AND GROUP CHAIRS

Range Sensing

> George Stockman (Chair), MSU
> Nelson Corby, GE
> Kevin Harding, ITI
> Avi Kak, Purdue
> Robert Sampson, ERIM

Early Processing

> Gerard Medioni, USC (Chair)
> Paul Besl, General Motors (Reporter)
> Patrick Flynn, MSU
> Richard Hoffman, Northrop
> Gerhard Roth, NRC-Canada and McGill
> Ishwar Sethi, Wayne State

Object Recognition

> Thomas O. Binford (Chair)
> Robert Bolles
> Francis Quek
> Richard Weiss

Sensor Integration

> Tom Henderson (Chair)
> Ramesh Jain
> Y.T. Chien
> Jake Aggarwal
> Ruzena Bajcsy

Navigation

> C.M. Brown (Chair)
> T. Kanade
> W.E.L. Grimson
> U.K. Sharma

Applications

> C.W. "Ron" Swonger, ERIM (Chair)
> Anil Jain, Michigan State University
> Martin Levine, McGill University

2

A Rule-Based Approach to Binocular Stereopsis

S. Tanaka and A. C. Kak [1]

2.1 Introduction

Before the famous random-dot stereogram experiments by Julesz [Jul60], it was generally believed that a necessary precursor to binocular fusion was a recognition of monocular cues in each of the two images. The experiments by Julesz caused a paradigm shift of sorts in the psychophysics of the human visual system; suddenly, the preponderance of the research effort shifted toward explaining practically all aspects of human stereopsis in terms of low-level processes, as opposed to high-level cognitive phenomena. One of the high points of this post-Julesz period was the development of the Marr-Poggio paradigm [MP79]. Marr and Poggio presented a computational theory, later implemented by Grimson, that provided successful explanation of the Julesz experiments in terms of the matchings of zero-crossings at different scales, the zero-crossings at each scale corresponding to the filtering of the images with a Laplacian-of-a-Gaussian (LoG) filter [Gri81a].

During the last few years it has been recognized that while the Marr-Poggio paradigm may be an elegant model of the low level mechanisms for generating depth information, not to be ignored are the higher level cognitive phenomena that are also capable of producing the same type of information. In a majority of these higher level phenomena, there is first an explicit recognition of monocular cues in each image; depth perception is then generated either directly from the monocular cues, or through their fusion in a stereo pair.

In this chapter, we will present a rule-based procedure that makes a modest attempt at combining the Marr-Poggio type of low-level processing with higher level knowledge-based processing that takes into account a priori knowledge of the geometric nature of object surfaces involved in the binocular fusion process. In our current effort, the higher level knowledge-based processing is limited to scenes with planar surfaces. One could say

---

[1] Robot Vision Lab, School of Electrical Engineering, Purdue University, W. Lafayette, IN 47907

that at this time we have limited ourselves to a polyhedral world. However, it is not hard to conceive of ways in which the present method could be extended to worlds with different types of curved surfaces simultaneously present.

Basically, our approach represents an integration – in an opportunistic framework – of the following methods for stereo matching: 1) dominant feature matching, 2) matching under geometric constraints, 3) zero-crossing contour matching, and 4) the full MPG matching. A rationale behind the integration is that while none of these methods by themselves is capable of yielding an adequately dense range map, their synergistic combination can be expected to provide more useful input for scene interpretation. Another rationale is that the first three methods provide us with mechanisms to inject higher level constraints into the MPG process. The only dominant features currently implemented are the straight line features; our implementation of the method for such features was inspired by the work of Medioni and Nevatia [MN85] and Ayache et al. [AFFT85]. For the geometric constraint based matching, we have been much inspired by the work of Eastman and Waxman [EW87] and Hoff and Ahuja [HA87]. The only geometric constraints currently incorporated in our system are those that are given rise to by planar surfaces. For zero-crossing contour matching – also called matching under figural continuity constraints – we have learned much from the work of Mayhew and Frisby [MF81] and Grimson [Gri85]. Our implementation of figural continuity is different but retains the spirit espoused in the earlier efforts.

The framework for the integration of the methods is opportunistic in the sense that, given all the available matching strategies, at each stage of processing the system invokes that matching strategy whose applicability conditions are best satisfied by evidence extracted so far from the image region. For example, if at the beginning of processing a pair of matchable dominant features is available in the two images, the system will go ahead and utilize them for the determination of the local depth information. However, in the absence of dominant features, the system will try to invoke other matching strategies.

The opportunistic framework for integration, implemented as a rule-based program, is intended to capture human intuitions about how higher level constraints should be injected into a low-level matching procedure such as the MPG algorithm. Our intuition, which is in concurrence with the BRPS conjecture made by Mayhew and Frisby [MF81], says that if a strong high-level feature can be extracted from an image, the human visual system will go ahead and do so; the stereoptic fusion will be subsequently driven by the constraints generated by the high-level feature.

We do not wish the reader to consider our approach to be a mere smorgasbord of the already well-known approaches to stereo matching. The different component approaches in the rule-based system are not complete duplicates of their earlier implementations by other investigators. As a case in point, when matching under geometrical constraints is invoked, only the output of fine zero-crossing channel is constrained by the expected geometric form of the object surface. This is contrary to the implementations proposed by Eastman and Waxman [EW87] and Hoff and Ahuja [HA87] where geometrical constraints are also applied to coarse-channel outputs. Our rationale is that the analytical properties of the coarse channel output may bear little resemblance to the analytical properties of the object surface. For example, for a planar object like a cube against a uniform background, the fine channel output, if free of mismatch errors, will correspond fairly closely to the three dimensional shapes of the visible surfaces of the cube; however, the coarse channel output will, in most cases, look like a blobular bell shaped function.

The above discussion leads us to the following dilemma: Ideally, any available geometrical constraints generated by hypothesized knowledge of object surfaces should be applied to zero-crossings at all scales; however, due to the large smoothing operators that come into play for coarse channels, the geometrical properties of coarse-channel disparities may not correspond to those of object surfaces. And, of course, applying the geometrical constraints to just the fine channel output is hazardous because of the mismatches in the coarse channel output.

To get around these difficulties, we have taken the following approach: Geometrical constraints are hypothesized and applied only if certain robust features are detected at the outputs of the finest channel. For example, we consider strong straight edges as robust features. If, at the output of the finest channel, the system detects zero-crossing contour segments that are straight and represent large changes in image brightness levels, the system then fuses these segments by a contour matching scheme. This fusion generates a straight line in the 3-D space of the scene. Geometrical constraints are then enforced by insisting that in the vicinity of this line in 3-D space, the disparities associated with the other zero-crossings be accepted only if the disparity values are close to that of the line.

There is a further mechanism built into our computational procedure for discarding a selected geometrical hypothesis : If in the vicinity of the zero-crossings generated by straight edges, a majority of the other zero-crossings cannot be fused under the disparity constraint just mentioned, the hypothesized geometrical constraint is discarded, and a search conducted for an alternative hypothesis.

Obviously, binocular fusion under geometrical constraints generated by straight edges would not be applicable everywhere in a scene. In other regions, where applicable, we invoke constraints generated by figural continuity. And if that is impossible, too, our rule-based system uses as a last resort the straightforward MPG matching scheme.

Evidently, in any passive stereo scheme, the nature of illumination has a considerable influence on the final results. We will report on experiments conducted with both natural lighting and under artificial unstructured light illumination. The latter type of illumination was pioneered by Nishihara [Nis84,INH$^+$86] in the PRISM system.

Since what we have done can, in a sense, be considered to be a modification of the Marr-Poggio-Grimson (MPG) procedure, in what follows we will begin with a brief review of this procedure in Section 2.2, where we also discuss some of the shortcomings associated with the MPG method. Hopefully, the discussion in Section 2.2 will convince the reader that there is a need to also invoke higher level constraints during the matching process. In Section 2.3, we will review the procedures that are currently available for enforcing high-level constraints. In Section 2.4, we present in detail the matching algorithms included in the rule-based procedure. Section 2.5 then reviews some of the rules in the system to give the reader a flavor of how the high-level control is organized. In Section 2.6, we show some experimental results. Finally, concluding remarks are made in Section 2.7.

2.2   The MPG Approach to Binocular Fusion

2.2.1   Brief Review of the Coarse-to-Fine Matching Strategy

Figure 2.1 illustrates what we usually refer to as the MPG process. Each retinal image is first convolved with a set of LoG functions, the function being of the form :

$$\nabla^2 G\,(\,x,\,y\,) \;=\; \left(\frac{x^2 + y^2}{\sigma^2} \,-\, 2\right)\,\exp\left(-\,\frac{x^2 + y^2}{2\,\sigma^2}\right). \qquad (2.1)$$

where ∇^2 stands for the Laplacian operator

$$\nabla^2 \;=\; \frac{\delta^2}{\delta x^2} \;+\; \frac{\delta^2}{\delta y^2} \qquad (2.2)$$

and $G(x,y)$ represents the smoothing kernel

$$G(x,y) \;=\; \sigma^2 \exp\left(-\frac{x^2 + y^2}{2\sigma^2}\right) \qquad (2.3)$$

Although the "width" of the LoG function, as described above, is characterized by the parameter σ, it is more frequently referred to by a parameter usually denoted by w_{2D}, the relationship between the two being

$$\sigma \;=\; \frac{w_{2D}}{2\sqrt{2}} \qquad (2.4)$$

The convolving functions in Figure 2.1 correspond to w_{2D} values of 63, 32, 16, and 8. As Grimson has pointed out, in the HVS there is physiological evidence for the presence of a fifth channel with w_{2D} equal to 4 [Gri81b].

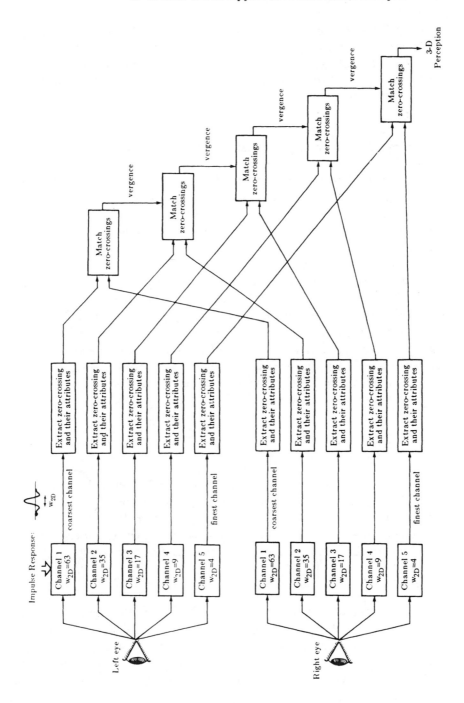

FIGURE 2.1. The Marr - Poggio - Grimson algorithm. The boxes under "Impulse Response" are where an image is convolved with a Laplacian-of-Gaussian operator.

For each image, the convolved outputs form a coarse-to-fine representation. Large scale variations manifest themselves via zero-crossings only in the coarser (large w_{2D}) channels, while the small scale variations generated by surface textures show mostly in the outputs of the finer channels. In Figure 2.1, there is an order to the matching of zero-crossings, which may or may not be representative of the human visual system but forms a good strategy for engineering implementations. As depicted in the figure, we first match the zero-crossings, taking into account the local orientations of the zero-crossing contours, in the coarsest channel. [Because of the nature of our rule-based superstructure, it is not necessary for us to directly enforce figural continuity constraints in the matching process, as was, for example, done by Grimson [Gri85]. In other words, the figural continuity considerations are subsumed by the rule-based procedure.] The disparity values thus generated form a coarse range map of the scene and are used for vergence control for the next channel – for a computer implementation, vergence control merely means that before matching a pair of zero-crossings in, say, the $w_{2D} = 32$ channel, the right-image zero-crossing is shifted by the local disparity value generated by the $w_{2D} = 64$ channel. Of course, it is unlikely that the $w_{2D} = 64$ disparity would be available exactly where it is needed, in that event a neighborhood is constructed around the right-image zero-crossing, and the average of the coarser disparities in the neighborhood is used for vergence control. Further details on such matters may be found elsewhere [Gri81b,Kak85].

2.2.2 SOME COMPUTATIONAL ASPECTS OF THE MPG ALGORITHM

The computational steps in each channel of the MPG algorithm consist of three steps: 1) extraction of zero-crossings, 2) matching of zero-crossings between the two images, and, 3) disambiguation if multiple candidates are available for matching. In the following subsections, we will briefly discuss the nature of computations involved in each of the steps.

Extraction of Zero-Crossings

In the implementation used for this research, the left and the right images were convolved with three LoG operators for w_{2D} equal to 16, 8 and 4. To save on computational time we did not use any larger operators. The larger operators simply permit the depth range to be greater; in our experiments we limited the maximal depth to what would correspond to a w_{2D} value of 16.

The double convolution implied by the kernel of Eq. 2.1 has considerable bearing on the computational efficiency of the MPG process. Until recently, the LoG function in Eq. 2.1 was not considered separable and the convolutions involved had to be implemented as two dimensional integrations. The only way around this difficulty was to approximate the LoG form by a difference of two Gaussion function and exploit the separability of a Gaussian kernel to reduce two dimensional integrations into sequences of one-dimensional integrations. However, more recently, Chen et al. [CHM86] have shown that it is possible to decompose the LoG kernel and express the decomposition as a sum of two parts, each part being separable in its x and y dependences. More specifically, the LoG kernel was shown to be expressible as:

$$\nabla^2 G(x, y) = h_{12}(x, y) + h_{21}(x, y) \tag{2.5}$$

where

$$h_{ij} = h_i(x) \times h_j(y) \tag{2.6}$$

$$h_1(\xi) = \sqrt{K}\left(1 - \frac{\xi^2}{\sigma^2}\right) e^{\frac{-\xi^2}{2\sigma^2}} \tag{2.7}$$

$$h_2(\xi) = \sqrt{K}\, e^{\frac{-\xi^2}{2\sigma^2}} \tag{2.8}$$

Note that the value of K does not affect the position of zero-crossings.

Representing Zero-Crossings

Although theoretically the zero-crossing contours are supposed to be closed, in practice if left-right scanning is used to detect the presence of a zero-crossing on each raster line (by looking for sign reversals in the LoG filtered output), the zero-crossings contours come out broken. The breaks are caused by the near-horizontal segments of what would otherwise be continuous contours, since in the vicinity of such segments it is difficult to detect left-to-right sign reversals. In general, breaks can also be caused by the magnitude of the pixel differences on the two sides of a zero-crossing not exceeding an acceptance threshold.

In order to obtain continuous zero-crossing contours, we use the following strategy. All the positive pixels in the LoG filtered image are marked as +1's, and all the negative values as 0's. The zero-crossing contours are then extracted by following the boundaries of the positive regions, where the boundaries are defined as the 4-connectedness neighbor of negative regions. During the contour extraction process, each zero-crossing is tagged as either 'p' or 'n', depending upon whether or not its immediate-left neighbor is lesser or greater than its immediate-right neighbor. If during the the left-to-right comparison, one of the neighbors is on the boundary, the zero-crossing is classified as '0', which is meant to stand for 'other.'

The above procedure results in the formation of two $N \times N$ character arrays, $L_w(x, y)$ and $R_w(x, y)$, for the two images, where N is the image size and equals 256 in our system. The contents of these arrays are

$$L_w(x, y) = \text{'}p\text{'} \quad \text{if a positive zero} - \text{crossing exists at } (x, y) \qquad (2.9)$$

$$\text{in the left image after the LoG operator is applied}$$

$$= \text{'}n\text{'} \quad \text{if a negative zero} - \text{crossing exists at } (x, y)$$

$$\text{in the left image after the LoG operator is applied}$$

$$= \text{'}0\text{'} \quad \text{else}$$

$$R_w(x, y) = \text{'}p\text{'} \quad \text{if a positive zero} - \text{crossing exists at } (x, y)$$

$$\text{in the right image after the LoG operator is applied}$$

$$= \text{'}n\text{'} \quad \text{if a negative zero} - \text{crossing exists at } (x, y)$$

$$\text{in the right image after the LoG operator is applied}$$

$$= \text{'}0\text{'} \quad \text{else.}$$

Determination of the Search Window Size

As shown in Figure 2.1, after the zero-crossings are extracted from each of the two images, the outputs of different channels must be matched and the zero-crossings from the left and right images paired in each of the channels. While this matching process is relatively straightforward for the coarsest channel, it must be preceded by vergence for the other channels. In this section, we will first describe how the search windows are set up to match the zero-crossings and the issues affecting this process.

In Figure 2.2, we show how a search window is set up to find a match in the right image for a left image zero-crossing. We transfer the coordinates of the left image zero-crossing into the right image and then construct a one-dimensional window of width $\pm w_{2D}$ around the resulting point.[2] Ideally, as was pointed out by Marr and Poggio [MP79], one should use a search window size of $\pm \frac{w_{2D}}{2}$, since in this case one can show theoretically that with 95% probability there will be only one right-image zero-crossing in the search window. In practice, $\pm \frac{w_{2D}}{2}$ sized search windows are too narrow to be practical, as difficulties are caused by shifts in zero-crossing contours, these shifts being produced by the interaction of gray level changes within the domain of support of the LoG operator [Ber84]. To demonstrate these

---

[2] Strictly speaking, this is only true of the coarsest channel in a multi-channel implementation. For finer channels, we add to the coordinates of the left image the disparities of all the coarser channels before setting up the search window. This, as was mentioned before, is called vergence control.

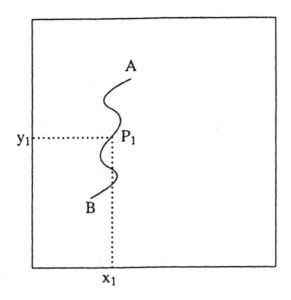

(a) Left Image.

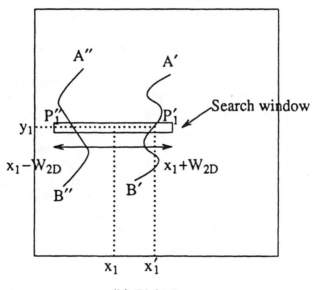

(b) Right Image.

FIGURE 2.2. Search window in the right-image for finding possible matches for a left-image zero-crossing. In the example shown, there exist two right-image zero-crossings, P_1' and P_1'', in the search window. The search window extends from $x_1 - w_{2D}$ to $x_1 + w_{2D}$, where x_1 is the horizontal coordinate of the left-image zero-crossing.

shifts, we have shown in Figure 2.3 the stereo images of a box scene with illumination arranged in such a manner that a shadow is cast on one side of the box in the left image only. To show how this shadow causes a shift in the placement of zero-crossings, we have used the notion of scale-space filtering, introduced first by Witkin [Wit83], and considered the gray levels on only the line PQ of the images. Figures 2.4a and 2.5a show the gray levels along PQ in the two images, respectively. Figures 2.4b and 2.5b show the zero-crossings obtained for different choices of w_{2D} for these gray levels. It is clear that the left image zero-crossings suffer greater shifts for larger w_{2D} than the right image zero-crossings, this being a consequence of the presence of the large gray level change at the shadow boundary in the left image.

Due to these shifts in the locations of zero-crossings, it is more common to use $\pm w_{2D}$ search windows, even though this implies that the probability of finding a single zero-crossing in the right image search window will be down to 50% and that in the rest of the cases there may be more than one candidate zero-crossing, leading to increased burden on disambiguation procedures.

If only a single zero-crossing is located within the search window, it is accepted as a match provided there is also a match in the orientations of the local zero-crossing contours. If the orientations do not correspond, then the left-image zero-crossing is simply left unmatched.

We will now describe how the zero-crossing orientation information is captured. A method to compute the local contour orientation was presented in a prior study [Kak85]. The approach there consisted of computing the x- and y - directional gradients by the application of Sobel operators and taking the arctan of the two, yielding a value for orientation which could take any value in the interval [0, 180 deg].

In our current implementation of the MPG procedure, we do not directly compute the orientations of the local zero-crossing contours. The contour orientation information is indirectly taken into account by comparing the local binary bit patterns in the binary images generated during the contour extraction procedure presented in Section 2.2.2. We believe this approach is much more efficient.

To explain the comparison of the bit patterns, let A_{il}, and A_{ir} be the values over 3 $\times$ 3 binary patches of the left and the right images, respectively, as shown in Figure 2.6. We assume that the pixel where information is sought about the orientation of the zero-crossing contour is located at the center of the 3x3 matrix. Let S be the matching magnitude computed by the following formula:

$$S = \sum_{i=0}^{7} NEG \, (\, A_{il} \; XOR \; A_{ir} \,), \qquad (2.10)$$

where XOR denotes the logical exclusive-or and NEG the logical nega-

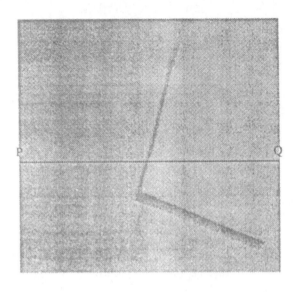

(a) Left Image.

(b) Right Image.

FIGURE 2.3. The scene consists of a box on a flat background.

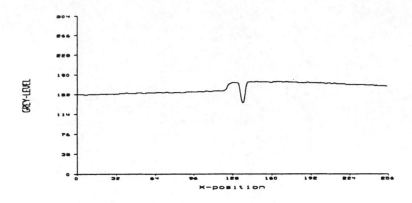

(a)

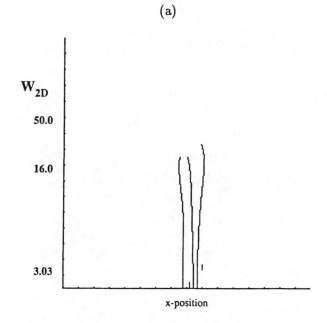

(b)

FIGURE 2.4. (a) Gray level variations across line PQ in the left image of Figure 2.3. (b) Locations of zero-crossings along PQ for different w_{2D}.

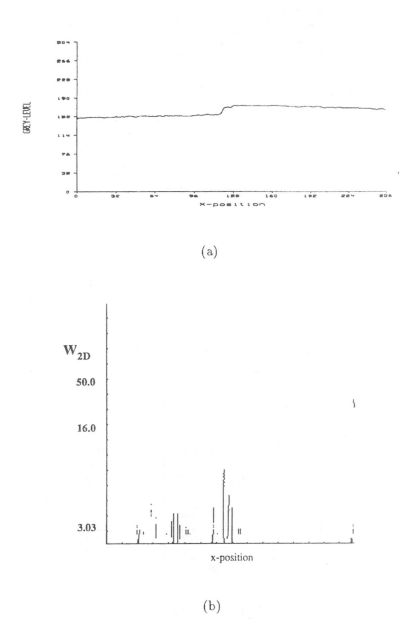

(a)

(b)

FIGURE 2.5. (a) Gray level variations across line PQ in the right image of Figure 2.3. (b) Locations of zero-crossings along PQ for different w_{2D}.

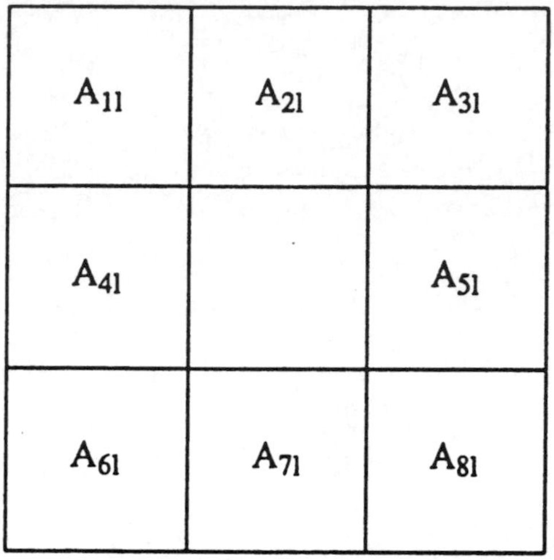

A_{11}	A_{21}	A_{31}
A_{41}		A_{51}
A_{61}	A_{71}	A_{81}

(a) Left Image.

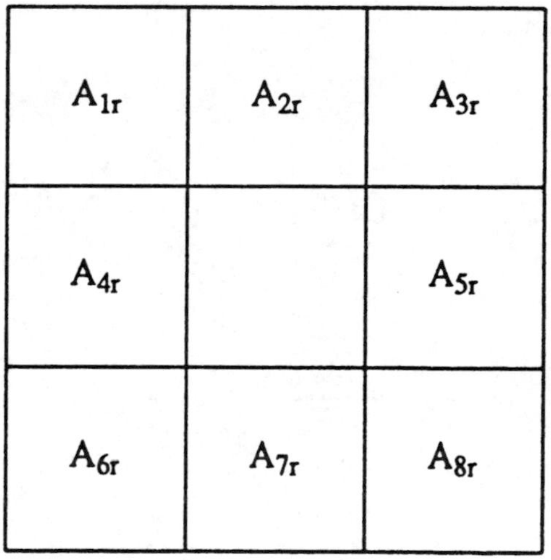

A_{1r}	A_{2r}	A_{3r}
A_{4r}		A_{5r}
A_{6r}	A_{7r}	A_{8r}

(b) Right Image.

FIGURE 2.6. Local orientations of zero-crossing contours are compared by exclusive-or of the bit patterns over 3×3 windows, the pixels where orientation comparisons are sought are at the centers of the windows.

tion. If all eight elements of the 3 × 3 matrices match, the value S is 8, meaning the two contours have identical orientations. If one of the eight elements differs, then S is 7, which, as should become evident from Table 2.1, corresponds to a maximum orientation difference of 27 degrees.[3] The orientation differences for a 1 bit disagreement can be found by comparing the orientations for the successive entries in the table. Again from the table, when the value of S is 6, meaning that two bits in the left and the right image patterns are in disagreement, the angular difference between the corresponding contours is at least 34 degrees. Since we did not want the contour orientations to differ by more than 30 degrees, we used a threshold of 7 on S. In other words, two zero-crossing orientations were considered to be the same if there was only a one bit disagreement between their corresponding neighborhood binary masks.

Our binary neighborhood comparison procedure has one advantage over methods that are more explicit in their usage of local orientations. Consider the following two binary patterns in the neighborhood of a zero-crossing.

$$
\begin{array}{ccc}
1 & 1 & 1 \\
0 & 1 & 1 \\
1 & 1 & 1
\end{array}
\qquad
\begin{array}{ccc}
0 & 0 & 1 \\
0 & 1 & 1 \\
0 & 0 & 1
\end{array}
$$

The Sobel operator would assign the same contour slope to the center point of both the patterns, since at the center point the first derivative in both cases is the same, only the second derivatives are different. Therefore, a matcher that uses gradient calculation based orientations would match the two zero-crossings corresponding to the patterns, although such a match would be erroneous. However, with our scheme, when two patterns are compared, the resulting value of S is 4, which is below the threshold, therefore the zero-crossings would not be matched.

Note that there is an implied assumption here that prior to the setting up of search windows in the manner described above, the two images are already rectified. Rectification means that the epipolar lines in the two images are parallel and correspond to the rows of the matrices representing the images. More specifically, it is assumed that the correspondents of all the pixels on the i-th row of the left image are on the i-th row of the right image. In general, this will not be the case, especially when the optic axes of the two cameras are not parallel. As discussed by Horn [Hor86], when the optic axes are convergent, the epipolar lines in each of the image planes are also convergent. For example, the epipolar lines in the left image must all radiate out from the left-image point corresponding to the camera center of the right image.

---

[3]The orientation entries in the table were generated by the application of 3x3 Sobel operators to the bit patterns shown in the second and the fourth columns. Note that the table itself is not used during the matching of zero-crossings. It is shown here only for the purpose of justifying the threshold used on S.

Orien-tation (deg)	3 × 3 patch (binary image patch)	Orien-tation (deg)	3 × 3 patch (binary image patch)
0	0 0 0 * 1 0 1 * 0 0 0 * 1 1 1 1 1 1 0 1 0 1 1 1 1 1 1 1 1 1	180	1 1 1 * 1 1 1 * 1 1 1 * 1 1 1 0 1 0 1 1 1 0 0 0 0 0 0 1 0 1
27	0 0 1 * 0 0 0 1 1 1 0 1 1 1 1 1 1 1 1	207	1 1 1 1 1 1 * 1 1 0 1 1 1 0 0 0 1 0 0
45	0 0 1 0 1 1 1 1 1	225	1 1 1 1 1 0 1 0 0
63	0 1 1 0 0 1 0 1 1 0 1 1 1 1 1 0 1 1	243	1 1 0 1 1 1 1 1 0 1 1 0 1 0 0 1 1 0
90	1 1 1 0 1 1 0 0 1 0 1 1 0 1 1 0 1 1 1 1 1 0 1 1 0 0 1	270	1 0 0 1 1 0 1 1 1 1 1 0 1 1 0 1 1 0 1 0 0 1 1 0 1 1 1
117	1 1 1 0 1 1 0 1 1 0 1 1 0 1 1 0 0 1	297	1 0 0 1 1 0 1 1 0 1 1 0 1 1 0 1 1 1
135	1 1 1 0 1 1 0 0 1	315	1 0 0 1 1 0 1 1 1
153	1 1 1 * 1 1 1 1 1 1 0 1 1 1 0 0 0 0 0	333	0 0 0 1 0 0 * 0 1 1 1 1 1 1 1 1 1 1 1

TABLE 2.1. 3 × 3 bit patterns and the associated edge orientations, as determined by actually applying a Sobel operator to the bit patterns, are shown in the table. Straight lines with orientations corresponding to the patterns marked * are not used for matching because these orientations are too close to being horizontal.

In case the concept is not already familiar to the reader, given a point in one of the two images of a stereo pair the epipolar line is defined as that line in the other image on which the corresponding point must lie. Given, say, a left-image point, we can argue that the object point must lie on the ray passing through the image point and the left camera center; if we project this ray onto the right image, we obtain the epipolar line for the left-image point in question. By analyzing the geometry associated with epipolar lines, it can be shown that when the optic axes are parallel, the epipolar lines must also become parallel. We demonstrate this with images of an object consisting of a lattice pattern, whose horizontal and vertical line are perpendicular, drawn on a sheet of paper. Figures 2.7a and b show a stereo pair of images obtained when the camera axes are convergent with an angle of 45 °. From the slight slant of the lines in the images, it is clear that in this case it would be inaccurate to use one-dimensional search windows for solving the correspondence problem. The process of rectification consists of transforming each of the images in such a manner that the transformed stereo pair corresponds to the case of parallel optic axes. In general, such transformations can be complicated. In our research, we have circumvented the difficulties of rectification by keeping the camera optic axes nearly parallel, usually within 10 °, and objects at a relatively large distance from the camera baseline. The camera baseline was typically 20 inches long and the object to baseline distance typically 110 inches. Figures 2.7c and d show stereo images of the 2-D lattice object taken under such conditions. Although visually there does not appear to be any distortion in the images, to be on the safe side we use a slight modification of the search described before the right image correspondents of the left image zero-crossings: we search in $\pm w_{2D}$ intervals in the row above and the row below. Thus we eliminate the need for rectification.

The reader should also note that a further correction is usually necessary before the zero-crossings can be matched even with the window modification we just described. In general, the plane containing the two optic axes will not intersect the image planes along lines parallel to the scan lines, assuming of course that the two axes are very nearly parallel and "containable in a plane. When this happens, the epipolar lines although parallel will not lie along the camera scan lines. To get around this difficulty, the two images must first be row-registered. Although one can visualize high-precision experimental set-ups where this would not be a problem, in our experiments, where the cameras are mounted on ordinary tripods, we must do the row-registration manually before matching. Our camera images are 512×480. From the left image, we first extract a 256×256 subimage. Then, from the right image, we extract a similar sized subimage that appears to be best row-registered with the left subimage.

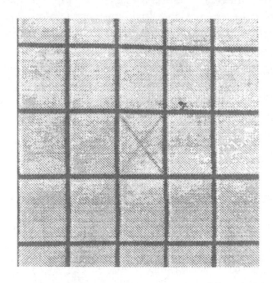

(a) Left image (angle = 45 deg.)

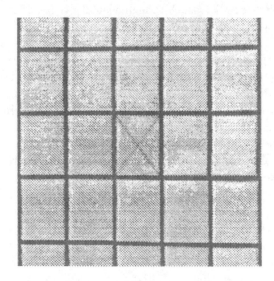

(b) Right image (angle = 45 deg.)

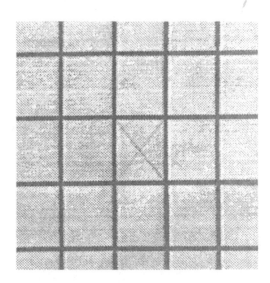

(c) Left image (angle = 10 deg.)

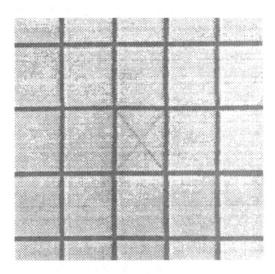

(d) Right image (angle = 10 deg.)

FIGURE 2.7. The stereo pair in a and b corresponds to the case when the optic axes of the two cameras are not parallel; as a result the horizontal lines in the images are slightly slanted. On the other hand, the optic axes are nearly parallel for the image pair in c and d.

Disambiguation

Since, statistically, there will be many cases where there are two or more candidate zero-crossings inside a search window of size $\pm w_{2D}$, one has to employ some disambiguation strategy to select one of the zero-crossings. Following Marr and Poggio [MP79], the notion of *pulling effect* is used by us for disambiguation. The pulling effect is intended to lend a certain measure of continuity to the calculated disparities values; meaning that since disparity variations can not be chaotic, if there is a choice one must use that value which is most consistent with the disparities in the neighborhood. Grimson [Gri85] implemented the pulling effect in the following manner: In the k th channel, let c_{k_i}, i=1,2,...,n, be the candidate zero-crossings in a right image search window set up for a given left image zero-crossing. Let d_{k_i} be the disparity of the i th candidate. We will accept that d_{k_i} for which we can find a coarser channel zero-crossing within a specified neighborhood of the left image zero-crossing, the disparity d_{k-1} that is associated with the coarser channel zero-crossing being such that

$$|d_{k_i} - d_{k-1}| \leq \frac{w_k}{2} \tag{2.11}$$

where w_k is the w_{2D} for the k-th channel. This pulling effect is illustrated in Figure 2.8a where C corresponds to d_{k-1}.

Our implementation is quite different from that of Grimson, since we do not at all use the coarser channel disparities for the pulling effect. Instead, we insist that a candidate zero-crossing be selected such that

$$\left| d_{k_i} - \sum_{disamb-neighborhood} d_{k_j} \right| \leq \frac{w_k}{4} \tag{2.12}$$

where *disamb-neighborhood* stands for a neighborhood around the left-image zero-crossing in question and the summation sign is actually an averaging operation over this neighborhood. In most of our programs, the size of this neighborhood is 20x20. This approach to the pulling effect is shown in Figure 2.8b where C' is the average shown in the above equation.

The size of our pulling-effect window was set empirically. We examined a large number of stereo pairs and concluded that a larger window, say of size $\pm w_{2D}$, allowed more than one candidate match to be accepted, which violated the entire purpose of disambiguation. And, of course, a smaller window, say of size $\pm \frac{w_{2D}}{8}$ rejected too often all the candidates.

2.2.3   PROBLEMS WITH THE MPG APPROACH

The disambiguation aspect of the MPG approach is not as defensible as the rest of the formalism. Of course, at a theoretical plane, the philosophy behind disambiguation appears to be sound – as it seeks to enforce continuity

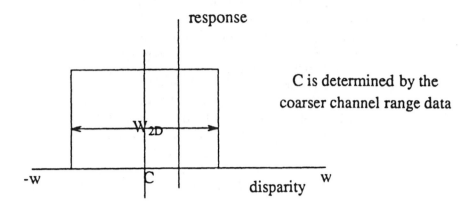

C is determined by the
coarser channel range data

(a) Grimson's Method

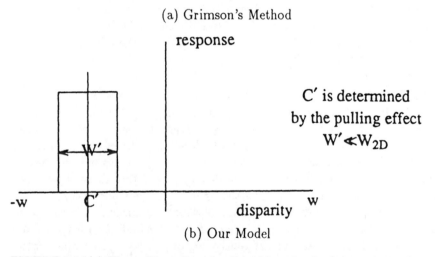

C' is determined
by the pulling effect
$W' \ll W_{2D}$

(b) Our Model

FIGURE 2.8. (a) The pulling effect for disambiguation in Grimson's implementation consists of selecting that right-image zero-crossing which is within a $\pm \frac{W_{2D}}{2}$ neighborhood of the disparity generated by the coarser channels. (b) In our implementation, the pulling effect consists of choosing that candidate right-image zero-crossing whose disparity is within a small neighborhood of the disparities corresponding to other proximal zero-crossings for the same channel.

and uniqueness on the computed disparities – however, there is a certain looseness in the implementation of the idea itself. For example, in our own implementation, the size of the window one uses for *disamb-neighborhood* depends upon how rapidly varying the depth values are, the nature of this dependence being poorly understood at this time. Our own selection for the size is made by trial and error. Clearly, a window designed for a class of scenes may not work well for another class. We maintain that the same is true for other implementations.

While the above difficulty is more in the nature of how a particular aspect of a theory should be implemented, we will now show, with the help of a simple example, a shortcoming of the MPG formalism that goes to the heart of the theory. We will show that a computational theory of depth perception must not only carry out bottom-up processing of the sensory information, as is done in the MPG approach, but it must also invoke top-down expectation-driven procedures.

For the example, assume that the object surface is made up of three panels, as shown in Figure 2.9. Also assume that the camera positions are such that panel 2 is not visible in the left image. If we assume that the surface of the object is randomly textured, it is highly probable that the zero-crossings in the panel 2 portion in the right image will match with some zero-crossings from either panel 1 or 3 in the left image. Figure 2.10 illustrates the calculated disparity values along line PQ shown in the previous figure.

To the human visual system, the object surface in Figure 2.9 presents no difficulties whatsoever when it comes to depth perception, even in the presence of occlusions, as shown there. We believe the human visual system uses higher level cognitive processing which invokes object level knowledge to place additional constraints on disparity values. We also believe that, in most cases, monocular processing is sufficient to generate these object level expectations that are then used in the process of binocular fusion.

It appears plausible that in the human visual system object-level knowledge for binocular stereopsis is triggered by strong high-level features in a scene. So, clearly, any attempt at generating object-level constraints on acceptable disparities must start with the detection of high-level features. In our work so far, the only high-level features we have used for this triggering process are straight edges that are strong and long. We refer to strong and long straight edges as dominant features.

Therefore, if a computational theory of depth perception is to not suffer from the kind of shortcoming exemplified by the three-panel example, the dominant features must first be detected and matched. The resulting structures in 3-D space must then trigger hypotheses about the orientations of surfaces in the vicinity of the dominant features. Finally, these hypotheses must generate constraints for acceptable disparities near the dominant features. Of course, if a sufficient fraction of the available zero-crossings can not be matched under a particular hypothesis, that hypothesis must

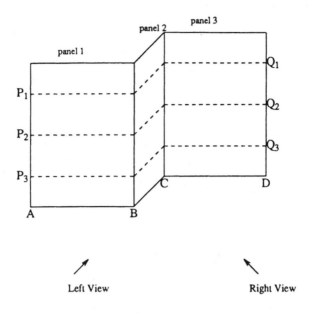

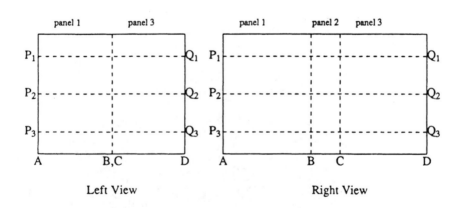

FIGURE 2.9. The three panels of the object shown at the top are arranged in such a manner that the middle panel is not visible in the left view, as shown by the two views in the lower half of the figure.

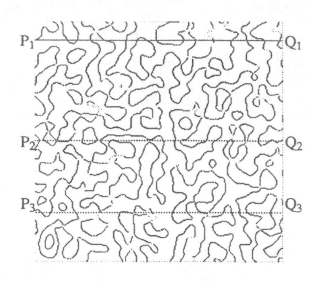

(a) Left contours

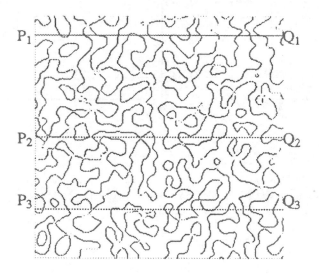

(b) Right contours

(c) Range on raster $P_1 - Q_1$

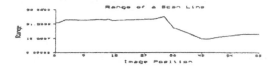

(d) Range on raster $P_2 - Q_2$

(e) Range on raster $P_3 - Q_3$

FIGURE 2.10. In parts a and b are shown the zero-crossing contours produced by one of the channels of the MPG process. When disparities are computed along the lines P_1, Q_1, P_2, Q_2, and P_3, Q_3, the results are as shown in c, d and e.

be rejected in favor of others. Clearly, if no hypotheses do justice to the zero-crossings in the vicinity of a structure generated by matching a pair of dominant features, then that structure should be discarded and other possibilities investigated for how the dominant features should be paired up. THIS IS THE ESSENCE OF OUR RULE-BASED APPROACH.

In the next section, we will briefly review the work done so far in stereo matching by invoking higher-level constraints. In the subsequent chapter, we will then discuss how some of these methods were modified for incorporation in our system.

2.3   Review of Procedures for Stereo Matching Under High-level Constraints

While the previous chapter discussed the MPG formalism and its shortcomings, this chapter will be a review of the stereo matching techniques that stand "at the other end. By the other end we mean the techniques that accomplish binocular fusion solely by high level, including object level, constraints on disparities.

2.3.1   MATCHING USING GEOMETRICAL CONSTRAINTS

In some of the existing approaches, geometrical constraints are explicitly used during the process of matching zero-crossings. For example, in the work done by Eastman and Waxman [EW87], a disparity functional is computed that estimates the coefficients of a local planar patch corresponding to a tentative match of a few adjacent zero-crossings in the left and right images. Matches may then be accepted or rejected based upon the magnitude of the disagreements between the disparity functional and the computed disparity. These authors have made the assumption that their scenes are continuous. In one of their methods, which they call the neighborhood-based algorithm, matching proceeds from the coarsest channel to the finest channel. Initially, for the coarsest channel, it is assumed that the scene is at a constant depth – which can be the average depth of the scene. Subsequently, the disparities computed at a given scale determine the location in the next finer channel of the windows to be used for searching for correspondents of zero-crossings.

The procedure proposed by Hoff and Ahuja [HA87] for enforcing geometrical constraints consists of two phases: In the first phase, as in the previous method, planar patches are fitted to tentative matches between zero-crossings, the coefficients of a planar patch being determined by the use of the Hough transform. Subsequently, in the second phase, the neighboring planar patches are clustered into quadratic surfaces by a least squares method. This then allows enforcement of geometrical constraints at the quadratic level. The control-flow for the propagation of matching information from the coarsest to the finest channels is the same as in the method of Waxman and Eastman – which is basically the same as in Grimson's implementations of the Marr-Poggio paradigm. First, in the coarsest channel, it is assumed that the scene can be represented by a constant (planar) surface at the average depth in the scene. And, then, the disparities computed are used to create a smooth curved surface for predicting the search windows for the next channel.

The notion of using geometrical constraints is, we believe, very useful, particularly for industrial vision applications. Such constraints form an important component of the rule-based approach that will be presented here.

2.3.2 THE CONSTRAINT ON THE ORDERING OF FEATURES

Images of scenes made of opaque object must observe an important constraint: monotonicity of rendition of object points. By monotonicity of rendition, we mean the following: Suppose we mark all the object surface points with a set of marks, no two of which are identical. On any line running through an image of the scene, the order of appearance of the marks must correspond to the order in the scene. In other words, there cannot be position reversals in, say, the left-right ordering of the marks. This constraint makes the stereo correspondence problem ideally amenable to solution by dynamic programming. Of course, since in practice it is not possible to mark up a scene, for using dynamic programming one has to first select a set of distinguished points from each image; how such points are selected sets apart the various implementations of this scheme. Another distinguishing aspects of the various implementations is the distance of function used for measuring the closeness of correspondence achieved between the gray levels along the epipolar lines in the two images.

To mention a few of the implementations that use the dynamic programming approach, Baker and Binford [BB81] have used for the distance-function features based on edge angles, gray levels on the two sides of an edge, relative disparities, (measured during a reduced resolution phase) and interval compression that is implied by the correspondence. The distance function used by Ohta and Kanade [OK85] uses the similarity of epipolar line intervals between successive distinguished points. In another study, by Lloyd, Haddow and Boyce [LHB87], the distance function is based upon distances between distinguished points, edge angles and average gray levels. The implementation of this last approach is along the lines of relaxation labeling. Note that in all three approaches, the distinguished points can, for example, be edge segments.

2.3.3 LOOSER ORDERING CONSTRAINT

In the dynamic programming approach, the ordering of image points declared distinguished must be strictly maintained in any matching of the two images along an epipolar line. If we loosen the constraint because of, say, the difficulty with the rectification process, the problem of matching image elements, such as edge segments, along epipolar lines can be cast as a graph search problem, as was done by Herman and Kanade [HK86]. Matching of edge segments along epipolar lines has also been carried out by Medioni and Nevatia [MN85] using a relaxation type approach.

2.3.4 SOME OTHER APPROACHES

We would now like to allude briefly to the fact that methods do exist for improving the overall accuracy of the calculated depth information that do not resort to the invocation of higher level constraint knowledge. For example, Nevatia [Nev76] has shown that if a progression of closely spaced views are fused together, it is possible to reduce mismatches in stereo correspondence without sacrificing accuracy in depth calculation. Moravec [Mor83] has also proposed a multi-view stereo-system, with similar results. Tsai [Tsa83] has used a statistical approach to combine eight views of a scene using joint moments and window variances.

2.4 Matching Methods Included in the Rule-based Program

We will now describe in greater detail the matching schemes that can be invoked by the rule-based system. At any given time, a 64 × 64 control matrix is used to store information on which matching scheme to invoke where in an image, which is usually of size 256 × 256. Each element of the control matrix, depending upon its integer value, indicates selection of a particular matching strategy. Later in this paper we will discuss how the values of this control matrix are initialized, and, subsequently, how these values are altered dynamically.

2.4.1 DOMINANT FEATURE MATCHING

In line with the discussion in the previous section, an important matching strategy consists of extraction and fusion of dominant features from the two images. At this time, the only type of dominant feature the system is capable of handling is the straight-line type. We will now describe the procedures used for first extracting straight lines and then fusing them. However, first we would like to point out that there is ample tradition in computer vision research in the use of straight line features for binocular stereopsis.

Baker and Binford [BB81] extracted edges from stereo pairs of images and represented each edge as a concatenation of piecewise straight segments, associated with each segment there being a set of attributes like orientation, side-intensities, etc. They then scanned each image row by row, and matched the segments on each row of the left image with the segments in the corresponding row of the right image by using the Viterbi algorithm. Herman and Kanade [HK86] also used a similar procedure except that in the fusion process they matched L-junctions formed by straight edge segments, instead of just straight lines. Medioni and Nevatia [MN85] extracted edges by using the Nevatia and Babu algorithm [NB80]; these edges were then matched by a relaxation-based procedure which minimized what they called differential disparity. In the Nevatia and Babu edge extraction procedure, edge points are first detected by using window operators, neighboring edge points are then connected to form continuous contours. The resulting contours are fitted with an iterative straight line fitting algorithm, which in the first iteration consists of joining the extremal points on the contour with a straight edge, and, later, if the this straight edge is too poor a fit to the contour, selecting a middle contour point for the purpose of fitting straight edges to the two segments thus formed, and so on. Ayache et al. [AFFT85] have also used straight line features for binocular fusion; the straight line features were extracted with a recursive approach similar to that of Nevatia and Babu.

Extraction of Straight Line Features

Our procedure for extracting straight line features from images uses a set of criteria that are a variation on those first proposed by Freeman [Fre74]. We believe our approach is more forgiving of small local deviations from strict straightness in linear features, whereas those used by previous investigators tend to be accomodating of departures from straightness at a more global level. In any case, our choice should be construed less as a categorical judgement on which approach might be best for the extraction of linear features and more as a matter of our own preference.

Freeman has suggested three criteria which must be satisfied by the chain code of a digital straight line [Ros74]:

1. At most two slopes occur in the chain, and if there are two, they differ by 45° exactly.

2. At least one of the two slopes occurs in runs of length 1.

3. The slope occurs in runs of at most two lengths (except possibly at the ends of the arc, where the runs may truncate) and, if there are two lengths, they must differ by 1.

These conditions, postulated for digital renditions of perfectly straight

Start

Contour

End

FIGURE 2.11. An almost straight line which violates the Freeman criteria for straightness.

lines, are not entirely satisfactory for straight lines extracted from images of objects and scenes. The "real world straight lines often exhibit small deviations from straightness; a line extraction algorithm must be forgiving of those. For example, a vertical line segment from an image might lead to the following chain code for its representation:

$$6666666766666666665666666$$

As is evident from Figure 2.11, this line, even though it violates the three Freeman criteria, would be called straight by most observers. Clearly, we need to "loosen the criteria in order to be able to process actual images. This we do in the following manner.

In the first Freeman criterion, not more than two code numbers are allowed in the chain code of a straight line; in our algorithm, up to three different codes are allowed. However, we require that when three different codes are present in a chain, the center code occur most frequently and that the values in the non-central bins not exceed a threshold T1, whose value is dependent on the length of the digital arc. By experimentation with the type of imagery that is of interest to us, we have found that an appropriate value for T1 is 3 when the length of the digital arc is 41. The reason for why we want our straight line segments to be 41 pixels long will be explained later. Figure 2.12a shows a digital arc whose length is 41 but whose chain code histogram, as shown in Figure 2.12b, is such that T1 is 4. Clearly, most observers would declare this arc as not straight.

The next Freeman criterion says that one of codes can only occur in unit lengths; we permit the maximum length of the code number that corresponds to the shortest run in the code sequence to be T2, which is also dependent on the arc length and is 2 in the current implementation. The number 2 was again arrived at through experimentation. Figure 2.13a shows a digital arc of length 41 whose histogram, as displayed in Figure 2.13b, is such that T2 is 3; this arc will again be declared as not straight by most observers. We do not at all use the third Freeman criterion.

In the rest of this section, we will first complete a description of our algorithm and then justify the underlying rationale with the help of a few examples. Note that our criteria imply that the decision about the straightness of a contour segment (meaning an arc) can be made entirely by examining its chain code histogram. Therefore, for each contour segment a chain-code histogram, represented by A, is constructed such that the bar corresponding to each code number – the code numbers go from 0 to 7 – represents the frequency of the appearance of the code number:

$$A = \{ i \mid C(i) \}, \qquad (2.13)$$

where $C(i)$ is the frequency of the chain code number i. We now use N to represent the cardinality of A, meaning the number of codes for which C(i) is non-zero:

$$N = \mid A \mid,$$

In terms of A and N, our procedure for extrating straight linear features may be stated more precisely as follows:

1. If the histogram has more than four bars ($N > 4$), this line is not straight. This line segment has at least four different orientations.

2. If the histogram has a single bar ($N = 1$), the line is purely straight, with the orientation of 0°, 45°, 90°, or 135° with the horizontal line.

3. If the histogram has two bars ($N = 2$), two cases need be considered (let the more frequently appearing code be the major code and the other code be the minor code):

   (a) If the two bars are adjacent to each other, again there are two cases:

      i. If the maximum run length of the minor code is less than a user specified threshold T2, the line is declared straight.

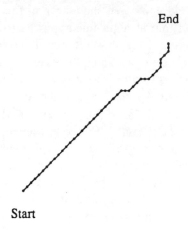

(a) A contour segment

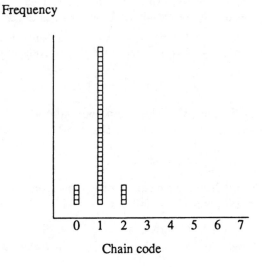

(b) Chain code histogram

FIGURE 2.12. A digital arc is shown in a and its chain-code histogram in b. This digital arc will not be declared straight because it violates the threshold T1.

(a) A contour segment

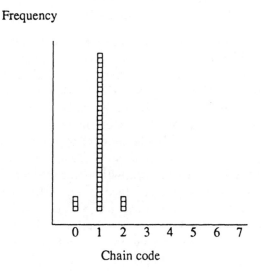

(b) Chain code histogram

FIGURE 2.13. A digital arc is shown in a and its chain-code histogram in b. This digital arc will not be declared straight because it violates the threshold T2.

        ii. If the maximum run length of the minor code is greater than T2, the line is declared as not straight.

    (b) If the two bars in the histogram are not adjacent, this arc is declared as not straight. This arc contains at least two different orientations, and the angles of these orientations differ by at least 90° difference.

4. If the histogram has three bars ($N = 3$), the following two cases need be considered.

    (a) If the three bars are adjacent to one another, the center bar is the largest, and the height of the closest neighboring bar is less than a user specified threshold T1, then there are the following two cases to consider:

        i. If the maximum run-length of the non-central code (meaning the value in the non-central bin in the histogram) is less than T2, the line is declared straight.

        ii. If the maximum run-length of the non-central code is greater than the threshold T2, the line is declared as not straight.

    (b) Of the three bars in the histogram if no two are adjacent, then the arc is declared as not straight. This arc has at least two different orientations, with angles differing by at least 90 °.

We would now like to provide empirical evidence in corroboration of our algorithm. Figure 2.14a shows a synthetic image consisting of a set of digital arcs; these have been numbered from 1 through 15. The arcs 1 through 5 satisfy all three Freeman criteria. However, the arcs 6 through 10 do not satisfy the Freeman criteria, but they do satisfy our criteria and would be considered as straight by most human observers. For example, for arcs 8 and 9 the value of N, the number of non-zero bins in the chain-code histograms, is 3. For that reason, these arcs would not be accepted as straight by the Freeman criteria. Although the chain codes for the arcs 6 and 7 contain only two slopes, which is one of the requirements of the Freeman criteria, both the slopes occur in runs of lengths more than one – which is a violation of the Freeman criteria. Similarly, arc 10 is accepted as straight by our method because we do not use Freeman's third criterion.

    The reader is probably wondering if some non-straight looking arcs would be accepted by our method. Note that the arcs 11 through 15 would not be considered straight by most observers and are also rejected by our criteria. While arc 11 is rejected because the two slopes differ by more than 90 degrees, arc 12 is not accepted because the run-length of the minor code is greater than the threshold used for declaring an arc short, which in these cases was set to 3. The minor codes of arc 13 appear more frequently than the shortness threshold value of 3. In the chain-code histograms of arc 14, the highest frequency chain-code is not at the center of the three

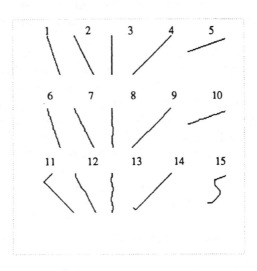

(a) A contour segment

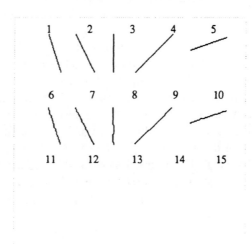

(b) Chain code histogram

FIGURE 2.14. When the straight line extraction algorithm is applied to the image in a, the result is the image in b.

consecutive non-zero frequency codes. The number of non-zero bins in the chain-code histogram for arc 15 is 4, which exceeds the maximum limit of 3. The application of the straight line extraction processing to Figure 2.14a results in Figure 2.14b.

The choice of the chain code length L in the straight line extraction algorithm is currently set to 41. The main determinant of L is the fact that longer an arc that meets our straightness criteria, the straighter it looks to a human observer. Although, this would imply that L should be made arbitrarily large, in practice if L is too large, few straight line segments would be extracted from an image. We have determined through experimentation that a value of 41 for L yields most of the straight edges for scenes of interest of us. The reader might also like to know that we have proven in [TK88] that for arcs satisfying our straightness criteria, longer L implies "greater straightness". In this proof, straightness of an arc was measured by the value of the radius of the smallest circumscribing circle of the arc; the larger the value of this radius, the straighter the arc.

Detection and Deletion of Horizontal Straight Lines

Straight line segments that are parallel, or nearly so, to epipolar lines – for our case these would be horizontal straight lines – cannot provide reliable disparity information. In general, when we establish correspondence between two straight line segments, we are in effect establishing correspondences between the pixels lying at the intersections of the line segments with the epipolar lines. For example, in Figure 2.15 if we say that line AB in the left image is the correspondent of line $A'B'$ in the right image, we are in effect saying that the points a_1, a_2, a_3, etc, which are on the intersections of line AB with the epipolar lines, are the correspondents of the points a'_1, a'_2, a'_3, etc, in the right image. When the line segments are nearly horizontal, there may be no well defined intersections between the segments and the epipolar lines, which can make impossible the calculation of disparities at such points. Therefore, it becomes necessary to detect and delete horizontal straight line segments. Note that we are not saying that an arc segment not contain any horizontal portions at all, only that if an arc segment is predominantly horizontal it should be deleted before the matching algorithm is applied.

As each contour segment is described by a chain code in our model, the detection of a horizontal line, or a nearly horizontal line is relatively easy. By the definition of chain codes, a horizontal portion of a digital arc is described by either the code 0 or the code 4. Note that straight line segments, each 41 elements long, are accepted as straight on the basis of their chain code histograms. All such histograms must have no more than three adjacent bins and the central bin must contain the largest count. If for a 41 element segment, the central bin corresponds to the chain codes 0 or 4, we reject such a segment from further considerations – since such a

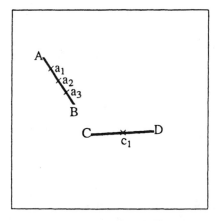

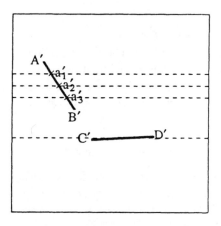

FIGURE 2.15. When these two images are fused by the straight line matching algorithm, disparity values result at the intersections of the straight lines with the epipolar lines.

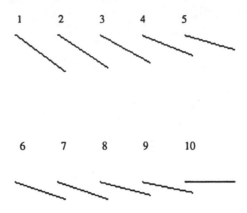

FIGURE 2.16. The procedure that detects and eliminates straight line segments that are nearly horizontal discards the segments labeled 6 through 10 before matching can begin.

segment would be mostly horizontal.

The digital arcs numbered 6 through 10 in Figure 2.16 are various examples of arc segments that were deemed as being too close to being horizontal. On the other hand, the digital arc segments 1 through 5 in Figure 2.16 contain many horizontal portions and yet were accepted for further consideration.

Binocular Fusion of Straight Line Features

We will now discuss the procedure used for the fusion of straight line features from the left and right images. For some applications, such fusion may be considered to be a special case of contour matching algorithms discussed in [SK84,Bur81,PA79,Pav79,SY81]. In most of these algorithms, a small set of parameters is used for measuring the relevant attributes of contours extracted from both images, the similarity between the corresponding contours is then established on the basis of the parameter values. For example, Pavlidis [PA79,Pav79] has used polygonal approximations for representing the contours; each contour is described by an ordered sequence of straight line arcs, there being a set of attributes associated with each arc. For each given contour in the left image, a corresponding contour is found in the right image on the basis of the similarity of these attributes. This work was followed by that of Sze et. al. [SY81], who used only one attribute for each straight line arc, the attribute being the slope of the arc.

Our approach is similar in spirit to that of Sze et al.; the difference lies in our use of chain codes for representing the straight line features, this being tantamount to using the finest possible polygonal approximation to a straight line arc. [The reader should note that, in keeping with the discussion in the preceding section, our straight lines are allowed to contain minor deviations from geometric straightness.] In another major departure from Sze et al., zero-crossing contours corresponding to straight line features are first represented by overlapping straight line segments to help us get around the difficulties caused by a straight line edge in the scene not appearing in its entirety in the final edge image; such a difficulty might be caused by the contrasts produced by illumination, etc. For example, Figure 2.17 shows four different edge images of a single scene with illumination sources placed at different angles. As the reader will notice, the same scene edge appears in different lengths in the edge images. By using overlapping segments, the straight line arcs generated by the same scene edge can be matched even when the two arcs are of unequal lengths in the two images. This notion is explained schematically in Figure 2.18. In Figure 2.18a, the arc is only 41 pixels long, while it is 60 pixels long in Figure 2.18b. The matching algorithm first constructs a list of all the 41 pixel long straight line segments it can discover in both images. In generating these overlapping segments, the starting pixels are not allowed to be within 4 pixels of one another; this is in keeping with our reduced resolution representation of disparity images computed by the rule-based stereo. In our example, for the left image, the list contains only 1 segment; while for the right image, the list consists of 6 segments. (Table 2.2 shows all the contour segments.) Each segment in the left image is then compared with every segment in the right image whose starting row index is within ±1 of the starting index of the left image segment. By making such comparisons, using a metric to be discussed below, the straight line matcher discovers that the left arc PB corresponds to the part P'B' of the arc in the right image. As the reader can see, this approach does alleviate the problems that might otherwise be caused by a part of scene edge not showing in one of the two images.

The straight line segments, each of which is 41 pixels long [see rationale for this length in Section 2.4.1], are then given chain code representations. Subsequently, the chain code for each straight line segment in the left image is compared with the chain codes of candidate segments from the right image for the purpose of finding a match. Our method for comparing two straight line segments is based on the notion that their chain codes must be similar. The following algorithm attempts to capture this notion.

In the overall algorithm for fusing straight line features, which is described in the rest of this section, first a data structure of overlapping segments in each image is created. Then candidate segments are matched by a comparison of their chain codes and a similarity score is computed. If the two segments are found matchable, the algorithm deletes from the left image data structure those segments whose starting pixels are on the segment that participated in the matching process. After all the matches have been discovered in this fashion, the last step carries out the compu-

Image	Contour No.	start-pix-col-index	start-pix-row-index	parity	chain code
Left [Fig. 23 (a)]	1	113	90	1	67677767....
Right [Fig. 23 (b)]	1	106	80	1	67777677....
	2	108	83	1	76777676....
	3	110	86	1	77676767....
	4	112	89	1	76767776....
	5	114	92	1	67776777....
	6	116	95	1	76777677....

Note:

"Start-pix-col-index" stands for the column index of the starting pixel of an arc.

"Start-pix-row-index" stands for the row index of the starting pixel of an arc.

"Parity" is either 1 or 0 corresponding to the positive or negative of contour parity.

TABLE 2.2. This table shows the data structure used for the straight line segments shown in Figures 23a and b. Since the segment in Figure 23a is only 41 elements long, only one chain code is required for its representation. On the other hand, the segment in Figure 23b, 60 pixels long, requires a set of overlapping chain codes.

(a) Illumination 1

(b) Illumination 2

(c) Illumination 3

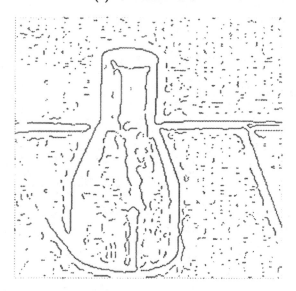

(d) Illumination 4

FIGURE 2.17. In general, even the corresponding edge segments in the two images of a stereo pair will have different lengths. To get around this difficulty, all straight and long edges are represented by an overlapping set of straight edges of fixed length; the fixed length in our current implementation is 41 pixels. To illustrate this idea, the left edge PB, which is 41 elements long, corresponds to the right edge P'B', which is 60 elements long. Due to its length, P'B' gives rise to many overlapping straight edge segments, each only 41 elements long. PB is matched with only one of them.

(a) Left digital arc

(b) Right digital arc

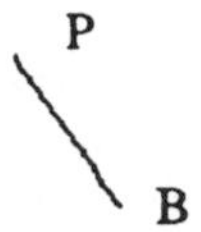

(c) Matched digital arc

FIGURE 2.18. Depending on its length, each line in the image will be represented by many fixed length straight line segments.

tation of range along the points in space that give rise to matched pairs of segments. The following is a step-by-step description of the algorithm.

THE STRAIGHT LINE MATCHING ALGORITHM

STEP-1 Each edge image is represented by a data structure which is a list of straight line segments. For example, the edge image in Figure 2.19 is represented by the list

$\{ segment_{AB(0)}, segment_{AB(1)}, segment_{AB(2)}, ..., segment_{AB(N1)},$

$segment_{CD(0)}, segment_{CD(1)}, segment_{CD(2)}, ..., segment_{CD(N2)},$

$segment_{EF(0)}, segment_{EF(1)}, segment_{EF(2)}, ..., segment_{EF(N3)},$

$segment_{GH(0)}, segment_{GH(1)}, segment_{GH(2)}, ..., segment_{GH(N4)} \}$
,

where $segment_{AB(i)}$ represent the i th 41-element long segment extracted from the arc AB.

STEP-2: Each straight line segment is represented by the following data structure

{ start-pixel-col-index, start-pixel-row-index, parity, chain-code }, where the first entries are self-explanatory, the third entry is +1 for straight line segments that represent positive zero-crossings – meaning the gray levels are increasing perpendicular to these segments as we go from left to right – and -1 for segments representing negative zero-crossings. Finally, the last item, which is the chain code for the segment, is a list which for the purpose of explanation will be denoted by

$$(L(1), L(2), ..., L(N))$$

for the left image arcs and by

$$(R(1), R(2), ..., R(N))$$

for the right image arcs. Note that both these chain code lists represent arcs that contain N+1 pixels.

STEP-3: In comparing the data structures for two segments from the two images, the algorithm first makes a check for the positional correspondence. This is done by examining start-pixel-col-index, start-pixel-row-index for the two segments. The difference of start-pixel-col-index's must be within the range of the maximum permissible value for the disparity. The difference of start-pixel-row-index's must be within a small value which is meant to account for any distortions that might be present in the epipolar geometry; this distortion might be caused by factors such as perspective effects, relative tilt between the cameras and their optic axes while being parallel in the horizontal plane but not so in the vertical plane. In the current implementation, the threshold is set to 1.

STEP-4: A similarity score, denoted by T, is computed for the two segments by comparing their chain codes. Initially, the value of T is set to 0. At step i, let the chain code elements from the two segments be $L(i)$ and $R(i)$. For each i, i $= 1,....,$N, the total score T is accumulated by using

$$\text{if } L(i) = R(i) \text{ then } T = T + 1$$
$$\text{if } L(i) = R(i\text{-}1) \text{ then } T = T + W$$
$$\text{if } L(i) = R(i\text{+}1) \text{ then } T = T + W$$

where $0 \leq W \leq 1$. The number W, which would always be set to a value greater than zero for matching straight line segments, captures the intuitive notion that if a chain code element is to be matched to a neighbor of its true correspondent then such a match must receive a reduced weight. In the current implementation, W has been set to 0.5, although we will show some matching results obtained by setting

W to different values. In the event the reader is still wondering about the necessity of using neighbors in the matching process, note the following difficulty caused by the digital representation of straight line segments. Figure 2.20 shows two straight line segments from the left and right images; these are represented by the following chain codes.

Arc segment A : 1212121212

Arc segment B : 2121212121

These two chain-code strings will represent similar digital contours to the human eye. By the algorithm shown above, the total similarity score T is zero when $W = 0$, However, with W set to 0.5, the similarity score increases to 10. Note that the second element of arc A is matchable with the first and the third element of arc B, each contributing 0.5 to the cumulative, and therefore both match possibilities contributing total score of 1. The symmetry of the similarity score associated with the two arcs A and B, which means the equality of the similarity score produced in either the case when A is in the left image and B is in the right image, or the case when B is in the left image and A is in the right image, is clearly guaranteed.

STEP-5: If the similarity score T does not exceed a pre-set threshold, denoted here by T3, delete the left image segment under consideration from the left image data structure created by STEP 1.

STEP-6: If the similarity score T exceeds the threshold T3, declare the two segments as matchable. Through experimentation with segments of length 41 pixels, we have found that an appropriate value for T3 is 50. Note that the similarity score of 10 for the example shown in the previous step really does not apply to 41 pixel segments. Delete from the left image data structure shown in STEP 1 the segment which is examined.

STEP-7: If the left image data structure created in STEP 1 is non-nil, go to STEP 3.

STEP-8: In this step, range values to the scene points that lie on the matched segments are computed by the following procedure: Let $D(i)$, $i=0,1,..,N$ be the disparity computed from the ith pixels in the left and the right image segments; as defined in STEP-2, the chain codes of these matching pixels being $L(i)$ and $R(i)$, respectively. The disparities, $D(i)$, is obtained from the chain codes $L(i)$ and $R(i)$ by the following formula in which A, A1, A2 are temporary variables:

D (0) ← CL - CR
>   where CL = start-pixel-col-index for the first pixel
>   in the left image segment
>   CR = start-pixel-row-index for the first pixel
>   in the right image segment

For i ← 1 step 1 until N do
begin
>   if (L (i) = (0, 1, or 7))
>   A1 = 1;
>   else if (L (i) = (2, or 6))
>   A1 = 0;
>   else if (L (i) = (3, 4, or 5))
>   A1 = -1;
>   if (R (i) = (0, 1, or 7))
>   A2 = 1;
>   else if (R (i) = (2, or 6))
>   A2 = 0;
>   else if (R (i) = (3, 4, or 5))
>   A2 = -1;
>   A = A1 - A2;
>   D (i) = D (i -1) + A;

end

Because the straight line segments are overlapping, a contour match may produce a new disparity value for a point where the disparity has already been computed. If this happens, the new value is simply discarded.

Although, in most cases, the range map computations are carried out over the 256 × 256 matrices used for representing images, for display purposes the range maps are down-sampled to 64 × 64. In Figure 2.21, twenty pairs of synthetic digital arcs are shown. The similarity score for each pair is shown in Table 2.3.

Effect of Scene Illumination on the Extraction of Dominant Features

How a scene is illuminated has a considerable bearing on the quality of results obtained with the matching of straight line features. In general, it is possible to use either normal room lighting, or, one can also use the unstructured light illumination proposed first by Nishihara [Nis84] for their PRISM system. Ordinarily, for object surfaces that are of uniform color and texture, and that, therefore, may not yield sufficiently many gray level variations, a large number of zero-crossings will be obtained with unstructured illumination. However, unstructured illumination will tend to obliterate the contrasts between adjoining surfaces, which under normal room

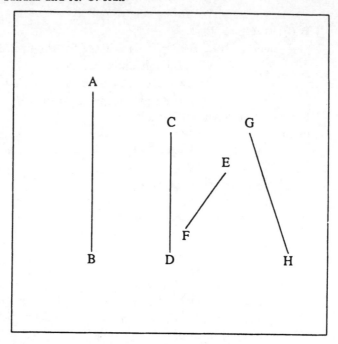

FIGURE 2.19. Depending on its length, each line in the image will be represented by many fixed length straight line segments.

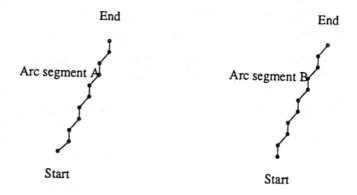

FIGURE 2.20. These two digital arcs possess different chain codes, yet they are visually identical. The differences at the two ends would not be considered important by most observers.

No.	Left Arc (Angle)	Right Arc (Angle)	Magnitude of Match	Matched? (Threshold=50)
1	71	56	47.5	no
2	71	63	49.5	no
3	71	71	54.0	yes
4	71	76	54.5	yes
5	71	90	58.0	yes
6	71	104	49.0	no
7	71	108	46.5	no
8	71	116	38.5	no
9	71	124	34.0	no
10	71	127	30.5	no
11	56	56	54.0	yes
12	56	63	52.0	yes
13	56	71	47.5	no
14	56	76	45.5	no
15	56	90	41.5	no
16	56	104	35.5	no
17	56	108	34.5	no
18	56	116	29.5	no
19	56	124	27.5	no
20	56	127	26.0	no

TABLE 2.3. In the fourth column are shown the similarity scores produced by the straight line matcher for line segments shown in Figure 2.21.

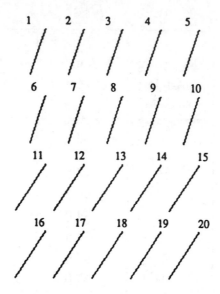

(a) Left Image

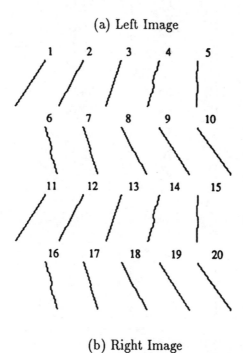

(b) Right Image

FIGURE 2.21. Similarity scores were computed for the left and right digital arcs possessing the same index. These scores are shown in Table 2.3.

lighting may cause the edges to become very noticeable. For this reason, for our experiments we use both illuminations. The images recorded under normal room lighting are used for the extraction of dominant features, while those recorded with unstructured light are used for the rest of the matching strategies.

To show the reader the different results that are obtained with these two illuminations, the image in Figure 2.22a was recorded with both types of illuminations present simultaneously; the upper half of the scene was illuminated with unstructured light, while normal room lighting was used for the lower half. Figure 2.22b shows the extracted zero-crossings, which bear out our claims about the relative advantages of the two illuminations.

Some Disparity Results Obtained with Just Straight Line Feature Matching

Figure 2.23a illustrates the surface structure of an object which is rather rich in straight edges; we will use stereo images of this object, shown in Figure 2.24, to illustrate the results obtained with straight line matching. The stereo images were taken under normal room illumination. The straight line features extracted from the two images are shown in Figure 2.25. Each image there shows two types of straight lines. We have used continuous dark lines for positive straight lines, these are lines across which the gray levels increase from left to right, and negative straight lines, across these the gray levels decrease in a left to right traversal. The disparities computed by matching the straight lines in the stereo pair of Figure 2.25 are shown in Figure 2.26. Table 2.4 displays a comparison of the computed disparities with those obtained from the ground truth information at a set of points marked as A through K in Figure 2.23.

2.4.2 GEOMETRICALLY CONSTRAINED MATCHING

The second major matching scheme invoked by the rule-based system utilizes matching under geometrical constraints. As will be explained later, this type of matching is invoked for image regions that are in the vicinity of the straight line features matched by the method discussed previously. Matching of straight lines from the left and the right images yields range information about a straight edge in 3D space, the geometrically constrained matching then extends this to space in the neighborhood of the straight edge.

Although the mathematical procedure used for matching under geometrical constraints is essentially the same as that used by Eastman and Waxman [EW87], there are important differences. As mentioned before, we only apply this type of matching to the zero-crossings produced by the finest LOG filter. Also, geometrically constrained matching is performed only in the vicinity of regions where we are able to match straight line features.

(a) Original Image

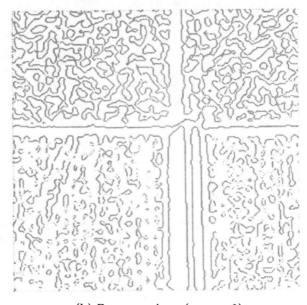

(b) Zero-crossings ($w_{2D} = 8$)

FIGURE 2.22. (a) This scene, which consists of a flat background with a rectangular ridge running through it vertically, is used to demonstrate the effect of illumination. The top half of the scene was illuminated with unstructured light and the bottom half with regular room light. (b) zero-crossing contours corresponding to the two halves.

Image Point	Disparity in terms of depth [inches]	Actual Depth [inches]
A	-0.8	-0.6
B	3.8	3.6
C	3.6	3.5
D	-1.5	-1.2
E	3.0	3.0
F	2.9	2.8
G	0.0	0.0
H	-1.1	-1.1
I	3.2	3.0
J	2.8	2.8
K	-1.9	-2.5

Image points A though K are the points marked as ×
in Figure 30 (a).

TABLE 2.4. Comparison of the depth values generated by the straight line matcher with ground truth. The image points labeled A, B, ... are shown in Figure 2.23.

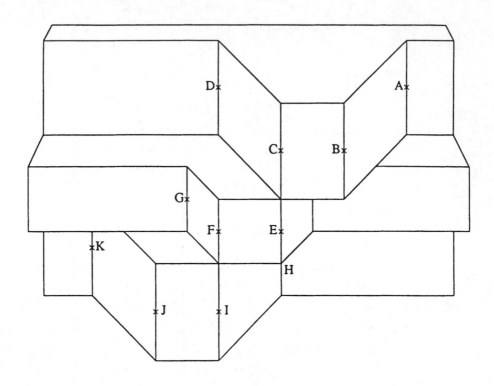

(a) Object Surface

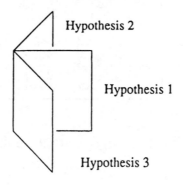

(b) Hypotheses

FIGURE 2.23. (a) To study the power of the straight line matcher, a cardboard scene rich in straight line detail was built. The three planar surfaces in (b) will be referred to in the section on matching under geometrical constraints.

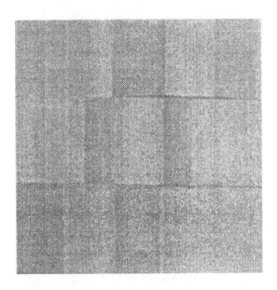

(a) Left Image

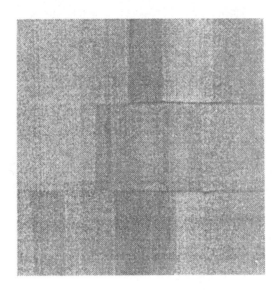

(b) Right Image

FIGURE 2.24. Stereo images of the object in Figure 2.23.

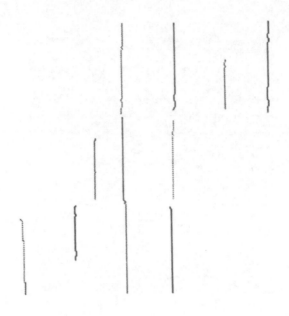

(a) Left Image

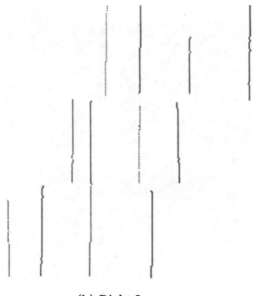

(b) Right Image

FIGURE 2.25. Lines extracted by the straight line extraction algorithm from the stereo images of Figure 24.

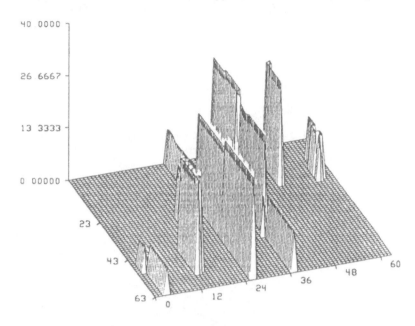

FIGURE 2.26. Depth map obtained by straight line matching.

Furthermore, a priori known hypotheses about planar surface orientations are used for the geometrical constraints.[4] This acts as a powerful constraint on the matcher and eliminates many false matches.

We will use the triples (x,y,z) to denote our disparity values with x and y taking integer values from 1 through 64, and z taking a floating point value from 0 to 31. As explained in the footnote, this constitutes a reduced resolution disparity map.[5] In 3D space, let L be a straight line segment derived by the straight line feature matching process discussed in the preceding

---

[4]There are important applications where we may assume that the orientations of the major surfaces are known and available to the stereo matcher. For example, for a mobile robot engaged in hallway navigation, we may safely assume that all the major surfaces are either vertical or horizontal. We believe that utilization of such knowledge, when available, can only lead to more robust stereo algorithms.

[5]Usually, the disparity maps tend to be of lower resolution than the images from which they are produced (see, for example, the work by Nishihara [Nis84]). In our processing, the images are usually of size 256×256, whereas the disparity maps tend to be defined only over 64×64 matrices. We will denote a disparity map by the triple (x,y,z), where x and y take integer values $0,1,2,.....,63$, and z takes floating point values that span the interval $[0,32]$. The reason why z is floating point over this interval has to do with the fact that when straight line features are matched, the disparities are computed over 256×256 images, implying that the range of computed disparities would be any integer from -128 to +128; in practice, of course, the disparity range is limited to a much smaller interval, usually [-15, 16]. When computing the reduced resolution disparity maps, the disparity values are averaged, leading to floating point numbers.

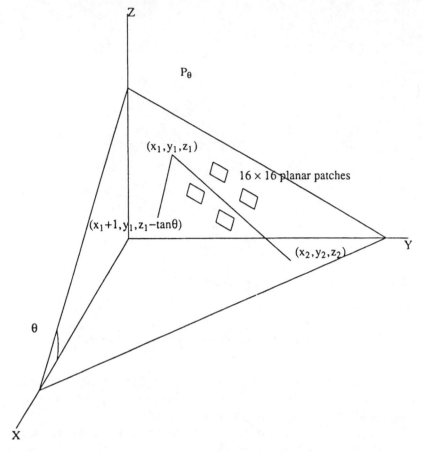

FIGURE 2.27. This figure shows how a hypothesized planar surface orientation is represented. The key parameters are the angle of the intersection of the planar surface with the xz-plane of the coordinate system and the end points of the straight line that must be contained in the planar surface.

section. Let the coordinates of the terminal points of L be (x_1, y_1, z_1) and (x_2, y_2, z_2). Let P_θ denote a hypothesized plane, of orientation θ, which contains L and which corresponds to one of the object surfaces. For our algorithms, the orientation is expressed in the following manner: we compute the intersection of the plane with the y=0 plane, the orientation of P_θ is then measured by the angle θ subtended by the intersection line with the x-axis; see Figure 2.27. As mentioned before, the orientation θ is assumed to be one of the set $\{\theta_1, \theta_2, \ldots \}$ of a priori known orientations of all planar surfaces in the scene.

Given an orientation θ for a hypothesized plane and the terminal points (x_1, y_1, z_1), (x_2, y_2, z_2), the complete equation of the plane is given by

$$\begin{vmatrix} x & y & z & 1 \\ x_1 & y_1 & z_1 & 1 \\ x_2 & y_2 & z_2 & 1 \\ x_1 + 1 & y_1 & z_1 + \tan\theta & 1 \end{vmatrix} = 0. \qquad (2.14)$$

which merely expresses the fact that the terminals points and the point $(x_1 + 1, y_1, z_1 + \tan\theta)$ must lie on the plane. The operator —.— stands for taking the determinant of its argument.

In geometrically constrained matching, our first task is to generate the plane that contains L and whose orientation corresponds to one of the hypothesized planes. In the 64 × 64 representation for disparity maps, this plane will extend to only 4 pixels on either side of the line (Figure 2.27). The choice of 4 is arbitrary and dictated by the nature of the scenes we are interested in. If it is believed that the planar surfaces in a polyhedral scene consist of large areas, then this number could be larger. Note that in terms of the row-column resolution in the original images, the width of 4 in the disparity space is equivalent to a width of 16.

In the implementation described by the following algorithm, a pass is made through the 64 × 64 disparity map and planar strips are fitted to all the straight lines at the same time, all the planar strips thus generated being of the same orientation. As described in Section 2.4.2, the geometrically constrained matching is carried over 16 × 16 square patches in each planar strip instead of enforcing the match within the entire planar strip at one time. This step is followed by fitting all the lines again with strips of another hypothesized orientation, and the process continued. For each hypothesized orientation, the computation of the geometrically constrained matching can be divided into two stages: *the planar strip generation stage* and *the geometrically constrained matching stage*. Before presenting further details on each of these stages, we will introduce a data structure, called the *control matrix.* for recording the matches generated by the geometrically constrained matcher and the other matchers to be discussed subsequently.

The Control Matrix

For our 256 × 256 image matrices, a 64 × 64 control matrix is used to organize the flow of control during the rule based implementation of binocular fusion. This control matrix also plays an important role in the execution of the geometrically constrained matcher, therefore we will define it in this subsection. The initial entries for the control matrix are provided by the results of matching the straight line features. To generate these initial entries, the image is divided into 64 × 64 non-overlapping blocks, each of size 4 × 4. If in a given 4 × 4 block, the system is able to successfully match a straight line feature, then in the control matrix an entry of 1 is made for that block. For all the blocks that overlapp with the regions grown around the straight lines features, the entry in the control matrix is 2. Elsewhere, the entry is 3.

During the execution of the rule-based system, the entries of the control matrix can be altered on the fly. For example, if it is concluded that a region cannot be matched with the help of zero-crossing contours, by the method discussed in Section 2.4.3, then the entries for all the blocks that are strictly within the region are set to 4.

In Section 2.5, we will discuss other computational mechanisms that are capable of altering the control matrix entries on the fly during the process of matching.

Planar Strip Generation Stage

For the purpose of generating planar strips around straight lines in 3D space, the control matrix entries are set to either 1 or 2, depending on

1. $C(x,y) = 1$: if the disparity at (x,y) is already known through dominant feature matching,

2. $C(x,y) = 2$: this will be true for those (x,y) that are in the vicinity of (x_1, y_1)' s where $C(x_1, y_1) = 1$. By vicinity we mean those pixels that are encompassed by four-fold growth of the regions where $C(x,y)$ is 1.

The algorithm that generates planar strips in 3D around lines corresponding to the fusion of straight line features in a stereo pair has been described in detail in [TK88]. In this algorithm, the first step consists of obtaining by region growing those (x, y)'s in the control matrix where we should have $C(x,y)=2$. The other steps then generate disparities maps in these regions for each of the hypothesized planar face orientations in the scene. In other words, if we know a priori that the scene can have planar faces at N possible orientations, then around each line in 3D space (obtained by fusing linear features), the algorithm will "fit planar strips for each of those N orientations. The algorithm then computes disparity fields corresponding to each of those strips. The algorithm in the next subsection then takes over and decides which if any of the planar strips constitutes a correct hypothesis by matching zero-crossings from the finest channel using for offsets the disparity fields corresponding to the different planar strips. The planar strip that leads to the largest number of zero-crossing matches is accepted as a validated planar face orientation in the vicinity of the edge.

Matching Zero Crossings Under Planar Strip Orientation Constraint

Suppose we have N hypotheses for planar surface orientations in a scene. The algorithm in the preceding section will, for each matched pair of straight line segments, generate a planar strip in 3-D space around the fused straight line feature. The next order of business is to accept only those hypotheses which lead to a maximum number of zero-crossing matches on these planar strips. Again from the previous section, each planar strip is represented as a disparity map on a 64 × 64 matrix. Therefore, for a pair of stereo images, at this point we will have N 64 × 64 disparity maps corresponding to the N hypotheses. In making the transition from 256 × 256 images to 64 × 64 disparity maps, the disparity of a pixel (i,j) in the image plane is stored at the coordinates $(x = \lceil \frac{i}{4} \rceil, y = \lceil \frac{i}{4} \rceil)$ in disparity map.

In enforcing the constraints corresponding to the different available hypotheses, in practice it is not advisable to use each strip in its entirety. This is owing to fact that an edge would in general form a boundary between planar faces of different orientations – the planar faces corresponding to different hypotheses. It is also possible that two or more objects might be lined up in just the right manner so that a long edge is created in the images, but, clearly, at different places along such an edge the planar faces would have different orientations. For all these reasons, each planar strip is divided into overlapping square patches, each of size M × M in the image space, and, therefore, of size M/4 × M/4 in the control matrix, as shown in Figure 2.28, where M equals 16, which is the case in our current implementation.

For example, a patch at location (x_0, y_0) in a disparity matrix spans the region within the range of $x_0 \leq x < x_0 + M/4$ and $y_0 \leq y < y_0 + M/4$. The same patch spans the region given by $4x_0 \leq i < 4x_0 + M$ and $4y_0 \leq j < 4y_0 + M$, in the image frame. When M is 16, note that in a disparity matrix, the maximal coordinate values for a patch are (61, 61); that is because for locations beyond these values, complete 16 × 16 patches cannot be accommodated in a disparity matrix. Also note that adjacent patches overlap for all but one row and one column. For example, the patches located at (x_0, y_0) and $(x_0 + 1, y_0 + 1)$ overlap as shown in Figure 2.28.

In the algorithm described below, two variables T and S play important roles in determining whether a given hypothesis is good or not. A hypothesis is considered to be valid if a sufficient number of zero-crossings can be matched on a planar patch, this number being a fraction of the total number of zero-crossings in the patch. The variable S is equal to the total number of zero-crossings in a patch and T the number of zero-crossings which can be successfully matched according to the constraints imposed by the hypothesis corresponding to the patch. The validity of the hypothesis is then established by comparing T/S against a threshold.

Say, a left image zero-crossing is located at coordinates (x,y). Then, in order to establish correspondence for the zero-crossing, we construct a search window of size $\pm\delta$ in the right image located at $x + d$ where d corresponds to the disparity value in the left image patch, the value of this disparity is given by $H_m(x/4, y/4)$. By trial and error, we have concluded that in practice the value of δ should be limited to unity. In other words, the search windows are of size ± 1.

We have also observed through experimentation that the acceptance threshold on T/S – this threshold will be denoted by T4 – should be a

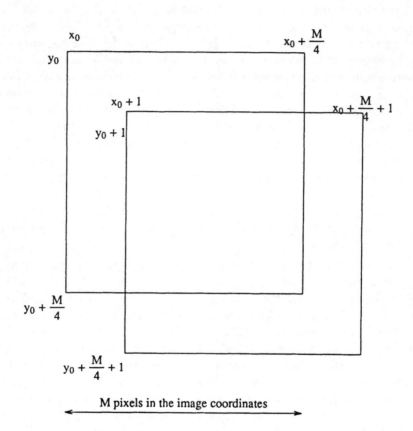

FIGURE 2.28. Each strip around a straight line is represented by overlapping planar patches. The planar surface orientation hypothesis is then tested for each patch separately.

function of the orientation of the plane corresponding to the hypothesis. For example, when the orientation of a plane is given by $\theta = 0$, meaning the plane is parallel to the image planes, the threshold T4 should be approximately 0.7, whereas for planes with $\theta = 45\,\deg$, the best value for T4 is around 0.5.

The following is an algorithmic description of the above procedure for accepting or rejecting a planar surface hypothesis in the vicinity of a straight edge. For a given patch, the procedure, which consists of two steps, STEP-1 and STEP-2, is invoked only if the control matrix entries for the entire patch are 2.

STEP-1: [Searching for correspondence]

For i and j spanning the range (0, 255), we define left and right image "zero-crossings matrices", denoted by LP and RP, in the following manner:

LP or RP (i , j) = $'p'$ if the pixel (i,j) in the image is
on a positive contour,

LP or RP (i , j) = $'n'$ if the pixel (i,j) in the image is
on a negative contour.

and

LP or RP (i , j) = 'h' if the pixel (i,j) is the image is
on a horizontal contour.

For every patch, let (x_0, y_0) be the patch coordinate in the disparity space. Now, the number T and S for the patch at (x_0, y_0) can be computed by the following algorithm.

```
S ← 0;
T ← 0;
for i ← 4 x₀ until 4 x₀ + M - 1
    for j ← 4 y₀ until 4 y₀ + M - 1
        begin
            if ( LP ( i, j ) = 'p' )
            begin
                T ← T + 1;
                if (RP(iₗ + H(⌈ iₗ/4 ⌉, ⌈ jₗ/4 ⌉), jₗ) =' p'
                or
                RP(iₗ + H(⌈ iₗ/4 ⌉, ⌈ jₗ/4 ⌉) + 1, jₗ) =' p',
                or
```

$$RP(i_l + H(\lceil i_l/4 \rceil, \lceil j_l/4 \rceil) - 1, j_l) =' p')$$
$$S \leftarrow S + 1;$$

end
if (LP (i, j) = $'n'$)
begin

$\quad$ T $\leftarrow$ T + 1;
$\quad$ if $(RP(i_l + H(\lceil i_l/4 \rceil, \lceil j_l/4 \rceil), j_l) =' n'$
$\quad$ or
$\quad$ $RP(i_l + H(\lceil i_l/4 \rceil, \lceil j_l/4 \rceil) + 1, j_l) =' n',$
$\quad$ or
$\quad$ $RP(i_l + H(\lceil i_l/4 \rceil, \lceil j_l/4 \rceil) - 1, j_l) =' n')$
$\quad$ S $\leftarrow$ S + 1;

$\quad$ end
end

STEP-2: This step is for computing the ratio R of T and S. If R exceeds a certain threshold, then the chosen planar surface hypothesis for this patch is regarded as correct.

R $\leftarrow \frac{T}{S}$

if (R $\geq$ T4) return (The chosen planar surface hypothesis for this patch is verified)

if (R < T4) return (The chosen planar surface hypothesis for this patch is not verified)

To demonstrate with an example the workings of the algorithm, consider the three-panel scene shown in Figure 2.29a. For this scene, the dominant straight lines, marked AB and CD, are matched by the method of Section 2.4.1. At this point, our system assumes that a set of hypotheses about planar surface orientations is available for matching regions around the dominant straight lines. For the sake of discussion, let's say that the available hypotheses are as illustrated in Figure 2.29b. This means that at each pixel in the vicinity of the matched straight lines, the system will invoke one of these hypotheses and select the best possible one on the basis of number of zero-crossings matched.

To demonstrate how well this procedure works, we have shown in Figure 2.30 a pair of stereo images of an actual 3-panel scene. As in the sketch in Figure 2.29a, the dominant edges in the scene are at the junctions of the panels. The top image in Figure 2.31a shows the pixels that were matched by the geometrically constrained matcher using planar orientation hypothesis corresponding to *hypothesis1* shown in Figure 2.29b. The figure has a blocky appearance because, as mentioned before, the computed disparity maps are over 64 x 64 matrices, while the results are displayed using

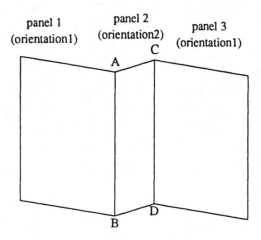

panel 1
(orientation1)

panel 2
(orientation2)

panel 3
(orientation1)

C

A

B

D

(a) The surface shape

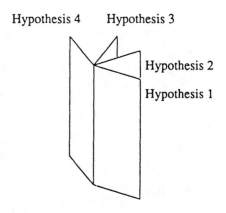

Hypothesis 4   Hypothesis 3

Hypothesis 2

Hypothesis 1

(b) Hypotheses

FIGURE 2.29. Matching under geometrical constraints will be demonstrated for the three panel scene shown in a. In b are shown the planar surface orientation hypotheses used in the matching process.

(a) Left Image

(b) Right Image

FIGURE 2.30. Stereo images of the three panel scene in Fig. 2.29a.

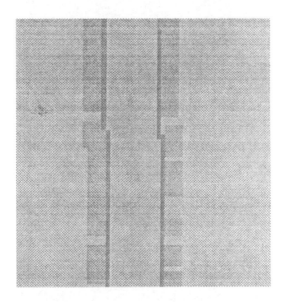

(a) Hypothesis 1

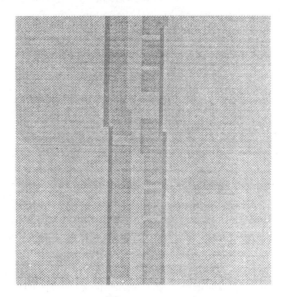

(b) Hypothesis 2

FIGURE 2.31. The regions where geometrically constrained matching was successful are highlighted.

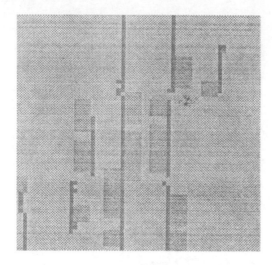

2.32(a) Hypothesis 1

256×256 matrices. The bottom plate in Figure 2.31b shows the pixels matched using *hypothesis2* for planar surface orientation, as displayed in Fig. 2.29b.

In Figure 2.32, we show the results obtained for the stereo images of Figure 2.24. We used the three hypotheses shown in Figure 2.23b for the orientations of the planes. The range maps generated by the three hypotheses are displayed in Figure 2.33.

2.4.3   MATCHING OF ZERO-CROSSING CONTOURS

A combined execution of the dominant-feature and the geometrically constrained matchers yields good depth maps in the vicinity of strong edges in a scene. Elsewhere, the system is dependent upon the two-level matcher that will be presented in this section and, if that does not work either, the full implementation of the MPG algorithm is used. The matcher is this section is based on the notion of figural continuity of zero-crossing contours; this continuity constraint says that when the planar surface is viewed from two neighboring viewpoints, the zero-crossing contours in both the stereo images must have nearly identical shapes. The idea of figural continuity was first suggested by Mayhew and Frisby [MF81] because they felt that the sign and the orientation of a zero-crossing contour did not constitute sufficient constraints for binocular fusion in the human visual system. Subsequently, figural continuity was incorporated by Grimson [Gri85] in the MPG algorithm.

In the two level matching scheme described here, figural continuity constraints are invoked for matching segments of the zero-crossing contours produced by the $w_{2D} = 8$ channel. The disparity map so obtained is then

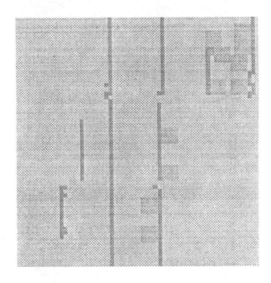

2.32(b) Hypothesis 2

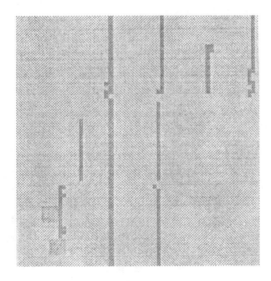

2.32(c) Hypothesis 3

FIGURE 2.32. For each of the three hypotheses in Figure 2.23b for planar surface orientations, parts a, b and c illustrate the regions where the geometrically constrained matching was successful.

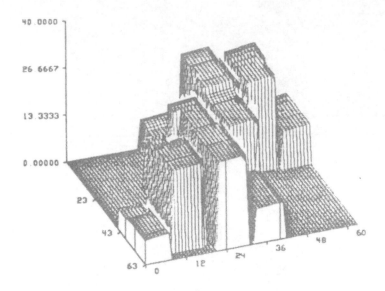

2.33(a) Hypothesis 1

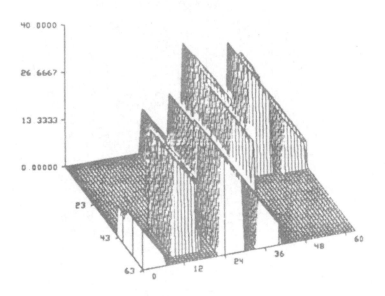

2.33(b) Hypothesis 2

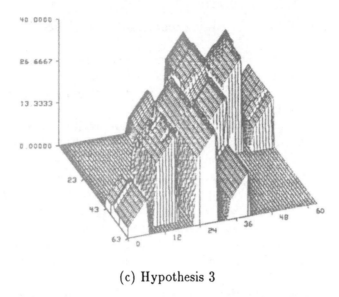

(c) Hypothesis 3

FIGURE 2.33. The three disparity maps shown correspond the matchings in parts a, b and c of Figure 2.32.

used to generate a higher resolution version by matching the zero-crossings for the finest channel for which w_{2D} is 4. The decision about the resolution level at which matching should be performed by invoking figural continuity constraints is not as arbitrary as it seems and is dictated by the procedure we use for testing the shape similarity of two contour segments. The shape similarity testing algorithm is such that it needs at least 10 pixels to arrive at reliable conclusions. The zero-crossing channel for $w_{2D} =4$ generates too many contours that are too short to be processed by the shape similarity algorithm. Note that random-dot illumination is used to generate images for all matching schemes except the first one that is based on the matching of straight line features. Our statement about too many contours being too short is applicable only under this illumination.

There is an important point to be made about why two channels are sufficient for generating depth values over large depth ranges with the scheme presented in this section. In the Marr-Poggio theory, if in each channel the search window for finding the correspondent in the right image of a left image zero-crossing is equal to $\pm w_{2D}/2$, then in over 95 percent of the cases there will be a single zero-crossing in the search window. If the search windows are made much larger than this, one has to contend with the problem of disambiguation; since large windows will contain multiple zero-crossings, from these one must be selected to serve as a correspondent of the left image zero crossing. On the other hand, if the search windows are much smaller, then the probability of completely missing the correspondent is increased. In practice, most implementations of the MPG algorithm use $\pm w_{2D}$ for search windows, this larger size being made necessary by the displacements in the zero-crossing contours that was discussed in Section 2.2.2.

Because, of the limitation on the maximum size of the search window in an MPG type of an algorithm, one is forced to use a number of channels, usually four, to cover a depth range over which humans are capable of perceiving depth through stereopsis.

The disambiguation problems are not as severe with the two level matcher discussed in this section. This is because the MPG matching process, even despite Grimson's figural continuity implementation, is essentially a pixel level matcher. On the other hand, the first level of the matching scheme described here implements stereopsis by actually fusing contour segments. This allows us to use larger search windows without suffering from the disambiguation problem. Contour segments tend to be much richer in detail compared to zero-crossing pixels even when contour slopes are associated with the latter. For this reason, it is sufficient for us to use two channels.

In the following subsections, we will first show with examples that the shapes of zero-crossing contours do indeed stay the same for the two viewpoints we use for stereo images. This observation is important since it forms the cornerstone of the matching strategy discussed in this section. We will then discuss our implementation of a figural continuity based matcher for zero-crossing contours.

Photometric Invariance in Stereo Vision

Photometric invariance refers to the fact that the corresponding areas in the left and right images exhibit similar gray level variations. Since gray level variations are captured by the zero-crossings generated by the application of LOG filtering to images, photometric invariance translates into the invariance of the shapes of the corresponding zero-crossing contours. In Figure 2.34, we have shown stereo images of a scene with large flat surfaces. Figure 2.35 displays the zero-crossing contours obtained via the w_{2D} channel. The similarity of the corresponding contours is evident. The similarity of zero-crossing contours is violated in the vicinity of range discontinuities and shadows. Some of the mechanisms that lead to distortions of the contours between the two images are the same as those discussed in Section 2.2.2.

Implementation of Matching by Enforcing Figural Continuity

Mayhew and Frisby [MF81] have shown that figural continuity of zero crossings plays an important role in binocular fusion in human stereopsis. As for the evidence, they presented the result of an experiment which measured the latency time for stereopsis for image pairs with and without figural continuity cues. Shown in Figure 2.36 is a random dot stereogram, superimposed on which are boxes that define the regions which undergo disparity

2.34(a) Left image

2.34(b) Right image

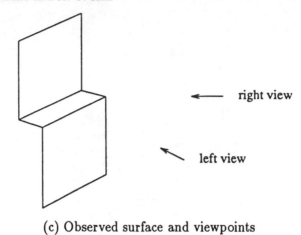

(c) Observed surface and viewpoints

FIGURE 2.34. Stereo images of a step scene are shown in parts a and b. Part c shows the arrangement of surfaces in the scene.

shifts from the left to the right image. Mahew and Frisby showed that the time it takes to fuse the stereogram is shorter when the box-shaped line features are present, in comparison with the time that it takes without the box outline. They argued that the structure of the box shaped outlines generated figural continuity cues that facilitated the process of stereoscopic fusion.

To quantify their results, Mahew and Frisby measured the ratios G/M in their experiments, where M is the number of zero-crossings on a zero-crossing contour in the left image and where $M+G$ is the total number of right-image candidate zero crossings within the respective search windows for the M left-image zero-crossings. G is referred to as the number of ghost zero-crossings and, ideally, we would want G to be zero. Clearly, G/M is a measure of the possibility of a false match.

Mahew and Frisby showed that in a particular experiment, G/M took a value of 2.17 when matching was accomplished on a raster line by raster line basis – meaning that for each zero-crossing in a given raster line in the left image the search window was constructed on the same raster line in the right image – provided no figural continuity information was used. On the other hand, with figural continuity enforced, the G/M ratio decreased to 0.317. For this particular result, for each left image zero crossing the figural continuity was enforced over 5 raster lines by comparing the horizontal coordinates of the contour segments associated with the left image zero crossing and a candidate right image zero crossing, and insisting that they be within ± 1. Further reductions in ghost matches could be obtained with figural continuity enforced over longer segments of zero-crossing contours; for example, instead of using five raster lines, we could use seven or nine.

Grimson [Gri85] implemented the concept of figural continuity such that a point P on a zero-crossing contour C in the left image was accepted as a

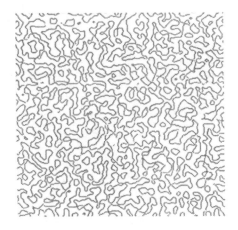

(a) Left image

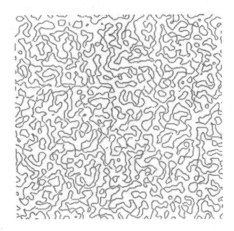

(b) Right image

FIGURE 2.35. The zero-crossing contours generated by the $w_{2D} = 8$ channel for the stereo images of Figure 2.34.

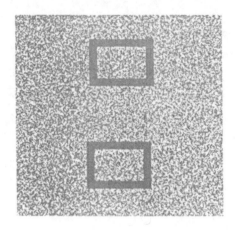

(a) Left image

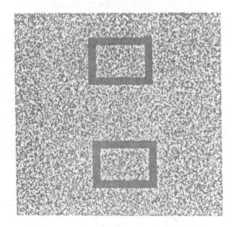

(b) Right image

FIGURE 2.36. A pair of synthetic stereo images with monocularly discriminable cues.

reasonable candidate to be matched if all points within a certain distance from P on C succeeded in finding correspondences in the right image.

Our algorithm for matching zero-crossing contours under the constraint of figural continuity is very similar to the straight line matching algorithm discussed previously. The following steps present this algorithm. It should be noted at the outset that whereas for straight line matching the straight line segments had to be 41 element long, for contour matching the zero-crossing contour segments need only be 15 elements long.

STEP-1: Each zero-crossing image is represented by a data structure which is a list of zero-crossing segments described as

$$\{segment_1, segment_2, segment_3, ...segment_M\}\,.$$

STEP-2: Each zero-crossing segment is represented by the following data structure

{ start-pix-col-indx, start-pix-row-indx, chain-code, start-pix-col-indx-of-conj, start-pix-row-indx-of-conj }

where the last two items are instantiated only after a right image contour segment is found that matches the left image contour segment with starting indices (start-pix-col-indx, start-pix-row-indx). The matching contour segment may be called the conjugate segment, hence the symbol 'conj.' In the event a left image segment matches more than one right image segment, the last two items can be replicated and instantiated with the corresponding starting values. Information about multiple matches this stored can be used subsequently when relational constraints are invoked. Each chain code is represented in the same manner as in straight line representation. For the discussion to follow, a contour segment from the left image will be denoted by

$$(L(1), L(2), ..., L(N))$$

and a segment from the right image by

$$(R(1), R(2), ..., R(N))$$

STEP-3: In comparing the data structures for two segments from the two images, the algorithm first makes a check for the positional correspondence. The positional correspondence is considered as sufficient if the following condition is satisfied:

$$|start - pixel - col - index_l - start - pixel - col - index_r| \leq D_{max}$$

and

$$|start - pixel - row - index_l - start - pixel - row - index_r| \leq 1,$$

where D_{max} is the range of the maximum permissible value for the disparity.

STEP-4: A similarity score, denoted by T, is computed for the two segments by comparing their chain codes. Initially, the value of T is set to 0. At step i, let the chain code elements from the two segments be L(i) and R(i). For each i, i = 1,....,N, the total score T is accumulated by using:

if L(i) = R(i) then T = T + 1

Note that the weight value W used in the straight line matcher is not employed here. This is because the alternation of two codes discussed in the straight line matcher is unlikely to occur in the case of zero-crossing contour segments extracted from random dot patterns used at this stage of our algorithm.

STEP-5: If the similarity score T does not exceed a pre-set threshold, denoted here by T5, delete the left image segment under consideration from the left image data structure created by STEP 1.

STEP-6: If the similarity score T exceeds a threshold, T5, declare the two segments as matchable. In the current computational model T5 and N are set to 11 and 15, respectively. Delete from the left image data structure shown in STEP 1 those segments whose (start-pixel-col-index, start-pixel-row-index) lie on the matched segment in the left image.

STEP-7: If the left image data structure created in STEP 1 is non-nil, go to STEP 3.

STEP-8: In this step, range values to the scene points that lie on the matched segments are computed by the following procedure: Let D(i), i=0,1,..,N be the disparity computed from the ith pixels in the left and the right image segments; as defined in STEP-2, the chain codes of these matching pixels are denoted by L(i) and R(i), respectively. The disparities, D(i), is obtained from the chain codes L(i) and R(i) by the following formula in which A, A1, A2 are temporary variables:

$$D(0) \leftarrow CL - CR$$

where CL = start-pixel-col-index for the first pixel
in the left image segment
CR = start-pixel-row-index for the first pixel
in the right image segment

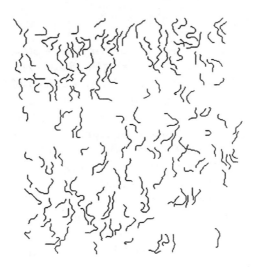

FIGURE 2.37. Shown here are those zero-crossing contour segments from the left frame of Figure 2.35 that were successfully matched by the figural continuity matcher.

```
For i ← 1 step 1 until N do
begin
        if ( L (i) = (0, 1, or 7) )
        A1 = 1;
        else if ( L (i) = (2, or 6) )
        A1 = 0;
        else if ( L (i) = (3, 4, or 5) )
        A1 = -1;
        if ( R (i) = (0, 1, or 7) )
        A2 = 1;
        else if ( R (i) = (2, or 6) )
        A2 = 0;
        else if ( R (i) = (3, 4, or 5) )
        A2 = -1;
        A = A1 - A2;
        D (i) = D (i -1) + A;
end
```

The disparity maps thus obtained are down-sampled to 64 × 64, similar to what was done in the straight line matching algorithm.

Figure 2.37 presents the contour segments that were successfully matched by this algorithm for the pair of images shown in Figure 2.35.

Matching of Individual Zero-Crossings

As described before, the figural continuity matching process is carried out at two levels: the contour segment level (the first level) in the $w_{2D} = 8$ channel and the pixel level (the second level) matching of individual zero-crossings in the $w_{2D} = 4$ channel. With the help of Figure 2.38, we will illustrate how the two levels act in concert. Parts a and b of Figure 2.38 depict a pair of zero-crossings contour segments extracted from the $w_{2D} = 8$ channel, where the parts c and d depict the zero-crossing contour segments extracted from the $w_{2D} = 4$ channel. Contour segment AB in the left image is matched with the contour segment A'B' from the right image by the figural continuity constraint on the first level. Note that when search for the matching contour segment for AB is conducted, we make sure that the horizontal coordinate of A' is within the horizontal coordinate of A $\pm\frac{D_{max}}{2}$, as shown in Figure 2.38 b. This match is used to compute a disparity map along each matched contour and the resulting disparities stored in a 64×64 matrix. Subsequently, the zero-crossings from the $w_{2D} = 4$ channel are matched individually, as in any channel of the MPG algorithm. For example, if P_2 is a zero-crossing produced by the $w_{2D} = 4$ channel with its x-coordinate equal to x_2, then to find its correspondent we first construct a search window of size $\pm\frac{w_{2D}}{2}$ around the point x_2+d, where d is the disparity value pulled out of the 64×64 disparity matrix montioned earlier.

The reader should note that the search window has half the size of those used in the MPG algorithms. Whereas each channel of the MPG algorithm uses a search window of $\pm w_{2D}$, the search window used here is only half that. As was pointed out in Section 2.2.2, theoretical considerations dictate that in the MPG algorithm the size of the search window be $\pm\frac{w_{2D}}{2}$, however when such algorithms are implemented the search windows are set to $\pm w_{2D}$ to account for the shifts in zero crossing contours caused by the interaction of different intensity variations in an image. To add to the discussion of Section 2.2.2, this interaction will be illustrated with the help of a one-dimensional gray level variation shown in Figure 2.39a. This pattern can be parametrized by the variables A and B, which control the relative heights of two of the levels in the pattern, and C which controls the separation of the spike from the other variation. Figure 2.39b shows the boundaries of the shifts in the zero-crossings for different normalized values of the parameters. For example, when the normalized value of separation is given by $\frac{C}{w_{2D}} = 0.5$ and the value of B/A is 0.06, the shift of the zero-crossing corresponding to the edge X is about $0.4w_{2D}$.

We believe that if the parameters of gray level variations in an image are such as to cause zero-crossing shifts comparable to, say, w_{2D}, then the resulting zero-crossing contours would be unmatchable by the figural continuity matcher. If this conjecture is true, then the matching of zero-crossing contour segments should provide us with an accurate disparity information wherever such a match can be accomplished. The point we

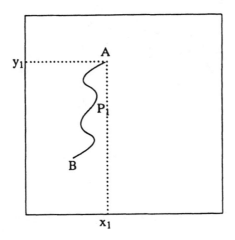

(a) Left contour image ($w_{2D} = 8$).

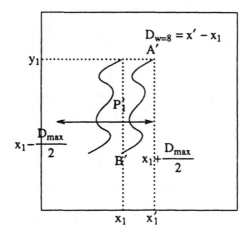

(b) Right contour image ($w_{2D} = 8$).

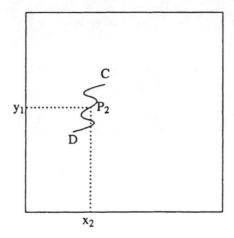

(c) Left contour image ($w_{2D} = 4$).

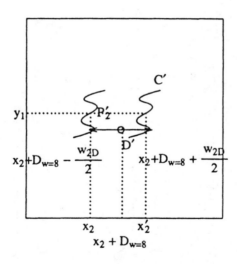

(d) Right contour image ($w_{2D} = 4$).

FIGURE 2.38. The disparities generated by matching the zero-crossing contour segments of the $w_{2D} = 8$ channel are used to match the individual zero-crossings in the $w_{2D} = 4$ channel. Parts a and b depict the figural continuity matching over the zero-crossing contours of the $w_{2D} = 8$ channel. The contour segment AB in the left image will be paired up with the segment A'B' of the right frame if the horizontal coordinate of A' is within a window of the horizontal coordinate of A and the chain codes associated with the contour segments exhibit sufficient similarity. Parts c and d show the matching of individual zero-crossings from the $w_{2D} = 4$ channel. $D_{w=8}$ corresponds to the local disparity generated by the figural continuity matcher in the $w_{2D} = 8$ channel.

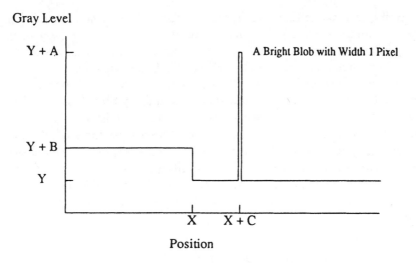

(a) 1-D synthetic image

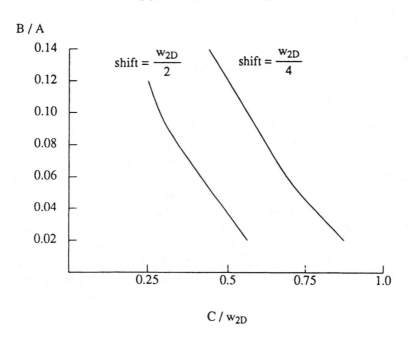

(b) Boundaries of misleading matching

FIGURE 2.39. The one dimensional gray scale variation in part a is used to illustrate zero-crossing shifts in part b as a function of the change in a.

are trying to make is that after matching contour segments, the resulting disparity information is quite robust and there is less of a reason to use $\pm w_{2D}$ windows for subsequent matching. Since smaller windows lead to fewer disambiguation problems, we chose the $\pm \frac{w_{2D}}{2}$ windows.

The point being made is that if the similarities between contour segments are such that they can be matched, then it is unlikely that there would any significant deviations in the zero-crossings at the next finer channel. After all, contour wise similarity arises because of area wide similarity between the two images. It is hard to conceive of a case where the photometric variances are such that there would be similarities at the $w_{2D} = 8$ channel for the contour matching to occur, yet there would be significant deviations at the $w_{2D} = 4$ level to require a search window larger than dictated by theory.

2.4.4   THE DEFAULT MATCHER

When all else fails, the systems invokes the full implementation of the MPG algorithm; so, in a sense, this is the default matcher.

2.5   A Review of Some Important Rules

2.5.1   OVERVIEW OF THE RULE-BASED PROCEDURE

Unless properly organized, a rule-based system can quickly outgrow the ability of a researcher to keep the entire system in mental perspective. Each rule usually embodies a small measure of control information; and, in a system with a large number of rules the interactions between the rules can be sufficiently overwhelming to the point that it may not be possible to feel confident about the robustness, stability and the convergence of the reasoning process. For these reasons, we have grouped the rules in our system in two different ways; the first type of grouping is simply to facilitate the comprehension of the system by a human, and the second type for the flow of control in the computer program. The first type of rule categorization is referred to as Groups and the second type Stages.

The three Groups of rules in the system can be described in the following manner:

GROUP-1 These rules are used for dynamically altering the entries of the control matrix. Note that the initial entries are generated by a deterministic procedure on the basis of the output of straight line matching. An important function of these rules is to generate the control matrix entries in such a manner that the straight lines extracted from the right image satisfy the relational constraints on their correspondents in the left image. This group also includes rules for invoking different possible surface-orientation hypotheses for the geometrically constrained matcher. A rule-based implementation here allows the incorporation of heuristics like: Of the many possible choices for surface orientations, we should first choose one that is the same as the orientation of one the neighboring surfaces; if that does not work then choose an orientation that is closest to that of one of neighboring surfaces. Of course, if no orientations are known in the immediate neighborhoods, then choose at random a permissible orientation hypothesis.

GROUP-2 Rules for determining the search window size for the implementation of the finest MPG channel. These rules make sure that if the MPG matching is being carried out without a prior geometrically constrained matching, then the search window size is set equal to $2 \times W_{2D}$. On the other hand, if the finest channel is being invoked as a follow-up on the geometrically constrained matcher, then these rules set the search window size to W_{2D}.

GROUP-3 These are metarules for coordinating the flow of control. These rules make sure that the alteration of an entry of the control matrix is followed up by the invocation of the appropriate matching strategy.

The stages represent another categorization of the same rules, as shown in Figure 2.40, where the symbols in the middle column are the names of the rules. As is made clear by the following description, the stages play important role in the organization of the flow of control.

Stage-1 In this stage, either the geometrically constrained match or the zero-crossing figure match is executed, depending upon the entry in the control matrix. This stage allows the generation of multiple hypotheses for both the surface orientations and the candidates for zero-crossing figure mathing. In the current implementation, although multiple candidates for figure matching are permitted, only a single hypothesis is retained for surface orientation.

Stage-2 In this stage, the best hypothesis or candidate is selected from amongst those generated in the previous stage. The hypothesis or candidate selection strategy includes examination of the valid hypotheses/candidates in neighboring regions.

Stage-3 The default matcher is called in this stage.

To give the reader some appreciation of the nature of the rules and how they are used, we will, in the rest of this section, review some of the rules; for a fuller discussion, the reader is referred to [TK88]. However, before we can do so, we need to mention what is meant by hypothesis arrays.

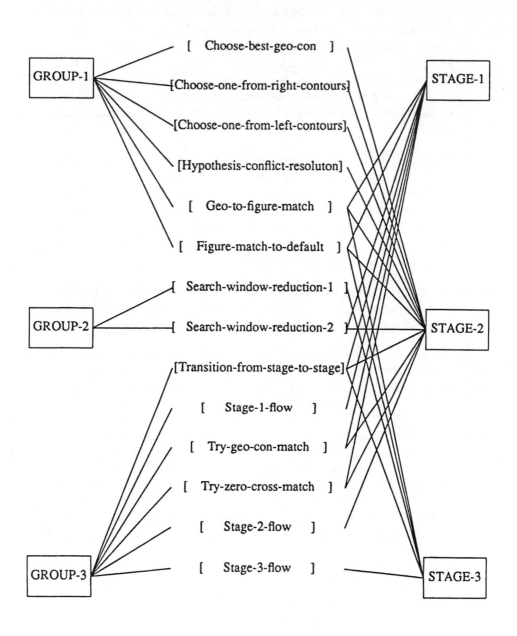

FIGURE 2.40. Two types of classification for the rules.

Hypothesis Arrays

In general, in geometrically constrained matching it will be possible for multiple surface orientation hypotheses to meet the hypothesis selection criteria. By the same token, in zero-crossing figure matching, for each zero-crossing contour in the left image there will be multiple candidates from the right image. The multiple orientation hypotheses and zero-crossing contour candidates are stored, respectively, in two arrays called Θ and Z.

As was explained earlier, a 256 × 256 image is divided into an array of 64 × 64 patches, each of size 4 × 4 pixels, for the construction of the control matrix and the calculation of disparities. Also, each orientation hypothesis is computed over an array of 4 × 4 patches – meaning 16 × 16 pixels – and, as can be seen from Figure 2.41, these patch arrays are overlapped. Therefore, the size of Θ matrix is 61 × 61 to represent orientations at all possible 16 × 16 pixel subarrays. Each entry in the Θ matrix is a list of all possible hypotheses for surface orientations at the corresponding 16 × 16 subarray of pixels; therefore, each such entry can be represented as the following list

$$\Theta(x, y) = \{ \ cardinality\_of\_entry, \ \theta_1, \theta_2, ..., \theta_K, \ \},$$

For example, if we have three hypotheses for a 16 × 16 subarray of pixels, $\Theta(x, y) = \{3, \theta_1, \theta_2, \theta_3\}$. When the i th hypothesis is tried and found to be unacceptable, it is removed from the list. In the discussion to follow, we will use the notation $\Theta(x, y, i)$ to describe the i-th hypothesis from the list at $\Theta(x, y)$. From the discussion in Section 2.4.3, it follows that the size of Z should be 64 × 64. Each entry in the Z matrix is again a list of possible candidates and can be represented by the following form: As is illustrated in Figure 2.41, the right-image candidate contour is stored as a list of disparities at the pixels of the left-image contour. Each entry in the Z matrix therefore looks like

$$Z(x, y) = \{ \ cardinality\_of\_entry, \ z_1, z_2, ... \ \},$$

where z_i is the list of disparity values computed by the zero-crossing figure matcher for the i-th candidate match.

Explanation on the rule description in the if-then form

We will now briefly describe the syntax used for the Group 1 rules. The rules will be shown with the help of IF-THEN forms. To improve the readability of presentation, some part of each rule may be presented as an English sentence. The following points are to be noted for the algorithmic parts of the rules: The reader should bear in mind the difference between the variables and constants, and also the differences between a C program

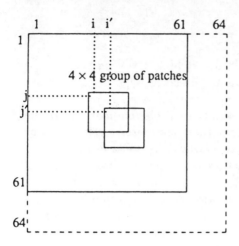

Θ (i,j) : a list with N+1 elements

$$\{ N, \theta_1, \theta_2, \cdots, \theta_N \}$$

N : The number of accepted hypothesis

θ_i : The orientation of the i th hypothesis

(The coordinates of Θ, (i,j), represent the patch spans within the range (i,i+3) horizontally and (j,j+3) vertically.)

(a) Hypothesis array Θ

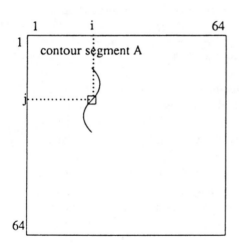

Z (i,j) : A list with M+1 elements

$$\{ M, \theta_1, \theta_2, \cdots, \theta_M \}$$

M : The number of disparity values computed by the zero crossing contour matching.

(The number M can be greater than 1 when more than two contours pass through the 4 × 4 patch specified by the coordinates (i,j).)

(b) Hypothesis array Z

FIGURE 2.41. Since both the geometrically constrained and the figural continuity matchers can result in multiple right-image matches for a left-image element, the high-level control must keep track of them. Hypothesis arrays Θ and Z are used for the purpose.

function and a logical predicate. The left hand side (LHS) of a rule can have both mathematical expressions and logical predicates, this being consistent with the syntax of OPS83. The following is a summary of the notation used for describing the rules:

1. The asterisk (*) indicates that the word following the asterisk stands for the purposes of explanation as a working memory element in OPS-83. Such a word can be matched with the LHS of a rule, and if the match is successful, the RHS of the rule can be executed. In RHS of a rule, a working memory element is created, modified, or removed by make, modify and remove commands, respectively.

2. A variable is denoted by a word whose first letter is capitalized.

3. A constant is denoted by a word with lower case letters. In the case of a string constant, it is denoted by the mark ' '.

4. A procedure written as a C-Program is denoted by a name with upper case letters.

2.5.2 SOME GROUP-1 RULES

These rules come into play when processing is in Stage-2. Therefore, these rules have the following two functions: 1) When for a given region of an image, as represented by an element of the control matrix, more than one hypothesis for the local planar surface orientation is found to be applicable, one of these rules must select the best of those by examining the hypotheses in the neighboring regions. 2) When for an arc of a zero-crossing contour in one of the images, the figural matching procedure yields more than one possible match from the other image, these rules must again select one on the basis of such decisions in the neighborhood.

[Rule Choose-best-geo-con]

IF two or more geometrical constraints are satisfied at a point (x_0, x_0) in the control matrix, THEN choose one by taking the neighboring hypotheses into account.

$$
\begin{aligned}
&\text{IF (Stage = 2} \\
&\quad \text{and } C(x_0,x_0) = 2 \\
&\quad \text{and } \Theta(x_0, y_0, 1) > 1 \ [\text{ more than two entries}] \ ) \\
&\text{THEN} \\
&\quad \{ \\
&\quad \text{CHOOSE\_MOST\_LIKELY\_THETA } (x_0,y_0,\Theta) \\
&\quad \text{make *stage\_2\_rule\_worked (status = 'yes')} \\
&\quad \}
\end{aligned}
$$

where CHOOSE_MOST_LIKELY_THETA (x, y, Θ) is a function, written in C, that examines the 8-neighbors of the location (x,y) in the control matrix by checking the entries for them in the Θ matrix. From this neighborhood, the function finds the most likely orientation hypothesis by counting the frequency of occurrences of the different hypotheses.

[Rule Choose-one-from-right-contours]

IF there are two or more candidates for the zero crossing figure match, as evidenced by the existence of multiple entries for an element of matrix Z, THEN choose one by polling the 8-neighbors using the Z-matrix neighborhoods. This situation will arise when an arc in the left image has more than one possible match in the right image.

> IF (Stage = 2
>   and $C(x_0,y_0) = 3$
>   and $Z(y_0, y_0, 1) > 1$ [two or more entries in Z])
>   THEN
>   {
>   CHOOSE_MOST_LIKELY_Z (x_0,y_0,Z)
>   make *stage_2_rule_worked (status = 'yes')
>   }

where the function CHOOSE_MOST_LIKELY_Z is defined in the last section. Basically, this function chooses a single disparity value from amongst the multiple choices available by taking into account those neighborhood disparities that are known unambiguously. Again, the neighborhoods used are those corresponding to the Z matrix.

[Rule Choose-one-from-left-contours]

IF two or more arcs from the left image have the same correspondent from the right image, THEN discard all but one of the matches by using the relational information with neighboring digital arcs; the relational information is being used only in the positional sense defined below.

In our model, only the horizontal relations corresponding to positional differences between the arcs are taken into account. (A study of stereopsis where more elaborate relations are utilized in stereopsis is presented in [BK88].) To illustrate what we mean by relational information generated by positional differences, consider the arcs A_0 in Figure 2.42 which can be matched with the digital arc A'. Let's say that the arc labeled A can also me matched with A' and that the neighboring arc B has only a single correspondent in B'. We will use REL(A, B) to denote the positional relation between two contour segments in an image. For the arc positions shown in Figure 2.42, we may write

$$REL(A_0,B) = x_0 - x_2$$
$$REL(A, B) = x_1 - x_2$$
$$REL(A',B') = x' - x_2'$$

Note that these relational values can easily be computed from the information that resides in the contour segment list. The rule under discussion will select either A or A_0 for matching with A' by using the relational values in the manner discussed below.

```
IF (Stage = 2
        and right digital A' has
        two left digital arcs, A and A_0,
        possibly to be matched )
THEN
        {
        Consider a nearest stereo pair B, and B'
        Compute
            REL(A_0,B)
            REL (A, B)
            REL (A',B')
        if ( | REL(A_0,B) - REL (A',B') | >
            | REL (A, B) - REL (A',B') | )
            {
            take A as the correct match
            CHANGE_C_MATRIX ( A_0);
            }
        else
            {
            take A_0 as the correct match
            CHANGE_C_MATRIX ( A );
            }
        make *stage_2_rule_worked ( status = 'yes' )
        }
```

The control matrix entries for elements corresponding to the regions through which the discarded left image arc traverses are changed to 4.

[Rule Hypothesis-conflict-resolution]

IF a planar-surface orientation hypothesis is not in agreement with orien-

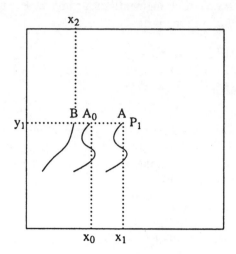

(a) Left contour image ($w_{2D} = 8$).

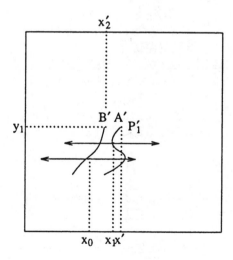

(b) Right contour image ($w_{2D} = 8$).

FIGURE 2.42. To illustrate how simple relational considerations are taken into account, we assume that the contour segment B in the left image is paired up with contour segment B on the right; and that both A and A_0 on the left get paired up with A' on the right. On of A and A_0 is discarded on the basis of the horizontal separations of the beginning pixels of each of these from beginning pixel of B vis a vis a similar separation between A' and B' in the right image.

tation hypotheses at any of neighbors in the THETA matrix whose images regions overlap with the region under consideration, THEN discard the hypothesis. A most important implication of this rule is that geometrically constrained matching will not be used in the immediate vicinity of corners formed by scene surfaces. Unfortunately, this has to be the case since orientation hypotheses are enforced at the same time over large image blocks – 16x16 to be precise – and so geometrically constrained matching would lead to erroneous matches in the vicinity of junctions between surfaces of different orientations. Therefore, in the immediate vicinity of surface junctions, the system must rely on other matchers.

$$\text{IF (Stage} = 2$$
$$\text{and } C(x_0, y_0) = 2$$
$$\text{and } \Theta(x_0, y_0, 1)$$
$$\text{and } \Theta(x_0, y_0, 2) \neq \Theta(x_1, y_1, 2))$$
$$[\text{ where } x_0 \leq x_1 < x_0 + 4, \text{ and } y_0 \leq y_1 < y_0 + 4]$$
$$\text{THEN}$$
$$\{$$
$$\text{discard } \Theta(x_0, y_0, 2) \text{ and } \Theta(x_1, y_1, 2)$$
$$\text{make *alter\_C\_request (X} = x_0, Y = y_0)$$
$$\text{make *alter\_C\_request (X} = x_1, Y = y_1)$$
$$\text{make *stage\_2\_rule\_worked (status} = \text{'yes')}$$
$$\}$$

[Rule Init-C-matrix-set]

IF the OPS83 program is initiated, THEN the control matrix must first be initialized.

$$\text{IF (Stage} = 1$$
$$\text{*start)}$$
$$\text{THEN}$$
$$\{$$
$$\text{CREATE\_INIT\_C\_MATRIX (C);}$$
$$\text{remove *start}$$
$$\text{In\_stage\_processing\_done} = \text{'no')}$$
$$\}$$

The control matrix is initialized on the basis of dominant feature matching; CREATE_INIT_C_MATRIX is the name of the function that does this initialization.

[Rule Geo-to-figure-match]

IF geometrically constrained matching is not successful, THEN the zero-crossing figure matching is to be invoked.

[Rule Figure-match-to-default]

IF neither geometrically constrained matching nor the zero-crossing figure matching is successful, THEN the default matching algorithm should be applied.

IF (*alter_C_request (X = x_0, Y = y_0))
THEN
    {
    if (C(x_0, y_0)= 2)
        then C (x_0, y_0) ← 3;
    else if (C(x_0, y_0) = 3)
        then C (x_0, y_0) ← 4;
    remove *alter_C_request (X = x_0, Y = y_0)
    }

This completes a review of some of the Group 1 rules. We were only trying to give the reader but a flavor of the rules in the system, we hope we succeeded in doing that with these rules. As was mentioned before, a longer discussion on the rules and their implementation can be found in [TK88].

2.6   Experimental Results

We will now show range maps computed using our rule based procedure and compare the results with those obtained with a straightforward application of the MPG algorithm. In addition to the range maps, we will also show the reduction in possible ambiguous matches with our scheme; a match is potentially ambiguous if for a zero-crossing in the left image there is more than one zero-crossing in the search window in the right image.

2.6.1   EXPERIMENTAL SETUP

A schematic of our experimental setup is shown in Figure 2.43. Random dot illumination is vertical and aimed straight down on objects placed on a table. The cameras are arranged in such a manner that their optic axes are nearly parallel, which eliminates the need for image rectification to satisfy the epipolar constraints. Any residual misalignments between the cameras are removed by hand adjusting their aiming angles until the images produced by them both are row-aligned. The random dot illumination is

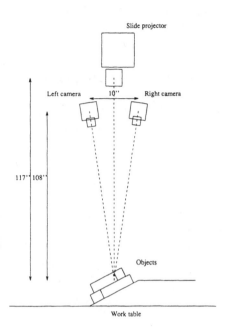

FIGURE 2.43. The geometry involved in the experiments.

produced by a slide projector using a computer generated 1024 × 1024 pixels random-dot pattern. For regular illumination, the same slide projector with a blank slide is used. The cameras are placed about 99 inches from the center of the scene and the camera aiming angle is about 2.3 degrees from the perpendicular to the work table, making for an angle of 4.6 degrees between the optic axes. The images were digitized over 512 × 480 matrices with 8 bits for representing each gray level. After LoG filtering, 256 × 256 pixel pictures were supplied to the pattern matching algorithm.

2.6.2 STEREO IMAGES AND DEPTH MAPS

The images observed by the left and the right cameras for a two box scene illuminated by regular room light are shown in Figures 2.44a and b. This pair of images is used for the dominant feature matching. The finest LoG operator is applied to these images. Then, as the dominant features, long straight lines are extracted. The zero-crossing contours, which are extracted through the finest LoG operator ($w_{2D} = 4$), are shown in Figures 2.45a and

b. The result of the dominant feature extraction, or straight line extraction, is shown in Figures 2.46a and b.

For the geometrically constrained matching, zero-crossing figure matching and default matching the same scenes lit by the unstructured (random-dot) lighting is utilized. Three different types of feature extracting LoG-operators, $w_{2D} = 16$, $w_{2D} = 8$, and $w_{2D} = 4$, are employed. After applying these operators, the locally steepest changes of the gray level were extracted as zero-crossing contours. For the illustration a pair of zero-crossing contours with $w_{2D} = 8$ is shown in Figure 2.47.

As described in the previous chapter, invocation of different matching procedures is controlled by the entries in the control matrix. For the scene under discussion, the control matrix as it exists just before the default matcher is invoked is shown in Figure 2.48. In the figure the control matrix entries are displayed by using different gray levels. The darkest grey level corresponds to the positions where the dominant feature matching is successful. The second darkest grey level represents the position where the geometrically constrained matching is successful. The third darkest gray levels correspond to the zero-crossing figure match. And, finally, the lightest grey level denotes the positions to which default matching is assigned. As was mentioned previously, the contents of the control matrix are not static and change during processing.

By invoking the default matching where dictated by the control matrix and computing the final disparities, the resulting depth map is shown in Figure 2.49. The depth is generated by using a zeroth order interpolation on the computed disparities.

2.6.3   COMPARISON WITH THE MPG ALGORITHM

We will now illustrate a few comparative results obtained with our method and with the MPG algorithm. The depth map obtained with the MPG algorithm for the stereo pair of Figure 2.44 is shown in Figure 2.50. The same zeroth order interpolation is used for the MPG case also.

While Figures 2.49 and 2.50 provide a qualitative comparison of the results obtained with our and the MPG methods, it is also possible to perform a quantitative comparison by keeping track of the number of left-image zero-crossings that have more than one possible zero-crossing in the right image for a potential match and for which one of these zero-crossings cannot be selected by the disambiguation process. If this number of zero-crossings is divided by the total number of zero-crossings available, we get a measure of robustness of the matching process.

As presented in the previous chapter, our method uses a narrow width disambiguation window. Therefore, the disparity value on some occasion, may nullify the values given by the matching. This nullification occurs in two cases : if the range provided by the coarser channel is entirely wrong,

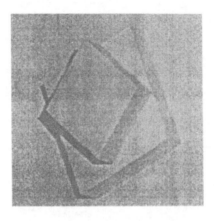

(a) Left image

(b) Right image

FIGURE 2.44. Stereo images of a two-box scene.

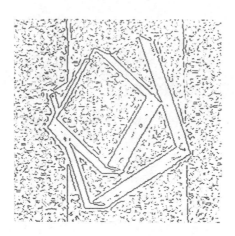

(a) Left image

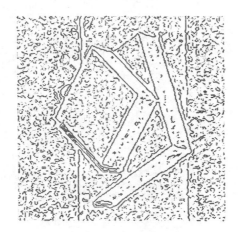

(b) Right image

FIGURE 2.45. Zero-crossing contours corresponding to the $w_{2D} = 4$ channel with regular room light illumination for the stereo images of Figure 2.44.

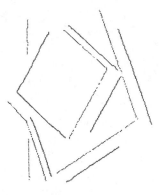

(a) Left image

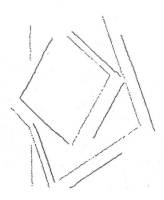

(b) Right image

FIGURE 2.46. Lines extracted as dominant features.

(a) Left image

(b) Right image

FIGURE 2.47. Zero-crossing contours for the $w_{2D} = 8$ channel with unstructured light illumination. These zero-crossing contours are used figural continuity matcher.

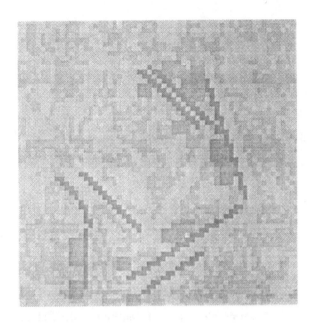

FIGURE 2.48. A gray level depiction of the control matrix.

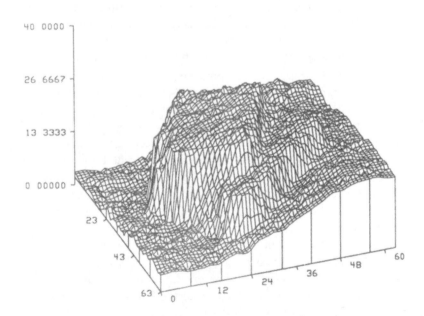

FIGURE 2.49. A depth map produced by our rule-based system.

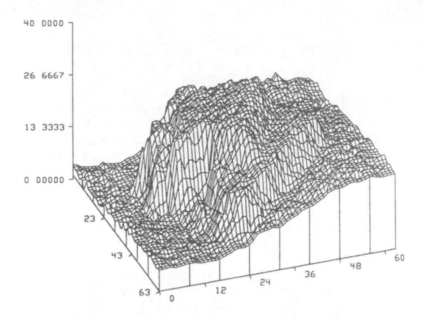

FIGURE 2.50. A depth map produced by the MPG algorithm.

or if the value given by the pulling effect is inconsistent with the currently measured disparity value. The latter case is likely to occur in both methods, the usual MPG and rule-based method, with almost the same rate. The difference of the rate of the occurrence of the nullification mostly reflects the amount of the misleading information by the coarser channel.

Table 2.5 shows the counts for different parameters in the disambiguation process for the four scenes shown in Figures 2.44 and 2.51. The stereo fusion was carried out by both the usual MPG method and the integrated rule-based approach. For each method, three numbers are counted: total number of left-image zero-crossings which have any zero-crossing matches at all (A), the number of left-image zero-crossings where the matching was entirely nullified by the disambiguation procedure (B), and the number of left-image zero-crossings where a matching right-image zero-crossing was chosen from amongst the available candidates by the disambiguation procedure (C). The upper number of each box of the table is for the usual MPG approach and the lower number for our rule-based procedure. As the total number of matches for each of the two methods is different, the ratios B/C, and C/A are also computed and shown percent fractions in Table 2.5. For the MPG method, matching is carried out in all the four channels, whereas for the case of the rule-based approach the numbers represent only the default matcher. In other words, for the rule-based approach, the counts shown are only for those regions of the images where the default matcher is invoked. Since the default matcher in the rule-based approach is identical to the

2.51(a) One box (image 2)

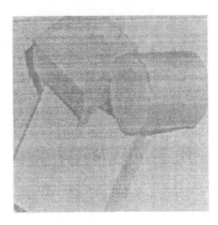

2.51(b) Three objects (image 3)

(c) Steps (image 4)

FIGURE 2.51. The three scenes shown here, together with the scene in Figure 2.44, are used for comparing the zero-matching statistics in Table 2.5.

full MPG matcher, the algorithms used in comparisons shown in Table 2.5 are exactly the same with regard to such issues as the matching criteria, disambiguation processing, search space size etc.

The numbers for both methods appearing in the column C/A are approximately the same. This is reasonable because the number of the feature points in a certain search space is completely determined by the relation between the LoG operator size and the search space size as shown by the Marr-Poggio theory. Looking closely at the table, one may find a weak tendency that the the lower number is larger than upper number. One possible explanation for this is that the ambiguous occasion will occur more likely when the zero-crossing figure match is not applicable. We assumed that the matching nullification occurs more frequently if the range measurement in the coarser channel was less accurate. If our claim is true, the difference of the number in the column B/A (expressed as percent) in the box corresponds to $W_{2D} = 8$. This indicates the difference of the frequency of the misleading information caused by the coarser channel, $W_{2D} = 16$. This value in the case of the usual method is 24.5 percent on the average of four images. The same value in the case of our model is 16.8 percent. Similarly, for the boxes corresponding to $W_{2D} = 4$ the values are 13.3 and 8.5 respectively. This sort of difference is not observed in the coarsest channel fusion. (The values are 15.0 and 15.0 respectively.) This is because there exists no coarser channel and the same fixation points (zero-disparity) are employed. It can be claimed that the misleading information by the coarser channel occurs more frequently in the usual method than our integrated rule-based method. This is because, for the fixation point determination prior to the medium channel ranging, the ranges determined by the geometrically constrained matching and zero-crossing figure match are taken into account in the rule-based model.

Another point to be discussed is the total number of the matches. As some part of the matching process in the MPG method is replaced by other methods, the number of point-wise matches normally appearing in the MPG method is significantly reduced. As this method uses the local orientation, and the sign of the zero-crossings as the attributes, the possibility of the erroneous correspondence in the usual MPG is occasionally higher than it is in other higher level matching. The reduction of the number of point-wise matches may lead to the reduction of the number of erroneous matching. The column of A in Table 2.5 indicates the total number of the point-wise matches. In the case where W_{2D} is 16 or 8, the reduction is about 56 percent. In the case where W_{2D} is 4, the reduction is about 14 percent.

2.7 Conclusions

In this report we have shown that the MPG procedure, although a landmark development in the evolving science of stereo vision, suffers from major deficiencies on account of its being a purely bottom-up approach. We pointed out that this procedure will generate disparity values at all those points which exhibit photometric differences. Since such points in a scene are a result of a complex interaction between illumination and the surfaces in the scene, their locations cannot be predicted in advance. Therefore, in most cases, especially if the scene surfaces are smooth, the pixels at which the disparities get calculated can be more or less randomly located, making difficult the process of interpolation for the purpose of computing continues looking depth maps.

In our work, our position has been that the problem with the MPG algorithm can be alleviated by injecting high level object knowledge into the matching process. In this report, we took a first step in that direction by assuming that all the object surfaces were planar and then this knowledge was directly used in the matching process.

Although, our use of object surface constraints by itself cannot be considered to be new, what is new in our work is the integration of such constraints with other approaches to the matching process – it seems plausible that such integration is also carried out by the human visual system. Since it is entirely likely that the human visual system latches on to any striking geometrical detail and since such details probably are fused at the outset – if only to facilitate the fusion of less striking scene details – in our combination method, we first extract dominant features, these being the straight lines constituted by joining of the planar faces of the scene objects.

In our rule based approach, we showed how the straight line feature matching was followed by the figural continuity matcher. And, the figural continuity matcher was followed by the default matcher, which is full blown implementation of the MPG algorithm. By embedding all these matching algorithms in a rule-based setting, the system became capable of invoking each of the methods on an opportunistic basis, meaning if, say, the figural continuity matcher did not produce acceptable results in a region of the image, the system could then automatically go ahead and invoke the default matcher. The bookkeeping for which matcher to apply where was done with the help of a 64 × 64 control matrix for 256 × 256 images.

Clearly, this report is only a first step in our attempt to inject high level knowledge into the process of binocular fusion. We are sure that future attempts would try to deal with higher order surfaces in scenes of greater complexity that what we have shown.

Image No.	W_{2D}	Total No. Matching A	No. Nullified by Disamb. B	(Ratio) $\frac{B}{A}\times100$	No. Disamb. Affected C	(Ratio) $\frac{C}{A}\times100$
1	16	3010	366	12	865	28
		1562	206	13	457	29
	8	5638	1408	24	2134	37
		2823	484	17	927	32
	4	7184	946	13	1538	21
		6419	555	8	1168	18
2	16	2554	367	14	834	32
		1482	209	14	463	31
	8	5789	1574	27	2557	44
		3492	648	18	1243	35
	4	6424	988	15	1885	29
		5470	510	9	1191	21
3	16	3044	511	16	928	30
		1378	244	17	466	33
	8	5787	1391	24	2270	39
		2765	476	17	1060	38
	4	7356	1004	13	1711	23
		6326	590	9	1223	19
4	16	3577	655	18	926	25
		920	143	15	258	28
	8	6163	1444	23	1769	28
		1722	281	16	496	28
	4	7207	898	12	1229	17
		5754	490	8	805	13

Upper numbers are for the usual MPG model

Lower numbers are for the integrated rule-based model

TABLE 2.5. This table compares two different statistics of zero-crossings matches for four images. In each box, the upper number was obtained with the MPG algorithm and the lower number with just the default matcher in our rule-based implementation. Of course, the default matcher is also the MPG algorithm, but note that it is only invoked wherever the other matching strategies cannot be invokded.

3

Geometric Signal Processing

Paul J. Besl[1]

3.1 Introduction

A wide variety of sensing techniques allow the direct measurement of the three-dimensional (3-D) coordinates of closely spaced points in a scene. A optical profilometer or a single light-stripe range sensor measures a one-dimensional depth profile $z_i = f(x_i)$ of a surface along a line specified by a y value. A single-view range imaging sensor [Bes88b] generates a two-dimensional set of samples $z_{ij} = f(x_i, y_j)$ that represent surface points in a scene. Such sensors might also yield surface dependent properties p_{ij} at each measured point, such as reflectance. Magnetic resonance imaging (MRI) systems [HL83] and computerized tomography (CT) systems [BGP83] measure various properties of 3-D points in a volume $p_{ijk} = f(x_i, y_j, z_k)$. A video camera is a good sensor for recovering planar curves $(x_i, y_i) = \vec{f}(s_i)$ that define the shape of a two-dimensional object in a plane specified by a fixed z value. In each case, a digital signal directly representing scene geometry is produced by the sensor. Typically, the signal is noisier than one would prefer and is therefore processed using digital signal/image processing techniques to clean up the digital sensor data for further computations, such as extracting descriptions of geometric primitives.

Unfortunately, most digital signal processing [OS75,RG75] and digital image processing [GW77,Pra78,RK82] techniques are not designed for the accurate recovery of geometric information from noisy digital signals. This is not surprising since most digital signal processing methods grew out of the needs of communications applications where the information content in a signal is concentrated in bands (frequency intervals) in the frequency domain. Filtering operations typically suppress noisy signal frequencies outside the bands of interest to clean up the signal for later processing.

In contrast, many geometric signal processing applications require the recovery of accurate geometric information from noisy geometric signals. High fidelity preservation of geometric features in a signal requires signal frequencies across the spatial frequency spectrum. The geometric information of interest is seldom concentrated in small spatial frequency bands be-

[1] Computer Science Department, General Motors Research Laboratories, Warren, Michigan 48090-9055, CSNet: besl@gmr.com

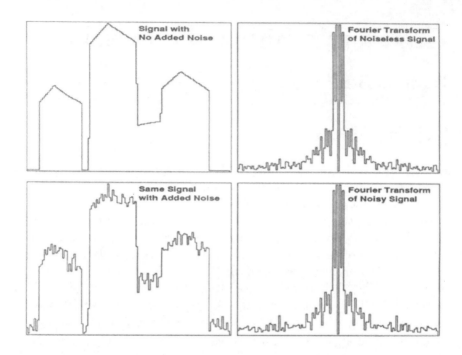

FIGURE 3.1. Discrete Fourier Transform of Geometric Signal with and without Noise.

cause sharp edges require lots of bandwidth. Figure 3.1 shows the amplitude of the discrete Fourier transform of a geometric signal with and without additive noise. The high frequency components of the Fourier transform are critical to sharp edges in the noiseless signal and do not look significantly different after the introduction of high frequency noise. Although conventional digital signal processing techniques are still quite useful in many circumstances, especially for signals with high noise levels, it is clear that as sensors get better and accuracy requirements increase, smoothing techniques more sophisticated than linear low-pass filtering will be useful and perhaps critical. We believe that a more cohesive theory of geometric signal processing is needed, and that the growing number of applications in this area would benefit greatly from a better theoretical foundation. Unfortunately, a cohesive theory of this sort does not yet exist.

In this work, the basic problems facing geometric signal processing will be defined in general terms. Our main goal is to focus attention on the fundamental issues in a dimension-independent manner, not to provide a complete geometric signal processing theory. First, machine perception is considered in a general context to provide a common background. Then we focus on geometric representations since most geometric signal processing applications are geared toward specific types of representations. A brief summary of geometric sensors is given next followed by a discussion of geometric signal structure. We then itemize first and second order descriptive quantities from differential geometry (tangent spaces and curvatures) in the one, two, and three dimensions. Finally, local and global approximation techniques are described which yield functions from which differential geometric properties can be computed. We discuss their relative advantages and disadvantages and conclude with a brief description of a robust approximation technique that should be able to overcome many of the disadvantages of conventional approximation methods.

The practical concerns of data abstraction in software development provide the main motivation for our dimension-independent thrust. Three-dimensional geometric data comes in so many different forms that it becomes necessary to standardize on relatively abstract entities in order to obtain a flexible software environment. Hence, the abstract notion of a geometric signal is adopted where the dimensions of the signal data are just properties of the geometric signal, and the appropriate approximation, tangent space, and curvature computations are invoked when needed based on signal dimension. In other words, we propose that a general-purpose geometric signal processing algorithm should not know whether a signal represents a curve, a surface, or a volume until execution. The flexibility of a machine perception system based on such algorithms would be significantly greater than that of any current systems, and we believe that such flexibility will be beneficial for the development of more capable machine perception systems.

3.2   Machine Perception

The general structure of many machine perception systems can be discussed in the context of the sets and mappings shown in Figure 3.2. The "real world" is sensed by one or more sensors (video, range, thermal, sonar, etc.) to create a time-varying spatially-varying multi-modal (vector-valued) image signal. Image (signal) processing techniques enhance the raw data for subsequent processing. A wide variety of data description processes may then be applied to the enhanced signal to isolate and extract information corresponding to physical features in an observed scene. If a machine perception system directly extracts geometric information (3-D points, curves, surfaces, or volumes) from the incoming signal, then the term *geometric signal processing* may be used to encompass both the enhancement processing and data description operations.

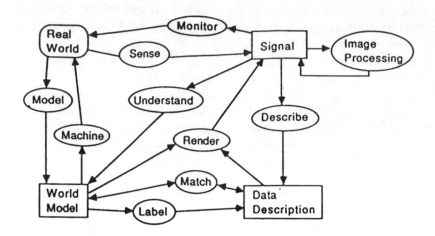

FIGURE 3.2. Machine Perception System Structure

The real world is usually modeled off-line prior to image processing and data description by the designer, and possibly the user, of a machine perception system to create an internal world model containing data corresponding to information recoverable from the input image signal. An intelligent "teach-by-example" system would also be able to derive specific model information dynamically from sensor input, as in e.g. [Pot83,Pot87,CA86], rather than requiring static, pre-specified models. In other words, geometric sensing and geometric signal processing may serve as components of an automated modeling (also known as reverse engineering) process as well as the basis for image understanding.

The primary goal of any machine perception system is to reliably establish meaningful relationships between observed signals and world knowledge. That is, the system must identify entities in the sensor data and interpret them as manifestations of modeled (or "model-able") entities. For example, interpretation might take the form of attaching the labels of modeled entities to segmented image regions. Correct interpretations (labelings), as judged by a human expert, indicate whether or not the system "understands" the signal.

In geometric signal understanding, interpretations are also judged according to approximation quality. A machine perception system provides a much stronger indication of correct signal understanding if, in addition to correctly labeling all parts of a signal, it can reconstruct a nearly identical version of a sensed signal based only on knowledge of the model entities detected in the signal ("tape recorders" not allowed). For example, if a person understands your spoken word, they can usually also pronounce it. In machine vision, a system should be able to render a version of the sensor data using only its understanding based on its internal world model. And just as a word can be repeated without knowing what it means, a vision system should also be able to render an accurate version of a signal from its data description alone without a formal model entity correspondence.

In summary, a machine perception system generally involves three data sets with increasing amounts of structure: (1) the voluminous signal data with very little structure (a list of numbers), (2) a more compact data description, e.g. isolated geometric structures, and (3) a world model, which includes information about world objects, data descriptions, and sensor data as well as the relationships between them and the real world. Sensing and modeling processes map the real world to signals and models respectively. An inverse modeling operation would be NC machining, which maps modeled objects back to real objects. The inverse sensing operation is signal reproduction; for example, a video monitor maps camera signals back to the real world. The description process is an inverse-rendering process that maps signals to unlabeled data descriptions. Matching and labeling are examples of processing between the description and model domains. The inverse-rendering mapping from the signal domain to the world model domain, denoted in Figure 3.2 as the complete signal understanding process, is usually a composite mapping of the description and matching processes.

3.3 Geometric Representations

A useful representation of the real world should at least be four dimensional (4-D) with three spatial dimensions and a time dimension. The internal world model for a general purpose machine perception system should also be at least 4-D if the system is to exhibit many capabilities of the human eye-brain system. In this section, 0-D, 1-D, 2-D, 3-D, and 4-D geometric entities are briefly considered and then summarized in Figure 3.3. Geometric entities can be represented in several forms:

1. A **parametric form** of an n-dimensional (n-D) geometric entity in an $n + m$-dimensional (($n + m$)-D) space is given by $\vec{x} = \vec{f}(\vec{u})$ where $\vec{u} \in \Re^n$ and $\vec{x} \in \Re^{n+m}$ and where $\Re$ is the set of real numbers. This form models geometry using a mapping of points $\vec{u}$ in a convenient parameter domain, such as the unit interval, the unit square, or the unit cube, to points $\vec{x}$ in an embedding space $\Re^{n+m}$ where $m \geq 0$. Polynomial parameterizations in the power basis and the Bernstein basis and piecewise-polynomial parameterizations in the B-spline basis are commonly encountered parametric forms. Since it is easiest and most stable to approximate geometric signal data with parametric forms, they are commonly used to obtain explicit geometric representations from geometric signals. In a later section, specific local and global parametric approximation techniques are given.

2. An **implicit form** of an n-D geometric entity in an n-D space is given by $g(\vec{x}) \leq 0$ where $\vec{x} \in \Re^n$. This form models geometry using an inequality constraint on all points inside or on the boundary of the geometric entity. An n-D entity in $(n+1)$-D space is specified implicitly as $g(\vec{x}) = 0$ where $\vec{x} \in \Re^{n+1}$. Some n-D entities in $(n+2)$-D space can be represented implicitly as the intersection of two implicitly defined entities in $(n+2)$-D space: $g_1(\vec{x}) = g_2(\vec{x}) = 0$ where $\vec{x} \in \Re^{n+2}$ (or $\vec{g}(\vec{x}) = \vec{0} \in \Re^2$). Algebraic geometric entities with polynomial implicit functions are usually considered. Implicit functions are most useful for applications in which the geometric signal data exhibits useful symmetries: e.g., spherical, cylindrical, or toroidal symmetries. Approximation using implicit functions is generally less stable and/or more computationally expensive than parametric approximation.

3. A **digital form** of an n-D geometric entity in an $(n+m)$-D space is an explicit list of all the $(n+m)$-D points that are members of the entity to within a specified spatial quantization. Since explicit lists require large amounts of computer memory for storage, other data structures that store the same information using less memory are commonly used. Digital forms can only approximate smoothly curved geometry albeit arbitrarily closely with increasing memory cost. Geometric sensors yield digital form descriptions of the observed scene, but the raw sensor data usually includes sensor noise mixed with the geometric information.

4. A **solution form** of an n-D geometric entity is a problem statement whose solution represents the given geometry. Some 1-D geometric entities in $(n+1)$-D can be represented as the solution to an ordinary differential equation (ODE) whereas some n-D entities in $(n+m)$-D can be represented as the solution to a partial differential equation (PDE). In general, differential equations are solved numerically resulting in explicit solutions that are either digital or piecewise-linear parametric. The solution forms of smooth space curves and smooth surfaces from differential geometry make invariance, existence, and uniqueness properties explicit.

5. A non-parametric, explicit **graph form** of an n-D geometric entity in a $(n+1)$-D space is very useful in many situations, but is not a general geometric form. It can only represent restricted classes of $(n+1)$-D entities. Graph forms of interest are $y(x), r(\theta), z(x,y), r(\theta,\phi), \rho(x,y,z)$, and $\rho(x,y,z,t)$ where (x,y,z) are Cartesian coordinates, (r,θ,ϕ) are spherical coordinates, and t is time. Graph functions exhibit properties of both parametric and implicit forms, but are inherently simpler than either one.

For each form above, it is possible in theory to construct representations based on each of the other forms.

A single instance of a geometric primitive form can be limited in its capability to describe shape. A geometric representation system should include the ability to flexibly combine geometric primitives to represent complex shapes. There are several methods often used to combine geometric primitives to create composite geometric entities:

1. The **boolean composition** method defines composite entities as expressions of primitives combined by the boolean operations of union ($\cup$), intersection ($\cap$), and difference ($-$). These operations are usually assumed to be regularized. A set is regular [RT78,KM76] if it is exactly equal to the closure of the interior of itself. A regularized boolean operation produces the closure of the interior of the usual set operations. For example, if the letters A to F represent geometric primitives with particular locations and orientations, then set expressions define a new composite entity: $G = (((A\cap B)\cup C)-D)\cup(E-F)$. Parsed expressions can be represented as **binary trees** where G is the root node, each branching node is a binary operator($\cup, \cap, -$), and geometric primitives are the leaf nodes. When the leaf nodes are 3-D volumetric solid models and the boolean operations are regularized, the composite 3-D models are known as **constructive solid geometry (CSG)** trees.

2. The **boundary composition** method defines n-D geometric entities in terms of $(n-1)$-D geometric entities. Representing 1-D intervals by their 0-D endpoints is the simplest case of boundary composition. If the boundary ∂V of a simply connected 3-D object volume V is a simple piecewise smooth 2-D surface primitive, then a representation of the bounding surface is a **boundary representation (B-Rep)** of the volume V [Req77]. If the boundary $\partial\Omega$ of a simply connected 2-D planar region Ω is a simple piecewise-smooth closed curve, then the bounding curve is a boundary representation of the region Ω.

3. The **sweep composition** method defines an $(n+1)$-D geometric entity in terms of (1) an n-D entity, (2) a 1-D curve entity along which the n-D entity is swept, and (3) a sweeping transformation function, which is often used to rotate or scale the n-D entity along the sweeping curve to obtain twisted or tapered geometric entities respectively. For example, a 2-D *ruled surface* entity can be represented as a 1-D straight line swept along a 1-D space curve. Some 3-D objects can also be represented by a space curve and the cross section of the object perpendicular to the curve tangent. If the cross section is defined by its boundary curve, e.g. $r(\theta)$, then the object is defined very simply and concisely in terms of two curve representations: the space curve, or spine curve, and the cross section boundary curve [SK83]. The

	1-D Space	2-D Space	3-D Space	4-D Space-Time
0-D Entity	Point	Point	Point	Point
	$x \in \Re$	$(x, y) \in \Re^2$	$(x, y, z) \in \Re^3$	$(x, y, z, t) \in \Re^4$
1-D Entity	Interval	Planar Curve	Space Curve	Point Trajectory
Parametric:	$[a, b] \subset \Re$	$\vec{f}(u) \in \Re^2; u \in [a, b]$	$\vec{f}(u) \in \Re^3; u \in [a, b]$	$\vec{f}(t) \in \Re^3$
Implicit:	$g(x) \leq 0$	$g(x, y) = 0$	$\vec{g}(x, y, z) = \vec{0} \in \Re^2$	$\vec{g}(x, y, z, t) = \vec{0} \in \Re^3$
2-D Entity	—	Region	Surface	Curve Trajectory
Parametric:		$\Omega \subset \Re^2$	$\vec{f}(u, v) \in \Re^3; (u, v) \in \Omega$	$\vec{f}(u, t) \in \Re^3; u \in [a, b]$
Implicit:		$g(x, y) \leq 0$	$g(x, y, z) = 0$	$\vec{g}(x, y, z, t) = \vec{0} \in \Re^2$
Boundary:		$\partial\Omega = $ Planar Curve	$\vec{f}(u, v) \in \Re^3; (u, v) \in \partial\Omega$	$\vec{f}(a, t), \vec{f}(b, t)$
3-D Entity	—	—	Volume	Surface Trajectory
Parametric:			$V \subset \Re^3$	$\vec{f}(u, v, t) \in \Re^3; (u, v) \in \Omega$
Implicit:			$g(x, y, z) \leq 0$	$g(x, y, z, t) = 0$
Boundary:			$\partial V = $ Surface	$\vec{f}(u, v, t); (u, v) \in \partial\Omega$
4-D Entity	—	—	—	Volume Trajectory
Parametric:				$H \subset \Re^4$
Implicit:				$g(x, y, z, t) \leq 0$

FIGURE 3.3. Primitive Geometric Entities by Dimension (from [Bes88b])

simplest example, a cylinder, is defined by a line segment and a circle. A sweep representation is known as a **generalized cylinder (GC)**, or generalized cone, in the computer vision literature.

The use of one composition method does not exclude the possible use of other methods, as in a hybrid world modeler [Req80]. Hybrid composite models might consist of a boolean composition of boundary representations and sweep representations.

To create composite models from geometric primitives, one must also specify orientations, positions, scales, possible joint relationships at attachment points, allowable deformations, or other geometry related features. These concerns do not often arise in the geometric signal processing of static geometric signals, and therefore we shall not discuss them further here. For a quick overview of some alternatives involved in geometric representations, refer to Figure 3.4.

Smooth surfaces are found mostly in man-made environments. Most natural objects and many man-made objects exhibit *texture*, which, like color, is useful for distinguishing surfaces and objects with similar shapes. For example, flat regions of carpeting, wood, grass, tile, and concrete approximated by planes cannot be distinguished from other planes based only on geometry. Rather than explicitly modeling the fine scale surface structure, one solution is to attach concise mathematical properties to a surface that represent its texture properties.

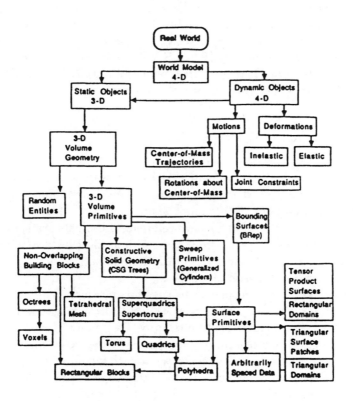

FIGURE 3.4. Geometric Representations for World Modeling

There are two types of perceivable texture: **visual texture** arising from surface reflectance or illumination variations and **physical texture**, i.e. geometric surface variations. A finished wood surface is visually textured because of reflectance variations, but is smooth to the touch. In contrast, a rough surface might have the same surface reflectance everywhere, yet it appears textured. Other surfaces exhibit both types of texture. Since visual texture is not physical geometry and can be modeled as a texture mapping on the given surface geometry [BN76,Hec86], it is not considered further here. Physical texture due to geometric surface variations is a separate issue and is discussed in the geometric signal model section.

3.4   Geometric Sensors

A *geometric sensor* is any combination of hardware and software capable of producing a *geometric signal* of a real-world scene under appropriate operating conditions. A *geometric signal* is a large collection of *three-dimensional points* (x, y, z) in a known reference coordinate system with the possible inclusion of the point properties, such as local surface reflectance, surface roughness, point velocity, vibration, polarization, temperature, X-ray attenuation, or magnetic properties.

A *volume sensor* is a geometric sensor that measures a property of 3-D points in a volume $p_{ijk} = f(x_i, y_j, z_k)$, such as a magnetic resonance imaging (MRI) or computerized tomography (CT) sensor. A *surface sensor*, such as a single-view range imaging sensor, measures a set of coordinates $z_{ij} = f(x_i, y_j)$ and possibly properties p_{ij} at each measured opaque surface point. A *profile sensor*, such as a static light-stripe sensor, measures one-dimensional depth profile $z_i = f(x_i)$ of a surface along a line specified by a fixed y value. A *planar curve sensor*, such as a video camera viewing 2-D objects on a plane, measures $(x_i, y_i) = \vec{f}(s_i)$ that define the shape of a planar curve in the plane specified by a fixed z value. A *space curve sensor* would measure values of the form $(x_i, y_i, z_i) = \vec{f}(s_i)$ that define the shape of a space curve. A *point sensor* measures the point coordinates (x_i, y_i, z_i) of a single point.

The terminology above indicates the functional relationship of the (x, y, z) coordinates for each type of sensor, but some sensors do not produce Cartesian coordinates directly. For example, many range imaging sensors output distance measurements that indicate range along 3-D direction vectors indexed by two integers (i, j). Such a range image is said to be in raster, or r_{ij}, form. Given an ideal orthographic range image where r_{ij} is the pixel value at the i-th row and the j-th column of the image, the 3-D coordinates (x_i, y_j, z_{ij}) would be given as

$$x_i = a_x + s_x i \qquad y_j = a_y + s_y j \qquad z_{ij} = a_z + s_z r_{ij} \qquad (3.1)$$

where the s_x, s_y, s_z values are scale factors and the a_x, a_y, a_z values are

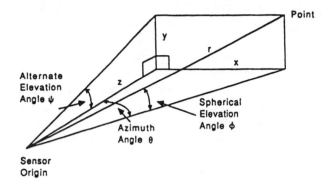

FIGURE 3.5. Cartesian, Spherical, and Orthogonal-Axis Coordinates

coordinate offsets. However, one more often encounters a spherical coordinate system, shown in Figure 3.5, where the (i, j) indices correspond to elevation (latitude) angles and azimuth (longitude) angles respectively. The spherical to Cartesian transformation is more complicated:

$$x_{ij} \;=\; a_x + s_r r_{ij} \cos(i s_\phi) \sin(j s_\theta) \qquad (3.2)$$
$$y_{ij} \;=\; a_y + s_r r_{ij} \sin(i s_\phi)$$
$$z_{ij} \;=\; a_z + s_r r_{ij} \cos(i s_\phi) \cos(j s_\theta)$$

where the s_r, s_ϕ, s_θ values are the scale factors in range, elevation, and azimuth and the a_x, a_y, a_z values are again offsets. The "orthogonal-axis" angular coordinate system, also shown in Figure 3.5, uses an "alternate elevation angle" ψ with the spherical azimuth definition θ. The transformation to Cartesian coordinates is

$$x_{ij} \;=\; a_x + s_r r_{ij} \tan(j s_\theta)/\sqrt{1 + \tan^2(i s_\theta) + \tan^2(j s_\psi)} \qquad (3.3)$$
$$y_{ij} \;=\; a_y + s_r r_{ij} \tan(i s_\psi)/\sqrt{1 + \tan^2(i s_\theta) + \tan^2(j s_\psi)}$$
$$z_{ij} \;=\; a_z + s_r r_{ij}/\sqrt{1 + \tan^2(i s_\theta) + \tan^2(j s_\psi)}.$$

The alternate elevation angle ψ depends only on y and z whereas ϕ depends on x, y, and z. The differences in (x, y, z) for Equations 3.2 and 3.3 for the same values of azimuth and elevation are less than 4% in x and z and less than 11% in y even when both angles are as large as $\pm 30°$.

Geometric signal processing algorithms must include provisions for such transformations to be performed on raw sensor data to yield the more desirable (x, y, z) coordinates. The exact stage of signal processing where one should introduce such a transformation, if needed, depends on the application and the sensor and is often not easy to determine. Performing the transformation too early may unnecessarily complicate certain types of processing for some applications whereas other applications, such as a vehicle that is rolling and pitching significantly during range image acquisition, require immediate transformation to Cartesian form in order to make sense out of the data.

Geometric signal processing algorithms should also include provisions for handling various types of noise models that will depend in general on the sensor and the application. Ideally, algorithms could be structured so that an application's sensor could be queried for a standardized description of its geometric and noise properties before geometric signals are processed, then appropriate operations could be performed given the idiosyncrasies of a given sensor.

A wide variety of physical principles have been used in geometric sensing:

1. Radar (Sonar): Range from Time, Phase, or Beat Frequency

2. Triangulation: Range from Disparity Angles and Baseline

3. Lens Focusing: Range from Blur

4. Moire Methods: Range from Grating Phase Modulation

5. Holographic Interferometry: Range from Optical Phase Modulation

6. Fresnel Diffraction: Range from Local Contrast

7. Imaging Constraints: Shape from Shading, Texture, Contour, etc.

8. Tactile and Proximity Sensing: Shape from Touch

9. Computerized Tomography: Structure from X-Ray or Ultrasound Attenuation

10. Positron and Single-Photon Emission Computerized Tomography.

11. Nuclear Magnetic Resonance Imaging: Structure from Magnetic Dipoles

The first six topics are discussed in detail in [Bes88b]. Imaging constraints are summarized in [Alo88] and tactile sensors were surveyed by [Har82]. The last three topics are used primarily in medical applications and have been described in [BGP83] (CT) [RHS+83] (X-ray CT) [Gre83] (Ultrasound CT) [Kno83] (SPECT) [RHK87] (PET) [HL83] (MRI). For our purposes, only the functional form, the noise characteristics, and the dimensionality of the data are of interest.

3.5   Geometric Signal Modeling

The parametric form is adopted for the geometric signal model. A *digital geometric signal* is defined as a collection of N discrete samples of an underlying function $\vec{f} : \Re^n \to \Re^m$

$$\vec{x}_i = \vec{f}(\vec{u}_i) \tag{3.4}$$

where $\vec{u}_i \in \Re^n$ and $\vec{x}_i \in \Re^m$ and $i = 1, \ldots, N$. The dimension n of the domain space and the dimension m of the range space depend on the particular geometric signal processing problem. Figure 3.6 lists various dimensions for signals of interest to machine perception and geometric modeling. The upper portion of the table lists non-geometric signals whereas the lower portion lists geometric signals.

Thus, a wide variety of signals of practical interest, both geometric and non-geometric, can be identified by two integers between one and four with a total of only sixteen possibilities. Hence, the first part of signal modeling, which is almost always an implicit step given an application, is the selection of the dimensions of the domain and the range spaces for a functional model.

Next, the structure of the function is considered. From a mathematical point of view, we have no right to impose any structure on our function until we are given more information. However, in most circumstances, we already know something about what to expect in a geometric signal acquired from real world geometry. We expect to see some obvious structure in a signal, such as smoothness, discontinuities, and texture, as well as sensor noise. If a signal appears to be totally random noise without any structure, then it is just random noise from a geometric signal processing point of view. For example, the signal processing involved in spread spectrum communications [Pro83], where information is hidden in signals that look like random noise, is essentially the opposite of geometric signal processing.

In most cases, a geometric signal is "reflected" from a scene containing a finite number of objects that have a finite number of relatively smooth surfaces (possibly textured) that meet at relatively distinct edges. Hence, a signal can be be decomposed into a finite number of partitions where each partition corresponds to some surface on some object. Our expectations of geometric information in a geometric signal then lead us to hypothesize that the data $(\vec{u}_i, \vec{x}_i)$ is explained by a function $\vec{f}$ that can be decomposed into the following form:

$$\vec{x} = \vec{f}(\vec{u}) = \sum_{k=1}^{K} \left(\vec{g}_k(\vec{u}) + \vec{t}_k(\vec{u}) + \vec{n}_k(\vec{u}) \right) \chi_k(\vec{u}) \tag{3.5}$$

where (1) K is the number of signal partitions, (2) $\vec{g}_k(\vec{u})$ is a smooth C^2 function (possesses continuous second derivatives) defined over a compact (i.e. closed, bounded) subset Ω_k of the domain $\Re^n$, (3) $\vec{t}_k(\vec{u})$ is a texture

n	m	Domain Variables	Range Variables	Signal Type
1	1	t (time)	A (voltage)	Audio Signal
1	2	t (time)	A_L, A_R (voltage)	Stereo Audio Signal
2	1	u, v (space)	I (intensity)	Static B&W Video Image
2	3	u, v (space)	R, G, B (color)	Static Color Video Image
2	4	u, v (space)	f_1, f_2, f_3, f_4	Static Multispectral Image
3	1	u, v, t (space-time)	I (intensity)	Time-Varying B&W Video Signal
3	3	u, v, t (space-time)	R, G, B (color)	Time-Varying Color Video Signal
3	4	u, v, t (space-time)	f_1, f_2, f_3, f_4	Time-Varying 4-Band Multispectral
1	2	s (arc-length)	x, y (space)	Image Edge, Planar Curve
1	3	s (arc-length)	x, y, z (space)	Range Image Edge, Space Curve
2	1	x, y (space)	z (depth)	Static Orthographic Range Image
3	1	x, y, t (space)	z (depth)	Time-Varying Range Image
2	3	u, v (space)	x, y, z (space)	Static Spherical Range Image
3	3	u, v, t (space)	x, y, z (space)	Time-Varying Spherical Range Image
2	2	x, y (space)	V_x, V_y (vector)	Static, Generic 2-D Vector Field
3	2	x, y, t (space-time)	V_x, V_y (vector)	Time-Varying 2-D Vector Field
3	1	x, y, z (space)	ρ ("density")	Static 3-D Volume Signal
4	1	x, y, z, t (space-time)	ρ ("density")	Time-Varying 3-D Volume Signal
4	4	u, v, w, t (space-time)	x, y, z, ρ ("density")	Time-Varying Parametric Volume
1	3	t (time)	x, y, z (space)	Point Space-Time Trajectory
2	3	u, v (space)	x, y, z (space)	Static Parametric Surface
2	1	x, y (space)	z (depth)	Static Graph Surface
3	3	x, y, z (space)	V_x, V_y, V_z (vector)	Generic Static 3-D Vector Field
4	3	x, y, z, t (space-time)	V_x, V_y, V_z (vector)	Generic Time-Varying Vector Field

FIGURE 3.6. Signals of Interest in Machine Perception

function with a zero first moment and a finite second moment which is also defined over Ω_k and describes the physical texture of the surface, (4) $\vec{n}_k(\vec{u})$ is a zero-mean stochastic (random) noise process which is in general non-normal, non-stationary, statistically correlated, and may depend on the sensed geometry $\vec{g}$ and the texture $\vec{t}$, and (5) $\chi_k(\vec{u})$ is the characteristic function of the domain subset Ω_k defined by

$$\chi_k(\vec{u}) = \left\{ \begin{array}{ll} 1 & \vec{u} \in \Omega_k \subset \Re^n \\ 0 & \text{otherwise} \end{array} \right. \tag{3.6}$$

where the subsets Ω_k are the largest subsets such that the $\vec{g}_k(\vec{u})$ geometry is still C^2. Thus, a geometric signal is modeled as piecewise-smooth geometry with texture plus sensor noise. It is important to note that without a priori information it is virtually impossible to distinguish some textures from sensor noise.

For geometry segmentation discussions, it is often convenient to associate a *region label function* $l(\vec{u})$ with the partitioning defined by the subsets Ω_k:

$$l(\vec{u}) = \sum_{k=1}^{K} k \, \chi_k(\vec{u}). \tag{3.7}$$

If $\vec{a}_k \in \Re^p$ is the vector of all p parameters needed to precisely specify the smooth function $\vec{g}_k(\vec{u})$ over its support region Ω_k, and if $\vec{b}_k \in \Re^q$ is the vector of all q parameters needed to specify the texture function $\vec{t}_k(\vec{u})$ over the same region, then any geometric signal that arises in our piecewise-smooth signal model may be represented as the piecewise-constant label function $l(\vec{u})$ with minimum value 1 and maximum value K and the list of K geometry parameter vectors $\{\vec{a}_k\}$ and K texture parameter vectors $\{\vec{b}_k\}$. This signal model is quite general and can be used to represent many types of signals unless multiplicative noise or some other type of non-additive noise is present.

The geometric *segmentation/reconstruction/extraction* problem may be stated as follows: Given only a geometric signal specified by the data set $(\vec{u}_i, \vec{x}_i)$ and denoted symbolically as observed function $\vec{f}$, find $\hat{K}$ approximating functions $\hat{g}_k(\vec{u})$ and texture functions $\hat{t}(\vec{u})$ defined over $\hat{K}$ domain regions $\hat{\Omega}_k$ such that the total geometric signal representation error

$$\epsilon_{tot} = \|\vec{f} - \hat{f}\| \tag{3.8}$$

between the reconstructed/extracted signal estimate $\hat{f}$, which is given by

$$\hat{f}(\vec{u}) = \sum_{k=1}^{\hat{K}} \left(\hat{g}_k(\vec{u}) + \hat{t}_k(\vec{u}) \right) \hat{\chi}_k(\vec{u}), \tag{3.9}$$

and the data is small and the total number of regions $\hat{K}$ is small. The function norm is left unspecified, but would conventionally be the max norm, the (Euclidean) root-mean-square error norm, or the mean absolute error norm.

There are two trivial solutions. The "one point per region" solution requires no computational effort and minimizes the approximation error (zero), but maximizes the number of regions (the number of data points). The "one region per signal" solution minimizes the number of regions (one), but maximizes the approximation error for any specified functional form. Although this can be useful in some cases and is considered later in the global approximation section, it does not really solve the problem in general. A good algorithm should tend to segment geometric signals into regions that can be directly associated with meaningful physical entities in a scene. The functions defined over the isolated regions should mathematically represent the shape of the scene geometry.

Although some progress has been made toward special-case solutions to this problem, such as the zero-texture assumption [BJ88], or the piecewise constant function assumption with certain non-zero textures (addressed in most texture analysis), a general purpose low-level segmentation algorithm has yet to be demonstrated.

3.5.1 GEOMETRIC NOISE MODELING

Sensor noise may be caused by several different phenomena depending on the type of sensor and the type of scene geometry being sensed. Nonetheless, noise in geometric signals may be broken down into different contributions: random uncorrelated, normally distributed sensor noise $\vec{n}_n$, quantization noise $\vec{n}_q$, systematic noise introduced by sensor imperfections $\vec{n}_s$, and other types of random non-normal noise $\vec{n}_r$ that might be analyzable. Even if most of the geometric sensor data can be explained by the above types of noise, it is common to have small amounts of the geometric data be completely corrupted. We use the term "outlier noise" $\vec{n}_o$ to represent any noise sources that have a large effect on a small percentage of the data. In range imaging for example, specular reflections, multiple reflections, steep relative surface angles, depth discontinuities, and other effects can produce wrong measurements not explainable by simple probabilistic models.

Given the above observations, the additive noise contribution at the i-th data point in a geometric signal may be decomposed into the following form:

$$\vec{n}(\vec{u}_i) = \vec{n}_n(\vec{u}_i) + \vec{n}_q(\vec{u}_i) + \vec{n}_s(\vec{u}_i) + \vec{n}_r(\vec{u}_i) + \vec{n}_o(\vec{u}_i). \qquad (3.10)$$

The choices for handling this model are the following: (1) pretend that the other terms besides the normally distributed noise do not exist, (2) try to analyze the noise process as thoroughly as possible using probabilistic techniques, or (3) use methods that are insensitive to the exact form of the noise probability distributions. The first option is the usual approach and it works surprisingly well in many cases. However, for accurate geometry extraction, there are definite problems that arise. The second option usually gets bogged down in either analysis or computation at some point. The third option however appears quite attractive. In a later section, we will briefly introduce one technique from a branch of statistics known as *robust statistics*. Robust statisticians have developed methods that are *distributionally robust* in the sense that they are fairly insensitive to the actual probabilistic nature of the noise. There is a huge body of useful literature that has remained untapped by computer vision researchers until recently. The methods are usually computationally intensive, but by judicious application to portions of the data where it is needed, practical techniques for real applications may be feasible.

3.6   Geometric Descriptions

At this point, we have discussed machine perception, geometric representations, geometric sensors, and mathematical signal and noise models. Now, suppose that we are given an unknown geometric signal in some representation and must describe its shape properties in detail. A general-purpose method must be able to describe arbitrary smooth shapes of curves, surfaces, and volumes in a manner that is independent of how the geometry is being viewed and how it is being represented, i.e., independent of parameterization if parametric forms are being used. Differential geometry defines quantities for describing arbitrary shapes that are independent of parameterization, rotation, and translation so such quantities have been the natural choice for geometric descriptions whenever the computation of such quantities is possible. At this point, we treat the description of geometric entities in different dimensions separately using only a basic knowledge of partial derivatives and linear algebra. For more information, the reader should consult one of the many texts that cover similar material [Gau85] [Dar96] [Eis09] [Wea27] [Pog58] [Kre59] [Wil59] [Str61] [Hic65] [O'N66] [Sto69] [Lip69] [DoC76] [Spi79] [Tho79] [FP79] [Hsi81] [BG84] [Bur85]. (The following journal articles are also recommended: [BPYA85] [BJ86] [Far86] [VMA86] [VA87].)

3.6.1   PLANAR CURVES

The behavior of univariate functions $y = f(x)$ is often described using properties of first and second derivatives. However, for curve shapes that can be represented by graph curves $(x = u, y = f(u))$, the first and second derivatives f_u, f_{uu} will of course depend on the x, y coordinate system in which the shape is represented. Subscript notation will used throughout to denote differentiation by a given variable

$$\vec{f}_u(u) = \frac{d\vec{f}}{du} \qquad \vec{f}_{uu}(u) = \frac{d^2\vec{f}}{du^2}. \qquad (3.11)$$

This convention is used instead of the dots or primes to be compatible with the partial derivative notation used for multivariate functions. For describing shape, it is desirable to have descriptive quantities like first and second derivatives, but the quantities should be independent of the coordinate system in which the shape is viewed as well as the mathematical parameterization by which it is described. In general, one should substitute the notion of tangent space for first derivative and curvature for second derivative.

For a parametric smooth curve segment C given by

$$C = \left\{ \vec{x}(u) \in \Re^2 : u \in [a, b] \subset \Re \right\}, \qquad (3.12)$$

where $\vec{x}(u) = (x(u), y(u))$ is a twice-differentiable vector function of a scalar argument u which is not assumed to be arc length, the quantities of interest are the speed function $\nu(u)$ given by

$$\nu(u) = \|\vec{x}_u\| = \sqrt{x_u^2 + y_u^2}, \qquad (3.13)$$

the unit tangent vector function $\vec{t}(u)$ given by

$$\vec{t}(u) = \frac{\vec{x}_u(u)}{\nu(u)}, \qquad (3.14)$$

and the curvature function $\kappa(u)$ given by

$$\kappa(u) = \frac{x_u y_{uu} - y_u x_{uu}}{\nu^3} = \frac{d}{du}\left(\tan^{-1}\left(\frac{y_u(u)}{x_u(u)}\right)\right). \qquad (3.15)$$

The speed function is a parameterization-dependent normalization factor that is independent of choice of coordinate system. Note that a parametric curve possesses a singularity wherever the curve's speed drops to zero. The unit tangent vector defines the tangent space (tangent line) of the curve at each point. The curvature function defines the local radius of curvature $1/\kappa$ at each point. These very fundamental concepts are shown in Figure 3.7.

For a given shape, the tangent space and the curvature at each point are invariant to parameterization changes and choice of coordinate system. For planar curves free of singularities, the curvature and speed functions uniquely determine curve shape. As one would expect, *almost every 2-D shape recognition technique that has appeared in the computer vision literature uses the curvature function, the tangent angle function, or the curve itself.* The challenge for 3-D shape recognition and geometric signal processing is the feasible, efficient, and correct extension of previous work.

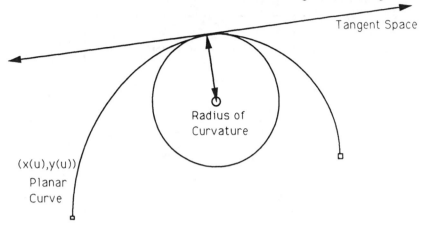

FIGURE 3.7. Differential Geometric Structure of a Planar Curve

For graph curves $(x = u, y = f(u))$, the speed is $\nu(u) = \sqrt{1 + f_u^2}$, the tangent vector is $\vec{t} = (1/\nu(u), f_u/\nu(u))$ (with tangent angle $\tan^{-1} f_u$), and the curvature simplifies to

$$\kappa(u) = \frac{f_{uu}(u)}{(1 + f_u^2)^{\frac{3}{2}}}. \tag{3.16}$$

These quantities are similar to those for graph surfaces and volumes as described later. Note the differences between these differential geometric quantities and the function's first and second derivatives.

3.6.2   SPACE CURVES

Planar curves are special cases of space curves. A parametric smooth space curve segment C is a 1-D geometric entity embedded in 3-D space:

$$C = \left\{ \vec{x}(u) \in \Re^3 : u \in [a, b] \subset \Re \right\} \tag{3.17}$$

where the three components of the vector function $\vec{x}(u) = (x(u), y(u), z(u))$ possess continuous second derivatives. For space curves, the speed function $\nu(u)$ is given by

$$\nu(u) = \|\vec{x}_u\| = \sqrt{x_u^2 + y_u^2 + z_u^2}, \tag{3.18}$$

the tangent unit-vector function $\vec{t}(u)$ is again given by

$$\vec{t}(u) = \frac{\vec{x}_u(u)}{\nu(u)}, \tag{3.19}$$

and the curvature function $\kappa(u)$ is given by

$$\kappa(u) = \frac{\|\vec{t}_u(u)\|}{\nu(u)} = \frac{\|\vec{x}_u \times \vec{x}_{uu}\|}{\nu(u)^3}. \tag{3.20}$$

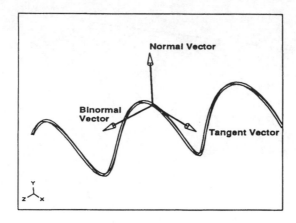

FIGURE 3.8. Tangent-Normal-Binormal Coordinate Frame on a Curve

These quantities correspond almost exactly to the planar curve expressions with the exception that curvature must be non-negative, and again singularities occur wherever the speed function is zero. Although curvature and tangent space notions are now defined, there exists an entire plane orthogonal to the space curve's tangent vector rather than a simple line as in the planar curve case. To quantify all the shape properties of a space curve, it is necessary to look at orthogonal basis vectors in this plane.

The normal unit-vector function $\vec{n}(u)$ may be computed from any of the following expressions:

$$\vec{n}(u) = \frac{\vec{t}_u(u)}{\|\vec{t}_u(u)\|} = \frac{\vec{t}_u(u)}{\kappa(u)\nu(u)} = \frac{\nu^2 \vec{x}_{uu} - (\vec{x}_{uu} \cdot \vec{x}_u)\vec{x}_u}{\kappa\nu^4}. \tag{3.21}$$

The binormal unit-vector function $\vec{b}(u)$ completes a right-handed coordinate system:

$$\vec{b}(u) = \vec{t}(u) \times \vec{n}(u) = \frac{\vec{x}_u \times \vec{x}_{uu}}{\|\vec{x}_u \times \vec{x}_{uu}\|} = \frac{\vec{x}_u \times \vec{x}_{uu}}{\kappa\nu^3}. \tag{3.22}$$

The tangent-normal-binormal coordinate system, known as a Frenet frame, is thus defined at each point of non-zero curvature on any space curve as shown in Figure 3.8.

The remaining descriptive quantity for space curves is the torsion τ, which is analogous to the third derivative. It can be defined as

$$\tau(u) = -\nu^{-1}(u)\vec{n}(u) \cdot \vec{b}_u(u) = \frac{(\vec{x}_u \times \vec{x}_{uu}) \cdot \vec{x}_{uuu}}{\|\vec{x}_u \times \vec{x}_{uu}\|^2} = \frac{(\vec{x}_u \times \vec{x}_{uu}) \cdot \vec{x}_{uuu}}{\kappa^2\nu^6}$$
$$\tag{3.23}$$

These six functions provide a complete differential geometric description of a space curve. For space curves free of singularities, the curvature, torsion, and speed functions uniquely determine curve shape.

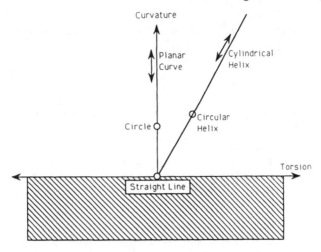

FIGURE 3.9. Curvature-Torsion Domain for Space Curve Description

Alternative Curvature Quantities

If we view the allowable two-dimensional space of curvature and torsion values, we see the half-plane as shown in Figure 3.9. An alternative method of representing this space is in terms of a polar coordinate transformation:

$$\rho^2(u) = \kappa^2(u) + \tau^2(u) \qquad \psi(u) = \tan^{-1}(\tau(u)/\kappa(u)). \qquad (3.24)$$

These curvature quantities are interesting for a number of reasons. The ρ function measures a total "bending energy" in the curve whereas the curvature κ measures bending only in the tangent-normal plane and the torsion τ measures bending out of that plane. The ψ function is a convenient way of formulating the torsion/curvature ratio as an angular quantity. If $\psi(s)$ is constant for all s on a curve, then the curve is known as a cylindrical helix and possesses the property that there exists a constant unit vector $\vec{a}$ such that the inner (dot) product of the curve's tangent vector with this vector is a constant for all s.

The following list summarizes several important special cases of space curve shape:

1. If $\kappa(u) = 0$, then $\tau(u) = 0$ and C is a straight line.

2. If $\tau(u) = 0$, then C is a planar curve.

3. If $\kappa(u) = \kappa_0 =$ positive constant and $\tau(u) = 0$, then C is a circle.

4. If $\kappa(u) = \kappa_0 =$ positive constant and $\tau(u) = \tau_0 \neq 0$, then C is a circular helix (τ_0 a constant).

5. If $\psi(u) = \tan^{-1}(\tau(u)/\kappa(u)) = \psi_0 =$ constant, then C is a cylindrical helix, i.e. the tangent vector to C always lies in a fixed cone. The

spherical image of C is a circular arc on the unit sphere. If the circular arc is a great circle, the curve is a circular helix.

3.6.3 SURFACES

The parametric form of a surface S in $\Re^3$ with respect to a known coordinate system is

$$S = \left\{ \vec{x} \in \Re^3 : \vec{x} = \left[\begin{array}{c} x(u,v) \\ y(u,v) \\ z(u,v) \end{array} \right], (u,v) \in \Omega \subseteq \Re^2 \right\} \tag{3.25}$$

This parametric representation is written more simply as $\vec{x}(u,v)$. Surfaces are also often represented implicitly as the zero set of a function F, the set of all (x,y,z) such that $F(x,y,z) = 0$, but such implicit representation will not be considered here. Only *smooth* surfaces are considered below in which all functions possess continuous second partial derivatives.

There are two basic mathematical entities that are considered in the differential geometry of smooth surfaces. In the classical mathematics of partial derivatives, they are known as the first and second fundamental forms of a surface. Modern mathematics uses differential forms and favors an equivalent formulation of these quantities in terms of the metric tensor and the Weingarten mapping (the "shape operator" [O'N66]). Complete knowledge of either of these forms at every surface point uniquely characterizes and quantifies general smooth surface shape. In general, the modern approach is preferred because it is a simpler formalism to work with once all the necessary terminology is established, but the classical approach is taken here since more people are familiar with partial derivatives than differential forms. The classical surface review begins by defining the fundamental forms of a surface in terms of a general surface parameterization $\vec{x}(u,v)$.

Basic Definitions

The first fundamental form I of a parametric surface $\vec{x}(u,v)$ evaluated at the point (u,v) in the direction (u_s, v_s) is given by

$$\begin{aligned}
I(u,v,u_s,v_s) &= \vec{x}_s \cdot \vec{x}_s \tag{3.26} \\
&= (\vec{x}_u u_s + \vec{x}_v v_s) \cdot (\vec{x}_u u_s + \vec{x}_v v_s) \\
&= \vec{x}_u \cdot \vec{x}_u u_s^2 + 2\vec{x}_u \cdot \vec{x}_v u_s v_s + \vec{x}_v \cdot \vec{x}_v v_s^2 \\
&= E u_s^2 + 2F u_s v_s + G v_s^2 \\
&= [u_s \ \ v_s] \left[\begin{array}{cc} g_{11} & g_{12} \\ g_{21} & g_{22} \end{array} \right] \left[\begin{array}{c} u_s \\ v_s \end{array} \right] \\
&= \vec{u}_s^T [g] \vec{u}_s
\end{aligned}$$

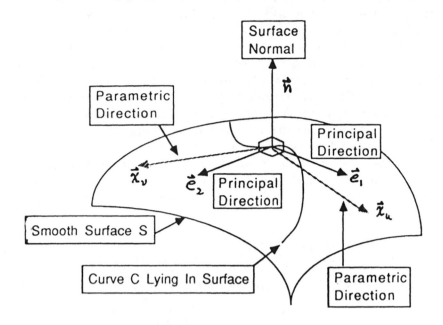

FIGURE 3.10. Local Coordinate Frame at Surface Point

where $\vec{u}_s = (u_s, v_s)$, where the [g] matrix elements are defined as

$$g_{11} = E = \vec{x}_u \cdot \vec{x}_u \qquad g_{22} = G = \vec{x}_v \cdot \vec{x}_v \qquad g_{12} = g_{21} = F = \vec{x}_u \cdot \vec{x}_v,$$
$$(3.27)$$

and where the subscripts denote the partial derivatives

$$\vec{x}_u(u, v) = \frac{\partial \vec{x}}{\partial u} \qquad \vec{x}_v(u, v) = \frac{\partial \vec{x}}{\partial v}. \qquad (3.28)$$

The vectors $\vec{x}_u$ and $\vec{x}_v$ are the *u-tangent vector* and the *v-tangent vector* functions respectively, and they may or may not be orthogonal to each other. These two tangent vectors are shown in Figure 3.10 and are said to lie in and form a basis for the tangent plane $T(u, v)$ (or tangent space) of the surface at the point $\vec{x}(u, v)$: $T(u, v) = \{\vec{x} \in \Re^3 : \vec{x} = a\vec{x}_u(u, v) + b\vec{x}_v(u, v), (a, b) \in \Re^2\}$. The [g] matrix is known as the first fundamental form matrix or the *metric* tensor of the surface. Since the vector dot product is commutative, this [g] matrix is symmetric and has only three independent components. The E,F,G notation of Gauss is used along with the matrix element subscript notation because both are useful in different circumstances, and both have occurred often in the differential geometry literature.

The first fundamental form $I(u, v, u_s, v_s)$ measures the small amount of movement $\|\vec{x}_s\|^2$ on the surface at a point (u, v) for a given small movement ds in the parameter plane direction (u_s, v_s). This form is invariant to surface parameterization changes and to translations and rotations of the surface. The first fundamental form depends only on the surface itself, and not on how the surface is embedded in 3-D space. Such properties are therefore referred to as *intrinsic* properties of a surface. In fact, the functions E,F,G determine all intrinsic properties of a surface. The *metric* 2x2 matrix function plays the same role as the scalar *speed* function does for curves. The intrinsic geometry of a curve is one-dimensional whereas that of a surface is two-dimensional.

In contrast, the second fundamental form of a surface is dependent on the embedding of the surface in 3-D space and is therefore known as an *extrinsic* property of the surface. The second fundamental form II is given by

$$
\begin{aligned}
II(u, v, u_s, v_s) &= \vec{x}_{ss} \cdot \vec{n} \qquad (3.29) \\
&= (\vec{x}_{uu} u_s^2 + 2\vec{x}_{uv} u_s v_s + \vec{x}_{vv} v_s s) \cdot \vec{n} \\
&= L u_s^2 + 2M u_s v_s + N v_s^2 \\
&= [u_s \quad v_s] \begin{bmatrix} b_{11} & b_{12} \\ b_{21} & b_{22} \end{bmatrix} \begin{bmatrix} u_s \\ v_s \end{bmatrix} \\
&= \vec{u}_s^T [b] \vec{u}_s \qquad (3.30)
\end{aligned}
$$

where the [b] matrix elements may be defined as

$$ b_{11} = L = \vec{x}_{uu} \cdot \vec{n} \qquad b_{22} = N = \vec{x}_{vv} \cdot \vec{n} \qquad b_{12} = b_{21} = M = \vec{x}_{uv} \cdot \vec{n} \tag{3.31} $$

where

$$ \vec{n}(u, v) = \frac{\vec{x}_u \times \vec{x}_v}{\|\vec{x}_u \times \vec{x}_v\|} = \text{Unit Surface Normal Vector} \tag{3.32} $$

and where the double subscripts denote the second partial derivatives

$$ \vec{x}_{uu}(u, v) = \frac{\partial^2 \vec{x}}{\partial u^2} \qquad \vec{x}_{vv}(u, v) = \frac{\partial^2 \vec{x}}{\partial v^2} \qquad \vec{x}_{uv}(u, v) = \frac{\partial^2 \vec{x}}{\partial u \partial v} = \vec{x}_{vu}(u, v). \tag{3.33} $$

The [b] matrix is the second fundamental form matrix and is also symmetric if the surface is well-behaved in the sense that the mixed partial derivatives $\vec{x}_{uv} = \vec{x}_{vu}$ are equal. The Gauss-like L,M,N notation is introduced again as above. The second fundamental form is also invariant to changes in the parameterization, orientation, or position of the surface.

Since $\vec{n}$ is defined to be orthogonal to both $\vec{x}_u$ and $\vec{x}_v$, we have

$$ 0 = (\vec{n} \cdot \vec{x}_s)_s = \vec{n}_s \cdot \vec{x}_s + \vec{n} \cdot \vec{x}_{ss} = 0 \tag{3.34} $$

which implies that

$$ II(u, v, u_s, v_s) = -\vec{n}_s \cdot \vec{x}_s. \tag{3.35} $$

The second fundamental form therefore measures the negative correlation between the change in the normal vector $\vec{n}_s$ and the change in the surface position $\vec{x}_s$ at a surface point (u, v) as a function of a small movement ds in the direction (u_s, v_s) in the parameter space. Since $\vec{n} \cdot \vec{n} = 1$, $\vec{n}_s \cdot \vec{n} = 0$, which implies that the normal vector derivative $\vec{n}_s$ always lies in the tangent plane $T(u, v)$.

Mean and Gaussian Curvature

The shape operator (Weingarten mapping) matrix [S] is defined by the matrix product $[S] = [g^{-1}][b]$. Hence, the [S] matrix combines the first and second fundamental form matrices into a single matrix.

$$[S] = \begin{bmatrix} E & F \\ F & G \end{bmatrix}^{-1} \begin{bmatrix} L & M \\ M & N \end{bmatrix} = \frac{1}{EG - F^2} \begin{bmatrix} GL - FM & GM - FN \\ EM - FL & EN - FM \end{bmatrix}$$
(3.36)

This matrix is a linear operator that maps vectors in the tangent plane to other vectors in the tangent plane at each point on a surface. The metric [g] is the generalization of the speed of a planar curve whereas the shape operator [S] is a generalization of the curvature of a planar curve. The concept of torsion is not relevant to surfaces since the dimension of the space orthogonal to the tangent space is only one just as it was in the case of planar curves. The *Gaussian curvature* function K of a surface can be defined from the first and second fundamental form matrices as the determinant of the shape operator matrix function as follows:

$$K = \det[S] = \det\left(\begin{bmatrix} E & F \\ F & G \end{bmatrix}^{-1}\right) \det\left(\begin{bmatrix} L & M \\ M & N \end{bmatrix}\right) = \frac{LN - M^2}{EG - F^2}.$$
(3.37)

The *mean curvature* function of a surface can be defined similarly as half the trace of the shape operator matrix function as follows:

$$H = \frac{1}{2}\text{tr}[S] \tag{3.38}$$

$$= \frac{1}{2}\text{tr}\left(\frac{1}{EG - F^2}\begin{bmatrix} GL - FM & GM - FN \\ EM - FL & EN - FM \end{bmatrix}\right) \tag{3.39}$$

$$= \frac{EN + GL - 2FM}{2(EG - F^2)}. \tag{3.40}$$

The surface curvature functions H and K are the two "natural" algebraic invariants of the 2x2 shape operator matrix (coefficients of the characteristic polynomial) and are independent of surface parameterization unlike the E,F,G,L,M,N functions themselves. In addition, Gaussian curvature uniquely determines the shape of convex surfaces [Min97,Che57,Hor84], and mean curvature uniquely determines the shape of graph surfaces under

	$K > 0$	$K = 0$	$K < 0$
$H < 0$	Peak T=1	Ridge T=2	Saddle Ridge T=3
$H = 0$	(none) T=4	Flat T=5	Minimal Surface T=6
$H > 0$	Pit T=7	Valley T=8	Saddle Valley T=9

FIGURE 3.11. Surface Type Labels from Surface Curvature Sign

various auxiliary conditions [GT83,Gui78,Bes88d,Bes88c]. The eigenvalues of [S] are the *principal curvatures* and the eigenvectors are the *principal direction vectors*. In the next two sections, we quickly rederive these quantities using basic relationships about curves in the surface which may make their properties easier to visualize.

A toleranced signum function

$$\text{sgn}_\epsilon(x) = \begin{cases} +1 & \text{if } x > \epsilon \\ 0 & \text{if } |x| \leq \epsilon \\ -1 & \text{if } x < \epsilon \end{cases} \tag{3.41}$$

may be used to compute a surface type label at each point based only on $\text{sgn}_{\epsilon_H}(H(u,v))$ and $\text{sgn}_{\epsilon_K}(K(u,v))$ using given zero thresholds ϵ_H and ϵ_K. A surface type label image may be computed as

$$L_{HK}(u,v) = 1 + 3(1 + \text{sgn}_\epsilon(H(u,v))) + (1 - \text{sgn}_\epsilon(K(u,v))). \tag{3.42}$$

With this definition, the values of the surface type labels will run from 1 to 9, excluding 4, as shown in Figure 3.11. These fundamental surface types are drawn in Figure 3.12.

Normal and Principal Curvatures

There are other ways of looking at surface curvature based on curves that lie in the surface. If $\vec{x}(s)$ is a parameterization of a curve that lies in a parametric surface $\vec{x}(u,v)$, then we can write down the derivatives of $\vec{x}$ as a space curve and as a part of the surface:

$$\begin{aligned} \vec{x}_s(s) &= \nu(s)\vec{t}(s) \\ \vec{x}_{ss}(s) &= \nu_s(s)\vec{t}(s) + \kappa(s)\nu^2(s)\vec{n}(s) \\ \vec{x}_s(u(s),v(s)) &= u_s\vec{x}_u + v_s\vec{x}_v \\ \vec{x}_{ss}(u(s),v(s)) &= u_{ss}\vec{x}_u + v_{ss}\vec{x}_v + u_s^2\vec{x}_{uu} + 2u_sv_s\vec{x}_u \cdot \vec{x}_v + v_s^2\vec{x}_{vv} \end{aligned}$$

$$\tag{3.43}$$

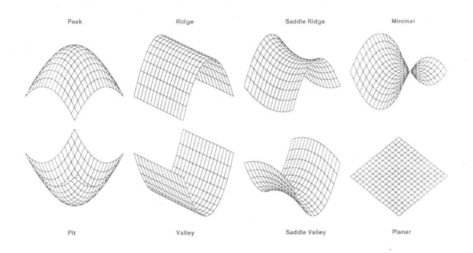

Peak   Ridge   Saddle Ridge   Minimal

Pit   Valley   Saddle Valley   Planar

FIGURE 3.12. The Eight Fundamental Surface Types

If the unit surface normal $\vec{n}(u(s), v(s))$ is aligned with the unit normal to the curve $\vec{n}(s)$, then taking the dot product of the expressions above with the surface/curve normal vector yields the *normal curvature* function

$$\kappa_n(u, v, u_s, v_s) = \frac{II(u, v, u_s, v_s)}{I(u, v, u_s, v_s)} \tag{3.44}$$

where the speed of the curve in the surface ν is specified by the first fundamental form: $\nu^2(u(s), v(s)) = \|\vec{x}_s(u(s), v(s))\|^2 = I(u, v, u_s, v_s)$. Rewriting this ratio using the quadratic form notation and $\vec{u} = (u, v)$ and $\vec{u}_s = (u_s, v_s)$, we get a so-called Rayleigh quotient form:

$$\kappa_n(\vec{u}, \vec{u}_s) = \frac{\vec{u}_s^T[\mathbf{b}(\vec{u})]\vec{u}_s}{\vec{u}_s^T[\mathbf{g}(\vec{u})]\vec{u}_s}. \tag{3.45}$$

The maximum and minimum normal curvature values at the point (u, v) must satisfy the condition $\partial \kappa_n / \partial \vec{u}_s = 0$. Applying the quotient derivative rule, we obtain

$$\partial \kappa_n / \partial \vec{u}_s = (\vec{u}_s^T[\mathbf{g}(\vec{u})]\vec{u}_s) \cdot 2[\mathbf{b}(\vec{u})]\vec{u}_s - (\vec{u}_s^T[\mathbf{b}(\vec{u})]\vec{u}_s) \cdot 2[\mathbf{g}(\vec{u})]\vec{u}_s = 0 \tag{3.46}$$

which implies that

$$[\mathbf{b}(\vec{u})]\vec{u}_s = \kappa_n[\mathbf{g}(\vec{u})]\vec{u}_s. \tag{3.47}$$

Solving for the minimum and maximum values of κ_n is an example of solving the generalized eigenvalue problem $A\mathbf{x} = \lambda B\mathbf{x}$. But since $[\mathbf{g}(\vec{u})]$ is always non-singular for any non-degenerate surface parameterization and since matrices commute with scalars, the problem is easily converted into a standard eigenvalue problem:

$$[S(\vec{u})]\vec{u}_s = \kappa_n \vec{u}_s. \tag{3.48}$$

Given $H = \text{tr}(S)/2$ and $K = \det(S)$ as defined above, the problem is easily solved using simple quadratic formula algebra to obtain the eigenvalues, which are the maximum and minimum principal curvatures:

$$\kappa_1 = H + \sqrt{H^2 - K} \qquad \text{(maximum principal curvature)} \tag{3.49}$$

$$\kappa_2 = H - \sqrt{H^2 - K} \qquad \text{(minimum principal curvature)}. \tag{3.50}$$

The eigenvectors of $[S]$ are the directions in the (u, v) parameter plane such that the normal curvature function achieves its maximum and minimum values. The *unnormalized* principal direction vectors $\vec{u}_1$ and $\vec{u}_2$ in the u-v plane for the corresponding principal curvatures κ_1 and κ_2 are given by

$$\vec{u}_1 = \begin{bmatrix} u_1 \\ v_1 \end{bmatrix} = \begin{bmatrix} GM - FN \\ \frac{1}{2}(EN - GL) + g\sqrt{H^2 - K} \end{bmatrix} \tag{3.51}$$

$$\vec{u}_2 = \begin{bmatrix} u_2 \\ v_2 \end{bmatrix} = \begin{bmatrix} \frac{1}{2}(EN - GL) + g\sqrt{H^2 - K} \\ FL - EM \end{bmatrix} \tag{3.52}$$

where $g = EG - F^2$. These directions are not in general orthogonal in the (u, v) parameter plane since the 2x2 Weingarten mapping matrix is not symmetric with respect to the surface parameterization. However, the Weingarten mapping itself is a symmetric linear operator on 3-D vectors in the 3-D tangent plane and the 3-D principal direction vectors of surface points are orthogonal in the tangent plane. This orthogonality property is seen directly by proving that $\vec{x}_1 \cdot \vec{x}_2 = 0$ where the *unnormalized* maximum and minimum principal direction vectors in 3-D space are given by

$$\vec{x}_1 = (u_1 \vec{x}_u + v_1 \vec{x}_v) \qquad \vec{x}_2 = (u_2 \vec{x}_u + v_2 \vec{x}_v). \tag{3.53}$$

The principal frame field of a surface is given by

$$(\vec{n}(u, v), \vec{e}_1(u, v), \vec{e}_2(u, v)) \quad = \quad \text{Principal Frame Field} \tag{3.54}$$

where $\vec{e}_i = \vec{x}_i / \|\vec{x}_i\|$ for $i = 1, 2$.

If $\vec{v} = \cos\theta \vec{e}_1 + \sin\theta \vec{e}_2$ is any unit direction vector in the tangent plane at a point, then the normal curvature $\kappa_n(\cdot)$ at (u, v) in the direction of $\vec{v}$ is a function of θ and the principal curvatures:

$$\kappa_n(u, v, \theta) = \kappa_1(u, v)\cos^2\theta + \kappa_2(u, v)\sin^2\theta. \tag{3.55}$$

If principal curvatures are given, one can easily compute the Gaussian and mean curvature in terms of the principal curvatures:

$$K = \kappa_1 \kappa_2 \qquad H = \frac{(\kappa_1 + \kappa_2)}{2}. \qquad (3.56)$$

The underlying relationship is that the principal curvatures κ_1 and κ_2 are the two roots of the quadratic equation:

$$\kappa^2 - 2H\kappa + K = 0. \qquad (3.57)$$

If $H^2 = K$ or $\kappa_1 = \kappa_2$ at a surface point, the point is known as an *umbilic* point to denote that the principal curvatures are equal and every direction is a principal direction. In other terms, the normal curvature function κ_n at an umbilic point is a constant function independent of direction since $\cos^2 \theta + \sin^2 \theta = 1$. A surface must be either locally flat or spherical in the neighborhood of an umbilic point. Saddle shaped (hyperbolic) surface patches are necessarily free of umbilic points.

Curve Networks in a Surface

It is often useful to characterize a surface based on the properties of curves C that lie in a surface S. However, rather than using the Frenet frame field to describe a space curve lying in surface, an alternative frame field, the Darboux frame field, is defined using the tangent vector to the curve $\vec{t}$ and the normal to the *surface* $\vec{n}$. The other vector in the tangent plane is given by $\vec{v} = \vec{n} \times \vec{t}$. Note that the surface normal and space curve normal are not the same in general.

This coordinate frame yields the following differential equation for unit-speed curves in a surface ($\nu(s) = 1$):

$$\frac{d}{ds} \begin{bmatrix} \vec{t}(s) \\ \vec{v}(s) \\ \vec{n}(s) \end{bmatrix} = \begin{bmatrix} 0 & \kappa_g(s) & \kappa_n(s) \\ -\kappa_g(s) & 0 & \tau_g(s) \\ -\kappa_n(s) & -\tau_g(s) & 0 \end{bmatrix} \begin{bmatrix} \vec{t}(s) \\ \vec{v}(s) \\ \vec{n}(s) \end{bmatrix} \qquad (3.58)$$

where $\tau_g = \vec{v} \cdot \mathbf{S}(\vec{t})$ is the geodesic torsion of the curve where $\mathbf{S}(\cdot)$ represents the shape operator acting on a 3-D vector rather that the 2x2 matrix, where $\kappa_n = \vec{t} \cdot \mathbf{S}(\vec{t})$ is the normal curvature of surface in the direction of the tangent vector of the curve, and where where $\kappa_g = \vec{v} \cdot \vec{x}_{ss} = \vec{n} \cdot (\vec{x}_s \times \vec{x}_{ss})$ is the geodesic curvature of the curve $\vec{x}(s)$ lying in the surface. This differential equation combines properties of surface geometry and curve geometry.

Several special types of curves in a surface are determined by letting each of the scalar shape description quantities above be zero.

1. A curve is a *geodesic* (curve) if the geodesic curvature is zero everywhere on the curve, i.e., if the curve's tangent-normal plane (osculating plane) is perpendicular to the surface. In other terms, $\vec{x}_{ss}$ is normal to the surface. There are an infinite number of geodesics

Curve Type	Zero Quantity	Restrictions
Geodesic	Geodesic Curvature = 0	None
Asymptotic	Normal Curvature = 0	$K \leq 0$
Principal	Geodesic Torsion = 0	$K \neq H^2$

FIGURE 3.13. Different Types of Curves Lying in a Surface

through every point on a surface and any straight line that lies in a surface is always a geodesic.

2. A curve is an *asymptotic* curve if the normal curvature is zero everywhere on the curve. Since $\kappa_n = \kappa_1 \cos^2 \theta + \kappa_2 \sin^2 \theta$, it is clear that an asymptotic curve can only exist on hyperbolic ($K < 0$) or parabolic ($K = 0$) regions of a surface where the direction of the curve is given by

$$\theta = \tan^{-1}\left(\pm\sqrt{\frac{-\kappa_1}{\kappa_2}}\right). \qquad (3.59)$$

The tangent-normal plane of an asymptotic curve coincides with the the tangent plane of the surface. On a hyperbolic surface, the asymptotic curves form a quadrilateral mesh, which is orthogonal only if the surface is minimal.

3. A curve is a *principal* curve, or a line of curvature, if the geodesic torsion is zero everywhere on the curve. The tangent vector of a principal curve always points in the principal direction of the surface. The lines of curvature form an orthogonal mesh everywhere on a surface except at umbilic points, which may be isolated singularities. In particular, any smooth hyperbolic surface possesses lines of curvature that are orthogonal everywhere.

These comments are summarized in tabular form in Figure 3.13.

Lines of curvature are perhaps the most useful geometric curve descriptions since asymptotic curves don't exist on elliptic regions of a surface and there are an infinite number of geodesics passing through each point, one in each tangent direction. Martin [Mar82] describes the advantages of principal patches, surface patches with isoparametric curves as the lines of curvature. Brady et al. [BPYA85] were the first computer vision researchers to attempt to compute the lines of curvatures from range images and to publicize the significance of such principal patches. Beck et al. [BFH86] computed the lines of curvature on Bezier surface patches along with other analytical properties. Sander and Zucker [SZ88a,San88] have recently investigated methods for locating the isolated umbilic points and for providing a stable principal frame field description at every point.

We believe that geometric descriptions based on lines of curvature will be increasingly important in the future. If the lines of curvature of a surface can be isolated and used as u-v parameter curves, then the first and second fundamental forms are diagonal and only four functions E,G,L,N are required to uniquely specify the shape of the surface (F=M=0). In this special case, the 2x2 Weingarten mapping matrix consists of the principal curvatures on the diagonal and zeros elsewhere. There are definite advantages to working with such a parameterization if it can be obtained or derived from given data. In theory, such patches can only be constructed locally because isolated umbilics cause significant topological problems in trying to establish consistent and complete u, v parametric domains. Owing to the importance principal patches and the difficulties in automatically deriving them from arbitrary data, the basic concepts associated with lines of curvature and isolated umbilics are covered below.

The definitions of the principal directions given above are also specifications of a coupled pair of nonlinear ordinary differential equations. By selecting an appropriate set of initial points, these differential equations can be solved via numerical methods, e.g. simple Runge-Kutta ODE solvers, to produce an (almost everywhere) orthogonal line of curvature mesh, as was done by Beck et al. [BFH86].

Umbilic Points (Singularities)

As we know, planar and spherical surface patches are umbilic everywhere and are easy to visualize. However, isolated planar and spherical umbilic points also exist on surfaces that never appear to be planar or spherical. There are exactly three generic types of isolated umbilics [Dar96,BH77, Por83]. The three generic isolated umbilics, known as star, lemon, and monstar, are shown in Figure 3.14. Non-generic umbilics are not usually treated by mathematicians. An example of the lines of curvature around one type of non-generic isolated umbilic can be pictured by thinking of the parallels and meridians around the north or south poles.

To characterize isolated umbilics, we examine the isotropic bicubic approximation of a surface at an umbilic point in the principal coordinate system with the z axis aligned with the surface normal and the x and y axes aligned with the principal directions:

$$z(x,y) = \kappa(x^2 + y^2) + ax^2y + bxy^2 + cx^3 + dy^3. \qquad (3.60)$$

The constant, x, y, and xy terms usually included in such an expansion are all zero by choice of the coordinate system. A discriminant D is useful for determining whether an umbilic is a generic star umbilic $D > 0$, not a generic star $D < 0$ (i.e., lemon or monstar), or not a generic umbilic $D = 0$:

$$D(a, b, c, d) = a^2 + b^2 - 3(ac + bd). \qquad (3.61)$$

Lemons and monstars can be distinguished by measuring the smoothness

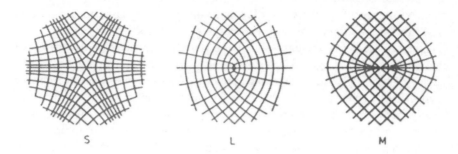

FIGURE 3.14. The Three Generic Isolated Umbilic Points (Star, Lemon, Monstar)

of the lines of curvature in a small neighborhood around the umbilic or by computing another discriminant given in Berry and Hannay [BH77]. In addition, umbilics are classified as either planar if $\kappa = 0$ or spherical if $\kappa \neq 0$. The following table shows coefficients for some example umbilics:

κ	a	b	c	d	D	Type
1	0	0	0	0	0	Spherical (Non-Generic)
1	1	1	0	0	2	Spherical, Star (Generic)
1	1	1	1	1	-4	Spherical, Lemon (Generic)
0	0	-3	1	0	9	Planar, Star (Generic)

Berry and Hannay [BH77] showed that on isotropic random Gaussian surfaces, 50% of the umbilics are stars, 44.7% are lemons, and 5.3% are monstars. Our experience has also been that monstars rarely occur on generic surfaces.

Umbilics can be detected by a variety of techniques. Sander and Zucker [SZ88b,San88] discuss a method for integrating principal directions around each point based on a technique given in Berry and Hannay [BH77]. Many other methods are also possible. The derivatives of both principal curvatures

$$\kappa_u = \frac{2\kappa H_u - K_u}{2(\kappa - H)} \qquad \kappa_v = \frac{2\kappa H_v - K_v}{2(\kappa - H)} \qquad (3.62)$$

as given in Farouki [Far86] do not exist and the principal direction fields $(\vec{u}_1, \vec{u}_2)$ are discontinuous at isolated umbilics which can provide other alternatives for detection if these quantities can be estimated well enough

(a) Surface Types from Principal Curvature Signs

	$\kappa_1 < 0$	$\kappa_1 = 0$	$\kappa_1 > 0$
$\kappa_2 < 0$	peak	ridge	saddle
$\kappa_2 = 0$	ridge	flat	valley
$\kappa_2 > 0$	saddle	valley	pit

(b) Surface Types from Mean and Gaussian Curvature Signs

	$K < 0$	$K = 0$	$K > 0$
$H < 0$	peak	ridge	saddle ridge
$H = 0$	(none)	flat	minimal
$H > 0$	pit	valley	saddle valley

FIGURE 3.15. Surface Types Determined By Surface Curvature Signs

from the geometric signal. If reliably detected, generic umbilic points could provide methods for matching surfaces.

Alternative Surface Curvature Quantities

Surface curvature has been viewed in principal curvature coordinates and in mean and Gaussian curvature coordinates. If only the sign of these quantities is considered, principal curvature sign allows one to identify points as peaks, pits, ridges, valleys, planes, and saddles as shown in Figure 3.15(a) whereas mean and Gaussian curvature sign allows one to subdivide saddle shapes into saddle ridges, saddle valleys, and minimal surfaces as shown in Figure 3.15(b).

Other surface curvature coordinates are also provide a useful way to look at surface curvature. In Figure 3.16, four different sets of surface curvature coordinates are shown. The eight fundamental types of surfaces are denoted for each pair of coordinates. Note that in principal curvature coordinates (or the $\kappa_1\kappa_2$-plane), umbilic points lie on the unit slope line whereas they lie on a parabola in the right half plane of the mean and Gaussian curvature space (or HK-plane). A forbidden region lies inside this parabola in the HK-plane which corresponds to the forbidden half-plane below the unit slope line in the principal curvature plane.

As a first alternative, a polar coordinate transformation is used to define (ρ, ψ) surface curvature similar to the space curve case:

$$\rho^2(u, v) \;=\; \frac{1}{2}(\kappa_1^2(u, v) + \kappa_2^2(u, v)) \tag{3.63}$$

$$\psi(u, v) \;=\; \tan^{-1}(\kappa_2(u, v)/\kappa_1(u, v)) - \frac{\pi}{4}. \tag{3.64}$$

The ρ function measures the total "bending energy" of the surface in both directions. In other terms, it is the distance of the curvature coordinates

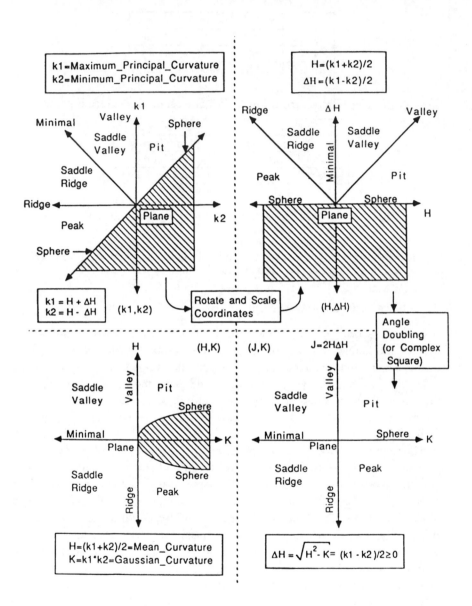

FIGURE 3.16. Four Surface Curvature Coordinate Systems

from the origin, i.e. ideal planarity [Bla84]. The ψ function indicates the angle in principal curvature plane; it is 0 for umbilic points and 90 degrees for minimal points.

As a second alternative, a simple rotation and scale transformation is performed on the principal curvature coordinates to obtain $(H, \Delta H)$ coordinates:

$$H \quad = \quad \frac{1}{2}(\kappa_1 + \kappa_2)$$

$$\Delta H \quad = \quad \frac{1}{2}(\kappa_1 - \kappa_2) \tag{3.65}$$

where $\Delta H(u, v) \geq 0$ always by definition of maximum and minimum principal curvatures. The inverse transformation is

$$\kappa_1 \quad = \quad H + \Delta H$$

$$\kappa_2 \quad = \quad H - \Delta H. \tag{3.66}$$

Note that $\Delta H = \sqrt{H^2 - K}$ using previous relationships. The same polar curvature coordinates (ρ, ψ) given above can also be defined in terms of the $(H, \Delta H)$ coordinates:

$$\rho^2 = H^2 + \Delta H^2 \qquad \psi = \tan^{-1}(\Delta H/H). \tag{3.67}$$

The $(H, \Delta H)$ coordinates provide perhaps the most convenient description of the forbidden region, the lower half plane $\Delta H < 0$, and the most convenient domain for defining "curvature probability densities" and computing surface curvature histograms (the upper half plane).

As a third alternative, suppose an angle doubling transformation is used to map the upper half plane to the whole plane such that the forbidden region disappears. In complex numbers, recall that if $z = \rho e^{i\psi} = H + i\Delta H$, then $z^2 = \rho^2 e^{2i\psi} = (H^2 - \Delta H^2) + 2iH\Delta H$. Hence, the complex squaring operation is a convenient angle doubling transformation. The transformed surface curvatures are denoted (J, K) where

$$K \quad = \quad H^2 - \Delta H^2 = \text{Gaussian Curvature}$$

$$J \quad = \quad 2H\Delta H. \tag{3.68}$$

The JK-plane is interesting in that each generic surface type (peak, pit, saddle ridge, saddle valley) corresponds to a separate quadrant. (Generic means type is not changed by small perturbations in surface curvature values.) The $K = 0$ axis corresponds to the non-generic ridges and valleys whereas the $J = 0$ axis corresponds to non-generic minimal and umbilic points. A subtle point of this representation is that there is a "cut" on the $J = 0, K$ positive axis such that elliptic points near the axis cannot be perturbed to cross the axis by small surface changes. The polar surface coordinates are obtained via

$$\rho^4 = K^2 + J^2 \qquad \psi = \frac{1}{2}\tan^{-1}(J/K). \tag{3.69}$$

In summary, surface curvature has many alternative representations: (κ_1, κ_2), (H, K), $(H, \Delta H)$, (J, K), (ρ, ψ) to name only a few.

An Example Surface

An interesting way to look at the fundamental surface types, as suggested by W.H. Frey, also indicates the numerical sensitivity of labeling computations. Consider the following 3x3 window of z values over a regular x, y grid:

0	2	8
-2	z_0	6
-8	-6	0

The interpolating tensor-product biquadratic graph surface for these points, which is defined over the unit square with the value -8 at $(0,0)$ and the z_0 value at $(1/2,1/2)$, is given by

$$f(u,v) = 8(u^2 - v^2) + 16v - 8 + 16z_0(u - u^2)(v - v^2). \qquad (3.70)$$

The derivatives *evaluated at the center point* $(1/2, 1/2, z_0)$ are

$$f_u = f_v = 8 \qquad f_{uu} = 16 - 8z_0 \qquad f_{vv} = -16 - 8z_0 \qquad f_{uv} = 0. \qquad (3.71)$$

The mean and Gaussian curvature at the center point $(1/2, 1/2, z_0)$ are then given by

$$H = -c_H z_0 \qquad K = c_K(z_0^2 - 4) \qquad (3.72)$$

where $c_H \approx 0.71$ and $c_K \approx 0.0038$. For these selected data points, the surface changes type at the center point with each value of z as shown in the following table:

Example z_0 Value	Surface Type	Valid Interval
3	Peak	$z_0 > 2$
2	Ridge (K=0)	$z_0 = 2$
1	Saddle Ridge	$0 < z_0 < 2$
0	Minimal (H=0)	$z_0 = 0$
-1	Saddle Valley	$-2 < z_0 < 0$
-2	Valley (K=0)	$z_0 = -2$
-3	Pit	$z_0 < -2$

This shows the progression of surface types as the position of a point changes relative to the other points in the window. In Figure 3.17, this surface type transition sequence is plotted in the four surface curvature domains mentioned in the previous section. The best separation of surface types for this example occurs in HK and JK coordinates. Given these surface type variations for one level changes in z_0 with other window values fixed, we can rightly expect that surface type will be sensitive to noise, especially in small windows.

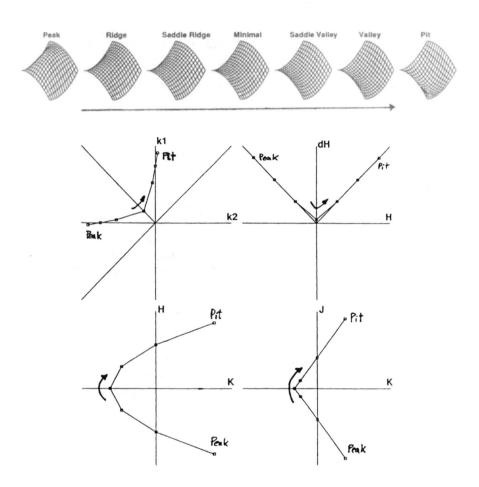

FIGURE 3.17. Surface Type Transition Sequence

Peak	$\Leftrightarrow$	Ridge	$\Leftrightarrow$	Saddle Ridge
$\Updownarrow$		$\Updownarrow$		$\Updownarrow$
Spherical Peak Umbilic	$\Leftrightarrow$	Planar		Minimal
		Umbilic	$\Leftrightarrow$	Surface
Spherical Pit Umbilic	$\Leftrightarrow$	Point		Point
$\Updownarrow$		$\Updownarrow$		$\Updownarrow$
Pit	$\Leftrightarrow$	Valley	$\Leftrightarrow$	Saddle Valley

FIGURE 3.18. Allowable Surface Type Transitions from Small Surface Changes

Surface Type Transitions

In the example above, the surface type label changed smoothly as a function of z_0. In general, as smooth surface shape is perturbed or as one moves along a smooth curve in a smooth surface, surface type will move along continuous paths in the surface curvature domain since mean and Gaussian curvature are both continuous. The allowable transitions between surface types are given in the table in Figure 3.18. The features of this allowable transition graph that distinguish it from the tables and the JK-plane plots given above are caused by the parabolic forbidden region in the HK-plane:

1. A spherical umbilic with positive mean curvature cannot transition to a spherical umbilic with negative mean curvature (and vice-versa) without becoming a planar umbilic point or a non-umbilic point.

2. As a result of the first exception, a peak point cannot transition to a spherical umbilic point and then to a pit point (and vice versa) without going through or around the planar umbilic state.

Boulanger [Bou88] has made use of these facts in a relaxation scheme that corrects surface type labels at pixels where forbidden transitions occur.

Graph Surfaces

Arbitrary 3-D surfaces cannot be represented as graph surfaces, but each parametric function of a parametric surface is a graph surface. Also, the set of all surface points visible from a particular direction form a piecewise smooth graph surface. Therefore, graph surfaces are of enough importance to merit special consideration.

The parameterization for a graph surface takes a very simple form: $\vec{x}(u, v) = [u \ v \ f(u, v)]^T$. (The T superscript indicates transpose so that $\vec{x}$ is a column vector by convention.) This yields the following formulas for the surface partial derivatives and the surface normal:

$$\vec{x}_u = [1 \ 0 \ f_u]^T$$

$$\vec{x}_v = [0 \ 1 \ f_v]^T$$

$$\vec{x}_{uu} = [0 \ 0 \ f_{uu}]^T \qquad (3.73)$$

$$\vec{x}_{vv} = [0 \ 0 \ f_{vv}]^T$$

$$\vec{x}_{uv} = [0 \ 0 \ f_{uv}]^T$$

$$\vec{n} = \frac{1}{\sqrt{1 + f_u^2 + f_v^2}} [-f_u \ -f_v \ 1]^T. \qquad (3.74)$$

These vectors are combined using the dot product definitions given earlier to form the six fundamental form coefficients:

$$E = g_{11} = 1 + f_u^2 \qquad F = g_{12} = f_u f_v \qquad G = g_{22} = 1 + f_v^2 \qquad (3.75)$$

$$L = b_{11} = \frac{f_{uu}}{\sqrt{1 + f_u^2 + f_v^2}}$$

$$M = b_{12} = \frac{f_{uv}}{\sqrt{1 + f_u^2 + f_v^2}} \qquad (3.76)$$

$$N = b_{22} = \frac{f_{vv}}{\sqrt{1 + f_u^2 + f_v^2}}.$$

Since the five partial derivatives $f_u, f_v, f_{uu}, f_{uv}, f_{vv}$ are all that is needed to compute the six fundamental form coefficient functions for a graph surface, this set of partial derivatives contains all shape information for a graph surface.

Gaussian curvature is the ratio of the determinants of the two fundamental form matrices. This ratio is written directly in terms of the graph surface function derivatives as follows:

$$K = \frac{f_{uu} f_{vv} - f_{uv}^2}{(1 + f_u^2 + f_v^2)^2} = \frac{\det(\nabla \nabla^T f)}{(1 + \|\nabla f\|^2)^2} \qquad (3.77)$$

where ∇ is the 2-D (u, v) gradient operator, and $\nabla \nabla^T$ is the Hessian matrix operator.

Mean curvature is half the trace of the shape operator and is written directly in terms of the graph surface function derivatives as follows:

$$H = \frac{1}{2} \frac{(1 + f_v^2) f_{uu} + (1 + f_u^2) f_{vv} - 2 f_u f_v f_{uv}}{(1 + f_u^2 + f_v^2)^{3/2}} \qquad (3.78)$$

$$= \frac{1}{2} \nabla \cdot \left(\frac{\nabla f}{\sqrt{1 + \|\nabla f\|^2}} \right).$$

where $(\nabla \cdot)$ is the divergence operator of 2-D vector calculus.

3.6.4 VOLUMES

In this section, three types of mappings from a 3-D parameter domain are considered briefly: $\Re^3 \to \Re^3$, $\Re^3 \to \Re^1$, and $\Re^3 \to \Re^4$. The third parameter is denoted w and may correspond to a spatial or temporal parameter. The first fundamental form I of a parametric volume $\vec{x}(u,v,w)$ evaluated at the point (u,v,w) in the direction (u_s, v_s, w_s) is given by

$$
\begin{aligned}
I(u,v,w,u_s,v_s,w_s) &= \vec{x}_s \cdot \vec{x}_s \qquad\qquad\qquad (3.79)\\
&= (\vec{x}_u u_s + \vec{x}_v v_s + \vec{x}_w w_s) \cdot (\vec{x}_u u_s + \vec{x}_v v_s + \vec{x}_w w_s)\\
&= [u_s\ v_s\ w_s] \begin{bmatrix} g_{11} & g_{12} & g_{13} \\ g_{21} & g_{22} & g_{23} \\ g_{31} & g_{32} & g_{33} \end{bmatrix} \begin{bmatrix} u_s \\ v_s \\ w_s \end{bmatrix}\\
&= \vec{u}_s^T [g] \, \vec{u}_s
\end{aligned}
$$

where $\vec{u}_s = (u_s, v_s, w_s)$, where the [g] matrix elements are defined as

$$
g_{11} = \vec{x}_u \cdot \vec{x}_u \qquad g_{22} = \vec{x}_v \cdot \vec{x}_v \qquad g_{33} = \vec{x}_w \cdot \vec{x}_w \qquad (3.80)
$$

$$
g_{12} = g_{21} = \vec{x}_u \cdot \vec{x}_v \qquad g_{23} = g_{32} = \vec{x}_v \cdot \vec{x}_w \qquad g_{31} = g_{13} = \vec{x}_w \cdot \vec{x}_u. \qquad (3.81)
$$

If $\vec{x} = (x,y,z) \in \Re^3$, then the metric represents all relevant differential geometric information about the deformation from the (u,v,w) space to the (x,y,z) space. If $\vec{x} = (x,y,z,p) \in \Re^4$ where p is a physical property of the point (x,y,z), then the surface mathematics generalizes by the defining the unit normal in the 4-dimensional space:

$$
\vec{n} = \frac{\vec{x}_u \otimes \vec{x}_v \otimes \vec{x}_w}{\|\vec{x}_u \otimes \vec{x}_v \otimes \vec{x}_w\|} \qquad (3.82)
$$

where $\otimes$ represents the cross-product operation in 4-D space which requires 3 vectors and may be defined in the usual determinant formulation.

The second fundamental form II of a parametric volume $\vec{x}(u,v,w)$ evaluated at the point (u,v,w) in the direction (u_s, v_s, w_s) is then given by

$$
\begin{aligned}
II(u,v,w,u_s,v_s,w_s) &= \vec{n} \cdot \vec{x}_{ss} \qquad\qquad\qquad (3.83)\\
&= [u_s\ v_s\ w_s] \begin{bmatrix} b_{11} & b_{12} & b_{13} \\ b_{21} & b_{22} & b_{23} \\ b_{31} & b_{32} & b_{33} \end{bmatrix} \begin{bmatrix} u_s \\ v_s \\ w_s \end{bmatrix} (3.84)\\
&= \vec{u}_s^T [g] \, \vec{u}_s
\end{aligned}
$$

where $\vec{u}_s = (u_s, v_s, w_s)$, where the [b] matrix elements are defined as

$$
b_{11} = \vec{n} \cdot \vec{x}_{uu} \qquad b_{22} = \vec{n} \cdot \vec{x}_{vv} \qquad b_{33} = \vec{n} \cdot \vec{x}_{ww} \qquad (3.85)
$$

$$
b_{12} = g_{21} = \vec{n} \cdot \vec{x}_{uv} \qquad b_{23} = g_{32} = \vec{n} \cdot \vec{x}_{vw} \qquad b_{31} = g_{13} = \vec{n} \cdot \vec{x}_{wu}. \qquad (3.86)
$$

Again, the shape operator may be defined as the inverse metric tensor times the second fundamental form matrix: $[S] = [g]^{-1}[b]$. The Gaussian curvature K is the determinant of the shape operator, the mean curvature H is one third of the trace of the shape operator, and a third algebraic invariant of the shape operator is given by the sum of the diagonal cofactors. There are now three principal curvatures $\kappa_1 \geq \kappa_2 \geq \kappa_3$, which are the eigenvalues of $[S]$ and the three principal directions in the tangent volume are given by the eigenvectors. Most of the results of the previous section on surfaces are readily extended to this higher-dimensional situation.

Graph Volumes

In analogy to graph surfaces, a graph volume is a simplified version of the general mapping above: $x = u$, $y = v$, $z = w$, and the fourth component representing a scalar property of the volume, such as density, is given by $p(u, v, w)$ or equivalently $p(x, y, z)$. This yields the following formulas for the surface partial derivatives and the surface normal:

$$\vec{x}_u = [1\ 0\ 0\ p_u]^T$$

$$\vec{x}_v = [0\ 1\ 0\ p_v]^T$$

$$\vec{x}_w = [0\ 0\ 1\ p_w]^T$$

$$\vec{x}_{uu} = [0\ 0\ 0\ p_{uu}]^T \tag{3.87}$$

$$\vec{x}_{vv} = [0\ 0\ 0\ p_{vv}]^T$$

$$\vec{x}_{ww} = [0\ 0\ 0\ p_{ww}]^T$$

$$\vec{x}_{uv} = [0\ 0\ 0\ p_{uv}]^T$$

$$\vec{x}_{vw} = [0\ 0\ 0\ p_{vw}]^T$$

$$\vec{x}_{wu} = [0\ 0\ 0\ p_{wu}]^T$$

$$\vec{n} = \frac{1}{\sqrt{1 + p_u^2 + p_v^2 + p_w^2}}[-p_u\ -p_v\ -p_w\ 1]^T. \tag{3.88}$$

These expressions can be plugged into the formulas above to obtain lengthy, explicit formulas comparable to those obtained for surfaces.

Very little has been done in computer vision with the differential geometry of graph volume mappings or the more general $\Re^3 \rightarrow \Re^4$ mappings. With CT, PET, and MRI sensors, detection of simple discontinuities has been adequate for many purposes [ZH81]. In intensity image sequence analysis, the signal is not fundamentally geometric so this differential geometric viewpoint has not been used even though the same partial derivatives are used. Deformable surface analysis [TPBF87] and range image sequence analysis can make use of this higher-dimensional case, and we expect to see differential geometric descriptions become more common in the future.

3.6.5 SUMMARY OF GEOMETRIC DESCRIPTIONS

Univariate, bivariate, and trivariate vector functions have been considered as geometric entities. The fundamental notions of metric, tangent space, curvature, and natural coordinate frames are encountered throughout and have provided us with all the mathematically descriptive quantities we need to know except for torsion of space curves, which arises because a 1-D entity is embedded in 3-D. Certainly, it should not be necessary for every distinct geometric signal processing application to develop its own software when such basic concepts are shared by what seem to be drastically different types of geometry. Practical, efficient software with the desired level of abstraction is certainly many years away, but it seems a worthwhile goal, and we have already begun to reap practical benefits by starting down this path.

3.7 Geometric Approximation

Differential geometry provides us with useful invariant geometric quantities if we can accurately estimate the necessary first and second partial derivatives (and third derivatives for space curves). In this section, derivative estimation based on local and global approximation techniques are described and their relative advantages and disadvantages are examined.

3.7.1 LOCAL APPROXIMATION METHODS

Given a point and its neighboring points, one can estimate derivatives at the given point by taking the appropriate differences in the point neighborhood. The appropriate differences can be determined by using a local curve, surface, or volume fitting model. The basic idea is to fit the point neighborhood with a function and estimate the derivatives at the point with the derivatives of the fitted function. Almost any useful finite difference scheme can be derived using this approach. In general, the results one gets depend on the order of the function being fitted to the data, the relative weights one places on the importance of the points in the neighborhood, and the type of error measure that is used to compare the estimated function to the data points. The speed of an implementation depends on the factors above as well as the separability of the weights, the spacings of the parameter values (if any are given), the number of points in each neighborhood, and the efficiency with which curves, surfaces, or volumes are fitted.

Discrete Orthogonal Polynomials

For a brief discussion of a useful technique for many geometric signal processing applications, we consider only equally spaced parameter values, the sum of squares error measure, square neighborhoods, and equal weights for all points. Surface fitting is discussed since it is more complicated than curve fitting, but not as complicated as volume fitting, and it applicable to range image processing. The method summarized below is based on a local least squares surface model using discrete orthogonal polynomials. This method has been used for many years and has been discussed in [All35, AH42,Dav63,Pre70,Hue73,Bea78,HW81,Pow81,BC84,HW81,HWL83,BJ85a, BJ86]. It is included here for comparison with the global approximation techniques in the next section.

Each data point in an $N \times N$ window (neighborhood) is associated with a position (u, v) from the set $U \times U$, where for convenience N is assumed odd:

$$U = \{-(N-1)/2, \ldots, -1, 0, 1, \ldots, (N-1)/2\} . \qquad (3.89)$$

The following discrete orthogonal polynomials (for odd size windows) provide the basic second order fit necessary for estimating first and second partial derivatives necessary for differential geometric descriptions:

$$\phi_0(u) = 1, \quad \phi_1(u) = u, \quad \phi_2(u) = \left(u^2 - M(M+1)/3\right) \qquad (3.90)$$

where $M = (N-1)/2$. A corresponding set of $b_i(u)$ functions are the normalized versions of the orthogonal polynomials $\phi_i(u)$ given by $b_i(u) = \phi_i(u)/P_i(M)$ where the $P_i(M)$ are normalizing constants (polynomials in M), which are defined as $P_i(M) = \sum_u \phi_i^2(u)$. The three normalization constants are given by

$$P_0(M) = N \qquad P_1(M) = \frac{2}{3}M^3 + M^2 + \frac{1}{3}M \qquad (3.91)$$

$$P_2(M) = \frac{8}{45}M^5 + \frac{4}{9}M^4 + \frac{2}{9}M^3 - \frac{1}{9}M^2 - \frac{1}{15}M.$$

The normalized $b_i(u)$ basis functions and the $\phi_i(u)$ basis functions satisfy the orthogonality relationship

$$\sum_{u \in U} \phi_i(u) b_j(u) = \delta_{ij} \qquad (3.92)$$

where $\delta_{ij} = 1$ if $i = j$ and $\delta_{ij} = 0$ otherwise (the Kronecker delta). There is nothing unique about the way these functions are defined with respect to the normalization constants. The normalization constants of the $b_i(u)$ functions could just as well have been grouped with the $\phi_i(u)$ functions, or the square root of the normalization constants could have been grouped with both functions so that there would be no distinction between them. The latter is perhaps the most common practice, but in image processing, it is convenient to have rational normalization constants with no square roots so that faster integer arithmetic can be used after appropriate scaling of quantities by the denominator.

The recipe for computing derivatives at a sample point using odd size data windows is simple since the $b_i(u)$ vectors may be precomputed for any given window size, and convolved with the image data to provide derivative estimates. A surface function estimate $\hat{f}(u, v)$ is obtained in the form

$$\hat{f}(u, v) = \sum_{i+j \leq 2} a_{ij} \phi_i(u) \phi_j(v) \tag{3.93}$$

that minimizes the total square error term

$$\epsilon^2 = \sum_{(u,v) \in U^2} w(u, v)(f(u, v) - \hat{f}(u, v))^2 \tag{3.94}$$

where the weights $w(u, v) = 1$ are assumed to be all equal to unity. The solution for the unknown coefficients is given by

$$a_{ij} = \sum_{(u,v) \in U^2} f(u, v) b_i(u) b_j(v). \tag{3.95}$$

This simple summation is obtained only because of the orthogonality of the basis functions. If we were not using orthogonal basis functions, the solution would have to be expressed using matrix inverses and the corresponding computations would be much more involved than a simple summation. The first and second partial derivative estimates are then given by

$$f_u = a_{10} \quad f_v = a_{01} \quad f_{uv} = a_{11} \quad f_{uu} = 2a_{20} \quad f_{vv} = 2a_{02}. \tag{3.96}$$

The total fit error is computed after the a_{ij} coefficients are determined:

$$\epsilon^2 = \sum_{(u,v) \in U^2} f^2(u, v) - \sum_{i,j} P_i(M) P_j(M) a_{ij}^2. \tag{3.97}$$

Since the discrete orthogonal quadratic polynomials over the 2-D window are separable in u and v as shown in the above equations, partial derivative estimates can be computed for an entire image using a separable convolution operator. This is much more efficient than non-separable convolution operations on a general purpose computer.

Disadvantages

One of the disadvantages of the local curve, surface, or volume fitting method for estimating partial derivatives is the consistency problem, a different function is fitted to the neighborhood of each point. No compatibility constraints are imposed on these surfaces so that the net continuous surface interpretation and the corresponding differential geometric properties will be meaningful and consistent. However, the experience of many researchers indicates that this approach, also known as the local facet model [HW81] approach, is one of the best image derivative estimation methods for the amount of computation required. There are no known methods that produce better results on average with less computation. Every method known to the author that can produce better results on average requires more computations per pixel. The simple global approximation technique described later does not suffer from this consistency problem, but has its own set of problems.

Another disadvantage of this approach is that the weights for each window are all equal and moreover cannot vary depending on the point neighborhood situation. For example, if a discontinuity runs through a window or an outlier is present in a window, any constant coefficient convolution operator will make errors in the derivative estimates. Even if we were to accept that fact as given, our intuition is contradicted when all columns or rows in a square neighborhood are weighted equally. If one uses a 9x9 window least squares estimate of the first derivative at a particular pixel, the data that runs four pixels away has the same impact on the final estimate as does the data that runs directly through the pixel where the derivative is being estimated. This situation can be modified using weighted least squares techniques, but then the question concerning the best set of weights arises. Gaussian or binomial weights are a good choice and are commonly used. However, rather than explicitly changing the weights used for function fitting in the derivative estimation, it is convenient to use a binomial weight pre-smoothing filter before equally-weighted derivative window operators are applied. As described below, such a step can save computation as well as providing a better weighting scheme. As far as optimal weights are concerned, the robust M-estimation techniques described later seem to be provide the best weighting scheme since it is locally adaptive.

An Example Application

It is found experimentally that relatively large $N \times N$ window sizes ($N \geq 7$) were needed to compute reliable estimates of curvature even in the presence of 8-bit quantization noise only. Since it is necessary to compute five different derivative estimates, the image could be smoothed first with a small $L \times L$ window operator (L odd) where the smoothed values could be stored with higher precision. This intermediate smoothed image could then be convolved with small $M \times M$ derivative estimation window operators (M odd) where $L + M = N + 1$ to achieve the same results as the $N \times N$ windows. Assuming window separability and linear time requirements, the $N \times N$ windows require time proportional to $5N$ whereas the $L \times L$ smoothing and $M \times M$ derivative windows require time proportional to $N + 4M + 1 < 5N$. For example, one 7x7 binomial weight (approximately Gaussian) smoother and five 7x7 equally-weighted least squares derivative estimation operators save about 30% of the computations required for the five equivalent 13x13 windows. These window operators are given explicitly below.

Since all operators are separable, window masks can be computed as the outer product of two column vectors. The binomial smoothing window may be written as $[S] = \vec{s}\,\vec{s}^T$ where the column vector $\vec{s}$ is given by

$$\vec{s} = \frac{1}{64}\begin{bmatrix} 1 & 6 & 15 & 20 & 15 & 6 & 1 \end{bmatrix}^T \qquad (3.98)$$

For a 7x7 binomial smoothing window, it is clear that an extra 12 bits ($12 = 2\log_2(64)$) of fractional information should be maintained in the intermediate smoothed image result. For an $L \times L$ binomial smoother, $2L-2$ bits of fractional information must be maintained. The equally-weighted least squares derivative estimation window operators are given by

$$\begin{array}{ccc} [D_u] = \vec{d_0}\,\vec{d_1}^T & [D_v] = \vec{d_1}\,\vec{d_0}^T & \\ [D_{uu}] = \vec{d_0}\,\vec{d_2}^T & [D_{vv}] = \vec{d_2}\,\vec{d_0}^T & [D_{uv}] = \vec{d_1}\,\vec{d_1}^T \end{array} \qquad (3.99)$$

where the column vectors $\vec{d_0}, \vec{d_1}, \vec{d_2}$ for a 7x7 window are given by

$$\vec{d_0} = \frac{1}{7}\begin{bmatrix} 1 & 1 & 1 & 1 & 1 & 1 & 1 \end{bmatrix}^T \qquad (3.100)$$

$$\vec{d_1} = \frac{1}{28}\begin{bmatrix} -3 & -2 & -1 & 0 & 1 & 2 & 3 \end{bmatrix}^T \qquad (3.101)$$

$$\vec{d_2} = \frac{1}{84}\begin{bmatrix} 5 & 0 & -3 & -4 & -3 & 0 & 5 \end{bmatrix}^T. \qquad (3.102)$$

The partial derivative estimate images are computed via the appropriate 2-D image convolutions (denoted $*$):

$$f_u = D_u * S * f \qquad f_v = D_v * S * f \qquad (3.103)$$

$$f_{uu} = D_{uu} * S * f \qquad f_{vv} = D_{vv} * S * f \qquad f_{uv} = D_{uv} * S * f. \qquad (3.104)$$

These methods are easily applied to curves and volumetric data in addition to surface case given here.

3.7.2   GLOBAL APPROXIMATION METHODS

One of the disadvantages of local approximation techniques is that the surface descriptions may be inconsistent for nearby points. In order to obtain a single globally consistent description of geometric data, one may fit a single piecewise polynomial form to all data in a geometric signal as was done by Naik and Jain [NJ88]. In this section, B-splines are considered since they are relatively simple to implement and provide a very computationally efficient method to handle curves, surfaces, and volumes. Surfaces and volumes are approximated using tensor-products, which have some disadvantages of their own, but such geometric descriptions can be extremely useful for many applications. B-splines have been used by computer vision researchers with increasing frequency in recent years and this trend is likely to continue. B-spline curves and surfaces are also an IGES standard for surface representation in commercial computer-aided geometric design (CAGD) systems making them even more important for practical applications. Some B-spline basics will be covered before discussing a global approximation algorithm, but first we discuss surface smoothing splines which have been discussed much more often in the computer vision literature.

Smoothing Splines

Smoothing splines and related techniques have been advocated by many computer vision researchers for global surface shape description, especially for irregularly-spaced sparse point data, such as is often obtained from point-matching stereo algorithms [Gri81b] [Gri82] [Ter83] [Ter84] [Ter86] [KLB85] [Bou86] [BK86] [Lee85] [Lee88] [BZ87a] [BPT88]. The disadvantages of smoothing splines are primarily of a practical nature: they are computationally expensive to solve for and evaluate (many logarithms and square roots are required in their evaluation) and the condition number of the associated linear system of equations grows significantly with the number of data points [Bou86]. On regularly-spaced rectangular grids, the linear system exhibits a block Toeplitz structure that affords some economies in computation [Lee85,Lee88]. Smoothing splines have some advantages in that they are intended for arbitrarily shaped surface regions, but there are techniques that can be used with tensor-product B-splines, which are intended for rectangular parameter domains, to handle arbitrarily shaped regions as well as long as the data still occurs on a rectangular grid. Both uniform-knot tensor product B-splines and smoothing splines in their standard form suffer ringing effects at discontinuities, which results in inaccurate geometric interpretations of the data. Since geometric signals from geometric sensors, such as range imaging sensors, are often obtained on a dense rectangular grid, we shall devote our attention to B-spline techniques owing to the relative computational efficiencies they can provide.

B-Spline Basis Functions

Splines generalize piecewise-linear forms and Bezier forms to piecewise-polynomial forms in a way that can allow local control of the curve shape and provide desired continuity [DeB78]. The B-spline (basis-spline) approach to splines is used in most geometric modeling literature as opposed to the variational approach found in the computer vision literature. A n-D spline curve $\vec{x}(t)$ of order m (degree $m - 1$) is a linear combination of $N \geq m$ control points $\vec{c}_i$ weighted by the order m B-splines $B_i^m(t;T)$

$$\vec{x}(t) = \sum_{i=0}^{N-1} \vec{c}_i B_i^m(t;T) \qquad \vec{c}_i \in \Re^n. \qquad (3.105)$$

where T is the *knot vector*, a set of $K \geq N + m$ non-decreasing constants $T = \{t_0, t_1, \ldots, t_{K-1}\}$ that subdivide the interval $[t_1, t_{K-2}]$. An individual B-spline function of order m can be defined [DH87] recursively in terms of

$m - 1$ order B-splines via the Cox-deBoor algorithm:

$$B_i^m(t;T) = \frac{t - t_i}{t_{i+k-1} - t_i} B_i^{m-1}(t;T) + \frac{t - t_{i+k}}{t_{i+1} - t_{i+k}} B_{i+1}^{m-1}(t;T) \qquad (3.106)$$

$$B_i^1(t;T) = \left\{ \begin{array}{ll} 1 & \text{if } t_i \leq t < t_{i+1} \\ 0 & \text{otherwise.} \end{array} \right. \qquad (3.107)$$

where $0/0 = 0$ by convention. If an explicit knot vector is not given, the unit-interval uniform knot vector $T_{m,N}$ with $K = N + m$ is used:

$$t_i = \left\{ \begin{array}{ll} 0 & \text{if } 0 < i < m, \\ \frac{1+i-m}{1+N-m} & \text{if } m \leq i \leq N, \\ 1 & \text{if } N \leq i < K - 1, \end{array} \right. \qquad (3.108)$$

where the first and last knot values are only constrained by the inequalities $t_0 \leq 0$ and $t_{K-1} \geq 1$. The second and second last knot values are duplicated $m - 1$ times which causes the spline to meet its first and last control points. Any spline defined as a linear combination of B-splines of order m is $m - 2$ times differentiable at every point in the open interval (t_1, t_{K-2}) as long as no interior knots are duplicated. Each time an interior knot is duplicated, the number of times the spline can be differentiated at that knot is decremented, but the rest of the spline remains $m - 2$ times differentiable.

The partition of unity condition $\sum_{i=0}^{N-1} B_i^m(t;T) = 1$ holds for any m and any knot vector T giving B-splines many desirable convexity properties [DeB78,FP79,FV82]. If $N = m$, B-splines are exactly the Bernstein-Bezier polynomials. If $m = 1$, B-splines are piecewise-linear on the control points. Figure 3.19 compares the cubic power basis functions to the univariate cubic (order 4) B-spline basis functions for a uniform knot vector and 8 control points. Figure 3.20 shows two cubic spline planar curves obtained using the basis functions in Figure 3.19 The control points in the left plot form a symmetric shape whereas the right plot shows the local effect of moving one control point.

Tensor-Product B-Spline Surfaces

A tensor-product spline surface $\vec{x}(u,v)$ of order (m,n) (degree $(m-1,n-1)$) is defined over a rectangle $[u_1, u_{K_u-2}] \times [v_1, v_{K_v-2}]$ partitioned by knot vectors T_u and T_v. A total of $N_u N_v$ control points are needed, and $K_u = N_u + m$ and $K_v = N_v + n$ if no interior knots are duplicated. The spline surface is a linear combination of control points weighted by separable bivariate tensor-product B-splines $B_{i,j}^{m,n}(u,v;T_u,T_v) = B_i^m(u;T_u)B_j^n(v;T_v)$:

$$\vec{x}(u,v) = \sum_{i=0}^{N_u-1} \sum_{j=0}^{N_v-1} \vec{c}_{ij} B_{i,j}^{m,n}(u,v;T_u,T_v). \qquad (3.109)$$

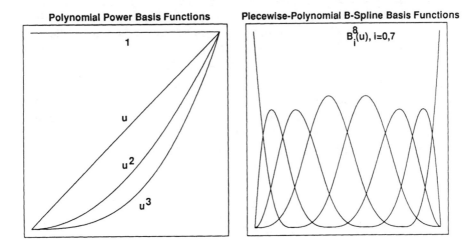

FIGURE 3.19. Cubic Power Basis Functions vs. Eight B-Spline Basis Functions

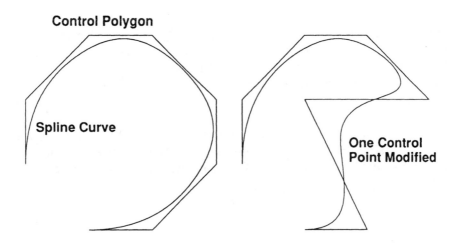

FIGURE 3.20. Planar B-Spline Curve Showing Local Control of Control Points

As well as being locally modifiable, the partition of unity condition holds in general for any m, n and any knot vectors T_u, T_v. There is a very efficient algorithm for fitting tensor-product spline surfaces to data on a discrete grid whenever a unit square parameter domain is appropriate [Die77]. This basic tensor-product approximation algorithm is included here for reference and is applicable to any set of basis functions, not just B-splines. For simplicity, we consider approximation of scalar functions $z = f(u, v)$ where the assignment the assignments $x = u$ and $y = v$ may be made to visualize a 3-D surface. If data for the functions $x(u, v)$ and $y(u, v)$ is also given, they are approximated separately by the same technique.

A tensor-product surface is the sum of coefficients multiplied by two univariate basis functions:

$$f(u, v) = \sum_{i=0}^{N_u-1} \sum_{j=0}^{N_v-1} c_{ij} B_i^m(u; T_u) B_j^n(v; T_v). \qquad (3.110)$$

If we are given $M_u M_v$ data points $\vec{f}(u_k, v_l)$ that we wish to approximate, then we should choose the control points to minimize the sum of the errors

$$\epsilon = \frac{1}{M_u M_v} \sum_{k=0}^{M_u-1} \sum_{l=0}^{M_v-1} \left(f(u_k, v_l) - \sum_{i=0}^{N_u-1} \sum_{j=0}^{N_v-1} c_{ij} B_i^m(u_k; T_u) B_j^n(v_l; T_v) \right)^2$$
$$(3.111)$$

We assume fixed knot vectors T_u and T_v (usually uniform) since selecting the best knots and the best control points simultaneously requires solving a nonlinear least squares problem, which can be done, but gets more complicated and is quite expensive. Good, suboptimal non-uniform knot vectors can be obtained, but it is difficult to guarantee the performance of such schemes.

The solution to the linear least squares problem with fixed knot vectors is expressed fairly conveniently by using matrix notation to represent the sets of numbers in the above equation. We define the following matrix elements:

$$U_{ki} = B_i^m(u_k; T_u) \qquad (M_u \times N_u) \qquad (3.112)$$

$$V_{lj} = B_j^n(v_l; T_v) \qquad (M_v \times N_v) \qquad (3.113)$$

$$F_{lk} = f(u_k, v_l) \qquad (M_v \times M_u) \qquad (3.114)$$

$$C_{ji} = c_{ij} \qquad (N_v \times N_u) \qquad (3.115)$$

In the tensor notation, where repeated subscripts imply summation over the relevant range, the approximation summation may be written as

$$F_{lk} \approx V_{lj} C_{ji} U_{ki} \qquad (3.116)$$

or in matrix notation,

$$F \approx VCU^T \qquad (3.117)$$

Sizes: $(M_v \times M_u) = (M_v \times N_v)(N_v \times N_u)(N_u \times M_u)$.

The least squares solution $\hat{C}$ minimizes the Frobenius norm of the difference matrix:

$$\epsilon = \|F - VCU^T\|^2. \tag{3.118}$$

The solution is given by

$$\hat{C} = (V^T V)^{-1} V^T FU(U^T U)^{-1} \tag{3.119}$$

Sizes: $(N_v \times N_u) = (N_v \times N_v)(N_v \times M_v)(M_v \times M_u)(M_u \times N_u)(N_u \times N_u)$.

The surface is reconstructed from the control points via matrix multiplication:

$$\hat{F}(u, v) = V(v)\hat{C}U^T(u). \tag{3.120}$$

If we wish to evaluate the derivatives of the estimated tensor-product surface, we could differentiate the basis function matrices:

$$\frac{\partial \hat{F}(u, v)}{\partial u} = V(v)\hat{C}\frac{\partial U^T(u)}{\partial u} \tag{3.121}$$

$$\frac{\partial^2 \hat{F}(u, v)}{\partial u^2} = V(v)\hat{C}\frac{\partial^2 U^T(u)}{\partial u^2} \tag{3.122}$$

$$\frac{\partial \hat{F}(u, v)}{\partial v} = \frac{\partial V(v)}{\partial v}\hat{C}U^T(u) \tag{3.123}$$

$$\frac{\partial^2 \hat{F}(u, v)}{\partial v^2} = \frac{\partial^2 V(v)}{\partial v^2}\hat{C}U^T(u) \tag{3.124}$$

$$\frac{\partial^2 \hat{F}(u, v)}{\partial u \partial v} = \frac{\partial V(v)}{\partial v}\hat{C}\frac{\partial U^T(u)}{\partial u} \tag{3.125}$$

In the case of B-splines, it is much more convenient to write down B-spline derivatives in terms of lower order B-splines and the differences of control points:

$$\frac{\partial f}{\partial u}(u, v) = \sum_{i=0}^{N_u-1} \sum_{j=0}^{N_v-1} c_{ij}^{1,0} B_i^{m-1}(u; T_u)B_j^n(v; T_v) \tag{3.126}$$

where the first partial derivative control points are given by

$$c_{ij}^{1,0} = \frac{(m-1)(c_{ij} - c_{i+1,j})}{(t_{i+m-1}^u - t_i^u)} \tag{3.127}$$

where the t_i^u is the i-th knot from the T_u knot vector. Higher derivatives are obtained by applying the derivative operation recursively for the appropriate argument. This changes the derivative formulas to the following forms where the order of the B-spline basis matrices are explicitly indicated in the subscripts:

$$\frac{\partial \hat{F}(u,v)}{\partial u} = V_n(v)\hat{C}_{10}U_{m-1}^T(u) \tag{3.128}$$

$$\frac{\partial^2 \hat{F}(u,v)}{\partial u^2} = V_n(v)\hat{C}_{20}U_{m-2}^T(u) \tag{3.129}$$

$$\frac{\partial \hat{F}(u,v)}{\partial v} = V_{n-1}(v)\hat{C}_{01}U_m^T(u) \tag{3.130}$$

$$\frac{\partial^2 \hat{F}(u,v)}{\partial v^2} = V_{n-2}(v)\hat{C}_{02}U_m^T(u) \tag{3.131}$$

$$\frac{\partial^2 \hat{F}(u,v)}{\partial u \partial v} = V_{n-1}(v)\hat{C}_{11}U_{m-1}^T(u) \tag{3.132}$$

where the control point matrices $\hat{C}_{ij}$ are the discrete finite-difference matrices of the original control point matrix $\hat{C}$.

Figure 3.21(a) shows a range image of the surface of a US penny depicting the head of A. Lincoln (courtesy of Y.R. Jeng, Fluid Mechanics Dept., General Motors Research Laboratories). A shaded image of this range image is shown in Figure 3.21(b). Note the high-frequency ripple from the range sensor used to obtain this range image. A global uniform-knot B-spline approximation to the Lincoln penny range image is shown in Figure 3.22(a). with its corresponding shaded image in Figure 3.22(b). The RMS error for this fit was 1.9 discrete levels in a range of 256. The control point image $\hat{C}_{ij}$ for the approximation is shown in Figure 3.23. The main advantage of this approach is that a globally consistent image description has been obtained for computing differential properties. The disadvantage is that the global B-spline approximation acts as a low-pass filter which "rings" at discontinuities owing to the loss of high spatial frequencies. However, the ringing problems are relatively minor in this case compared to the problems that local approximation techniques suffer from when ripple is present in the raw data.

3.7.3   FUNCTION APPROXIMATION COMPARISONS

The following comparisons are equally valid for local and global approximation methods.

Curve fitting typically involves linear regression on a sum of basis functions:

$$x(u) = \sum_i c_i \phi_i(u). \tag{3.133}$$

If we are given N data points and M basis functions, least squares approximation produces M coefficients:

$$\vec{c} = (\Phi^T \Phi)^{-1} \Phi^T \vec{x} \tag{3.134}$$

FIGURE 3.21. Lincoln Penny (a) Range Image and (b) Shaded Image

FIGURE 3.22. B-Spline (a) Approximation Surface and (b) Shaded Image

FIGURE 3.23. Control Points of B-Spline Surface Viewed as Range Image

where $\vec{c}$ is the vector of coefficients, $\vec{x}$ is the vector of dependent data samples, Φ is the matrix of basis functions evaluated at the independent data samples. The inverted matrix is of size $M \times M$. If we weight data samples $(u_j, x(u_j))$ individually as to their relative importance to the fitted solution with the weights w_j, we get the weighted least squares solution:

$$\vec{c} = (\Phi^T W \Phi)^{-1} \Phi^T W \vec{x} \qquad (3.135)$$

where W is a diagonal matrix of weights w_j. These matrix equations give an indication of the amount of computation required to perform a given approximation. Although one should not numerically compute least squares solutions via the above equations, the size of the "inverted" matrix can be used as a gauge of the amount of work required to obtain an approximation. In curve fitting over arbitrary parameter sets, linear least squares techniques can be ordered according to the amount of work required to "invert" the $M \times M$ matrix $(\Phi^T W \Phi)^{-1}$. For example, if orthogonal polynomials are used on fixed parameter sets, e.g., equally spaced points, this matrix is diagonal and can be inverted by taking the reciprocals of the diagonal elements. This is the least amount of work possible. If B-splines are used, this matrix is banded with the bandwidth proportional to the order of the splines used. For arbitrary basis functions, the matrix will in general be dense requiring more work than orthogonal polynomials or B-splines. In general, least squares curve fitting via linear regression with M basis functions requires work related to the amount of work to solve an $M \times M$ linear system of equations.

It must be noted that if the same set of u values over which the curve functions are being approximated is fixed, then the matrix inversion part of the solution need only be done once. Approximation solutions are then carried out by forming the matrix $(\Phi^T W \Phi)^{-1} \Phi^T W$ once and doing matrix multiplication with the vector of dependent sample data to get the desired coefficients.

In general, the amount of work involved in least squares surface or volume approximations with M basis functions is about the same as that for curves with M basis functions. However, more basis functions are required for any given order. For example, an (isotropic) quadratic fit requires 3 basis functions for graph curves $(1, u, u^2)$, 6 basis functions for graph surfaces $(1, u, v, uv, u^2, v^2)$, and 10 basis functions for graph volumes $(1, u, v, w, uv, vw, wu, u^2, v^2, w^2)$. For an isotropic degree-m graph approximation in n variables, $(m + n)(m + n - 1)/2$ basis functions are required.

For multivariate approximation of surface or volume geometry, it is convenient and sometimes appropriate to use tensor-product basis functions as described above in the section on global approximation via B-splines. For a tensor-product quadratic surface fit, the nine basis functions are $(1, v, v^2, u, uv, uv^2, u^2, u^2v, u^2v^2)$. The advantage of this tensor-product basis is that the least squares approximation can be computed by inverting two

3x3 matrices rather than inverting a single 9x9 matrix:

$$C = (V^T V)^{-1} V^T X U (U^T U)^{-1} \qquad (3.136)$$

where X is the matrix of data samples, U is the matrix of basis function values for $(1, u, u^2)$, and V is the matrix of basis function values for $(1, v, v^2)$, and C is the matrix of tensor product coefficients.

If a separable weight matrix is used i.e., $w(u_i, v_j) = w_u(u_i) w_v(v_j)$, the weighted least squares solution can still benefit from the tensor-product decomposition:

$$C = (V^T W_V V)^{-1} V^T W_V X W_U U (U^T W_U U)^{-1} \qquad (3.137)$$

However, if a non-separable weight matrix used, this destroys the ability to decompose the linear system, and the full size matrix solution $M^2 \times M^2$ must be computed.

The main points of this section are summarized in Figure 3.24 by considering an example in which one wishes to obtain a bicubic surface approximation to a square 15x15 window of image data. If we choose an isotropic bicubic polynomial, we could determine 10 coefficients by solving a 10x10 linear system. The use of orthogonal basis functions would make this system diagonal whereas the use of local support B-splines makes the system banded (non-zero values directly above and below the matrix diagonal). If we chose a tensor-product bicubic polynomial (or a bicubic Bezier patch), we could determine 16 coefficients by solving two 4x4 linear systems independently if the weight matrix is separable; otherwise, a 16x16 linear system would need to be solved. A separable-weight tensor-product B-spline surface with N control points ($4 \le N \le 15$) in each direction would require solution of two $N \times N$ linear systems (maximum size 15 x 15). If the weight matrix is not separable, a single linear system of size $N^2 \times N^2$ would need to be solved (maximum size 225 x 225). To compare some other surface types, the C^2 smoothing spline (or "thin-plate" spline) advocated by [Gri81b,Ter84,KLB85,Lee85,Bou86] would require the solution of a 228x228 block Toeplitz linear system for each possible smoothing parameter. The weighted C^1 spline of Foley [Fol87], being tested for computer vision purposes by Sinha [Sin88], requires the solution of a sparse 675x675 linear system. In general, as the amount of computation increases the approximating surface follows the data more closely. However, approximations that follow the data closely also tends to incorporate noise, too.

3.7.4   OTHER METHODS OF INTEREST

Rather than determine differential properties of geometry by explicit fitting, other methods can be used to compute the same information. As an example, we discuss the use of covariance matrices for surface normal estimation and the computation of curvature from surface normals. These

Approximating Surface	Linear System Size
Isotropic Bicubic	10 × 10
Tensor-Product Bicubic:	
Separable Weights	(2) 4 × 4
Non-Separable Weights	16 × 16
Tensor-Product B-Spline:	$N \leq 15$
Separable Weights	(2) $N \times N$
Non-Separable Weights	$N^2 \times N^2$
C^2 Smoothing Spline	228 × 228
Weighted C^1 Spline	675 × 675

FIGURE 3.24. Computational Effort to Approximate One 15x15 Image Window

methods are particularly useful for arbitrarily spaced data points where there is no preferred direction for making measurements, such as the viewing direction.

Covariance Matrix Determination of Normals

Let $S = \{\vec{x}_i\}$ be a discrete set of (x, y, z) points that may interpreted as surface points. A neighborhood $N(k, r)$ of a point $\vec{x}_k$ is the set of all points in S that lie within a radius r of that point:

$$N(k, r) = \{\vec{x}_i \in S : \|\vec{x}_i - \vec{x}_k\| \leq r\}. \qquad (3.138)$$

The covariance matrix $C(k, r)$ of the neighborhood $N(k, r)$ is defined as the expectation of the outer product of the difference vectors in the neighborhood:

$$C(k, r) = \frac{1}{|N|} \sum_{\vec{x}_i \in N(k,r)} (\vec{x}_i - \vec{x}_k)(\vec{x}_i - \vec{x}_k)^T = \left(\frac{1}{|N|} \sum_{\vec{x}_i \in N(k,r)} \vec{x}_i \vec{x}_i^T \right) - \vec{x}_k \vec{x}_k^T$$

$$(3.139)$$

where $|N|$ is the number of points in the neighborhood $N(k, r)$. The covariance matrix is a symmetric 3x3 matrix. It is typically of full rank for all neighborhoods with more than 3 data points from a real sensor. Let $\sigma_1 \leq \sigma_2 \leq \sigma_3$ be the eigenvalues for the matrix $C(k, r)$ and let $\vec{v}_1$, $\vec{v}_2$, and $\vec{v}_3$ be the corresponding unit eigenvectors. If the data points are noisy samples from a flat or gently curving smooth surface, then the surface normal at the k-th point is given by

$$\vec{n}_k = \vec{v}_1 \qquad (3.140)$$

and the principal directions are given by the other two eigenvectors. The value σ_1 is a measure of planar fit error in the direction specified by the surface normal $\vec{v}_1$.

Surface Curvature from Surface Normals

If a surface normal is assigned to every surface point in a neighborhood, then surface curvature properties can be computed as in Hoffman and Jain [HJ87b]. The normal curvature for a curve passing through the points $\vec{x}_j$ and $\vec{x}_k$ is given by

$$\kappa_n(k,j) = \frac{\|\vec{n}_k - \vec{n}_j\|}{\|\vec{x}_k - \vec{x}_j\|}. \tag{3.141}$$

The minimum and maximum principal curvatures are determined by comparing the normal curvatures of all points $\vec{x}_j$ in the neighborhood. The mean and Gaussian curvatures are computed as the average and the product of the principal curvatures.

3.8   Robust Approximation

As described above, it is a common practice in image processing and computer vision to convolve rectangular constant coefficient windows with digital images to perform local smoothing and derivative estimation for edge detection and other purposes. If all data points in each image window of interest belong to the same statistical population, this practice is reasonable and fast. But, as is well known, constant coefficient window operators produce incorrect results if more than one statistical population is present within in a window, e.g. if a gray level or gradient discontinuity is present. This section describes robust M-estimation as a replacement for any type of least squares approximation. For practical applications, algorithms will have to weight the benefit of robust approximation against the additional computational expense incurred by a more complicated procedure. More details about a local approximation application are available in [BBW88].

Robust statistics is the branch of statistics that studies the sensitivity of statistical procedures to departures from their underlying assumptions. (The technical term "robust" was apparently first coined by Box [Box53] in the early fifties, but robust estimation techniques date back to at least 1885 [Sti73].) The formal theory of robust statistics arose in the sixties [Tuk60,Tuk62,Hub64,Ham68]. Of specific interest to geometric signal processing is the concept of distributional robustness. For example, least squares techniques, optimal for independent, identically distributed (i.i.d.) normal random variables, can yield poor results if sample data are from non-normal distributions. An ideal robust estimator yields very good estimates when the sample data is distributed according to a given distribution and yields reasonable results if the data is contaminated with points from other distributions. In statistics, the term *efficiency* refers to the ability of a procedure to yield optimal estimates under ideal conditions whereas the term *robustness* refers to the ability to yield reasonable estimates under less than ideal conditions. There is a fundamental tradeoff between efficiency and robustness: the most efficient procedures cannot be the most robust and the most robust procedures cannot be the most efficient in statistical terms. However, procedures are available that can tolerate up to 49.9% "bad" sample data and yield reasonable estimates (90-95% efficient) of the properties contained in the good portion of the data.

Computer vision has employed a variety of techniques that have a flavor similar to the formal robust statistical methods [BF81,DR78,HR84,Ter84, GP85,HSHD87]. The Hough transform is perhaps the best known procedure [DH72] for detecting particular functions and fitting those functions to the data obtaining function parameters to within some quantization error. It is a memory intensive method involving many simple computations whereas robust statistical procedures are typically computationally intensive, but require little memory as will be described below. The Hough transform can detect geometric entities, such as lines, in samples where more than half of data points are bad, but it becomes quite impractical for functions with six parameters, such as an isotropic biquadratic surface. Robust statistical algorithms are ideal for curve, surface, and volume fitting in the presence of non-normal noise and outliers.

3.8.1   ROBUST M-ESTIMATION

We naively introduce robust regression using ρ-functions and ψ-functions to explain the basic concepts. We intentionally avoid rigorous definitions of influence functions, change of variance functions, change of bias functions, and other concepts found in the textbooks [HRRS86,Hub81] since these underlying concepts are not strictly necessary for gaining insight into the basic procedures.

Suppose we are given a set of N data samples $\{(u_i, z(u_i))\}$ for which we hypothesize a model function $\hat{z} = \hat{f}(\vec{a}, u)$ with parameter vector $\vec{a}$ to account for the structure of the data. In M-estimation (short for Maximum likelihood type estimation), one seeks to minimize an error metric $\epsilon(\vec{a})$, which is usually the sum of the norm $\rho(\cdot)$ of the residual errors $e(u_i) = z(u_i) - \hat{f}(\vec{a}, u_i)$:

$$\epsilon(\vec{a}) = \sum_{i=1}^{N} \rho(e(u_i)/s) = \sum_{i=1}^{N} \rho\left((z(u_i) - \hat{f}(\vec{a}, u_i))/s\right) \quad (3.142)$$

where s is known as the scale estimate which may or may not be of importance depending on the nature of the ρ-function. If $\rho_1(x) = |x|$, then finding the parameters $\vec{a}$ of the function $\hat{f}$ is a standard L_1 regression problem [Abd80]. If $\rho_2(x) = x^2$, then finding the parameters $\vec{a}$ of the function $\hat{f}$ is a standard least squares (L_2) regression problem [LH74,GL83]. Note that both L_1 and L_2 regression problems are independent of the scale estimate s.

For any given ρ-function associated with any given M-estimation proce-

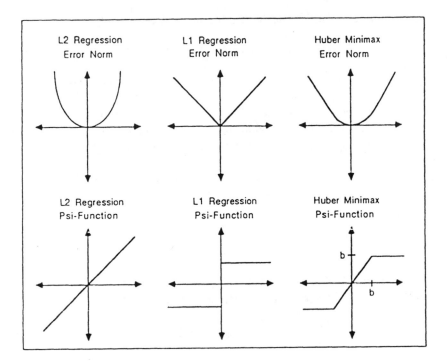

FIGURE 3.25. ρ, ψ-Functions for L_1, L_2 Regression; Huber Minimax Functions.

dure, we may define the ψ-function $\psi(x)$ as

$$\psi(x) = \frac{d\rho(x)}{dx}. \tag{3.143}$$

In general, $\rho(x)$ should be an even function in which case $\psi(x)$ is odd. The ρ-functions and ψ-functions $\psi_1(x)$ and $\psi_2(x)$ for L_1 and L_2 regression are shown in Figure 3.25. We can qualitatively see that L_1 regression is less sensitive to contaminated data sets than L_2 regression because the "influence" of statistical outliers is constant rather than linearly increasing. In other words, L_1 regression is fairly robust compared to L_2, but is only efficient for the double exponential distribution $\exp(-|x-\mu|/\sigma)$ [MP80]. L_2 regression is not very robust and is only efficient for normal distributions.

Huber [Hub64] introduced the minimax ψ-function $\psi_b(x)$ with cutoff b. This function qualitatively yields the efficiency of L_2 regression with the robustness of L_1 regression and provides a better general-purpose estimator than either:

$$\psi_b(x) = \min(b, \max(x, -b)) \qquad \text{(Huber minimax)}. \tag{3.144}$$

It is clear that the Huber minimax function is dependent on the scale estimate s, which means it must be known or estimated from the data. Although somewhat *ad hoc*, the robust statistics community uses the median absolute deviation (MAD) scale estimate almost exclusively:

$$s(\vec{a}) = 1.4826 \, \mathrm{median}(|e(u_i) - \mathrm{median}(e(u_i))|) \qquad (3.145)$$

where $e(u_i)$ are the residuals from some initial function fit $\vec{a}_1$ and the factor $1.4826 = 1/0.6745$ is chosen to make s a consistent estimator of the standard deviation provided that model error terms are normally distributed random variables. In what follows, zero values of s will be handled separately as a special case so that we may assume $s(\vec{a}) \neq 0$ for generic situations.

The solution $\vec{a}$ is now given for the case where the approximating function $\hat{f}(\vec{a}, u)$ is a linear combination of K linearly independent basis functions $\{\phi_k(u)\}$:

$$\hat{f}(\vec{a}, u) = \sum_{k=1}^{K} a_k \phi_k(u) \qquad (3.146)$$

where a_k is the kth component of the parameter vector $\vec{a}$. The necessary minimization conditions for the multivariate function $\epsilon(\vec{a})$ are

$$\frac{\partial \epsilon}{\partial a_k} = 0 \qquad \text{for all } k = 1, \ldots, K. \qquad (3.147)$$

which implies that

$$\sum_{i=1}^{N} \psi(e(u_i)/s)\phi_k(u_i) = 0 \qquad \text{for all } k = 1, \ldots, K. \qquad (3.148)$$

If we define a set of weight parameters $w(u_i)$ as

$$w(u_i) = \begin{cases} \dfrac{\psi(e(u_i)/s)}{e(u_i)/s} & \text{if } e(u_i) \neq 0 \\ 1 & \text{if } e(u_i) = 0 \end{cases}, \qquad (3.149)$$

then the K conditions above may be written as

$$\sum_{i=1}^{N} \phi_k(u_i)w(u_i)e(u_i) = 0 \qquad \text{for all } k = 1, \ldots, K. \qquad (3.150)$$

Substituting the expression for the residual error, one obtains

$$\sum_{i=1}^{N} \sum_{j=1}^{K} \phi_k(u_i)w(u_i)\phi_j(u_i)a_j = \sum_{i=1}^{N} \phi_k(u_i)w(u_i)z(u_i) \qquad (3.151)$$

for each k, which can be written in matrix form as

$$\Phi^T W(\vec{a}) \Phi \vec{a} = \Phi^T W(\vec{a}) \vec{z} \qquad (3.152)$$

where the ith component of the $\vec{z}$ vector is $z(u_i)$, the ijth element of the $N \times K$ matrix Φ is $\Phi_{ij} = \phi_j(u_i)$, and the $N \times N$ weight matrix is specified by $W_{ij}(\vec{a}) = w(u_i)\delta_{ij}$ where δ_{ij} is the standard Kronecker delta. Note that this weighted least squares relationship is nonlinear in the coefficients $\vec{a}$ since the weight matrix W depends upon the coefficients. This nonlinear matrix equation can be solved iteratively via several different methods, but iteratively reweighted least squares (IRLS), attributed to Beaton and Tukey [BT74], is among the most popular methods. It always converges to a unique solution for a *monotonically nondecreasing* ψ-functions regardless of the initial fit for any given fixed value of the scale estimate [Bir80]. This unique convergence property must be viewed with some caution though because the final unique solution is dependent upon the scale estimate constant, and the scale estimate is dependent upon the initial fit coefficients used. More caution is required when using nonmonotonic redescending ψ-functions since there are no guarantees of convergence to a unique solution although problems seldom occur in practice.

The IRLS M-estimation algorithm is summarized. Suppose a judiciously chosen parameter vector $\vec{a}_m$ is given (where initially $m = 0$) and the $(m+1)$-th parameter vector $\vec{a}_{m+1}$ is to be obtained. First, the N residuals at the mth iteration are computed:

$$e_m(u_i) = z(u_i) - \sum_{i=1}^{K} a_k^m \phi_k(u_i). \tag{3.153}$$

The residuals are used to compute the weights $w(u_i)$ according to the general expression given above. In particular, when the Huber minimax ψ-function ψ_b is used, the explicit expression for the weights is given by

$$w(u_i) = \begin{cases} 1 & \text{if } |e_m(u_i)| \le bs \\ \dfrac{bs}{|e_m(u_i)|} & \text{if } |e_m(u_i)| > bs \end{cases}. \tag{3.154}$$

This form shows explicitly that all "inliers" receive unit weights whereas questionable data points are "downweighted" proportional to the magnitude of the residual error. Although this is a desirable effect, the weights are never exactly zero unless the residuals are infinite. It can be even more desirable to allow so-called redescending ψ-functions that have the property that $\psi(x) = 0$ for $|x| > c$ where c is the final cutoff value. This allows total elimination of the effects of data points with very large residual errors. Figure 3.26 shows several different redescending ψ-functions from the robust statistics literature [HRRS86,Hog79] Empirical studies show that the detailed shape of the ψ-function is not very important. The most critical features are the maximum ψ points and the final cutoff value c.

The notion of completely cutting off the effects of large residuals is related to the breakdown point concept in robust statistics. Roughly speaking, the *breakdown point* of an estimator, usually denoted as ϵ^*, is the limiting fraction of arbitrarily bad data that the estimator can cope with. For example,

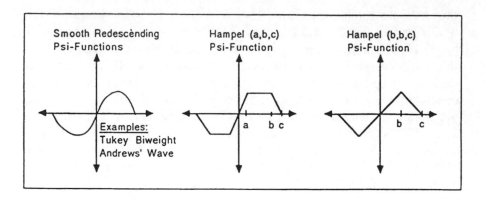

FIGURE 3.26. Redescending ψ-Functions for Robust Regression

$\epsilon^* =0\%$ for L_1, L_2, L_p regression estimation since no matter how large a finite set of sample data is, these estimators can be made to give bad estimates by inserting a few bad data points ("leverage points") and letting them diverge toward infinity. It is possible to achieve an $\epsilon^* =50\%$ breakdown point with robust M-estimation on discrete image data located on a regular image grid. This is also the best that other robust methods, such as least median squares procedures [Rou84,RL87], can offer, but the IRLS procedure is more computationally efficient as well as statistically efficient for multivariate regression.

3.8.2   BASIC EXAMPLES

Suppose we do a surface fit to the data points in the following step edge window

1	1	1
1	1	0
1	0	0

which is shown graphically in Figure 3.27. The robust fit planar equation is $z = 1$ with MAD=0. The function normal at the center of the window is computed to be pointing straight up: $\hat{n} = (0, 0, 1)$. Compare this with the least squares planar fit $z = (2-u-v)/3$ and its normal $\hat{n} = (-1, -1, 3)/\sqrt{11}$ and an RMS error of $\sqrt{2/3} \approx 0.82$. One can correctly compute derivatives and function normals to within one-half of a pixel from an edge without preliminary detection of the edge.

Similarly, suppose we do a surface fit to the data points in the following roof edge window:

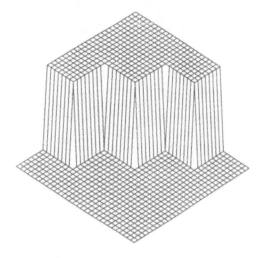

FIGURE 3.27. 3x3 Window Containing a Step Edge

1	2	3
2	3	4
3	4	3

which is shown graphically in Figure 3.28. The planar equation for the window is $z = 3 + u + v$ with a MAD=0. The function normal at the center of the window is computed to be pointing at an angle: $\hat{n} = (-1, -1, 1)/\sqrt{3}$. Compare with the least squares planar fit $z = (25 - 6u - 6v)/9$ and its normal $\hat{n} = (-2, -2, 3)/\sqrt{17}$ and an RMS error of 1.49. In this noiseless case, we can compute derivatives and function normals to within one pixel of a roof edge without preliminary detection of the edge.

These simple examples demonstrate the capability of robust methods to ignore inconsistent data. Although the potential for improvement in many geometric signal processing applications is significant, robust methods are not a panacea for all signal processing problems though and should be used with care. Model selection and scale estimation are critical issues for noisy data.

3.9 Emerging Themes

Although no new research has been presented here, this work has attempted to gather in one place the rudiments of what will be needed in a useful geometric signal processing theory. The same fundamental issues occur regardless of the dimension of the signal, and techniques are desired that work well in any dimension. Given a geometric signal, partial derivatives

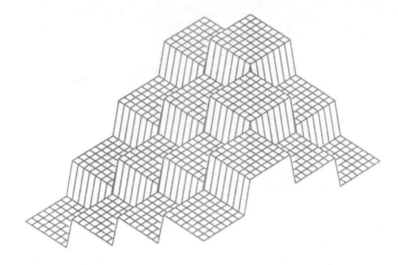

FIGURE 3.28. 3x3 Window Containing a Roof Edge

must be estimated in order to locate step, normal, and curvature discontinuities and compute metrics, tangent spaces, curvatures, and coordinate frames on the smooth pieces of the data. Derivatives can be estimated using local or global approximation techniques, but each approach has its own advantages and disadvantages. Some non-approximation techniques were also given for estimating normals and curvature. As in most of computer vision, the lack of an objective application-independent criteria for evaluating algorithm performance prevents us from choosing the method which is best for all cases of interest. Local and global approximation techniques can interact with each other in region growing based on geometric fitting as described in Besl [Bes88d] in a dimension-independent manner. Robust statistical techniques are directly useful for eliminating the effects of outliers and non-normal noise, but have only recently begun to be explored by computer vision researchers [For87,Har88a]. (These techniques began to be used by signal processing researchers in the early 1980's [MT82].) We believe that a continuing evolution of geometric signal processing algorithms can be built on the basic concepts outlined here. Eventually, we would like to see a standardization of geometric signal formats so that unified software implementations will indeed be capable of handling data for curves, surfaces, and volumes automatically without elaborate application specific programming. Such developments would aid research efforts as well as application developments.

Acknowledgements: The author would like to thank L. Watson, J. Birch, R.B. Tilove, W.H. Frey, Y.R. Jeng, R.C. Jain, and P. Boulanger, as well as all those who expressed their ideas at the RIV workshop at MSU.

4

Segmentation versus object representation – are they separable?

Ruzena Bajcsy
Franc Solina
Alok Gupta[1]

4.1   Introduction

When vision is used for moving through the environment, for manipulating or for recognizing objects, it has to simplify the visual input to the level that is required for the specific task. To simplify means to partition images into entities that correspond to individual regions, objects and parts in the real world and to describe those entities only in detail sufficient for performing a required task. For visual discrimination, shape is probably the most important property. After all, line drawings of scenes and objects are usually sufficient for description and subsequent recognition. In computer vision literature this partitioning of images and description of individual parts is called segmentation and shape representation. Segmentation and shape representation appear to be distinct problems and are treated as such in most computer vision systems. In this paper we try to disperse this notion and show that there is no clear division between segmentation and shape representation. Solving any one of those two problems separately is very difficult. On the other hand, if any one of the two problems is solved first, the other one becomes much easier. For example, if the image is correctly divided into parts, the subsequent shape description of those parts gets easier. The opposite is also true when the shapes of parts are known, the

[1]GRASP Laboratory,Computer and Information Science Department, University of Pennsylvania, Philadelphia, PA 19104, USA. This work was supported in part by the following contracts and grants: NSF DCR-84-10771, NSF ECS-84-11879 and DMC-85-12838, US Postal Service contract 104230-87-H-0001/M-0195, Air Force F49620-85-K-0018, F33615-83-C-3000, F33615-86-C-3610, DARPA/ONR grants NOO14-85-K-0807, NOOO14-85-K-0018, ARMY DAAG29-84-K-0061 and DAAG29-84-9-0027, NSF-CER MCS-82-19196, DCR-82-19196 A02, NIH NS-10939-11 as part of the Cerebrovascular Research Center, by DEC Corp., and the LORD Corp.

partitioning of the image gets simpler. Since neither of them can be easily solved in isolation, at least not on the first try, we argue that they should interact to guide and correct each other. Hence, segmentation and shape recovery should not be studied separately. The complete visual interpretation problem is even more complex because the initial data acquisition process should not be separated from the later segmentation and shape representation. How data acquisition can interact with the interpretation stage is investigated in computer vision under the heading of active vision [Baj85]. In this paper we concentrate only on the interaction between segmentation and shape representation, assuming an image taken from a particular viewpoint is given.

A more formal problem definition of the topic of this paper is the following. Given an arbitrary spatial arrangement of static, three dimensional solids, imaged by a noncontact sensor, answer the following three questions:

1. What are the geometric primitives that (possibly uniquely) describe the data?

2. What are the processes that carry out this decomposition?

3. What is the overall control strategy to explain the measured data?

While the first two questions represent the analysis aspect of the problem, the last one can be explained as the synthesis or integration of the whole system.

In the rest of the paper we assume that a complete depth map of a scene is given. Obtaining a depth map is one of the stated goals of low level vision modules, such as stereo and shape from shading. The computation of the depth map or 2-1/2 D sketch was once considered to be the harder part and that image interpretation from there on would be easy. Although dense and accurate depth maps are now available from laser range scanners, the interpretation of those images is still difficult. A depth map as the starting point, obtained either with a laser scanner or from low level image techniques on gray level images, does not simplify neither segmentation nor shape recovery in any large extent. For the examples in this paper we use range images taken from a single viewpoint [Tsi87]. Due to self occlusion, not all points on the surface of an object are given. Since the supporting surface is fixed, range points from the support can be easily removed at the start of scene interpretation.

When the necessity for interaction between segmentation and shape representation is acknowledged, control strategies that implement this strategy in a vision system become important. The influencing factors on the design of the control strategy are the goal of the vision system, the scene complexity and the dimensionality of the objects in the scene. Typical goals of a vision system are locating obstacles in a scene for mobile robot navigation, enabling manipulation with robot hands or identifying objects by matching recovered shape descriptions to a given data base. The complexity problem is to find out whether the scene contains a single convex object, a non-convex object consisting of parts, or more than one object. Scene classification according to its complexity can greatly simplify the control structure for interpretation. Establishing dimensionality is to find out if a scene can be interpreted only in terms of volumetric models, flat-like models or rod-like models. Global measures such as center of gravity and moments of inertia give such estimates. The importance of dimensionality parameters is that, depending on the dimensionality, different geometric primitives come into play. For example, in the case of a scene with flat-like objects only, surface primitives should be sufficient and no volumetric primitives would be required. A segmentation system for intensity images that uses such adaptable parameters, provided by the user and computed from the image data, is described in Anderson et al [ABM88].

Depending on all those influencing factors, different geometric parameters can be used for shape discrimination to recover volumetric, surface or boundary properties. One of the hardest problem that the computer vision community has tried to solve during the last 20 years is the extraction of geometric shape properties. The rest of the paper is organized as follows: problems and issues in selecting the type of shape primitives are in section 4.2, section 4.3 is on segmentation, and section 4.4 on the overall control structure. In section 4.5 we compare the actual occluding boundaries of objects in range images to the boundaries of volumetric models fitted to the data to point out the different scope of those models. Section 4.6 is a summary.

4.2   The Role of Shape Primitives

Decomposition into parts, units or primitives is the basis of scientific methodology. Because of the limits on how much information we can process at a time, we have to simplify and view the world at various levels of abstraction. In shape decomposition, one tries to follow the principle of orderliness, which means partitioning things in the simplest possible way. Such partitioning normally reflects the structure of the physical world quite well due to the principle of parsimony [Arn74]. The choice of primitives can be guided by some general requirements such as a unique decomposition into primitives, that the primitives cannot be further decomposed or that the set of primitives is complete. Some of the shape representation criteria are designed primarily to facilitate object recognition when models recovered from images are matched to a model data base. For a discussion of different criteria for shape representation we refer the reader to [Bra83]. Unfortunately, all those principles have not been applied to any general shape representation scheme for 3-D objects. A review of computer vision literature which reveals the large variety of geometrical primitives that were investigated for their applicability to shape representation is a testimony to the difficulty of shape description [BJ85b]. Another discipline involved in representing shape is computer graphics, but from a synthesis (generating) point of view. Some commonly used 3-D representations in graphics are wire-frame representation, constructive solid geometry representation, spatial-occupancy representation, voxel representation, octree representation, and different surface patch representations. Splines are used for surface boundary representation.

In early days of computer vision, most shape primitives were borrowed from computer graphics. But requirements for shape primitives in computer vision are different from the ones for computer graphics. Foremost, shape primitives for computer vision must enable the analysis (decomposition) of shape. Common shape primitives for volume representation are polyhedra, spheres, generalized cylinders, and parametric representations such as superquadrics. Different orders of surface patches (planar, quadratic, cubic) are used for surface representation. For boundary description one can use linear, circular or other second order models for piecewise approximation, and higher order spline descriptions. In the rest of this section we will discuss what influences the selection of shape primitives in computer vision.

If only one shape primitive is chosen, the segmentation process is relatively simple. But the resulting segmentation may not be natural! The data can be artificially chopped into pieces to match the primitives. An example of such unnatural decomposition is when a circle is represented piecewise with straight lines or when a straight line is represented with circular segments. If the scene consists of both straight lines and circles, then neither straight lines nor circles alone would enable a natural segmentation. A natural segmentation, on the other hand, would partition an image into entities that correspond to physically distinct parts in the real world. A solution to such problems is to use more primitives. How many primitives are required for segmentation of more complicated, natural scenes is then the crucial question. The larger the number of primitives, the more natural and accurate shape description and segmentation is possible. But the larger the number of primitives, the more complicated gets the segmentation process. Finding the right primitive to match to the right part of the scene leads potentially to a combinatorial explosion. This argues for limiting the number of different shape models.

Another influencing factor on the number of different models is the level or granularity of models. A large number of low level models is required for scene description because of their small size or granularity. Low level models can fit to a large variety of data sets but bring little prior information to the problem. Hager [Hag88] calls low level models descriptive as opposed to prescriptive and are as such used mostly in data-driven vision systems. Substantial manipulation is required to obtain further interpretation of the data by aggregating low level models into models of larger granularity

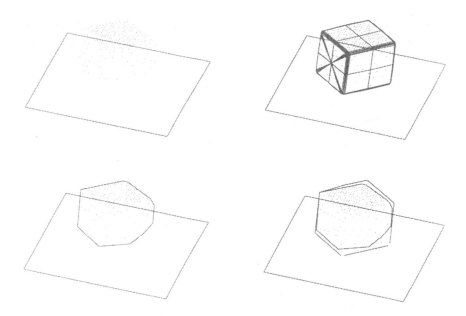

FIGURE 4.1. Top left is a laser range image of a cube. Top right is a superquadric volumetric model recovered by least-squares fitting of a parametric function to the 3-D points. This model gives probably the best overall explanation of the imaged object, an explanation, that most human observers would likcly agree with. A closer examination by following the occluding contour reveals, however, that some points are missing from the lower right corner of the cube. Bottom left is a line approximation that closely follows the local shape of the occluding boundary. From this edge model alone is quite difficult to conclude that the object is roughly shaped as a cube. This difficulty is due to the fairly low level of line models which bring very little prior information to the interpretation problem. Volumetric models, on the other hand, are of larger granularity. By bringing additional information in form of internal parametrization such volumetric models constrain the recovery problem and find a plausible solution.

which correspond to real world entities. Such aggregation techniques often fail because it is not possible to distinguish data from noise or account for missing data only on the basis of local information. Higher level models, on the other hand, are prescriptive in the sense that they bring in more constraints and provide more data compression. But higher level models might miss some important features because they cannot encompass those data variations within their parametrization. A concise model which adequately describes the data will enable partitioning or segmentation of images into right parts and ignore noise and details beyond the scope of the task.

In everyday life, people use most of the time a default level of representation, called basic categories [Ros78]. Basic categories seem to follow natural breaks in the structure of the world which is determined by part configuration [TH84]. Shape representation on the part level is then very suitable for reasoning about the objects and their relations in a scene. For part level description in vision, a vocabulary of a limited number of qualitatively different shape primitives [Bie85] and different parametric shape models have been proposed. Parametric models describe the differences between parts by changing the internal model parameters. In computer vision, the most well known parametric models suitable for representing parts are generalized cylinders but superquadrics with global deformations seem to have some important advantages when it comes to model recovery [BS87,Pen86]. This is discussed later in this section.

It is sometimes possible to know a priori that a certain class of geometric models is sufficient to describe observed data. Another possibility is to somehow evaluate the complexity of the scene and the dimensionality of the objects in the scene. Knowing the complexity of the scene can greatly simplify the control structure for segmentation and shape recovery while knowing the dimensionality of objects simplifies the selection of shape models.

The objective of a vision system, whether the goal is to avoid obstacles during navigation, to manipulate objects with robotic grippers and hands or to identify objects by matching them to a data base, is another constraint during shape model selection. For object avoidance, only representation of occupied space is necessary, often allowing to largely overestimate the size of obstacles. In addition to location and orientation, grasp planning for robotic hands requires knowing more precisely the size and overall global shape of the object. For object recognition, more specific, identifying features are needed. Different shape primitives are better at representing different aspects of shape and at different scales. Volumetric representation provides information on integral properties, such as overall shape, enabling classification into elongated, flat, round, tapered, bent, and twisted primitives. They can best capture the overall size and volume since they must make an implicit assumption about the shape of the object hidden by self occlusion. Surface representation is better at describing details that pertain to individual surfaces which can be part of larger volumetric primitives. Surface primitives can differentiate planar surfaces versus curved surfaces, concave versus convex, and smooth versus undulated surfaces. Boundary representation lies, in scope, somewhere between volumetric and surface representation. On one hand, it is a local representation of curvature and surface near the boundaries, on the other hand, by delineating the boundaries of an object from the background, it defines the whole object.

Coming back to the problem of segmentation, which is to match the right kind of shape model with the right parts of data in an image, brings up the question of facilitating this matching process. Instead of a combinatorial search, one should find a way of determining from the data, which models to use where. A possible way to cut the search is by using a coarse to fine strategy. To find such a shortcut leads back to the question in the title of this paper is segmentation separable from shape representation? By now it should be clear that the segmentation process and its results depend on the selected shape primitives. To facilitate segmentation we believe that for a general purpose vision system one needs volumetric, surface and boundary shape primitives.

We now outline the criteria for selection of shape primitives, in particular the superquadrics family of shapes as volumetric primitive. As mentioned before, complexity and dimensionality of the scene determine the shape primitives that will adequately describe the scene. The primitives should be able to define local as well as global characteristics of the parts of objects in the scene. In a general scene objects can have parts and parts themselves consist of parts. In this paper we are addressing the issue of segmenting parts of an object in the scene. The problem of segmenting individual objects in a complex scene can be handled as an extension of current approach. The object shape can be described at three levels of complexity, each contributing to the overall shape :

1. Description in three dimensions using superquadrics shape primitive.

2. Description in two dimensions using surface primitives.

3. Description in one dimension using contour primitive.

Low level models like contours and edges have low granularity (see figure 4.1) and are too local to capture or make use of the gross structure of the world. They are sensitive to local changes and difficult to put together in a global context. However, this characteristic allows them to capture local details of shape that would be missed or smoothed out by more global primitives. When analyzed as a whole, contour primitives have the remarkable capability of describing global shape and segmenting an object into parts, as demonstrated in [HR85].

The next level of shape description is achieved by describing local and overall surface characteristics. Binford [Bin82] has argued that parts should be defined by continuity. Human perception defines objects as collection of surfaces and does not necessarily segment objects at surface discontinuities. Nonetheless, surfaces play important role in human perception of shape. A lot of effort in computer vision has been spent on describing complex surfaces as piecewise continuous patches. In order to arrive at a global interpretation, a surface representation scheme that combines relevant surface characteristics (e.g. lines of curvature) with the surface patches is needed. This would enable us to describe object shape at a higher level (e.g, The surface has 3 pleats) than that described by individual patches.

Parametric models like generalized cylinders and their derivatives have been used as volumetric primitives by vision researchers because they give compact overconstrained estimate of overall shape. This overconstraint comes from using models defined by a few parameters to describe a large set of 3-D points. Researchers have developed rule-based systems to recover generalized cylinders from image data. In such systems monitoring of progress is difficult and a direct evaluation criteria of results is not available. Also, they can recover only a restricted subset of generalized cylinders, such as linear straight homogeneous generalized cylinders [NB77]. Superquadric models use least squares minimization for recovery of their parameters. An important advantage for ease of model recovery is that the superquadric surface is defined by an analytic function, differentiable everywhere. Superquadric shapes form a subclass of shapes describable by generalized cylinders. Shape deformations like bending and tapering can be defined with global parametric deformations. Superquadrics with parametric deformations encompass a large variety of natural shapes yet are simple enough to be solved for their parameters. Due to their built-in symmetry, superquadric models predict the shape of occluded parts conforming with the principle of parsimony - among several hypotheses select the simplest [Gom62].

If one accepts the need for multiple representations, one has to have a control strategy to bring all of them together. But first, one has to decide what is needed for segmentation.

4.3   Segmentation Process

There are two basic strategies for segmentation:

1. Proceed from coarse to fine discrimination by partitioning larger entities into smaller.

2. Start with local models and aggregate them into larger ones.

Both of these strategies have been used in the past [DH73,Pav77]. The advantage of the coarse to fine strategy is that one gets first a quick estimate about the volume/boundary/surface of the object which can be further refined under control of some higher level process which determines how much details on wishes to know. The disadvantage of this approach is that the amount of detectable detail is not always sufficient without switching to a different kind of representation. For example, to describe smaller shape details one might have to go from volumetric to surface representation. This progression of looking at data at different scales is more formalized in scale-space [Wit84] and in different multiresolution signal decomposition techniques [Mal88]. The important idea that these methods convey is that progressive blurring of images clarifies their deep structure [KvD79]. Large scale structure constrains the structure at finer levels so that adding details only entails adding information and does not require changing the larger structure. Although these multiresolution techniques do not correspond to structural decomposition of images into parts, one assumes that the same principle applies there, also. When a part model must be subdivided into smaller parts to gain finer resolution it should not affect the original partitioning. In that sense, backtracking to change prior decisions would not be necessary.

The second strategy, which goes from local to global, starts with local features and incrementally builds larger representations. This can be an advantage or disadvantage at the same time. Some details could help the classification process early on by excluding any hypothesis that clearly does not include such particular details. On the other hand, keeping track of too many details at once can lead to a combinatorial explosion. As already mentioned, aggregation of low level models into models of larger granularity is difficult in presence of noise or when data is missing. It is also necessary to ignore details that cannot be represented in the next higher level of representation. Recovering from mistakes or erroneous aggregations by rearranging the low level models in new ways should be possible.

Both methods of segmentation, top-down and bottom-up have their benefits and problems. Both methods should be used in a general vision system and the question is how to combine them in a fruitful way. Another possible way of dividing segmentation methods is by the type of shape primitives they use. The following three subsections are on segmentation using volumetric, boundary, and surface representation.

4.3.1 SEGMENTATION USING VOLUMETRIC REPRESENTATION

Although many different methods for partitioning into volumetric primitives exist, we shall focus only on two examples that typify such use of volumetric primitives. The first one is the work by Binford and Nevatia [NB77] who used generalized cylinders for describing parts of objects. They start from local edge models, cross sections and aggregate them into parts, each of them represented with a generalized cylinder. Many improvements of this basic method exist, both by the original authors and others ACRONYM being probably the most well known system [Bro83]. This is an example of a strategy going from local to global aggregates.

An example of the global to local method of segmentation is the superquadric fitting method by Solina [Sol87]. Here the goal is to decompose objects or scenes into parts which can be represented with a single superquadric model enhanced with global deformations such as tapering and bending. Since a superquadric surface can be described with an analytic function, an iterative least-squares minimization of a fitting function can be used for shape recovery. Consider a depth map of an arbitrary scene. The initial model is an ellipsoid in the right position, orientation and of the right size to cover all of the 3-D points. During the least-squares minimization, the shape of the initial model starts to change so that the given range points would lie on or close to the surface of the model. If the model can reject and accept 3-D points, the model can actively search for a better fit, resulting in a recursive subdivision of the scene into parts. The simplest case is when only a single part is present in the scene. Then the model must incorporate all of the points. When several parts or objects made up of multiple parts are present, a suitable distance measure must be used to decide which 3-D points should be included in a particular volumetric model and which points should be excluded. This question has not yet been successfully solved. The same problem of sensitivity and robustness, however, is present in the aggregation method where the setting of the similarity parameters for joining features into larger entities must be robust enough to bridge small gaps in measurements due to noise and imperfect fit, yet sensitive enough to distinguish between different parts.

Given some complexity measures for the scene, the segmentation process can be changed accordingly. In the one-object scenario one can first fit a volumetric model and then analyze how well the model fits the data and adjust the shape and deformation parameters for a better fit. If several objects are present, one should apply segmentation to each cluster individually. In the difficult case, when a heap of objects is given with multiple occlusions, one might concentrate only on the top most object and treat it in the same way as in the one object scenario.

4.3.2   SEGMENTATION USING BOUNDARY INFORMATION

The segmentation process using boundary information is based on the detection of discontinuities both in depth values as well as in orientation. Given discontinuities in depth and orientation, similar adjoining segments can be merged and curve fitting, using splines or some other piecewise model can be performed. Partitioning that corresponds to the human notion of parts can be achieved using changes in curvature of the occluding boundary to detect concavities which indicate part boundaries [HR85]. Occluding contours play a large role in human perception. Strong spatial impressions arise from seeing only silhouettes of objects in a general orientation. Koenderink relates this to the capability of inferring from occluding boundaries the shape of the near lying surface [Koe84]. Ramachandran [Ram88] shows how boundaries influence also the interpretation of shaded surfaces. When information from shading underdetermines the interpretation, information from borders helps to resolve ambiguity throughout the image.

4.3.3   SEGMENTATION USING SURFACE PRIMITIVES

A large portion of computer vision literature is on different methods for surface reconstruction. A recent overview of different surface reconstruction approaches can be found in [BZ87a]. The reason for the widespread interest in surface reconstruction is that this fits well into the prevalent bottom-up approach in vision and that surface is a much more tangible property than volume. Surface segmentation can be based either on merging similar local surface models, or by defining region boundaries in terms of differential geometry [BJ86]. The aggregation process begins with small local neighborhoods which are then combined if they are similar in depth values, surface normal values or some curvature measurements. The result is a scene segmented into surface regions with similar surface characteristics. The difficulty with both surface segmentation approaches is that it is sensitive to local variations which are not important but are difficult to eliminate unless the larger context is taken into account. Since this larger context can be much easier accounted for by volumetric models, it should be here where the surface, volume and boundary segmentation could cooperate. We have implemented such segmentation process in Gupta [Gup88].

4.4 Control Structure

The problem that we wish to address in this section can be stated in the following way. Given that we have all three different modules for extracting volume, surface and boundary properties, how should they be invoked, evaluated and integrated? There are two extreme possibilities. The first one is to apply all three modules simultaneously. The second is to apply them strictly in a predetermined sequence. In the parallel approach conflicting hypothesis can arise that would have to be resolved. The sequential method may lead the segmentation process in a wrong direction so that backtracking would sometimes be necessary. A combined approach where all three methods could interact would not be so vulnerable. This opens up the problem of evaluating and comparing information embedded in models built by different aggregation methods. What do you do if different types of models do not mutually reinforce each other? In such cases, one would normally prefer models of smaller granularity that are less prescriptive models that closely follow the data in the image . But this has to be distinguished from the case when the information that could give rise to low level models is not present. A good example are the well known phenomena of illusory contours in human perception. We can perceive solid shapes although a large part of boundary lines physically do not exist. In conflicting situations information has to be reorganized and the control system adapted. Anderson et al [ABM88] designed an adaptive system for 2-D segmentation of intensity images based on on the general assumption that the gradient value at region borders exceeds the gradient within regions. An adaptive control system that has to reconcile conflicting shape models might use also some result from the recent study of active reduction of uncertainty in multi-sensory systems [Hag88].

To incorporate the best of the coarse to fine and fine to coarse segmentation strategy we propose to perform volume and boundary fitting in parallel, followed by surface description. The volumetric shape recovery that we have in mind is a global, holistic method going from very coarse to fine fitting on the part level while boundary detection and description which is local by the nature of the data can guide segmentation. These two processes are complementary in the approach of explaining the data, accounting for global position, orientation, size and shape such that the local boundary confirms with the boundary obtained from the volumetric fitting. Surface modeling is necessary for representing details that cannot be encompassed by part-level volumetric models. Surface fitting can be used also to reaffirm segmentation into parts by testing the surface continuity or discontinuity between parts.

The control structure has to determine the reliability of information obtained from each primitive. Superquadrics being part-models, need to be compared with the bounding contour and available surface points to evaluate suitability of the recovered model. Surfaces, for most part, complement the information provided by bounding contours. Bounding contours are viewpoint dependent and may not account for all relevant contours needed for complete segmentation or description. This is obviously the case when viewpoint is not general. Thus, in some cases, surface information along with bounding contour can determine if the object is in most general position or not and ask for information from different viewpoint (or rotate the object). For some objects, it may not possible to obtain data from a viewpoint such that the object can be segmented by analyzing only the contour. In such a case, if surface information strongly suggests segmentation along a surface discontinuity, bounding contour should not lower our confidence in surface information. On the other hand, if contour suggests a possible segmentation and there is no support from surfaces, a decision will have to be made about the possibility of segmentation assuming a smooth join between part and object body.

Superquadrics essentially provide global description of individual parts and give the feedback as to the possibility of further segmentation of that part. They lack the local information needed to suggest possible segmentation sites. Contour and Surfaces, on the other hand, actively hypothesize and carry out segmentation. The process continues until a satisfactory description of parts is achieved.

During the segmentation process the control module has also to decide on part/whole (or part/detail) relationships. This requires determining the scale of a potential part given the overall size of the object and deciding to consider it a part or just a detail of the object that can be ignored (implying that current description is adequate).

The global control program must have many parameters and thresholds that would have to be predetermined or, if possible, adjusted during the process. Some of those parameters are the following:

- the size (or range of sizes) of the local neighborhood for local processing,

- the size (or range of sizes) of volumetric models,

- the number (or range) of expected segmented units,

- all the thresholds (for partitioning and aggregation),

- the level of details that we wish to explain.

4.5   Results

We applied the volumetric shape recovery procedure [Sol87] to a set of range images of single objects (Figures 4.2, 4.3 and 4.4). The contour obtained by tracking the occluding boundary and the contour of the recovered volumetric model are compared in all cases. While the volumetric model gives a holistic explanation of the whole object it can miss details that are beyond the scope of the model. An overall measure of goodness of fit, like the residual from least-squares fit [Sol87], does not always give an accurate evaluation of the appropriateness of the volumetric model. Although models can have about the same overall goodness of fit, like the volumetric models in Figures 4.2 and 4.3, they can be more or less acceptable representations of the actual object. Comparing the local boundary of range points with the boundary of the recovered volumetric model can point out the aberrations of the volumetric model and suggest improvements in segmentation or refinement in shape representation. When boundaries do not coincide, preference should be given to actual boundary in the range image, but the possibility of missing data (i.e. occlusion) must be considered also. For example, the actual occluding boundary in Figure 4.2 is without doubt a better representation of the object while the actual boundary shown in Figure 4.1 probably differs from the boundary of the volumetric model because of missing range data.

4.6   Summary

In this paper we discuss some general issues concerning shape representation and segmentation in computer vision. The selection of shape models should be guided by the task of the vision system, the complexity of the scene and the dimensionality of objects in the scene. We argue that shape representation and segmentation should not be approached separately. By picking a particular shape model we restrict the possible ways of partitioning or segmenting an image. Volumetric, boundary and surface models

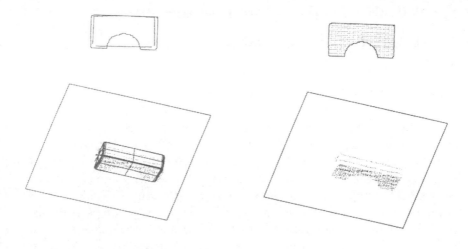

FIGURE 4.2. Range image of a block with a circular cutout. Top left is the original range image. Top right is the best fitting volumetric model. Bottom left is a the line-approximation of the occluding contour as seen from top. Bottom right is the comparison of the occluding boundary with the boundaries of the volumetric model from above. The circular cutout was not accounted for by the volumetric model.

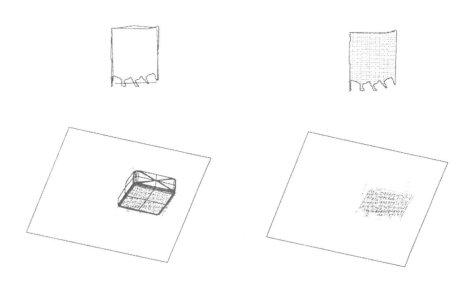

FIGURE 4.3. Range image of a block with a jagged edge. Top left is the original range image. Top right is the best fitting volumetric model. Bottom left is the line-approximation of the occluding contour as seen from top. Bottom right is the comparison of the occluding boundary with the boundaries of the top volumetric model. Since the differences between the two outlines are small in comparison with the overall size of the object the jagged edge could be brushed away as a detail.

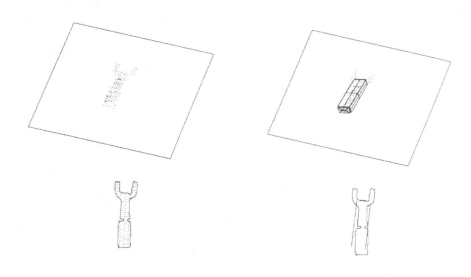

FIGURE 4.4. Top left is the original range image of a wrench. Top right is the best fitting volumetric model. Bottom left is the line-approximation of the occluding contour as seen from top. Bottom right is the comparison of the occluding boundary with the boundaries of the top volumetric model. The two boundaries coincide only in part of the image alerting to the fact that the object consists of more than one part.

represent different types of features and at a different scale. In a general vision system, all three types of shape models should be used. We propose a control structure for such a general system which follows a coarse to fine strategy. It starts with recovery of volumetric models, constrained by occluding contours for segmentation. In order to describe finer details that cannot be encompassed with volumetric models, one has to switch to surface representation. We show some examples of how comparing the occluding boundaries can guide or correct the recovery of volumetric models. In the discussion of control structure, we stress the importance of checking not only the global goodness of fit of the applied shape models but also the local alignment in order to correct or refine the representation. The control system should also adapt to different task requirements and complexities of the scene.

5

Object Recognition

George Stockman[1]

5.1 Introduction

Humans recognize many objects effortlessly. A chair is easily recognized by us; so is a screwdriver. Biederman roughly estimates that a six-year-old can recognize 30,000 distinguishable objects at a time when his vocabulary is roughly 10,000 words [Bie87]. In order to construct flexible robots for industry, navigation, and the home, computer vision must provide the capability of recognizing many of these objects. Objects need to be recognized for inspection, for grasping and manipulation, including assembly, or, in order to attack them or plan path around them. However, current vision systems don't come close to the recognition ability of a six-year old.

Recognition of objects implies the activation of other processes. First of all, there must be an access to memory where a representation of the object is stored. Appropriate representations or *models* are important items of research in computer vision. Secondly, there must be a *matching* process where observations are collected, normalized, and matched to the memory representations to effect recognition. In computer implementations, models are usually represented as *data structures* while matching processes map into *algorithms*, or *control structures*. The purpose of this chapter is to investigate some of the representation and matching techniques.

There are several recognition systems which have been successful on a limited object domain [BH86,GLP84] and some of their principles will be reviewed in this chapter. For example, it is generally agreed that polyhedral objects can be recognized, even when there is occlusion due to multiple objects. However, the issue fast becomes cloudy when more generality is needed. What class of objects should computer vision next attack? Is it possible to employ a single modeling scheme and a single matching strategy to recognize a rich class of objects? What is the suitable object representation and what is the successful matching strategy? Given that a large number of object types must be recognized, can the system automatically learn the object representations?

---

[1]Computer Science Department Michigan State University East Lansing, MI 48824. This work was supported in part by NSF Grants DCR-8600371 and IRI-8743697 to Michigan State University.

At the outset, there are some philosophical issues which are not often broached in the computer vision literature, but which should be brought up here in order to provide a better backdrop for the approaches treated. First of all, it is not always obvious what an *object* is! Clearly, a screwdriver or a chair is an object. But what about a swamp, a fence, a vehicle? After considering these, the reader might want to reconsider the obvious chair object–the reader is challenged to construct a model of a chair. The reader is also invited to read Dreyfus' discussion on chairs where some sticky problems are discussed [Dre85, pp183-184]. Even if we could define *chair* in terms of static visible properties, accounting for most of the real world variations that are possible would be very difficult. Recognition of objects that have single rigid iconic models, such as a 12 oz soda can, might be relatively easy, but we are going to have much more difficulty with object types which permit varying shape, or are defined in terms of some composition of parts. A second difficult issue is underscored by Dreyfus' statement that What makes an object a *chair* is its function. (See also Gibson's *ecology theory* [Gib79].) Determination of the function of an object must call into play a great deal of other memory structure and perhaps common sense reasoning to operate on the properties observed in an image of the object. Thus, for example, a can or a hand or a cap may in fact function as a cup! Surely Winston's arches [Win84] should be recognized as much by their function as by the relationships of their parts.

There are several points to be made from the previous discussion. First of all, it will be difficult to get a general modeling scheme which goes significantly beyond the set of objects for which a rigid prototype is available. Secondly, object recognition in natural environments, as opposed to man-made environments, will be a more difficult problem–partly for reasons related to the first point. Finally, recognition of some objects may require inference about the function of the object, which implies arbitrary consideration of how the object relates to its context in the scene and the general culture–recognition in this case goes beyond use of visible properties and may require common sense reasoning processes, which seem to be the most difficult processes to automate.

Having given the above caveats we focus the discussion on the current accomplishments and goals of research work in object recognition. In such a broad field, only certain aspects can be emphasized. Attention will be focused on man-made objects, rigid parts, and geometrical features. Human vision is based upon a complex interaction of perceptual processing of intensity, color, depth, motion, and shape [LH87,Liv88]. Here we will only consider the use of intensity, depth, and shape. Availability of range (depth) data will be assumed. Section 5.2 discusses the various aspects of the recognition problem and gives some of the choices that must be made in attacking it, while Section 5.3 introduces the properties of object models treated in the remainder of the chapter. Three different paradigms for object representation and recognition are given in Sections 5.4, 5.5 and 5.6.

A summary and assessment is given in the final Section 5.7. This chapter is not meant to be a comprehensive review of published work , but instead tries to provide motivation and general lines of approach. For more detailed review of recent work in this area, primarily from the engineering viewpoint, the reader can consult the fine surveys by Besl and Jain [BJ85b] and Chin and Dyer [CD86] and the collection of papers in Fischler and Firschein [FF87].

5.2   Aspects of the Object Recognition Problem

In this section we identify the various constraints and choices that define particular object recognition problems. There are many dimensions along which one can classify or constrain an object recognition problem: some of these are as follows.

- **Is the interest engineering or cognitive science?** In case we want to engineer a solution to an immediate practical problem, our problem may be specific enough to be simple [BH86,GLP84,Ike87]. For example, we may have to grab a steel cylinder from a jumble of many of them. On the other hand, our interest may be in understanding human object recognition. This implies development of a very general theory which is consistent with multifarious psychological data–a difficult problem [BS87,Bie87,Gib79,Pen87]. In this book, a chapter by Corby and Mundy emphasizes engineering approaches to industrial problems, for example the inspection of the tubing of a refrigerator, while another chapter by Bajcsy et al takes a more general view toward the difficult problem of segmenting scenes containing general objects.

- **Natural or manufactured objects?** Manufactured objects are usually more regular than natural ones. Moreover, there are rigid iconic prototypes for many man-made objects, making several known matching paradigms applicable. Natural objects are created by processes (geological, biological, etc.) which produce a great deal of variety which is hard to model. Moreover, the context of natural objects may be less constrained and predictable than the context in which manufactured objects are found. Thus the problem of object recognition for autonomous navigation seems to be much more difficult than that for factory automation. Another chapter by Herbert et al addresses the problems of navigation in natural environments.

- **Rigid or nonrigid objects?** Most machine vision work has been done using rigid objects (e.g. cups) rather than non-rigid objects (e.g. cats). Data sensed from a rigid object can be registered to a stored prototype using a rotation, scaling, and translation; a common matching paradigm. Nonrigid objects may have to be recognized as an articulated composition of parts, which seems to be a harder problem.

- **Regular or sculpted objects?** Many recognition projects have dealt only with polyhedra, which makes modeling particularly simple. Recently, researchers have turned toward use of quadric surfaces, which it is claimed can model about 85% of manufactured objects. The major convenience is that the modeling and the sensed data are readily put into the same primitives, possibly with some fitting of parameters. It is not clear how best to model sculpted objects even when they are rigid objects. A sculpted object, such as a sports car, turbine blade, or iceberg, may have many different smoothly blending surface features which are not easily segmented into simple primitives. Approximations using polyhedral or quadric models for example are possible, but there may be a loss of efficiency or discriminability due to an unnaturally large number of meaningless primitives being used in the object representation.

- **One object in the scene or many?** Some object recognition schemes assume that objects to be recognized are presented in isolation. This may or may not be possible to engineer in the task domain. Multiple object environments are typically harder because object features will be both masked and intermixed. Global feature methods work well only for single objects. The *segmentation problem* can be acute in multiple object environments.

- **What it the goal of the recognition?** We might need to recognize an object for inspection, grasping, or object avoidance. For inspection, we would look at the small details of at least part of the object –modeling and measurement precision must be good. Grasping an object has different requirements. Not only does the task require some rough geometrical knowledge, but it must also consider balance and strength and accessibility of the object in the workspace. A robot recognizing that an object in its path must be avoided must only have a rough idea of the size, shape, and location of that object [Gen79].

- **2D or 3D sensed data?** Humans can operate quite well with the image from only one eye. Several researchers have designed systems that use only 2D intensity images as input [Goa83,HU87,SE85]. 2D features from the object image are related to a 3D model via the view transformation; usually the matching process has to discover this transformation as well as the object identity. Matching should be easier if 3D (or 2 1/2 D) data is directly available and this is the reason why many current researchers are working with range data [BJ85b, BH86,FH83,GLP84]. The belief is that the surface shape of objects and their positions can be directly sensed; this in turn provides a direct index into possible object models and also reduces the amount of ambiguity in computing the registration transformation. In another chapter, Bajcsy et al emphasize that object recognition and scene segmentation is still a difficult problem, even with 3D range data as input.

- **Are models to be learned or preprogrammed?** Object models may contain a large amount of precise data which is very difficult for humans to provide. CAD data is becoming more available and will usually have all the necessary geometric detail. However, some additional organization of that data, such as emphasizing features, is often necessary. Having a system learn object geometry by presenting the object to its sensors is an attractive possibility. Such learning might even occur before a CAD model is available, and, in fact, may be needed to create a CAD model. Work in model-building has been done by several researchers [CA87,HB85,HJ88,FH83] but most research in object recognition up to this point has been done with a set of specific models where the model-building task was not studied.

5.3   Recognition via Matching Sensed Data to Models

Object models provide the memory structure necessary for the process of object recognition. The higher levels of image analysis provide a representation that is suitable for matching to the stored memory structure to effect recognition. Pentland [Pen87] gives two major requirements for such a representation. 1) It must have *descriptive adequacy*. This means that the important structures in the image are represented in a natural way and the insignificant details are suppressed. 2) The representation of image structure must be *stable* with respect to a) **scale** (no change of the representation for small scale changes and a hierarchical change of representation for large scale changes), b) **image noise**, and c) **configuration** (no change in representation with change in viewpoint or object articulation). In studying object modeling, Pentland takes the cognitive viewpoint and is primarily interested in modeling articulated forms, such as bodies, trees, and furniture. Besl and Jain take an engineering viewpoint and discuss requirements of an object recognition system [BJ85b, p82]. Some of their seven requirements overlap those of Pentland; but the following points related to performance are worth adding. An object recognition system 3) should be able to handle a large number of objects in arbitrary locations and positions (*poses*) with significant occlusions; 4) should be quick and accurate; 5) should be able to alter its representations via learning; and 6) should be able to express a degree of confidence in its results.

It is difficult to discuss object modeling schemes without an integrated discussion of the processes that use them in the task of recognition. Therefore, each of three different paradigms for object recognition are treated in the following three sections. Each section contains a discussion of the representation and the matching algorithms for only one paradigm. Considering only the modeling methods, the three paradigms are 1) representation of an object by a set of global features (statistical pattern recognition approach), 2) representation of the object as a rigid set of geometric features (CAD approach), and 3) representation of an object as a set of parts attached and composed in constrained ways (structural pattern recognition or parts theory approach). Table 5.1 highlights these modeling schemes which are discussed in more detail in the next three sections.

TABLE 5.1. Three idealized modeling schemes

	Model	Recognition Scheme
M1	object as a prototype feature vector	SPR: (statistical pattern recognition): classification via nearest neighbor or decision tree rule.
M2	object as geometric aggregate	REG: (matching via registration): match k observed features to k model features; derive registration transformation; verify by mapping other model features to data space.
M3	object as articulated set of primitive parts	RBC: (recognition by components): identify some parts and attachments; index into model memory; verify other parts and compute pose.

5.4   The Statistical Pattern Recognition Approach

In the pattern recognition approach, an object is represented as a list, or vector, of its features. Objects are recognized by comparison of the features of the object instance to those of a prototype. There are several ways to do this, including use of discriminant functions, the k-nearest-neighbor classifier, and decision tree classifier [DH73,Fuk72].

5.4.1   OBJECT AS FEATURE VECTOR

Global features useful for object classification include volume (area), surface area (perimeter), lengths along the principle axes, moments of inertia about those axes, number of holes, number of corners, etc. Thus, an object is represented by a feature vector $\mathbf{x} = (x_1, x_2, ..., x_n)$. Object recognition

	cucumber	tomato	donut
longest axis	150	100	100
height	50	100	50
elongation	3	1	1
volume	280000	500000	200000

FIGURE 5.1. Four features measured for three prototype objects.

is achieved by some decision procedure which decides the class of an object after observing $\mathbf{x}$. The class of the object is c_i where $i \epsilon \{1, ..., m\}$ and m is the number of models. For most 2D objects, such features are readily measured and are effective for recognition, as indicated by the success of the so called SRI vision module. With good range data, perhaps taken from several views, enough features may be available for robust recognition of 3D objects. An example of using this representation for three simple household objects is shown in Figure 5.1, where four measured features are shown for three objects. If feature x_i for object c_j is normally distributed with mean μ_{ij} and standard deviation σ_{ij}, then it is easy to represent objects in the class as a list of the mean feature values along with a list of the standard deviations to be used to interpret how close an unknown feature vector is to the prototype means. Because of self- occlusion, some object features may not be observable, rendering some pattern recognition techniques useless, a one-shot decision procedure weighting all expected object features, for example. However, a decision tree approach which uses only a subset of the features may still be effective. More details of recognition procedures are given in the next section.

Advantages of the feature vector approach are as follows. The representation is extremely compact compared to other methods. There is a large body of techniques for classification and for learning classification procedures from training samples. The disadvantages of this approach are well known. Most features can only be extracted from isolated objects and most are not available from a single view of a 3D object. Also, the representation is insufficient for generation of an iconic object, making it inadequate for thorough matching or for detailed object inspection.

Viewsphere or *property sphere* models are variations which allow the feature vector approach to remain applicable to 3D objects [DH73,KD87, Goa83]. A covering set of viewpoints (perhaps 200 or more) of the prototype object are selected, and a feature vector is computed for the projection onto 2D from each of these views. The features are not invariant 3D features but should be invariant 2D features for each particular viewpoint. When features are extracted from the 2D image of an object, the pattern recognition procedure must now sift through a much larger set of prototypes to recognize not only an object but also a viewpoint. A similar technique was also used in the CONSIGHT system [HRW79] for 3D object recognition. For each stable state of a 3D object resting on the conveyor a 2D prototype silhouette was used: thus, each 3D object resulted in several 2D objects with the same classification label. The number of stable states for most objects is much less than the number of views used in viewsphere models to capture all significant viewpoints of the object.

5.4.2   THE PATTERN RECOGNITION PARADIGM

The previous paragraphs introduced the idea of representing an object by a vector of its observed features $x = (x_1, ..., x_n)$. This idea has been fairly successful for the recognition of 2D objects that do not overlap with other objects. Rather standard software is now available for extracting the connected components (objects) of a binary image and computing the features on-the-fly. In fact, hardware also exists to bring the processing down to only a few TV frame times.

The mechanism of object recognition is to compute an object class label from the feature vector x. This will be easy to do if the feature vectors of exemplars of each object model are separable, i.e. cluster, in the n-dimensional feature space. The concept of *separability* can be studied at a very formal level using probability theory or at an intuitive level using notions of geometry. Using the notion of probability, the ideal case occurs when for any observed feature vector x exactly one object class is likely and all others are unlikely. From the geometrical viewpoint, the ideal case occurs when all the measurement vectors for each object class are close together in n-space and are far away from the measurement vectors from other object classes. It turns out that effective discrimination procedures can be constructed starting from either theoretical standpoint and guided by feature vector samples (training samples) from all of the object classes to be discriminated [DH73,Fuk72]. Moreover, the actual implementation of the decision-making may be the same regardless of theoretical viewpoint.

5.4.3   PIECEWISE LINEAR DECISION SURFACES

Suppose that we take representative sample measurements from object exemplars and study the feature vectors in n-space. Assume the optimistic case where object exemplars cluster in such a way that each cluster can be contained in a convex region defined by a set of h hyperplanes (a convex polyhedra if n=3), and assume that there is no overlap of any pair of convex regions. The decision that a sample feature vector x belongs to a cluster c_j can then be made by checking to see that h dot products are positive (the dot product of x with the coefficients defining each hyperplane) indicating that x is inside of the region for c_j. If x is found in none of the defined regions, it is a *reject* and the system must take some special action. If there are many classes, it may not be efficient to sequentially check to see if x is inside of each defined region. Instead, a hierarchy af regions may be defined so that at the first decision level, an entire set of objects may be ruled out. Piecewise linear decision surfaces are easy to implement and it may be worth searching for appropriate features that will separate the sample data.

5.4.4   K-NEAREST NEIGHBORS

Another popular approach to making classification decisions is the k-nearest neighbor decision procedure. All of the labeled sample feature vectors from all of the object classes are stored in the same memory. A k-d tree [Ben75] is an efficient data structure for such storage. When an unknown feature vector x is to be classified, the k vectors in memory that are nearest it are fetched and their class labels examined. Vector x is classified as from the object class having the majority of the labels among the k neighbors. Although k should be odd, it is possible that x is in an ambiguous region of the feature space and a majority decision does not result: this will require special treatment. The k-nearest neighbor method is straightforward in implementation and is known to approximate optimal statistical decision making [Fuk72, ch4] in the limit as k goes to infinity. Feature vectors from samples of objects as in Figure 5.1 should readily admit to this kind of classification.

5.4.5   PROTOTYPE MATCHING

Suppose that each object class c_j can be represented by some ideal prototype such that all measured features for object exemplars are normally distributed about the prototype features. Thus the entire class c_j can be represented by one feature vector $\mu_j = (\mu_{j1}, \mu_{j2}, ..., \mu_{jn})$. Further, assume that measurements are normalized to have the same variance; that is, unit differences of a measurement from the nominal measurement have the same significance for all measurements. Under this situation, which is fairly representative for a set of manufactured parts, an unknown x can be classified as belonging to class c_j where the Euclidean distance between x and μ_j is the smallest. This scheme should work well for the objects shown in Figure 5.1. The representation is very compact since only one prototype feature vector needs to be saved for each class. Also, the decision computation is simple unless there is a large number of classes. This technique is effectively an optimal statistical technique under the assumption that all features are statistically independent and have a Gaussian distribution with the same variance.

5.4.6   SEQUENTIAL DECISION-MAKING

It is possible to make many classification decisions without using all of the features that can be computed. Not only can some decision-making computations be saved, but a good deal of feature extraction work may also be unnecessary. Formally, we should take enough features, $x_1, ..., x_k = \mathbf{x}^k$ until a classification is highly likely. This will happen when $p(c_j|\mathbf{x}^k) >> p(c_l|\mathbf{x}^k)$ for all $l \neq j$, where $p(c_j|\mathbf{x}^k)$ is the posterior probability of class c_j given the feature vector $\mathbf{x}^k$. At any point in this sequential decision process, three distinct changes to the state are possible; 1) a class decision is made and the process ends, 2) a next feature is chosen depending upon the previous features and the current class possibilities, and 3) the set of possible classes is changed depending on the features and the previous possibilities. A *reject option* is included in the tree to provide for the cases where it is known that the extracted features do not correspond to any of the object classes. A plan for all such decisions is a *decision tree* – Figure 5.2 shows a decision tree for the simple data of Figure 5.1. Decision tree classifiers have been popular because they are efficient on conventional computers and are easy to implement. Although formal methods are available for tree construction which reduce the probability of error, most decision trees are heuristically constructed.

5.5   Object Represented as Geometric Aggregate

Perhaps the most intuitive modeling scheme, at least for rigid objects, is the one used by CAD systems. Objects are modeled by a set of points or other geometric primitives in a common coordinate system. *Wire frame* models are convenient for representing polyhedra because they faithfully represent vertices and edges, which completely characterize the object. *Surface models* directly represent only the surfaces of objects while *volumetric models* represent their volumes. There are many types of surface and volume models. Good descriptions of these may be found in other survey literature [Req80,BJ85b,BH87,CD86], and are not taken up in detail here. It is important to note that a representation from one modeling scheme can usually be converted to another modeling scheme, provided that both schemes are adequate. Often, neither scheme is superior for all demands, and such conversions are necessary. For example, a volumetric model may have to be converted to a surface model for graphical rendering. Most CAD modeling

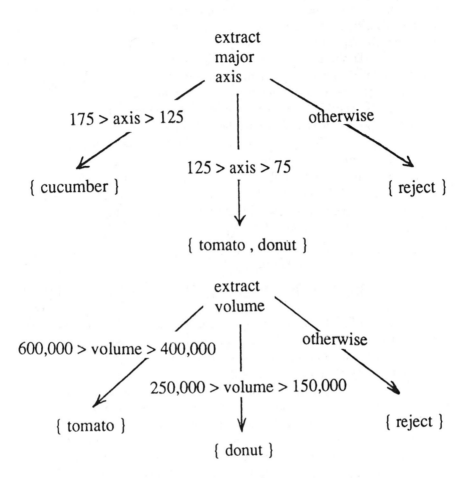

FIGURE 5.2. One possible decision tree for the data of Figure 5.1.

schemes are not immediately useful for general object recognition. CAD models are highly developed due to their widespread use in manufacturing, yet they are undergoing more evolution due to increasing demands on object modeling, such as use in process planning or in object recognition and inspection [BH87].

A general 3D surface can be implicitly defined as a set of points via some function F and some domain for the variables to which it applies. An example of a quadric surface is given in Equations 5.1 and 5.2 ; where the function is specified by 10 parameters, 9 of which are free. 3 of the parameters specify surface shape while the other 6 specify the pose of the surface in 3D space. The quadric surface model can exactly model most of the surfaces of manufactured objects. It was hoped by many researchers that observed data could be fit by the quadric form and that the resulting parameters could be interpreted to deduce the surface shape and index into complete object models (see [HTMS82] for example). This is now known to be a troublesome task [Gol83,FJ88].

$$S \; = \; \{ \, (x,y,z) \; : \; F(x,y,z) \; = \; 0 \, \} \tag{5.1}$$

$$F_{quadric}(x,y,z) = Ax^2 + By^2 + Cz^2 + Gxy + Hyz + Ixz + Ux + Yy + Wz + D \tag{5.2}$$

Besl and Jain [BJ85b, p90] list eight types of surface patch models. These models have been developed for convenience in computer-aided design and not for recognition. The problem is that it is difficult to map back from range or intensity observations through surface patch models to a consistent object or part model. Mathematically defined surface patches may not be the right primitive elements in which to define a recognition process due to the problem of noise, occlusion, and segmentation of observed data. Parametric surface models will continue to be used to precisely define geometric data, but they probably will have to be augmented with other information more useful for recognition as has been done by Bolles and Horaud [BH86]. The CAD industry is developing *feature-based modelers* to be more useful for planning object manufacturing operations, which should also help in automating object recognition [HB85,BH87].

For geometric matching, salient geometric features are especially useful [BAM86] [BH86] [HU87] [LSW88] [SKB82] [Sto87] [VA88]. Salient features are local features which have some contextual information available to restrict the matching possibilities. Such information might be the topology of an intersection [SKB82] or the measure of the dihedral angle of a fold [BH86,HJ87a], for example. Vemuri and Aggarwal have shown that a single special salient feature can be used to compute object pose [VA88]. Table 5.2 lists some of these local feature types. Note that each feature has location information and orientation information to be used for computation of object pose and some contextual information to restrict matching. Low and middle level processing is necessary for extraction of such features as discussed in the other chapters. Combination of such features to deduce a registration transformation is discussed below.

TABLE 5.2. General Primitive Features for Recognition by Registration

Feature	2D	3D	Example of Context
Point(P)	(x,y)	(x,y,z)	"L" intersection
Normal(N)	$(x,y),\vec{N}$	$(x,y,z),\vec{N}$	Concave neighborhood
Edge(E)	$(x1,y1),(x2,y2)$	$(x1,y1,z1),(x2,y2,z2)$	Dihedral angle
Planar patch (S)	-	3 points	Area
Boundary (B)	curve	patch	Saddle
Vector (V)	2 points	2 points	2 point tags

Assuming that the object is rigid and has an iconic model, the object can be taken to be an instance of the model placed in space by a rotation, scaling, and translation (**RST** transformation). Actually, more general transformations can be used, such as one that bends or twists, to register object and model features. But, for this type of modeling scheme we insist that there is only one such transformation that applies globally to all features. Nonrigidity will add difficulties in practice but does not change the paradigm. Only rigid transformations will be treated here, as is common in the literature. Object recognition is achieved by discovering an object model and a transformation that acceptably registers the model features to the observed object features. The notion of *acceptability* must include both the notions of geometric tolerance and the appropriate number of matching features. Where there is occlusion, including self-occlusion, it will not be possible to observe all model features. Also, we usually want to recognize objects that are imperfect, or variants, due to added or deleted features relative to the model. Methods of matching a stored model to observed data under this paradigm are now considered.

5.5.1 The Registration Paradigm

Under the registration paradigm there exists a transformation that maps the geometric features of the model onto the geometric features extracted from the image(s) of the object. If the transformation is rigid, all parts of the object rotate, scale, and translate in the same way. Sensed features will be denoted S_1, S_2, etc. while model features will be denoted M_1, M_2, etc. Often, a combination of features is necessary to completely specify a transformation. For example, if sensed data and model data are both 2-D then 2 pairs of matching points (or one pair of matching abstract edges) are sufficient to specify scaling, rotation, and translation. Essentially, what is desired is enough information to estimate how a model-oriented coordinate

frame is posed in the sensed data. In 3D, assuming no change of scale, such a frame can be established from two pairs of matching straight edge segments which are neither colinear nor parallel. Table 5.3 summarizes some of the possible structure correspondences that yield the specification of a frame. For example, Huttenlocher and Ullman [HU87] have published the computations necessary for registering a 3D model to a 2D image using a set of three corresponding feature points.

TABLE 5.3. Example feature structures for registration

Data Dimension	Sensed Structure	Model Dimension	Reference
2D	2 points (PP)	2D	[SKB82,Sto87]
2D	2 points (PP)	3D	[SE85]
2D	3 points (PPP)	3D	[HU87]
3D	3 points (PPP)	3D	[Cra86, ch2]
3D	3 normals (SSS)	3D	[Che86,GLP84]
3D	2 edges (EE)	3D	[Che86,Sto87]
3D	2 norm., 1 edge (SSE)	3D	[Che86]

The most common case in the recent literature requires the matching of 3D model features to 3D features from range data. Assuming a 3D sensor calibrated such that a scaling of 1.0 can be used, the pose of the model in 3D space can then be conveniently specified by six independent parameters –the rotational parameters of roll, pitch, and yaw, and the translational parameters $\Delta x, \Delta y, \Delta z$. The transformation can also be specified by a 4 x 4 homogeneous matrix of 12 parameters, where ROT is a 3 x 3 rotation matrix and $TRANS$ is a 3 x 1 translation vector.

$$\mathbf{T} = \begin{bmatrix} ROT & TRANS \\ 0 & 1 \end{bmatrix} = \begin{bmatrix} r_{11} & r_{12} & r_{13} & \Delta x \\ r_{21} & r_{22} & r_{23} & \Delta y \\ r_{31} & r_{32} & r_{33} & \Delta z \\ 0 & 0 & 0 & 1 \end{bmatrix} \qquad (5.3)$$

Methods for converting between the three independent rotational parameters and the nine elements of the rotation matrix are given in [Cra86].

Global matching of rigid geometry implies that certain pairwise relations between features are preserved by **T**. For example, if two features are distance d apart in the model then any sensed features matched to them must be a distance d apart as well. Other relations that must be preserved are angular relations, betweenness, and connectivity. Thus if there is a relation R between sensed features S_i and S_j, denoted as $S_i R S_k$, then the relation $M_j R M_l$ must also necessarily hold in the model if these model features are to match the pair of sensed features. Preservation of such relations is a necessary but not sufficient condition for matching via a rigid transform, however, such conditions can often be checked more easily than the stronger one, and this allows for efficient pruning of hypotheses [GLP84].

Given that certain sets of features, or structures, as shown in Table 5.3 have been extracted from the sensed data, and that models represent objects using the same kinds of structures, the task of matching is to put the appropriate sensed and model structures into correspondence and determine the pose transformation in the process. The number of sensed features and model features is almost never the same. Each sensed structure S_i may be paired with none, one, or several of the model structures M_j. Each compatible pairing may produce a candidate pose. In general, we must allow for both false alarms and false dismissals. Extra structure can be expected in the scene due to artifacts or the presence of multiple objects and missing structure is the expected result of occlusion or imperfect feature detection. Missing structures in either sensed data or model are indicated by the symbol **NIL**, following the convention used by Grimson and Lozano-Perez [GLP84]. If a pose candidate T_{ij} is computed from compatible structures S_i *and* M_j , then it will correctly match the *local* geometry of the structures but may not correctly match the global geometry of the entire object. The *hypothesize-and-test* (**H&T**) procedure will attempt to verify a hypothesized transform **T** by transforming other model features and verifying them in the observed data; if enough of them are found near where they are predicted, then **T** is accepted. The pose clustering approach will accept a pose **T** to be correct when there are many other independently derived candidate poses that agree with it. Each structure correctly extracted from the sensed data should provide a vote for the correct pose. A sketch of the pose clustering procedure is given below. This procedure is given first because it is, in fact, easier to describe than the **H&T** procedure, which uses sequential control and several decisions.

5.5.2   POSE CLUSTERING ALGORITHM

It is assumed that features are detected via lower level processing of intensity and/or range imagery and that, where necessary, these features have been combined into structures for matching. This algorithm simply pairs structures of the same type and local geometry and attempts to derive a transformation from each such correspondence. A globally acceptable transformation is detected as a cluster in the space of all such candidate transformations. For purposes of explanation, specialized data structures are not used.

Pose Clustering Procedure

Objective: Find best pose transformation(s)

Data: sensed structures S_i: i=1,n and

model structures M_j: j=1,m

Procedure: PC
    for each pair of match evidence (S_i , M_j) do in parallel
      if S_i and M_j are compatible
        then begin
          attempt to compute pose candidate T_{ij}
          if pose candidate exists then place T_{ij}
             in parameter space
      end
    find clusters in parameter space to get the best pose candidate(s)
    and supporting evidence.

It is important to note that the convention is that tranformation T_{ij} will be applied to the model feature M_j to map it onto the sensed feature S_i. Figure 3 shows three candidate poses computed for a model block matched to 3D features extracted from structured light data. The three pose candidates were computed from the different types of feature matching **EE**, **SSS**, and **SSE** respectively (refer to Table 5.3). Each candidate pose transformation **T** was evaluated by transforming the corners of the model and recording the distances between the object corners and the transformed model corners. Despite the different computational procedures, and the slightly different transformations computed, each pose candidate transformed the model such that the maximum coordinate difference between transformed model corners and the object corners was 5 mm and the average difference was 2 mm. The object diameter is 155 mm and the average error in each of the coordinates of measured points is about 1 mm. The translational parts of the three pose candidates are in agreement relative to the error of the 3D sensor. Methods of clustering are discussed in detail in [Sto87]. An interesting algorithm called *geometric hashing*, which is a distant relative of pose clustering, has been proposed by Lamden et al [LSW88] for registering images of flat objects to 2D models via affine transformation.

5.5.3 SEQUENTIAL HYPOTHESIZE AND TEST

In sequential matching, a sequence of correspondences is constructed by pairing sensed and model features. When a new pairing is made, all constraints in the sensed features are checked against the model. If any constraint fails, the process backs up to attempt a different pairing: if all constraints are satisfied, the new pairing is added to the sequence being developed and yet another pairing is tried. When the sequence of paired features is long enough to allow computation of an accurate registration transformation, the process shifts to the test mode. Model features are transformed into the data space and the data is checked for presence of the appropriate feature. Due to occlusion, the feature may not be present in the scene data, or due to error, the feature may be slightly misaligned with its predicted pose – both of these effects must be taken into consideration by the process which attempts to verify or evaluate the hypothesis at hand.

A classical backtracking algorithm is sketched below. At any time in the process a stack contains a consistent set of pairs (S_1, M_{j1}), (S_2, M_{j2}), ... , (S_i, M_{ji}). The pairs are mutually consistent in the sense that whenever relation $S_i R S_k$ holds in the sensed data then relation $M_{ji} R M_{lk}$ holds in the model. The sequential matching being done will form enough pairs until a registration transform T can be computed. This algorithm is very similar to depth-first search. Revisions which replace the stack by a queue or priority queue attempt to find a global match in less time, usually trading off a good deal of space in exchange. In our discussion all of these variations on sequential search are regarded as fundamentally similar.

Sequential Matching Procedure

Objective: Match each sensed feature to a model
feature such that the interpretation
is compatible with a rigid transformation T .

Data: sensed features and model features

Procedure: H&T
push pair (S_1, M_0) onto the stack

while the stack is not empty do

pop pair (S_i, M_j) off the stack

find the next unassigned model feature M_l
which matches the type of S_i

if M_l has been found

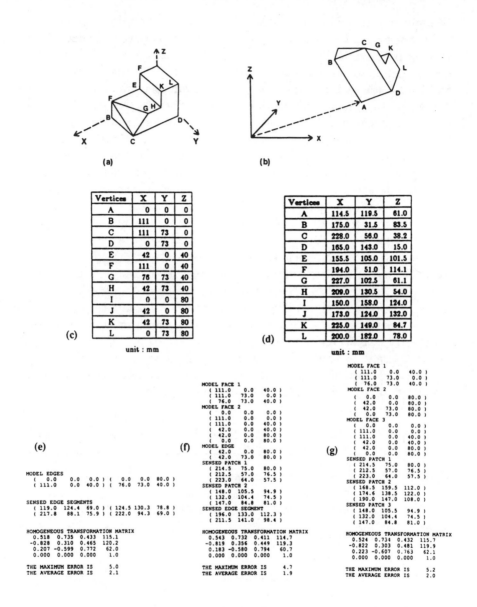

(a) model, (b) object instance, (c) model vertices,
(d) instance vertices, (e) pose from EE-match,
(f) pose from SSE-match, (g) pose from SSS-match .

FIGURE 5.3. Object pose computed from three different structure matches.

then begin

push the pair (S_i, M_l) onto the stack

if CONSISTENT (stack)
  then if enough evidence in the stack,
    then compute **T**
      if VERIFY (**T**) then exit

  else push (S_{i+1}, M_0) onto the stack

end

else failure, back-up implemented at top of while loop

empty stack indicates matching failure; nonempty stack
contains matching evidence.

The predicate CONSISTENT checks to see if all the appropriate relations $M_k \, R \, M_l$ in the model data also hold in the corresponding sensed data. The predicate VERIFY uses **T** and returns TRUE iff **T** adequately registers the remaining model features to sensed data. This type of algorithm has been very popular in recent robot vision work [FH83,BH86,GLP84,BAM86]. There are many ways to incorporate heuristics, for example, by consideration of the features in some special order [FH83,BH86] or by using quick constraint checking [GLP84]. The RANSAC algorithm proposed by Fischler and Bolles [FB81] is a variation of this general procedure. Random samples of matched sensed features and model features are paired to compute a candidate pose **T** which is then immediately evaluated on the rest of the feature evidence. If **T** provides a satisfactory consensus, then the algorithm terminates; otherwise sampling is continued from scratch. Each sampling corresponds to one path of the search tree searched by the **H&T** procedure given above; except that it would be possible to repeat paths using RANSAC if feature samples can be repeated. In the work of Grimson and Lozano-Perez [GLP84], sensed feature to model feature matches are exhaustively considered via an *interpretation tree* which is the explicit search space of the above algorithm. On the basis of (S_i, M_j) symbol pairing alone, **H&T** algorithms appear to be $O(m^n)$; however, using constraints of real objects available to the procedure CONSISTENT(stack), the practical behavior can be much better. Making many general assumptions to more formally define the problem, Grimson has recently shown that if all the sensed data is known to be drawn from one object the complexity of the IT search is only quadratic, but with the object in a cluttered background the search is exponential [Gri88].

5.5.4   COMPARISON OF PC and H&T

Although several projects have successfully used pose clustering [BS81, BM87,SKB82], hypothesize and test has been the most popular paradigm because most computers working at the symbolic level are of the Von Neumann type. Programs are sequential and heuristics are easy to apply. However, an H&T algorithm may not know whether it has derived an optimal answer, and because of the sequential character of the decision-making, the algorithm is inherently limited in speed. For those who adhere to the approach of cognitive science, H&T is an unlikely model for human object recognition. H&T execution time can vary greatly depending upon the order of examining the evidence. Under simplifying assumptions, RANSAC can take between one and 48 units of time to find four correctly matching point pairs given that any pairing has $p = 0.5$ chance of being correct [FB81]. (We would like four point pairs in order to compute a good registration transformation T.) A value of $p = 0.2$ might be more appropriate for a bin picking application, and then the execution time range is from one to 375 units of time. On any type of computer, for a given set of data, the runtime of the PC algorithm will not vary: it can neither benefit nor suffer from reordering features. Both PC and H&T share common problems. The combinatorics of grouping must be addressed. If there are n sensed features and m model features, there are nm pairs and $\binom{nm}{2}$ pairs of pairs, etc. This problem is greatly exacerbated when there is a multiple object scene and mixed sets of sensed features are being matched to model features. If the scene has two objects with 10 features each, the probability of choosing at random three features from a given object is only about 0.1. If three such features are needed to compute pose hypothesis T, then 90 percent of the time the search will go to level 4 or more in the IT. If there are 10 features from a given object mixed with 40 features from other objects, then the probability of getting 5 matching features by level 10 of the IT is less than 0.01. It would be better if most feature pairings never were generated in the first place. Higher level features would allow indexing to avoid the inefficient arbitrary pairings; they would also reduce the size of n and m. One way to do this is to do a better bottom-up job of segmenting the scene into objects and segmenting objects into parts. Also, the features used in Table 5.3, while readily available from polyhedra, may not be available for sculpted or curved objects. The RBC theory covered in the next section addresses this problem by attempting to extract parts from nonaccidental feature relationships.

5.6   Object as an Articulated Set of Parts

Recently, several researchers have argued that humans use models that
are a composition of parts and that the early stages of human vision are
concerned with extraction of such parts from an image [BS87,Bie87,HR85,
Pen87]. Moreover, the parts of the models in memory are 3D primitives,
whereas the parts sensed from the world must be extracted from 2D images.
Bajcsy [BS87] discusses broad philosophical and psychological arguments
for recognition by components (RBC) while Biederman [Bie87] reports on
many experiments with humans which support his RBC theory. Older computer vision work which viewed objects via parts and the relationships of
the parts was done by Barrow and Popplestone [BP71] and Shapiro et al
[SMHM84].

Modeling via parts theory is the most energetic scheme studied here and
research is just beginning to attack the several difficult problems involved
with its implementation. First of all, the concept of *part* is difficult to make
precise. It is generally agreed that the *principle of transversality* applies–a
part can be segmented from an object by following lines of extreme negative
curvature [HR85]. Thus a human head can be segmented from the torso
at the neck, the crown of a tree from its trunk, the leg of a chair from
the chair, the handle of most any object that has one from the rest of the
object, etc. But, the general segmentation problem is not easy because it
is in a sense just the *whole-parts-problem* all over again. The uniform and
simple structure of a part is perhaps just as important in defining it as
is its attachment to the whole – the human head is roughly spherical, the
tree trunk cylindrical, the chimney of a house a prism, etc. Extracting a
part representation from the image of a part in either an intensity image
or range image is a difficult problem, especially in light of the problems of
segmentation and occlusion. Unique segmentations should not be expected:
Pentland [Pen87] points out that a human foot may be represented by an
ellipsoid segmented from the leg at the ankle, but a fitting procedure might
also fit both the foot and ankle as a bent cylinder.

Biederman proposed generalized cylindrical models of parts [Bie87].
Thirty six volume primitives called *geons* (for geometric ions) are defined
in terms of parameters of the cross section, edges, and axis. Examples
are shown in Figure 5.4. A 2-geon lamp and a 3-geon lamp are shown in
Figure 5.5. One of Biederman's strongest arguments is that humans seem
to be able to infer such geons from nonaccidental arrangements of edge
data –range data does not seem to be needed. Biederman has not done
experiments with machine vision implementation of his theory, but work
by computer vision researchers toward computation of such geons from
intensity images has begun [HJ87a,XT87]. Also, there is an interesting point
made by Pentland [Pen87, 4.3], that his fitting method appeared to work
even on range data with so little variation that it was nearly the equivalent
of just silhouette data.

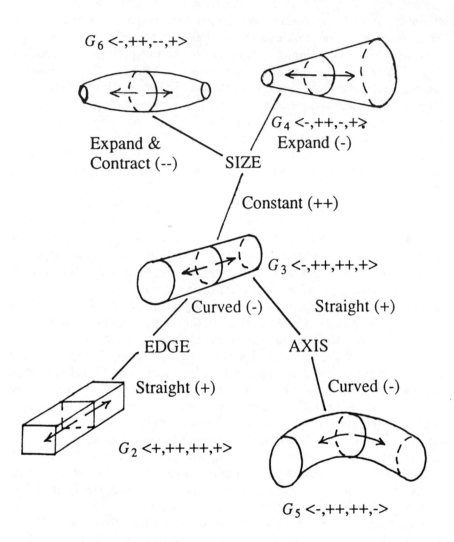

G_6 <-,++,--,+>

Expand &
Contract (--)   SIZE

G_4 <-,++,-,+>
Expand (-)

Constant (++)

G_3 <-,++,++,+>

Curved (-)   Straight (+)

EDGE   AXIS

Straight (+)   Curved (-)

G_2 <+,++,++,+>

G_5 <-,++,++,->

FIGURE 5.4. Five of the 36 geons proposed by Biederman

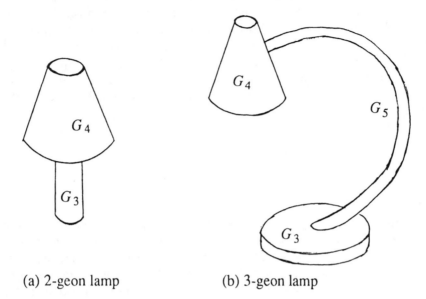

(a) 2-geon lamp   (b) 3-geon lamp

G_4 : <-,++,-,+> lamp shade
G_3 : <-,++,++,+> lamp base
same size G_3 , G_4
top connected
end-to-end
join short side G_4
join short side G_3

(c) symbolic coding for 2-geon lamp

FIGURE 5.5. An example of Biederman's object representation: a) 2-geon lamp, b) 3-geon lamp, c) symbolic coding for 2-geon lamp.

Pentland has recommended the use of *superquadrics* to model object parts. These forms are similar to generalized cylinders as can be seen by comparing Figures 5.4 and 5.6, but they are perhaps more tractable mathematically. They are also a generalization of the primitives used in the constructive solid geometry (CSG) approach to CAD. A point $\mathbf{P} = [x, y, z]^t$ on the surface of a superquadric is defined mathematically in equation 5.4. The variables ν and ω are latitude and longitude with $-\pi/2 \le \nu \le \pi/2$ and $-\pi \le \omega < \pi$, while the parameters α and β control the shape of the surface.

$$\mathbf{P}[\nu, \omega] = \begin{bmatrix} x \\ y \\ z \end{bmatrix} = \begin{bmatrix} C_\nu^\alpha C_\omega^\beta \\ C_\nu^\alpha S_\omega^\beta \\ S_\nu^\alpha \end{bmatrix} \quad where \quad C_\nu = \cos \nu \; ; \; S_\omega = \sin \omega$$

$$(5.4)$$

Pentland's modeling system uses 14 parameters to model an instance of a part. These include the two shape parameters α and β along with others that specify the pose of the part and any distortion. There are three parameters each for position and orientation (pose) and there are three parameters for scale along each axis. Finally there are two parameters for bending along two of the axes and one parameter for tapering along the major axis of the part. Recognition of a part in observed data is achieved by fitting a part model to the data: the results of the fit specify the pose via the 6 pose parameters, and the shape via the 8 other parameters. Several of the shape parameters provide natural modeling for some of the processes that humans often use to describe objects –such as a squashed sphere or bent cylinder.

If the superquadric shape parameters provide a natural method of modeling shape, then they can be used to index a very large data base of models. It has been estimated (see [Bie87] for example) that humans can recognize roughly 30,000 object exemplars from 3000 object types – the object type *lamp* may have 15 or more structurally different *exemplars*, for example. Biederman has shown that 75,000 two-part objects can be constructed using the 36 geons. There are 36 x 36 pairs of geons, 3 size relations $(G1 > G2, G1 < G2, G1 = G2)$, and another factor of about 20 for the combinations of attaching G1 to G2. A symbolic encoding for the 2-geon lamp shown in Figure 5.5a is given in Figure 5.5c. Similar rough combinatorics reveals a possible 150 million 3-geon objects. Thus, in terms of the variety of objects modeled and the effort involved in accessing object descriptions stored in memory, Biederman's RBC theory seems to be adequate. Along with this combinatoric evidence for adequacy, Biederman has support from experimenting with human subjects for a *3-geon rule* that states that memory access and object recognition is based on only 3-geons. Consideration of more geons and geon surface texture requires more time from the human visual system [Bie87,Liv88]. For manufacturing tasks, such

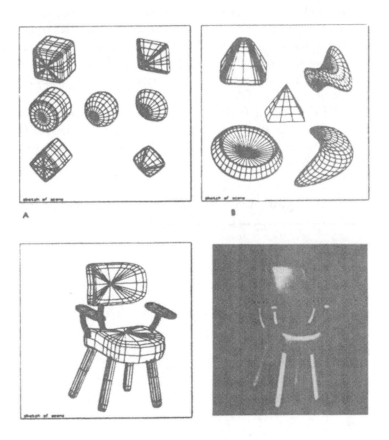

FIGURE 5.6. Pentland's superquadric primitives (a),(b) and composite chair (c) (From "Recognition by Parts," by A. Pentland, *Proc. ICCV-87*, 1987, pp. 612-620. Used with permission.)

as tolerance checking, more detailed geometric information would have to be added to such models – not an easy task.

In addition to the advantages already cited, RBC models provide for the modeling of the backsides of objects and easily allow 3D rotation, and hence are at a higher level than surface models. The 14 parameters used by Pentland compares well to the 10 needed for a quadric surface patch and the 5 to 10 used for curvature-based classifications at each object surface point. On the negative side, the fitting procedure will be fairly demanding and there are tough decisions to be made concerning attachments of parts, with lots of ambiguity possible.

Although RBC theory is fairly comprehensive implementations are still in progress. Because the level of abstraction is greater than that of the prior two paradigms, the RBC paradigm will not be discussed at the implementation level. A high level description is given below.

Recognize Object in Scene using RBC

Extraction of Parts
        edge extraction
        detection of nonaccidental properties
        segmentation of regions at concavities
Determine Attachments of Parts
Encode Parts and Attachments (possibly ambiguously)
Match Scene Representation to Stored Representations
        index memory using only 2 or 3 geons
        detailed verification of response set with
            respect to scene representation

The first step is perhaps the most difficult–extraction of object parts. It is implied that there is a general solution to the image segmentation problem, which does not employ object models. Several general principles are subscribed to by proponents of this theory. Edges are very important along with nonaccidental relationships among edge elements [Bie87,Low85]. Also, part contours are to be segmented at cusps, or regions of extreme negative curvature [Bie87,HR85]. The psychologists promote the sufficiency of edge data for inference of 3D primitives: recent work by computer vision researchers has tried to implement this [HJ87a,XT87].

Pentland finds superquadric parts by RANSAC fitting of range imagery [Pen87]. Range samples are taken and then a superquadric is fit to them by first broadly searching over the parameter space and then making refinements according to goodness of fit criteria. Once the 14 parameters of the shape and its pose are set, range and edge data can be rendered from the model and compared to the sensed data. By histogramming differences between the model and the data, Pentland can obtain a subset of the sensed data that fits the model. The fitting process is then continued on the data which remain. Bajcsy and Solina [BS87] have a different fitting approach. They have assumed that objects are isolated and that the axes of the superquadric forms may be inferred from simple 2D processing.

Not only must parts be identified in the sensed data, but their attachments to each other must also be characterized. Philosophically, it seems that the parts and their attachments must be revealed at the same time [HR85]. Given 3D data, such as used by Pentland and Bajcsy and Solina, the attachments of parts should be available from the adjacencies of the set of parts. An approach using only intensity data has been taken by Ferrie [FL88].

The parts and their attachments can be symbolically encoded, perhaps according to Biederman's scheme, and the symbolic representation used as a key for search into a similarly encoded data base of models. A possible encoding for the 2-geon lamp of Figure 5.5a is given in Figure 5.5c. According to Biederman's thinking, only 2 or 3 geons and their attachments are needed to reference the stored models. File and data base theory provide many alternatives for quick access to models with the same characteristics. A detailed verification of the memory response set to the scene representation and original data is the final step. Such verification may include the matching of finer detail, such as looking at the fine texture of a surface, looking for hair on a head, etc. For some manufacturing tasks, which require more than just object recognition, the coarse models discussed so far would need some detailed refinements and the recognition/inspection procedure would also.

5.7   Concluding Discussion

Object recognition is one of the prime cognitive skills of humans. It is also crucial in many robotics and computer vision applications. Many aspects of the general object recognition problem were discussed in section 5.2. No theory, and hence no working system, has been able to deal with all aspects of the problem. Applications and research projects must make specific limiting assumptions. The problems of factory automation and all terrain robotic vehicles are of primary interest to the authors of this book. While factory automation problems can often assume controlled circumstances, the navigation problem seems to run the gamut of all possibilities. One conclusion of this work is that recognition of natural objects in natural environments is much harder than recognition of manufactured objects in factory environments. Much of the difficulty seems to stem from the availability of adequate models in the latter case and the lack of them in the former case.

Three broadly differing object modeling/recognition paradigms were presented. Each paradigm has assets and liabilities relative to specific applications. In the pattern recognition approach an object is represented by a prototype and the corresponding feature vector of its nominal features. The representation is compact, there are a variety of well-known recognition procedures, and there are viable learning schemes. On the negative side, the representation may not be viable if there are thousands of objects and it is insufficient for tasks such as detailed inspection or grasping because it cannot produce an iconic object model. On the other hand, recognition by registration depends totally on having a geometrically faithful iconic object representation and the ability to compute a transform to register object model to sensed data. This approach is akin to CAD and is the one of choice for rigid manufactured objects. Object models are elaborate. There does not seem to be a single modeling scheme that applies well to all object types – sheet metal, castings, sculpted forms, and assemblies of such. Recognition by registration has shown success in several applications, but typically where the number of possible objects was small and where salient features such as corners, edges, and holes were prevalent. In order to handle general objects, which are combinations of parts, possibly which move relative to one another, the recognition by components paradigm has been proposed. It is the most general and least developed of the paradigms studied here. Each of the subtasks of this paradigm presents difficulties – part modeling, part segmentation, memory organization and matching – and are current topics of research in both the cognitive science and computer vision communities.

It is useful to identify some of the problems common to different object recognition approaches. First of all, all depend on lower level processing to deliver some good features such as edges, corners, and surface patches. Moreover, all require some solution to the *segmentation problem* . The combinatorics of using specific object models to help with segmentation are discouraging when there are more than just a few models [Gri88]. General object recognition will profit greatly from advances in general bottom-up segmentation processes. Another pervasive problem is that of using numerical assessment of fit error between model and data. Many researchers have discovered that formal mathematical methods do not always capture the type of matching desired. In a similar vein, only the pattern recognition approach has dealt extensively with assessment of errors in classification. Recent works by Hoffman, Jain, and Flynn [HJ87a,FJ88] have investigated the error inherent in surface classification, but this must be extended to the entire process of object recognition. Finally, we note that there are classes of objects that are somewhat unique and application specific. As a result, a single theory for representation and recognition may not be feasible or even desirable: the quest for a uniform system may not be worth the trouble in applying it to the several special cases.

There are many exciting research projects for the future. Certainly feature extraction and segmentation methods from multiple sensors must be advanced. CAD models must be extended to include representation of more meaningful features. Organization of memory for storage of a large number of object models needs to be examined as well as methods for automatically learning those models. While the problems are, in general, very hard, progress is to be expected in certain cases where the potential gain is great.

6

Applications of Range Image Sensing and Processing

N. R. Corby
J. L. Mundy[1]

6.1 Introduction

In any machine vision problem, one is concerned with analyzing an image so as to produce a description of the image relevant to the task at hand. Most industrial problems have to do with the inspection, manipulation or measurement of three dimensional objects in a three dimensional workspace. Thus, machine vision systems used in these problems are often required to provide geometric descriptions of object and and workspace. The desired descriptions can be formed by *implicit* or *explicit* methods. Classical machine vision research seeks to construct three dimensional representation of objects in the field of view *implicitly* from one or more gray scale luminance images. The central idea behind this approach is that shape characteristics can be inferred from luminance variations observed in the image through the use of a variety of physical, optical and conceptual models. The system forms a description of the scene based on the information from the models, features from the images and control flow supplied by the particular reasoning approach used.

Attempts at development of implicit systems have indicated the difficulty of producing shape descriptions that are accurate and complete enough to use in practical applications. Researchers interested in applying machine vision in the workplace recognized the value of techniques that could *explicity* supply sets of points derived from actual measurement of an object surface. The sets of measured surface points typically are quite dense and potentially can serve as the basis of highly accurate surface representations. In practice, as can been seen from other papers in this volume, the path from initial surface point measurements to useable global surface and object descriptions is not a simple and straight forward one. However, in spite of the difficulties, applications that have used explicit approaches have generally met with reasonable amounts of success. Many of the constraints on object type and variety, object arrangement, object pose and lighting

---

[1] General Electric Research and Development Center, Schenectady, NY 12301.

present in implicit approaches have been relaxed or eliminated.

Measured surface shape data is usually referred to as range data and collections of range points comprise range images. Range images tend to have a sufficient number of individual points to "cover" or span the important surfaces of the object at a sufficiently high density. Techniques that give only one or at most a few range values for an entire object are used in specialized applications (e.g. air traffic control), but in most applications, images with a much higher density are required. Since this workshop is concerned with the production, processing and exploitation of explicit range data, we will restrict our discussions to applications classes that rely on explicit range data of reasonable density.

Range can be measured *actively* or *passively*. The earliest approaches to acquiring range data were passive and used the principle of stereopsys. In principle, the technique is capable of providing precise data from object surfaces. However, in practice a number of difficulties have prevented this technique from providing general, uniform precise range imagery. Work is still continuing in passive stereo as well as other passive techniques such as depth from focus, however most sensor approaches being investigated today are active in nature. These techniques emit energy which has been "shaped" in some way (e.g. spatially, spectrally or temporally) and make a measurement of the interaction of the energy and the object surface with some form of transducer or detector. Calculations based on detector signals and knowledge of the emitter and detector geometry result in measurements of range.

The second section of this report identifies some generic classes of industrial applications and discusses the characteristics and requirements of each class. These applications have implications regarding sensor design and processing approach and architectures. The third section of this paper lists some of the major obstacles which currently are restricting further application of range image based techniques to industrial problems. Many obstacles are related to sensor characteristics (e.g. resolution, accuracy, density and measurement rate) while others are related to processing the resultant range images.

6.2   Major Industrial Application Areas

Functionally, applications of range image sensing and processing can be broken down into five major categories:

- Integrity and Placement Verification

- Surface Inspection

- Metrology

FIGURE 6.1. Compressor Assembly

- Guidance and Control

- Modeling

The section dedicated to each category will give a definition of the scope and will provide some examples of applications. Important parameters such as required spatial resolution, data acquisition and processing rate will be discussed. Problems and difficulties associated with the specific applications will be discussed in the following section on obstacles to use.

6.2.1 INTEGRITY AND PLACEMENT VERIFICATION

This application category is characterized by the need to verify that the object of concern contains all parts and components that are expected to be present and that no additional or unwanted parts or features are present. In many applications there is not a specific or precise geometry template against which the part or assembly has to be checked. Often only fairly loose tolerance bounds exist and the part is deemed good if the feature being measured lies within the bounds. The major area of application has primarily been in assembly and configuration control applications.

A practical example is illustrated in figure 6.1. The photograph shows the sealed compressor assembly for a home refrigerator. The central black cylinder is the rotary compressor. The two copper tubes are refrigerant lines which run to and from the evaporator and condensor. Since the compressor vibrates considerably under operating conditions, the two tubes must be positioned so that they are at least an inch or so apart at any point along their length. Also the near tube must be at least an inch from the compressor body at the point of closest approach. If these separations are not maintained during manufacture, then during the course of the life of the refrigerator, the tubes may begin to rub against one another or the compressor causing noise and eventually failure of the tubing. There is no exact shape specified for the tube in the factory fabrication procedure. The compressor assemblies are manufactured at a rate of one every one to two seconds. In addition, the are approximately a half-dozen sizes and types of compressor assemblies.

In these types of applications, the size of the sub-parts will determine the absolute spatial measurement resolutions. To measure a surface feature reliably (e.g. tubing diameter) requires approximately 10 lateral sample points distributed across the smallest dimension of the smallest surface of interest. For most applications of this class, the smallest features are nominally 0.1 inches across, thus requiring a minimum lateral resolution of about 0.010 inches. For larger sections, lateral resolutions of 0.10 inches may be adequate. In many of these applications there is no preferred orientation which implies that depth resolution be approximately equal to lateral resolution.

Typically there may be from 10 – 100 surfaces per object that require checking with between 100 and 1000 raw sample points per surface being commonly required for surface measurement. Object presentation rates from 0.1 to 1 per second are common with some presentation rates running as high as 10 per second. This can result in peak measurement rates of up to 10^6 range points per second. The usual range of rates commonly encountered is 10^4 to 10^6 range points per second.

6.2.2   SURFACE INSPECTION

In surface inspection applications, the entire surface to be inspected is exhaustively scanned to determine surface flaws and component defects. The required measurement resolutions are intermediate between those of integrity checking and those of metrology applications. Surface flaws that are to be detected in surface inspection may vary considerably in size and type, ranging from large and imprecise flaws such as surface "dents" which could approach 40 to 50 percent of the surface area of a part surface, to extremely fine cracks, pits and pores, which may be as small as 0.0005 inches.

Two examples are aircraft turbine blade inspection and solder joint shape inspection. Figure 6.2 is a photograph of a typical turbine blade from a GE jet engine. Typically engines are rebuilt periodically and during that

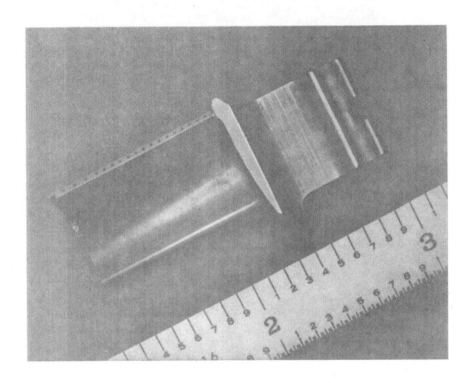

FIGURE 6.2. Example Turbine Blade

FIGURE 6.3. Example Integrated Circuit Solder Joint

period all parts are examined for flaws. In particular, the turbine blades, (which are subject to extreme temperatures and rotational stresses), must be examined carefully for any signs of deterioration such as the presence of small cracks. Range sensors have been developed which are capable of scanning the entire surface of the blade at 0.0005 inch resolution laterally. Typical blades may have 10 – 20 square inches of blade surface and may need to be scanned in time intervals of 10 seconds to one minute with lateral sampling resolutions of 0.00001 inches. This can result in sensor data rates from 10^5 to 10^8 points per second.

The second example concerns the inspection of soldered joints in electronic circuit assemblies. Figure 6.3 shows a typical integrated circuit package designed to mount on the surface of a printed circuit board. The results of some current research suggests that the actual shape of the solder joint between the IC lead and the circuit pad is related to the lifetime of joint. Thus, there are a number of efforts to develop sensors that can acquire explicit range images of the leads of the IC. Current lead width/pitch dimensions are on the order of 0.050 inches. In the future this is expected to trend towards 0.010 inches or less. Experiments have shown that lateral resolutions of 0.0001 inches are required for the higher density devices. Figure 6.4 shows a range image of the same IC lead area acquired at a lateral resolution of 0.0005 inches.

A typical high value circuit board may contain 5 to 20 such devices with an allowed scan time of 30 to 300 seconds. Other circuit boards may contain an order of magnitude more integrated circuits with roughly the same allowed scan time. The actual time available for scanning all of the leads of a given IC may be as small as 0.1 seconds in some applications.

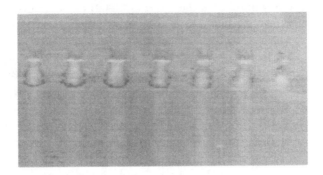

FIGURE 6.4. Range Image of IC Solder Joint

More typical times are on the order of 0.5 to 5 seconds. The total lead area is in the range from 0.1 to 0.4 square inches per IC. At a scan density of 10^8 points per square inch (0.0001 inch resolution) the sensor scan rates required are in the range quoted above - 10^5 to 10^8 points per second.

6.2.3 METROLOGY

Metrology applications are perhaps the most demanding in terms of overall accuracy of measurement of part features. Metrology applications deal with spot measurements as well as feature measurements. Most current approaches use a coordinate measurement machine which makes a spot measurement by actually contacting the surface with a stylus. The stylus consists of a slender needle-like rod with a small spherical probe tip. The probe is instrumented in such a way that contact force can be accurately prescribed. The touch probe tip is delivered to the point of measurement by a Cartesian gantry arrangement. The gantry is constructed in such a way that deflections in the beams of the apparatus are small. Optical noncontact equivalents for these mechanical touch probes are now routinely in use. The accuracy of these optical probes are on the order of 100 microinches. Interferometric devices exist which can accurately determine relative and absolute positions down to wavelengths of light.

It is difficult to specify bounds on sensor accuracies in metrological applications. In most applications, the individual spot measurements are not used independently but are combined to produce *feature* measurements, e.g. hole diameters, lengths, widths, thicknesses, angles between surfaces, concentricity measurements. Also, the actual feature measurement accuracies desired will vary from application to application. The number of feature measurements for a complex piece (e.g. an automobile engine block or jet engine housing) may number in the thousands, but for more ordinary parts, the number of measurements is on the order of a few dozen. Accuracies of a few ten-thousanths of an inch are common in many feature measuremnts for precision manufacturing industries. Most mechanical tolerances will be better than +/- 0.010 inches. Manufacturers currently tend to use more direct methods for measurement of features and feel more comfortable if the spot measurement accuracy equals or exceeds the desired feature measurement accuracy. Over time, better measurement systems and a better understanding of the statistical nature of the measurement process may allow the use of sensor data of reduced accuracy.

Since the gantry carrying the sensing head cannot be repositioned rapidly, most current range sensors are designed to acquire many range points from a local neighborhood after being positioned by the gantry system. This is achieved by parallel sensing schemes or by scanning a spot measurement sensor rapidly and accurately over the small local neighborhood. If the feature of interest is contained in the neighborhood, then the relative feature measurement accuracy is likely to be improved. This is because the sensor head measurement accuracy locally can be significantly better in many cases than the accuracy of the mechanical positioning system.

Discussions of measurement rate are complicated by the fact that the envelope of most parts of interest can be quite large and complex. In general, the motions of the apparatus positioning the measurement head dominate the measurement rate. The gantry will usually require at least a few seconds to move from one site to another. If the sensor can acquire only one measurement per position, the sensor data rate will be only one measurement every few seconds. Parallel or locally scanned measurement systems can usually gather hundreds or thousands of individual sub-measurements for a given positioning of the sensor head. The time to gather such data can be as small as a millisecond or so but is more often on the order of 50 – 100 milliseconds. Most feature measurements may require from 10 – 100 spot measurements and will allot about 10 – 100 seconds for the feature measurement. All of the factors discussed above result in a very wide variation in sensor data rate. A range of 10 – 100,000 points per second is common.

6.2.4   GUIDANCE AND CONTROL

The previous three sections have dealt with systems which make sets of measurements to be used to measure and inspect various objects with resolution roughly increasing from class to class. In most of the applications it was desirable to make the measurements as rapidly as possible to maximize system throughput. In guidance and control applications the proper operation of the system being controlled often requires real-time response from the sensor system. The major tasks of vision in guidance and control are object detection, object recognition, and pose estimation.

Many applications can be described as "look-identify-move" cycles. In these situations the operations need to be done rapidly but real-time speeds are not generally required. Many of these applications have been attempted by gray-scale or binary vision systems in the past. With the advent of reasonably priced, accurate and fast explicit range imaging systems, these applications are being readdressed with greater sucess. Most systems are model-driven to a large extent. The are many individual approaches to processing and matching the range data to the model data. Some of them are treated elsewhere in this volume.

The resolutions required vary somewhat with the application and are dependent primarily on the features being used for recognition, but typical resolutions are in the range of 0.010 – 0.5 inches. The cycle time depends on the allowed time for the robotic operation. Cycle times from 0.5 – 5 seconds are common. The surface sampling in many applications dealing with recognition can be fairly sparse, perhaps 30 – 100 points per surface. In pick and place type applications where specific small features may have to be located (e.g. to grip the handle of a cup), the sampling may have to be more dense or may involve sparse placement of dense sampling neighborhoods. Some examples are:

- part sorting

- palletizing

- pick and place operations

- fastener insertion and removal

- bin picking

Another important category of guidance and control applications are those characterized by the need for "continuous" geometric information. Continuous in this context means that the rate at which image-derived decisions can be produced is fast enough that results of the processing can be used to influence incremental actions or movements by tools or manipulators. In contrast to the large grained movements and actions of the previous class, continuous applications are characterized by finer grained sensing-motion cycles. Cycle rates of 10 – 100 per second are common. This translates into a sensor measurement rate of perhaps 10^3 to 10^6 points per second. The processing rates involved in going from measurements to a major result such as object pose, can be three to four orders of magnitude higher - perhaps 10^6 to 10^{10} operations per second. For applications in which the result is simpler or more directly related to the input measurements (e.g. determining the location and orientation of the gap between two metal plates for an automatic welding application), processing requirements may be in the range of 10^4 to 10^7 operations per second. Some examples of "visual servoing" are:

- Seam tracking for welding

- edge or surface following for grinding and deburring

- sealant deposition

- vehicle navigation and collision avoidance

6.2.5 MODELING

The production of geometric models is vital to many applications. Models are used in visual simulation, model-driven image understanding systems, as well as many aspects of product design and product engineering. Much of the design, engineering and production in modern industry is done with the aide of powerful CAD systems. For objects designed with CAD systems, models will exist. However, in a very large number of cases no apriori models exist. Often what is required is to create a surface or solid model from an original physical object. In many instances a specific object will have undergone some changes through use. The object is scanned and a model created. The model can then be used to quantify the location and nature of the changes or can be used to analyze the reasons for the change. If a part of an assembly needs to be replaced and no CAD models or drawings exist, then range-based modeling systems can be used to create a copy which fits the existing assembly perfectly.

The sensor measurement accuracies for most modeling applications need to be fairly high. Typical accuracies range from 0.0001 – 0.010 inches. The sensor data rates required are still fairly high even though there is a reasonable time in which to make all the pertinent measurements. The rates typically are very high because a large number of samples must be measured for each surface of the object. In some ways modeling combines the need for precision encountered in metrology applications with the extremely close surface coverage encountered in surface inspection applications. Thus the time to survey a part is often very long in modeling applications. Sensor data rates required are in the range of 10^4 to 10^6 range points per second.

6.3 Obstacles to Practical Application

There has been rapid progress in the development of range sensors in terms of speed, resolution and range accuracy. However there are still many obstacles to be overcome before 3D range data can be broadly applied in industrial applications.

6.3.1   REFLECTANCE DYNAMIC RANGE

It is not difficult to encounter very large variations in the surface reflectance of objects of interest in industrial application. For example, in the inspection of solder surfaces the reflectance dynamic range can approach 10^5. Even for common metal casting surfaces, the variation can be 10^3.

This reflectance variation places considerable demands on the light sensor in the range camera. Useful range accuracy cannot be maintained if the light sensor is operating outside of its linear range. This problem is even more severe for range determination techniques that involve interpolation of a structured light intensity pattern.

In this range sensing approach, the spatial distribution of the image intensity pattern determines the range values by interpolating the image to subpixel accuracy. If the intensity ranges beyond the upper and lower saturation limits of the sensor, the interpolation scheme will produce wildly inaccurate results.

This problem is even manifested in time-of-flight sensors. Here the calculation of the return phase of the modulated light intensity is disturbed by saturation in the receiver.

The main avenue for progress here is the development of image sensors with a high dynamic range. At present, only the photomultiplier can support these enormous signal variations. The photomultiplier is a single point detector, so the image must be formed by optical scanning means. As a consequence the overall pixel rate of the range camera is limited to perhaps 1 million points per second. This rate could be increased through the use of parallel channels, with attendant cost and system complexity.

In any case, many industrial applications will not be achieved unless the design of the range sensing system is immune to this rather harsh reflectance dynamic range requirement.

6.3.2   SURFACE REFLECTANCE ARTIFACTS

A related problem is manifested in range sensors that depend on the spatial distribution of the received intensity of a structured light pattern. For example consider the simple case of a single light stripe. In order to determine range, the image position of light stripe is determined by locating the peak in image intensity associated with the stripe.

The stripe intensity pattern is shown at the top of Figure 6.5.

Now suppose that the surface reflectance has a pulse-like variation as shown in the middle plot. This variation produces a rather distorted received intensity pattern, as shown in the bottom plot. The range value computed from the distorted stripe image will be corrupted by the effective shift in the peak of the stripe image. The actual shift error will depend somewhat on the method used to determine the center of the stripe. The shift illustrated in the figure assumes that an intensity moment calculation

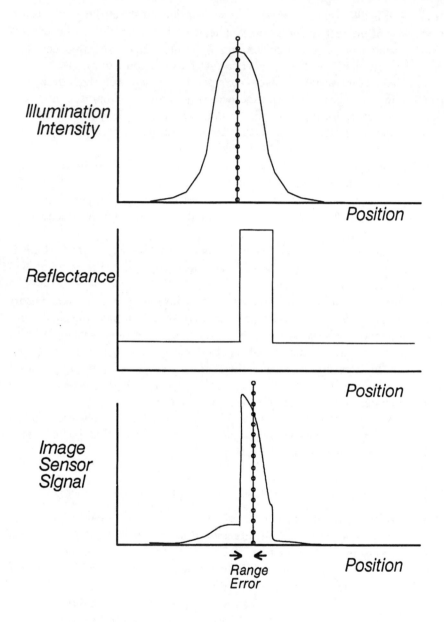

FIGURE 6.5. Reflectance range artifacts. A structured light intensity pattern (top) is corrupted by a reflectance variation (middle). The received light intensity is distorted and produces an error in range (bottom).

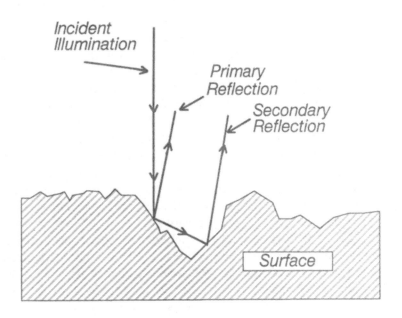

FIGURE 6.6. Geometry of Secondary Reflections

is used to determine the peak.

For significant reflectance variations, the shift error can be comparable to the width of the illumination stripe or spot. The error can be minimized by projecting as fine a stripe as possible. On the other hand, sharp stripe focus cannot be maintained over a large depth of field.

This effect would seem to place an upper limit on the spatial resolution that can be obtained in range sensing. Since most industrial applications require considerable lateral resolution as well as depth range, the presence of reflectance artifacts is a serious barrier.

6.3.3 SECONDARY REFLECTIONS

Since many applications involve metallic surfaces, secondary reflection is also a significant issue. Consider the situation shown in Figure 6.6. For the case of an optical sensor, an incident beam of light strikes the surface of the part. After interaction with the surface, the incident beam re-emerges as the primary reflection ray. This ray is detected by a receiver and processed in a manner consistent with the particular measurement approach being used. For example, in a triangulation sensor, the emitter and detector assemblies would be located some distance apart and the angle of the returned ray would be of interest. For time-of-flight approaches, the emitter and detector would be coaxially located and the measurement of interest would be the difference in time (or phase) between the incident and reflected rays. Consider now the geometry shown in Figure 6.6. Some of the incident energy is reflected towards a second surface. At the second surface, energy is reflected towards the detection apparatus giving rise to a secondary indication. Depending on surface conditions, a number of errors can result. If the primary surface is very specular and the secondary surface angle is appropriate, only the secondary reflection will be detected. If the first surface is not purely specular then a mixture of the two reflected rays will be detected with highly unpredictable results. In most practical cases there is no guarantee that the primary reflection will be stronger than the secondary. In many cases, the measured strength of the secondary was 10^2 to 10^3 time the primary. For many highly regular structures such as the soldered leads on an integrated circuit package, the interaction of the many regular specular surfaces can cause very confused situations. It is possible to minimize the effects of secondary reflections to some extent through the use of specific optical and signal processing designs. It has not been possible thus far to completely eliminate the effects of secondary reflections.

6.3.4 SHADOWING AND OCCLUSION

In all active sensors there exist regions of the object being sensed that cannot be imaged from specified vantage points. This can result from the geometry of the object or the geometry of the measurement system. For example, most systems are unable to image all sides (front, back, top and bottom) of an object simultaneously. Consider the situations shown in Figure 6.7. There are many cases (triangulation systems being the primary example) in which an illumination source and an intensity sensor are located at different locations in space. For the arrangement shown, measurements are only possible in the cross hatched area where the field of view of the illumination system intersects with the field of view of the detector. The other zones correspond to areas that can be illuminated but not sensed or areas that can be sensed but are not illuminated. In addition, other objects in either path or other parts of the object being imaged can interfere by shadowing or occluding either field of view. Thus, in triangulation systems for example, one typically cannot image to the bottom of a hole unless the hole diameter is greater than the triangulation baseline distance and the combined field of view of the system is within the hole width. Even in coaxial systems such as time-of-flight sensors, one can encounter shadowing by self-occlusion. This is shown in the lower part of Figure 6.7.

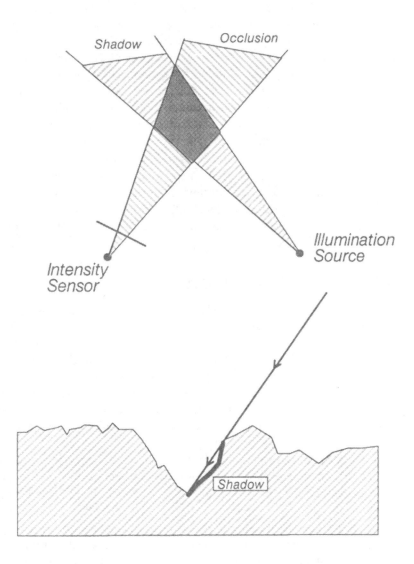

FIGURE 6.7. Occlusion and Shadowing in Active Range Measurement

6.3.5   Sensor Scanning and Transport

In virtually all sensor systems, the desired surface coverage will exceed the instantaneous field of view of the measurement system. This will require the use of mechanical, electro-optical or electro-mechanical positioning systems to position the sensor and / or part to achieve the desired vantage points. In order to maintain the overall system accuracy, either the positioning systems must be capable of accuracies on the order of the sensing system or strategies must be adopted that allow for compensation of modeled errors. "Whole surface" scanning of complicated objects will usually require complicated positioning systems which kinematically are difficult to program. In order to scan the entire surface, automatic procedures have to be created that are intelligent enough to automatically generate "scan plans" that will adequately and efficiently position the sensor over the entire surface of the part. The generation of scan plans must make use of knowledge of sensor characteristics (such as shadowing, occlusion and nonuniform spatial sampling), transport mechanism kinematics, and surface feature characterization. Engineering issues such as complexity, durability and cost are very important to applications.

6.3.6   Surface Feature Extraction

As mentioned previously in the section on surface inspection, the nature of surface flaws can vary widely depending on the industry involved. Defects can range from large, imprecise flaws such as dents with gradually sloping edges covering large areas to extremely fine cracks. In addition, the location and grouping of flaws is often very important. In order for a flaw to be detected, the geometric nature of flaw must be characterized in such a way that automatic methods can evaluate if a detected three dimensional feature corresponds with a given class of defect and if the defect meets the inspection criteria.

A common method of defining surface flaws in industry is to maintain books of photographs of flaws together with physical examples or physical fragments that exhibit the type of flaw being defined. There have been and continue to be efforts at expressing the geometry of the flaw in quantitative terms, but to date, the number of defect classes that have been translated is very small. Figure 6.8 shown some examples of surface flaw types.

Another problem is the amount of data that typically must be processed and the rate at which it must be processed in a surface inspection task. In the case of detecting small cracks, the surface must be scanned laterally at resolutions that are a small fraction of the crack width. In typical cases this can amount to 10^8 points per square inch of surface area. In many cases, the amount of surface area to be scanned can be hundred or thousands of square inches. Processing rates can reach very high levels, depending on the time available in which to make the inspection. In many cases, the

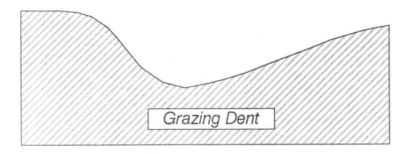

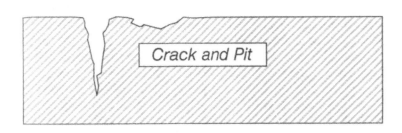

Surface Feature Extraction

FIGURE 6.8. Typical Features for Surface Feature Extraction

inspection is of a continuous nature (for example, inspecting rolls of painted sheet metal) which calls for drastically different processing strategies than those that would be encountered on smaller areas or on parts for which all the scanned data is available for review and reprocessing.

6.4   Conclusion

Active range sensing systems are being applied in more and more situations. The accuracies and speeds of the sensors are improving daily. Processing the resultant data continues to be an area of active research. As costs decrease, active range sensors will become even more widespread. The future challenges will be in the areas of increased dynamic range and clutter rejection and the areas of representation and interpretation of the range data.

7

3-D Vision Techniques for Autonomous Vehicles

Martial Hebert
Takeo Kanade
InSo Kweon [1]

7.1   Introduction

A mobile robot is a vehicle that navigates autonomously through an unknown or partially known environment. Research in the field of mobile robots has received considerable attention in the past decade due to its wide range of potential applications, from surveillance to planetary exploration, and the research opportunities it provides, including virtually the whole spectrum of robotics research from vehicle control to symbolic planning (see for example [Har88b] for an analysis of the research issues in mobile robots). In this paper we present our investigation of some the issues in one of the components of mobile robots: perception. The role of perception in mobile robots is to transform data from sensors into representations that can be used by the decision-making components of the system. The simplest example is the detection of potentially dangerous regions in the environment (*i.e.* obstacles) that can be used by a path planner whose role is to generate safe trajectories for the vehicle. An example of a more complex situation is a mission that requires the recognition of specific landmarks, in which case the perception components must produce complex descriptions of the sensed environment and relate them to stored models of the landmarks.

There are many sensing strategies for perception for mobile robots, including single camera systems, sonars, passive stereo, and laser range find-

---

[1]The Robotics Institute, Carnegie Mellon University, 5000 Forbes Avenue, Pittsburgh PA 15213. This research was sponsored in part by the Defense Advanced Research Projects Agency, DoD, through ARPA Order 5351, monitored by the US Army Engineer Topographic Laboratories under contract DACA76-85-C-0003, by the National Science Foundation contract DCR-8604199, by the Digital Equipment Corporation External Research Program, and by NASA grant NAGW-1175. The views and conclusions contained in this document are those of the authors and should not be interpreted as representing the official policies, either expressed or implied, of the funding agencies.

ers. In this report, we focus on perception algorithms for range sensors that
provide 3-D data directly by active sensing. Using such sensors has the advantage of eliminating the calibration problems and computational costs
inherent in passive techniques such as stereo. We describe the range sensor
that we used in this work in Section 7.2. Even though we tested our algorithm on one specific range sensor, we believe that the sensor characteristics
of Section 7.2 are fairly typical of a wide range of sensors [Bes88a].

Research in perception for mobile robots is not only sensor-dependent but
it is also dependent on the environment. A considerable part of the global
research effort has concentrated on the problem of perception for mobile
robot navigation in indoor environments, and our work in natural outdoor
environments through the Autonomous Land Vehicle and Planetary Exploration projects is an important development. This report describes some of
the techniques we have developed in this area of research. The aim of our
work is to produce models of the environment, which we call the *terrain*,
for path planning and object recognition.

The algorithms for building a terrain representation from a single sensor
frame are discussed in Section 7.3 in which we introduce the concept of
dividing the terrain representation algorithms into three levels depending
on the sophistication of the path planner that would use the representation, and on the anticipated difficulty of the terrain. Since a mobile robot
is by definition a dynamic system, it must process not one, but many observations along the course of its trajectory. The 3-D vision algorithms
must therefore be able to reason about representations that are built from
sensory data taken from different locations. We investigate this type of algorithms in Section 7.4 in which we propose algorithms for matching and
merging multiple terrain representations.

Finally, the 3-D vision algorithms that we propose are not meant to be
used in isolation, they have to be eventually integrated in a system that
include other sensors. A typical example is the case of road following in
which color cameras can track the road, while a range sensor can detect
unexpected obstacles. Another example is a mission in which a scene must
be interpreted in order to identify specific objects, in which case all the
available sensors must contribute to the final scene analysis. We propose
some algorithms for fusing 3-D representations with representations obtained from a color camera in Section 7.5. We also describe the application
of this sensor fusion to a simple natural scene analysis program.

Perception techniques for mobile robots have to be eventually validated
by using real robots in real environments. We have implemented the 3-D
vision techniques presented in this report on three mobile robots developed by the Field Robotics Center: the Terregator, the Navlab, and the
Ambler. The Terregator (Figure 7.1) is a six-wheeled vehicle designed for
rugged terrain. It does not have any onboard computing units except for
the low-level control of the actuators. All the processing was done on Sun
workstations through a radio connection.

We used this machine in early experiments with range data, most notably the sensor fusion experiments of Section 7.5.

The Navlab [SW88] (Figure 7.2) is a converted Chevy van designed for navigation on roads or on mild terrains. The Navlab is a self-contained robot in that all the computing equipment is on board. The results presented in Sections 7.3.3 and 7.3.4 come from the 3-D vision module that we integrated in the Navlab system [THKS88]. The Ambler [BW88] is an hexapod designed for the exploration of Mars (Figure 7.3). This vehicle is designed for navigation on very rugged terrain including high slopes, rocks, and wide gullies. This entirely new design prompted us to investigate alternative 3-D vision algorithms that are reported in Section 7.3.5. Even though the hardware for the Ambler does not exist at this time, we have evaluated the algorithms through simulation and careful analysis of the planetary exploration missions.

FIGURE 7.1. The Terregator

7.2   Active range and reflectance sensing

The basic principle of active sensing techniques is to observe the reflection of a reference signal (sonar, laser, radar..etc.) produced by an object in the environment in order to compute the distance between the sensor and that object. In addition to the distance, the sensor may report the intensity of the reflected signal which is related to physical surface properties of the

FIGURE 7.2. The Navlab

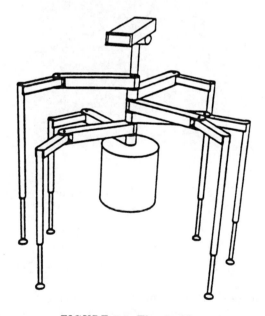

FIGURE 7.3. The Ambler

object. In accordance with tradition, we will refer to this type of intensity data as "reflectance" data even though the quantity measured is not the actual reflectance coefficient of the surface.

Active sensors are attractive to mobile robots researchers for two main reasons: first, they provide range data without the computation overhead associated with conventional passive techniques such as stereo vision, which is important in time critical applications such as obstacle detection. Second, it is largely insensitive to outside illumination conditions, simplifying considerably the image analysis problem. This is especially important for images of outdoor scenes in which illumination cannot be controlled or predicted. For example, the active reflectance images of outside scenes do not contain any shadows from the sun. In addition, active range finding technology has developed to the extent that makes it realistic to consider it as part of practical mobile robot implementations in the short term [Bes88a].

The range sensor we used is a time-of-flight laser range finder developed by the Environmental Research Institute of Michigan (ERIM). The basic principle of the sensor is to measure the difference of phase between a laser beam and its reflection from the scene [ZPFL85]. A two-mirror scanning system allows the beam to be directed anywhere within a 30° × 80° field of view. The data produced by the ERIM sensor is a 64 × 256 range image, the range is coded on eight bits from zero to 64 feet, which corresponds to a range resolution of three inches. All measurements are all relative since the sensor measures differences of phase. That is, a range value is known *modulo* 64 feet. We have adjusted the sensor so that the range value 0 corresponds to the mirrors for all the images presented in this report. In addition to range images, the sensor also produces active reflectance images of the same format (64 × 256 × 8 bits), the reflectance at each pixel encodes the energy of the reflected laser beam at each point. Figure 7.5 shows a pair of range and reflectance images of an outdoor scene. The next two Sections describe the range and reflectance data in more details.

7.2.1   FROM RANGE PIXELS TO POINTS IN SPACE

The position of a point in a given coordinate system can be derived from the measured range and the direction of the beam at that point. We usually use the Cartesian coordinate system shown in Figure 7.4, in which case the coordinates of a point measured by the range sensor are given by the equations[2]:

$$x = D\sin\theta \tag{7.1}$$
$$y = D\cos\phi\cos\theta$$

---

[2] Note that the reference coordinate system is not the same as in [HK85] for consistency reasons

$$z \ = \ D \sin \phi \cos \theta$$

where ϕ and θ are the vertical and horizontal scanning angles of the beam direction, and D is the measured distance between the scanner and the closest scene point along the direction (ϕ, θ). The two angles are derived from the row and column position in the range image, (r, c), by the equations:

$$\begin{aligned} \theta &= \theta_0 + c \times \Delta\theta \\ \phi &= \phi_0 + r \times \Delta\phi \end{aligned} \tag{7.2}$$

where θ_0 (respectively ϕ_0) is the starting horizontal (respectively vertical) scanning angle, and $\Delta\theta$ (respectively $\Delta\phi$) is the angular step between two consecutive columns (respectively rows). Figure 7.6 shows an overhead view of the scene of Figure 7.5, the coordinates of the points are computed using Eq. (7.3).

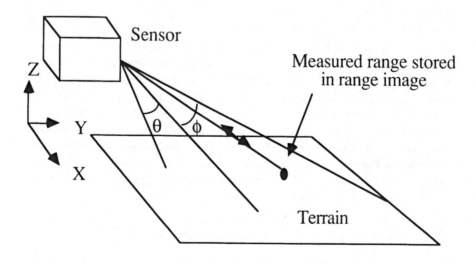

FIGURE 7.4. Geometry of the range sensor

7.2.2   REFLECTANCE IMAGES

A reflectance image from the ERIM sensor is an image of the energy reflected by a laser beam. Unlike conventional intensity images, this data provides us with information which is to a large extent independent of the environmental illumination. In particular, the reflectance images contain no shadows from outside illumination. The measured energy does depend,

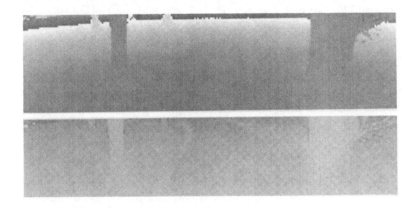

FIGURE 7.5. Range and reflectance images

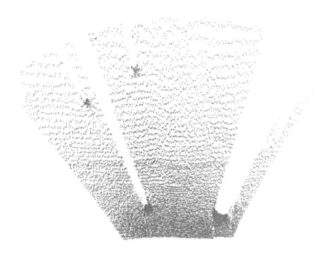

FIGURE 7.6. Overhead view

however, on the shape of the surface and its distance to the sensor. We correct the image so that the pixel values are functions only of the material reflectance. The measured energy, P_{return}, depends on the specific material reflectance, ρ, the range, D, and the angle of incidence, γ:

$$P_{return} = \frac{K\rho \cos\gamma}{D^2} \qquad (7.3)$$

Due to the wide range of P_{return}, the value actually reported in the reflectance image is compressed by using a log transform. That is, the digitized value, P_{image} is of the form [WPZ87]:

$$P_{image} = A\log(\rho\cos\gamma) + B\log D \qquad (7.4)$$

where A and B are constants that depend only on the characteristics of the laser, the circuitry used for the digitization, and the physical properties of the ambient atmosphere. Since A and B cannot be computed directly, we use a calibration procedure in which a homogeneous flat region is selected in a training image; we then use the pixels in this region to estimate A and B by least-squares fitting Eq. (7.4) to the actual reflectance/range data. Given A and B, we correct subsequent images by:

$$P_{new-image} = (P_{image} - B\log D)/A \qquad (7.5)$$

The value $P_{new-image}$ depends only on the material reflectance and the angle of incidence. This is a sufficient approximation for our purposes since for smooth surfaces such as smooth terrain, the $\cos\gamma$ factor does not vary widely. For efficiency purposes, the right-hand side of (7.5) is precomputed for all possible combinations (P_{image}, D) and stored in a lookup table. Figure 7.5 shows an example of an ERIM image, and Figure 7.7 shows the resulting corrected image.

FIGURE 7.7. Corrected reflectance image

7.2.3 RESOLUTION AND NOISE

As is the case with any sensor, the range sensor returns values that are measured with a limited resolution which are corrupted by measurement noise. In the case of the ERIM sensor, the main source of noise is due to the fact that the laser beam is not a line in space but rather a cone whose opening is a 0.5° solid angle (the instantaneous field of view). The value returned at each pixel is actually the average of the range of values over a 2-D area, the *footprint*, which is the intersection of the cone with the target surface (Figure 7.8). Simple geometry shows that the area of the footprint is proportional to the square of the range at its center. The size of the footprint also depends on the angle θ between the surface normal and the beam as shown in Figure 7.8. The size of the footprint is roughly inversely proportional to $\cos \theta$ if we assume that the footprint is small enough and that θ is almost constant. Therefore, a first order approximation of the standard deviation of the range noise, σ is given by:

$$\sigma \propto \frac{D^2}{\cos \theta} \tag{7.6}$$

The proportionality factor in this equation depends on the characteristics of the laser transmitter, the outside illumination, and the reflectance ρ of the surface which is assumed constant across the footprint in this first order approximation. We validated the model of Equation 7.6 by estimating the RMS error of the range values on a sequence of images. Figure 7.9 shows the standard deviation with respect to the measured range. The Figure shows that σ follows roughly the D^2 behavior predicted by the first order model. The footprint affects all pixels in the image.

There are other effects that produce distortions only at specific locations in the image. The main effect is known as the "mixed point" problem and is illustrated in Figure 7.8 in which the laser footprint crosses the edge between two objects that are far from each other. In that case, the returned range value is some combination of the range of the two objects but does not have any physical meaning. This problem makes the accurate detection of occluding edges more difficult. Another effect is due to the reflectance properties of the observed surface; if the surface is highly specular then no laser reflection can be observed. In that case the ERIM sensor returns a value of 255. This effect is most noticeable on man-made objects that contain a lot of polished metallic surfaces. It should be mentioned, however, that the noise characteristics of the ERIM sensor are fairly typical of the behavior of active range sensors [BJ85c].

7.3 Terrain representations

The main task of 3-D vision in a mobile robot system is to provide sufficient information to the path planner so that the vehicle can be safely steered through its environment. In the case of outdoor navigation, the task is to convert a range image into a representation of the terrain. We use the word "terrain" in a very loose sense in that we mean both the ground surface

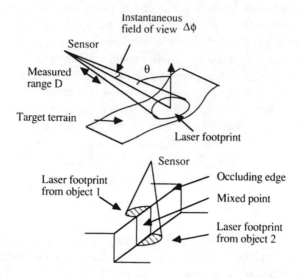

FIGURE 7.8. Sources of noise in range data

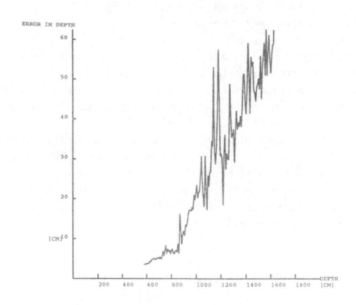

FIGURE 7.9. Noise in range data

and the objects that may appear in natural environments (*e.g.* rocks or trees). In this Section we discuss the techniques that we have implemented for the Navlab and Mars Rover systems. We first introduce the concept of the elevation map as a basis for terrain representations and its relationship with different path planning techniques. The last four Sections spell out the technical details of the terrain representation algorithms.

7.3.1   THE ELEVATION MAP AS THE DATA STRUCTURE FOR TERRAIN REPRESENTATION

Even though the format of the range data is an image, this may not be the most suitable structuring of the data for extracting information. For example , a standard representation in 3-D vision for manipulation is to view a range image as a set of data points measured on a surface of the equation $z = f(x, y)$ where the $x-$ and $y-$axes are parallel to the axis of the image and z is the measured depth. This choice of axis is natural since the image plane is usually parallel to the plane of the scene. In our case, however, the "natural" reference plane is not the image plane but is the ground plane. In this context, "ground plane" refers to a plane that is horizontal with respect to the vehicle or to the gravity vector. The representation $z = f(x, y)$ is then the usual concept of an elevation map. To transform the data points into an elevation map is useful only if one has a way to access them. The most common approach is to discretize the (x, y) plane into a grid. Each grid cell (x_i, y_i) is the trace of a vertical column in space, its *field* (Figure 7.10). All the data that falls within a cell's field is stored in that cell. The description shown in Figure 7.10 does not necessarily reflect the actual implementation of an elevation map but is more of a framework in which we develop the terrain representation algorithms. As we shall see later, the actual implementation depends on the level of detail that needs to be included in the terrain description.

Although the elevation map is a natural concept for terrain representations, it exhibits a number of problems due to the conversion of a regularly sampled image to a different reference plane [KHK88a]. Although we propose solutions to these problems in Section 7.3.5, it is important to keep them in mind while we investigate other terrain representations. The first problem is the sampling problem illustrated in Figure 7.11. Since we perform some kind of image warping, the distribution of data points in the elevation map is not uniform, and as a result conventional image processing algorithms cannot be applied directly to the map. There are two ways to get around the sampling problem: We can either use a base structure that is not a regularly spaced grid, such as a Delaunay triangulation of the data points [OR87], or we can interpolate between data points to build a dense elevation map. The former solution is not very practical because of the complex algorithms required to access data points and their

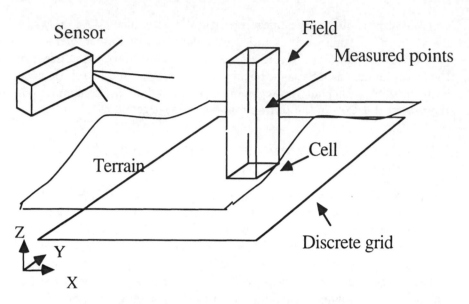

FIGURE 7.10. Structure of an elevation map

neighborhoods. We describe an implementation of the latter approach in Section 7.3.5. A second problem with elevation maps is the representation of the range shadows created by some objects (Figure 7.12). Since no information is available within the shadowed regions of the map, we must represent them separately so that no interpolation takes place across them and no "phantom" features are reported to the path planner. Finally, we have to convert the noise on the original measurements into a measure of uncertainty on the z value at each grid point (x, y). This conversion is difficult due to the fact that the sensor's uncertainty is most naturally represented with respect to the direction of measurement (Figure 7.13) and therefore spreads across a whole region in the elevation map.

7.3.2 TERRAIN REPRESENTATIONS AND PATH PLANNERS

The choice of a terrain representation depends on the path planner used for actually driving the vehicle. For example, the family of planners derived from the Lozano-Perez's A^* approach [LP79] uses discrete obstacles represented by 2-D polygons. By contrast, planners that compare a vehicle model with the local terrain [DHR88,Ste88] use some intermediate representation of the raw elevation map. Furthermore, the choice of a terrain representation and a path planner in turn depend on the environment in which the vehicle has to navigate. For example, representing only a small number of discrete upright objects may be appropriate if it is known in advance that the terrain is mostly flat, (e.g. a road) with a few obstacles (e.g. trees) while cross-country navigation requires a more detailed description of the eleva-

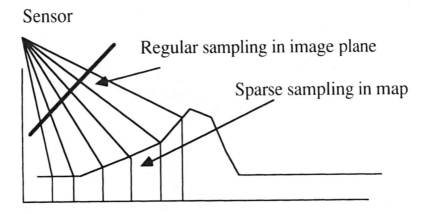

FIGURE 7.11. The sampling problem

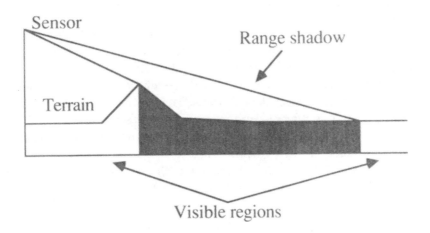

FIGURE 7.12. An example of a range shadow

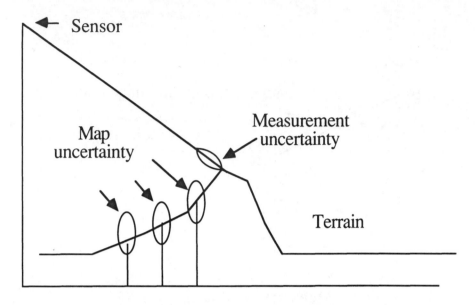

FIGURE 7.13. Representing uncertainty

tion map. Generating the most detailed description and then extracting the relevant information is not an acceptable solution since it would significantly degrade the performance of the system in simple environments. Therefore, we need several levels of terrain representation corresponding to different resolutions at which the terrain is described (Figure 7.14). At the low resolution level we describe only discrete obstacles without explicitly describing the local shape of the terrain. At the medium level, we include a description of the terrain through surface patches that correspond to significant terrain features. At that level, the resolution is the resolution of the operator used to detect these features. Finally, the description with the highest resolution is a dense elevation map whose resolution is limited only by the sensor. In order to keep the computations involved under control, the resolution is typically related to the size of the vehicle's parts that enter in contact with the terrain. For example, the size of one foot is used to compute the terrain resolution in the case of a legged vehicle.

7.3.3   LOW RESOLUTION: OBSTACLE MAP

The lowest resolution terrain representation is an obstacle map which contains a small number of obstacles represented by their trace on the ground plane. Several techniques have been proposed for obstacle detection. The Martin-Marietta ALV [DM86,Dun88,TMGM88] detects obstacles by computing the difference between the observed range image and pre-computed images of ideal ground at several different slope angles. Points that are far

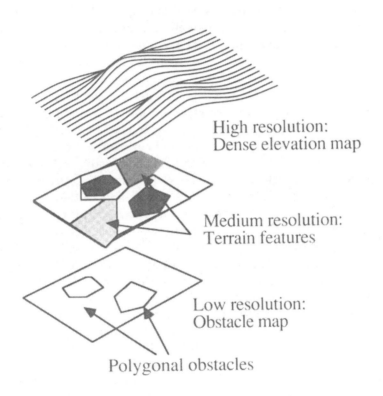

High resolution:
Dense elevation map

Medium resolution:
Terrain features

Low resolution:
Obstacle map

Polygonal obstacles

FIGURE 7.14. Levels of terrain representation

from the ideal ground planes are grouped into regions that are reported as obstacles to a path planner. A very fast implementation of this technique is possible since it requires only image differences and region grouping. It makes, however, very strong assumptions on the shape of the terrain. It also takes into account only the positions of the potential obstacle point, and as a result a very high slope ridge that is not deep enough would not be detected.

Another approach proposed by Hughes AI group [DHR87] is to detect the obstacles by thresholding the normalized range gradient, $\Delta D/D$, and by thresholding the radial slope, $D\Delta\phi/\Delta D$. The first test detects the discontinuities in range, while the second test detects the portion of the terrain with high slope. This approach has the advantage of taking a vehicle model into account when deciding whether a point is part of an obstacle. We used the terrain map paradigm to detect obstacles for the Navlab. Each cell of the terrain contains the set of data points that fall within its field (Figure 7.10). We can then estimate surface normal and curvatures at each elevation map cell by fitting a reference surface to the corresponding set of data points. Cells that have a high curvature or a surface normal far from the vehicle's idea of the vertical direction are reported as part of the projection of an obstacle. Obstacle cells are then grouped into regions corresponding to individual obstacles. The final product of the obstacle detection algorithm is a set of 2-D polygonal approximations of the boundaries of the detected obstacles that is sent to an A^*-type path planner (Figure 7.15). In addition, we can roughly classify the obstacles into holes or bumps according to the shape of the surfaces inside the polygons.

Figure 7.16 shows the result of applying the obstacle detection algorithm to a sequence of ERIM images. The Figure shows the original range images (top), the range pixels projected in the elevation map (left), and the resulting polygonal obstacle map (right). The large enclosing polygon in the obstacle map is the limit of the visible portion of the world. The obstacle detection algorithm does not make assumptions on the position of the ground plane in that it only assumes that the plane is roughly horizontal with respect to the vehicle. Computing the slopes within each cell has a smoothing effect that may cause real obstacles to be undetected. Therefore, the resolution of the elevation map must be chosen so that each cell is significantly larger than the typical expected obstacles. In the case of Figure 7.16, the resolution is twenty centimeters. The size of the detectable obstacle also varies with the distance from the vehicle due to the sampling problem (Section 7.3.1).

One major drawback of our obstacle detection algorithm is that the computation of the slopes and curvatures at each cell of the elevation map is an expensive operation. Furthermore, since low-resolution obstacle maps are most useful for fast navigation through simple environments, it is important to have a fast implementation of the obstacle detection algorithm. A natural optimization is to parallelize the algorithm by dividing the elevation

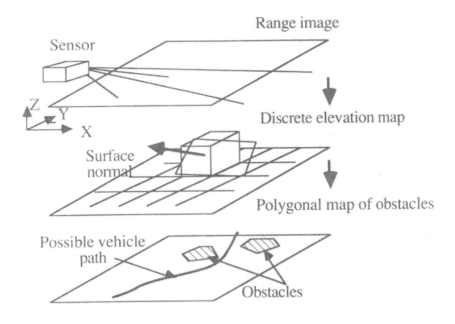

FIGURE 7.15. Building the obstacle map

map into blocks that are processed simultaneously. We have implemented such a parallel version of the algorithm on a ten-processor Warp computer [WK86,KW87]. The parallel implementation reduced the cycle time to under two seconds, thus making it possible to use the obstacle detection algorithm for fast navigation of the Navlab. In that particular implementation, the vehicle was moving at a continuous speed of one meter per second, taking range images, detecting obstacles, and planning a path every four meters.

7.3.4 MEDIUM RESOLUTION: POLYGONAL TERRAIN MAP

Obstacle detection is sufficient for navigation in flat terrain with discrete obstacles, such as following a road bordered by trees. We need a more detailed description when the terrain is uneven as in the case of cross-country navigation. For that purpose, an elevation map could be used directly [DHR88] by a path planner. This approach is costly because of the amount of data to be handled by the planner which does not need such a high resolution description to do the job in many cases (although we will investigate some applications in which a high resolution representation is required in Section 7.3.5). An alternative is to group smooth portions of the terrain into regions and edges that are the basic units manipulated by

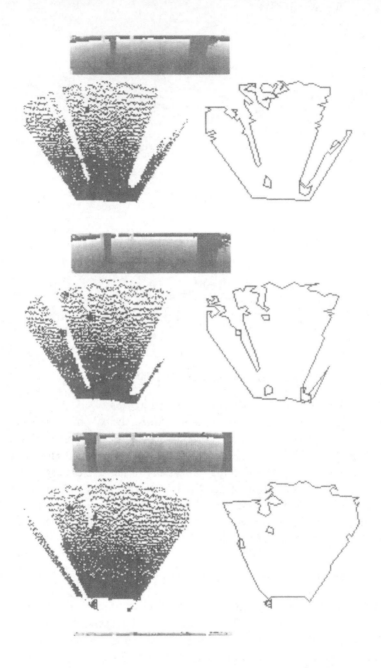

FIGURE 7.16. Obstacle detection on a sequence of images

the planner. This set of features provides a compact representation of the terrain thus allowing for more efficient planning [Ste88].

The features used are of two types: smooth regions, and sharp terrain discontinuities. The terrain discontinuities are either discontinuities of the elevation of the terrain, as in the case of a hole, or discontinuities of the surface normals, as in the case of the shoulder of a road [BC86]. We detect both types of discontinuities by using an edge detector over the elevation map and the surface normals map. The edges correspond to small regions on the terrain surface. Once we have detected the discontinuities, we segment the terrain into smooth regions. The segmentation uses a region growing algorithm that first identifies the smoothest locations in the terrain based on the behavior of the surface normals, and then grows regions around those locations. The result of the processing is a covering of the terrain by regions corresponding either to smooth portions or to edges.

The final representation depends on the planner that uses it. In our case, the terrain representation is embedded in the Navlab system using the path planner described in [Ste88]. The basic geometric object used by the system is the three-dimensional polygon. We therefore approximate the boundary of each region by a polygon. The approximation is done in a way that ensures consistency between regions in that the polygonal boundaries of neighboring regions share common edges and vertices. This guarantees that no "gaps" exist in the resulting polygonal mesh. This is important from the point of view of the path planner since such gaps would be interpreted as unknown portions of the terrain. Each region is approximated by a planar surface that is used by the planner to determine the traversability of the regions. Since the regions are not planar in reality, the standard deviation of the parameters of the plane is associated with each region.

Figure 7.18 shows the polygonal boundaries of the regions extracted from the image of Figure 7.17. In this implementation, the resolution of the elevation map is twenty centimeters. Since we need a dense map in order to extract edges, we interpolated linearly between the sparse points of the elevation map. Figure 7.17 shows the interpolated elevation map. This implementation of a medium resolution terrain representation is integrated in the Navlab system and will be part of the standard core system for our future mobile robot systems.

7.3.5 HIGH RESOLUTION: ELEVATION MAPS FOR ROUGH TERRAIN

The elevation map derived directly from the sensor is sparse and noisy, especially at greater distances from the sensor. Many applications, however, need a dense and accurate high resolution map. One way to derive such a map is to interpolate between the data points using some mathematical approximation of the surface between data points. The models that

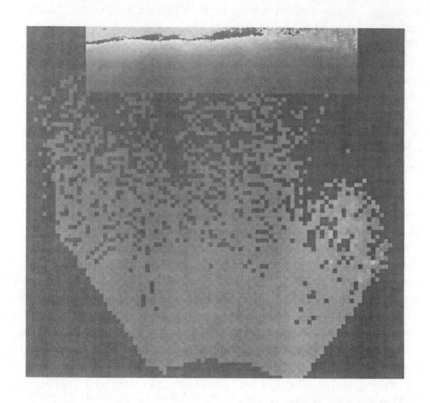

FIGURE 7.17. Range image and elevation map

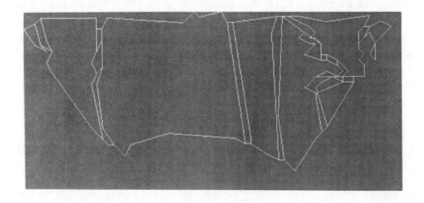

FIGURE 7.18. Polygonal boundaries of terrain regions

can be used include linear, quadratic, or bicubic surfaces [OR87]. Another approach is to fit a surface globally under some smoothness assumptions. This approach includes the family of regularization algorithms [BZ87b] in which a criterion of the form:

$$\int \|h_{data} - h_{interpolation}\|^2 + \lambda \int f(h_{interpolation}) \qquad (7.7)$$

is minimized, where f is a regularization function that reflects the smoothness model (*e.g.* thin plate). Two problems arise with both interpolation approaches: They make apriori assumptions on the local shape of the terrain which may not be valid (*e.g.* in the case of very rough terrain), and they do not take into account the image formation process since they are generic techniques independent of the origin of the data. In addition, the interpolation approaches depend heavily on the resolution and position of the reference grid. For example, they cannot compute an estimate of the elevation at an (x, y) position that is not a grid point without resampling the grid. We propose an alternative, the *locus* algorithm [KHK88a], that uses a model of the sensor and provides interpolation at arbitrary resolution without making any assumptions on the terrain shape other than the continuity of the surface.

The locus algorithm for the optimal interpolation of terrain maps

The problem of finding the elevation z of a point (x, y) is trivially equivalent to computing the intersection of the surface observed by the sensor and the vertical line passing through (x, y). The basic idea of the locus algorithm is to convert the latter formulation into a problem in image space (Figure 7.19). A vertical line is a curve in image space, the *locus*, whose equation as a function of ϕ is:

$$D = D_l(\phi) = \sqrt{\frac{y^2}{\cos^2 \phi} + x^2} \qquad (7.8)$$

$$(7.9)$$

$$\theta = \theta_l(\phi) = \arctan \frac{x \cos \phi}{y}$$

where ϕ, θ, and D are defined as in Section 7.2. Equation (7.9) was derived by inverting Equation (7.2), and assuming x and y constant. Similarly, the range image can be viewed as a surface $D = I(\phi, \theta)$ in ϕ, θ, D space. The problem is then to find the intersection, if it exists, between a curve parametrized by ϕ and a discrete surface. Since the surface is known only from a sample of data, the intersection cannot be computed analytically. Instead, we have to search along the curve for the intersection point. The search proceeds in two stages: We first locate the two scanlines of the range image, ϕ_1 and ϕ_2, between which the intersection must be located, that is the two consecutive scanlines such that, $Diff(\phi_1) = D_l(\phi_1) - I(\phi_1, \hat{\theta}_l(\phi_1))$ and $Diff(\phi_2) = D_l(\phi_1) - I(\phi_2, \hat{\theta}_l(\phi_2))$ have opposite signs, where $\hat{\theta}_l(\phi)$ is the image column that is the closest to $\theta_l(\phi)$. We then apply a binary search between ϕ_1 and ϕ_2. The search stops when the difference between the two angles ϕ_n and ϕ_{n+1}, where $Diff(\phi_n)$ and $Diff(\phi_{n+1})$ have opposite signs, is lower than a threshold ϵ. Since there are no pixels between ϕ_1 and ϕ_2, we have to perform a local quadratic interpolation of the image in order to compute $\theta_l(\phi)$ and $D_l(\phi)$ for $\phi_1 < \phi < \phi_2$. The control points for the interpolation are the four pixels that surround the intersection point (Figure 7.20). The final result is a value ϕ that is converted to an elevation value by applying Equation (7.2) to $\phi, \theta_l(\phi), D_l(\phi)$. The resolution of the elevation is controlled by the choice of the parameter ϵ.

The locus algorithm enables us to evaluate the elevation at any point since we do not assume the existence of a grid. Figure 7.21 shows the result of applying the locus algorithm on range images of uneven terrain, in this case a construction site. The Figure shows the original range images and the map displayed as an isoplot surface. The centers of the grid cells are ten centimeters apart in the (x, y) plane.

We can generalize the locus algorithm from the case of a vertical line to the case of a general line in space. This generalization allows us to build maps using any reference plane instead of being restricted to the (x, y) plane. This is important when, for example, the sensor's (x, y) plane is not orthogonal to the gravity vector. A line in space is defined by a point $u = [u_x, u_y, u_z]^t$, and a unit vector $v = [v_x, v_y, v_z]^t$. Such a line is parametrized in λ by the relation $p = u + \lambda v$ if p is a point on the line. A general line is still a curve in image space that can be parametrized in ϕ by eliminating λ. We can then compute the intersection between the curve and the image surface by using the same algorithm as before except with the new equation of the locus curve.

The representation of the line by the pair (u, v) is not optimal since it uses six parameters while only four parameters are needed to represent a line in space. For example, this can be troublesome if we want to compute the Jacobian of the intersection point with respect to the parameters of the line. A better alternative [KM63] is to represent the line by its slopes in x and y and by its intersection with the plane $z = 0$ (See [Rob88] for a complete survey of 3-D line representations). The equation of the line then becomes:

$$x = az + p \qquad (7.10)$$
$$y = bz + q$$

We can still use the same technique to compute the locus because we can switch between the (a, b, p, q) and (u, v) representations.

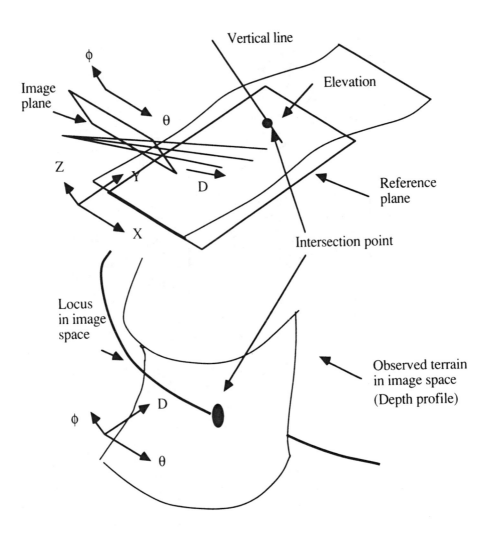

FIGURE 7.19. The locus algorithm for elevation maps

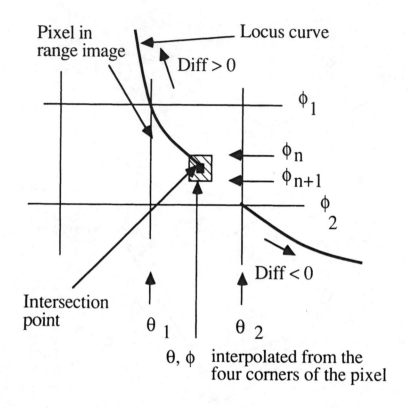

FIGURE 7.20. Image interpolation around the intersection point

grid.Multi.seq25.gif(view1)

FIGURE 7.21. The locus algorithm on range images

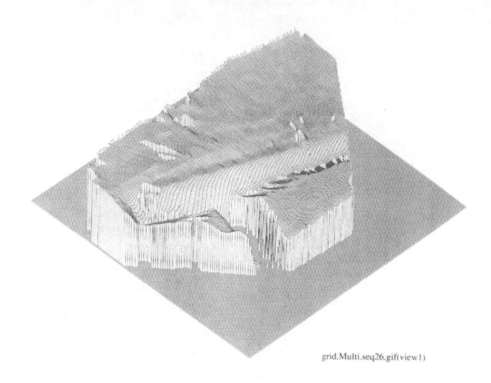

grid.Multi.seq26.gif(view1)

FIGURE 7.21. The locus algorithm on range images (Continued)

grid.Multi.seq27.gif(view1)

FIGURE 7.21. The locus algorithm on range images (Continued)

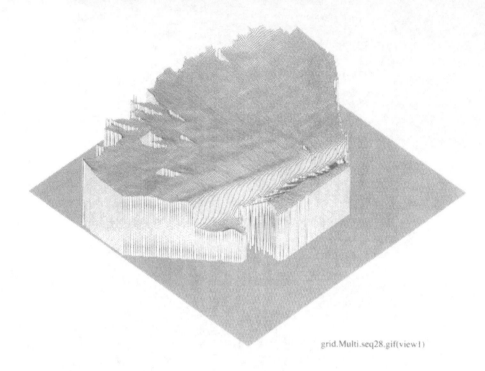

grid.Multi.seq28.gif(view1)

FIGURE 7.21. The locus algorithm on range images (Continued)

Evaluating the locus algorithm

We evaluate the locus algorithm by comparing its performance with the other "naive" interpolation algorithms on a set of synthesized range images of simple scenes. The simplest scenes are planes at various orientations. Furthermore, we add some range noise using the model of Section 7.2.3 in order to evaluate the robustness of the approach in the presence of noise. The performances of the algorithms are evaluated by using the mean square error:

$$E = \frac{\sum_{i=1}^{N}(h_i - \tilde{h}_i)^2}{N} \tag{7.11}$$

where h_i is the true elevation value and $\tilde{h}_i$ is the estimated elevation. Figure 7.22 plots E for the locus algorithm and the naive interpolation as a function of the slope of the observed plane and the noise level. This result shows that the locus algorithm is more stable with respect to surface orientation and noise level than the other algorithm. This is due to the fact that we perform the interpolation in image space instead of first converting the data points into the elevation map.

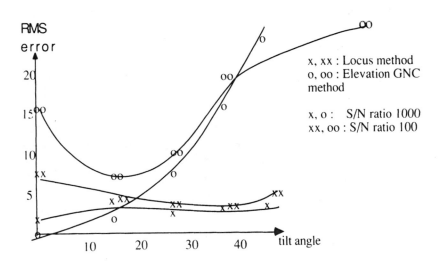

FIGURE 7.22. Evaluation of the locus algorithm on synthesized images

Representing the uncertainty

We have presented in Section 7.2.3 a model of the sensor noise that is a Gaussian distribution along the direction of measurement. We need to transform this model into a model of the noise, or uncertainty, on the elevation values returned by the locus algorithm. The difficulty here is that the uncertainty in a given range value spreads to many points in the elevation map, no matter how the map is oriented with respect to the image plane (Figure 7.13). We cannot therefore assume that the standard deviation of an elevation is the same as the one of the corresponding pixel in the range image. Instead, we propose to use the nature of the locus algorithm itself to derive a meaningful value for the elevation uncertainty. To facilitate the explanation, we consider only the case of the basic locus algorithm of Section 7.3.5 in which we compute an elevation z from the intersection of the locus of a vertical line with a depth profile from a range image. Figure 7.23 shows the principle of the uncertainty computation by considering a locus curve that corresponds to a line in space and the depth profile from the range image in the neighborhood of the intersection point, each point on the depth profile has an uncertainty whose density can be represented by a Gaussian distribution as computed in Section 7.2.3. The problem is to define a distribution of uncertainty along the line. The value of the uncertainty reflects how likely is the given point to be on the actual surface given the measurements.

Let us consider an elevation h along the vertical line. This elevation corresponds to a measurement direction $\phi(h)$ and a measured range $d'(h)$. If $d(h)$ is the distance between the origin and the elevation h, we assign to h the confidence [Sze88a]:

$$l(h) = \frac{1}{\sqrt{2\pi}\sigma(d'(h))} e^{-\frac{(d(h)-d'(h))^2}{2\sigma(d'(h))^2}} \tag{7.12}$$

where $\sigma(d'(h))$ is the variance of the measurement at the range $d'(h)$. Equation 7.12 does not tell anything about the shape of the uncertainty distribution $l(h)$ along the h axis except that it is maximum at the elevation h_0 at which $d(h) = d'(h)$, that is the elevation returned by the locus algorithm. In order to determine the shape of $l(h)$, we approximate $l(h)$ around h_0 by replacing the surface by its tangent plane at h_0. If α is the slope of the plane, and H is the elevation of the intersection of the plane with the z axis, we have:

$$\sigma(d'(h)) = K\frac{H^2(a^2 + h^2)}{(a\tan\alpha + h)^2} \tag{7.13}$$

$$\frac{(d(h) - d'(h))^2}{2\sigma(d'(h))^2} = \frac{(h - h_0)^2(a\tan\alpha + h)^2}{K^2H^4(a^2 + h^2)} \tag{7.14}$$

where a is the distance between the line and the origin in the $x - y$ plane and K is defined in Section 7.2.3 by $\sigma(d) \approx Kd^2$. By assuming that h is close to h_0, that is $h = h_0 + \epsilon$ with $\epsilon \ll h_0$, and by using the fact that $H = h_0 + a\tan\alpha$, we have the approximations:

$$\sigma(d'(h)) \approx K(a^2 + h_0^2) \tag{7.15}$$

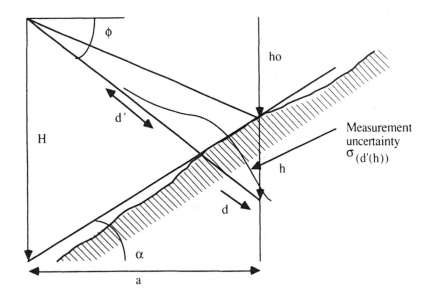

FIGURE 7.23. Computing the uncertainty from the locus algorithm

$$\frac{(d(h) - d'(h))^2}{2\sigma(d'(h))^2} \approx \frac{(h - h_o)^2}{2K^2 H^2(a^2 + h_o^2)}$$

(7.16)

In the neighborhood of h_o, Equation 7.16 shows that $(d(h) - d'(h))^2/2\sigma(d'(h))^2$ is quadratic in $h - h_o$, and that $\sigma(d'(h))$ is constant. Therefore, $l(h)$ can be approximated by a Gaussian distribution of variance:

$$\sigma_h^2 = K^2 H^2(a^2 + h_o^2) = K^2 H^2 d_o^2$$

(7.17)

Equation 7.17 provides us with a first order model of the uncertainty of h derived by the locus algorithm. In practice, the distance $D(h) = (d(h) - d'(h))^2/2\sigma(d'(h))^2$ is computed for several values of h close to h_o, the variance σ_h is computed by fitting the function $(h - h_o)^2/2\sigma_h^2$ to the values of $D(h)$. This is a first order model of the uncertainty in the sense that it takes into account the uncertainty on the sensor measurements, but it does not include the uncertainty due to the locus algorithm itself, in particular the errors introduced by the interpolation.

Detecting the range shadows

As we pointed out in Section 7.3.1, the terrain may exhibit range shadows in the elevation map. It is important to identify the shadow regions
because the terrain may have any shape within the boundaries of the shadows, whereas the surface would be smoothly interpolated if we applied the
locus algorithm directly in those areas. This may result in dangerous situations for the robot if a path crosses one of the range shadows. A simple
idea would be to detect empty regions in the raw elevation map, which are
the projection of images in the map without any interpolation. This approach does not work because the size of the shadow regions may be on the
order of the average distance between data points. This is especially true
for shadows that are at some distance from the sensor in which case the
distribution of data points is very sparse. It is possible to modify the standard locus algorithm so that it takes into account the shadow areas. The
basic idea is that a range shadow corresponds to a strong occluding edge
in the image (Figure 7.12). An (x, y) location in the map is in a shadow
area if its locus intersects the image at a pixel that lies on such an edge
(Figure 7.24).

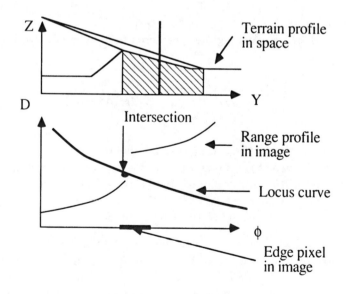

FIGURE 7.24. Detecting range shadows

We implement this algorithm by first detecting the edges in the range
image by using a standard technique, the GNC algorithm [BZ87b]. We
chose this algorithm because it allows us to vary the sensitivity of the
edge detector across the image, and because it performs some smoothing

of the image as a side effect. When we apply the locus algorithm we can then record the fact that the locus of a given location intersects the image at an edge pixel. Such map locations are grouped into regions that are the reported range shadows. Figure 7.25 shows an overhead view of an elevation map computed by the locus algorithm, the white points are the shadow points, the gray level of the other points is proportional to their uncertainty as computed in the previous Section.

FIGURE 7.25. Shadow regions in an elevation map

An application: footfall selection for a legged vehicle

The purpose of using the locus algorithm for building terrain is to provide high resolution elevation data. As an example of an application in which such a resolution is needed, we briefly describe in this Section the problem of perception for a legged vehicle [Kwe88]. One of the main responsibilities of perception for a legged vehicle is to provide a terrain description that enables the system to determine whether a given foot placement, or *footfall*, is safe. In addition, we consider the case of locomotion on very rugged terrain such as the surface of Mars.

A foot is modeled by a flat disk of diameter 30 cms. The basic criterion

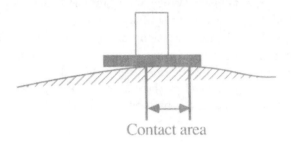

FIGURE 7.26. Footfall support area

for footfall selection is to select a footfall area with the maximum support area which is defined as the contact area between the foot and the terrain as shown in Figure 7.26. Another constraint for footfall selection is that the amount of energy necessary to penetrate the ground in order to achieve sufficient support area must be minimized. The energy is proportional to the depth of the foot in the ground. The support area is estimated by counting the number of map points within the circumference of the disk that are above the plane of the foot. This is where the resolution requirement originates because the computation of the support area makes sense only if the resolution of the map is significantly smaller than the diameter of the foot. Given a minimum allowed support area, S_{min}, and the high resolution terrain map, we can find the optimal footfall position within a given terrain area: First, we want to find possible flat areas by computing surface normals for each footfall area in a specified footfall selection area. Footfalls with a high surface normal are eliminated. The surface normal analysis, however, will not be sufficient for optimal footfall selection. Second, the support area is computed for the remaining positions. The optimal footfall position is the one for which the maximum elevation, h_{opt} that realizes the minimum support area S_{min} is the maximum across the set of possible footfall positions. Figure 7.27 shows a plot of the surface area with respect to the elevation from which h_{min} can be computed.

Extracting local features from an elevation map

The high resolution map enables us to extract very local features, such as points of high surface curvature, as opposed to the larger terrain patches of Section 7.3.4. The local features that we extract are based on the magnitude of the two principal curvatures of the terrain surface. The curvatures are computed as in [PB85] by first smoothing the map, and then computing the derivatives of the surface for solving the first fundamental form. Figure 7.28 shows the curvature images computed from an elevation map using the locus algorithm. The resolution of the map is ten centimeters. Points of high curvature correspond to edges of the terrain, such as the edges of

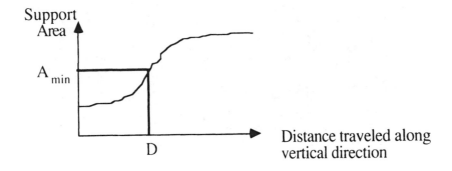

FIGURE 7.27. Support area versus elevation

a valley, or to sharp terrain features such as hills, or holes. In any case, the high curvature points are viewpoint-independent features that can be used for matching. We extract the high curvature points from both images of principal curvature. We group the extracted points into regions, then classify each region as point feature, line, or region, according to its size, elongation, and curvature distribution. Figure 7.28 shows the high curvature points extracted from an elevation map. The two images correspond to the two principal curvatures. Figure 7.29 shows the three types of local features detected on the map of Figure 7.28 superimposed in black over the original elevation map. The Figure shows that while some features correspond merely to local extrema of the surface, some such as the edges of the deep gully are characteristic features of the scene. This type of feature extraction plays an important role in Section 7.4 for combining multiple maps computed by the locus algorithm.

7.4   Combining multiple terrain maps

We have so far addressed the problem of building a representation of the environment from sensor data collected at one fixed location. In the case of mobile robots, however, we have to deal with a stream of images taken along the vehicle's path. We could ignore this fact and process data from each viewpoint as if it were an entirely new view of the world, thus forgetting whatever information we may have extracted at past locations. It has been observed that this approach is not appropriate for mobile robot navigation, and that there is a need for combining the representations computed

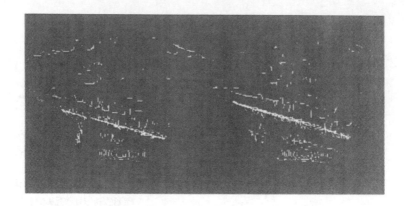

FIGURE 7.28. The high curvature points of an elevation map

FIGURE 7.29. Local features from a high resolution elevation map

from different vantage points into a coherent map. Although this has been observed first in the context of indoor mobile robots [FAF86,GCV84], the reasoning behind it holds true in our case. First of all, merging representations from successive viewpoints will produce a map with more information and better resolution than any of the individual maps. For example, a tall object observed by a range sensor creates an unknown area behind it, the range shadow, where no useful information can be extracted (Section 7.3.1). The shape and position of the range shadow changes as we move to another location; merging images from several locations will therefore reduce the size of the shadow, thus providing a more complete description to the path planner (Figure 7.30). Another reason why merging maps increases the resolution of the resulting representation concerns the fact that the resolution of an elevation map is significantly better at close range. By merging maps, we can increase the resolution of the parts of the elevation map that were originally measured at a distance from the vehicle.

The second motivation for merging maps is that the position of the vehicle at any given time is uncertain. Even when using expensive positioning systems, we have to assume that the robot's idea of its position in the world will degrade in the course of a long mission. One way to solve this problem is to compute the position with respect to features observed in the world instead of a fixed coordinate system [SC86,MS87]. That requires the identification and fusion of common features between successive observations in order to estimate the displacement of the vehicle (Figure 7.31). Finally, combining maps is a mission requirement in the case of an exploration mission in which the robot is sent into an unknown territory to compile a map of the observed terrain.

Many new problems arise when combining maps: representation of uncertainty, data structures for combined maps, predictions from one observation to the next etc. We shall focus on the terrain matching problem, that is the problem of finding common features or common parts between terrain maps so that we can compute the displacement of the vehicle between the two corresponding locations and then merge the corresponding portions of the terrain maps. We always make the reasonable assumption that a rough estimate of the displacement is available since an estimate can always be computed either from dead reckoning or from past terrain matchings.

7.4.1   THE TERRAIN MATCHING PROBLEM: ICONIC *vs.* FEATURE-BASED

In the terrain matching problem, as in any problem in which correspondences between two sets of data must be found, we can choose one of two approaches: feature-based or iconic matching. In feature-based matching, we first have to extract two sets of features (F_i^1) and (F_j^2) from the two views to be matched, and to find correspondences between features,

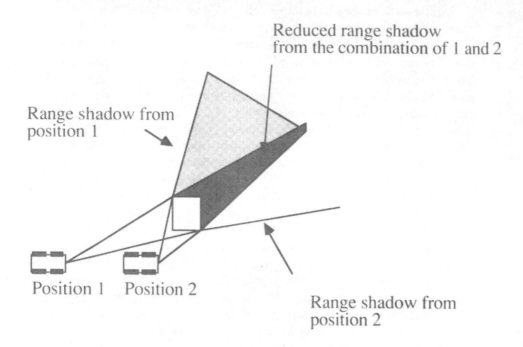

FIGURE 7.30. Reducing the range shadow

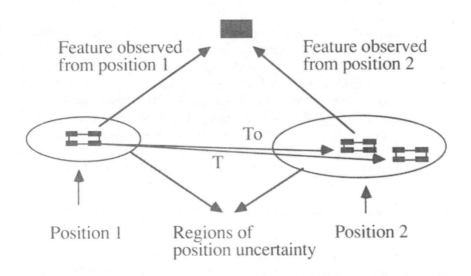

FIGURE 7.31. Matching maps for position estimation

$(F^1_{i_k}, F^2_{j_k})$ that are globally consistent. We can then compute the displacement between the two views from the parameters of the features, and finally merge them into one common map. Although this is the standard approach to object recognition problems [BJ85c], it has also been widely used for map matching for mobile robots [FAF86,KTB87,MS87,Bro85,Asa88,Tho84]. In contrast, iconic approaches work directly on the two sets of data points, P^1 and P^2 by minimizing a cost function of the form $F(T(P^2), P^1)$ where $T(P^2)$ is the set of points from view 2 transformed by a displacement T. The cost is designed so that its minimum corresponds to a "best" estimate of T in some sense. The minimization of F leads to an iterative gradient-like algorithm. Although less popular, iconic techniques have been successfully applied to incremental depth estimation [MS87,Luc85] and map matching [Sze88b,Elf87].

The proponents of each approach have valid arguments. The feature-based approach requires a search in the space of possible matches which may lead to a combinatorial explosion of the matching program. On the other hand, iconic approaches are entirely predictable in terms of computational requirements but are usually quite expensive since the size of the points sets P^i is typically on the order of several thousands. As for the accuracy of the resulting displacement T, the accuracy of iconic techniques can be better than the resolution of the sensors if we iterate the minimization of F long enough, while any feature extraction algorithm loses some of the original sensor accuracy. Furthermore, feature matching could in theory be used even if no a-priori knowledge of T, T_0, is available while iconic approaches require T_0 to be close to the actual displacement because of the iterative nature of the minimization of F.

Keeping these tenets in mind, we propose to combine both approaches into one terrain matching algorithm. The basic idea is to use the feature matching to compute a first estimate $\hat{T}$ given a rough initial value T_0, and then to use an iconic technique to compute an accurate estimate $\hat{\hat{T}}$. This has the advantage of retaining the level of accuracy of iconic techniques while keeping the computation time of the iconic stage under control because the feature matching provides an estimate close enough to the true value. We describe in detail the feature-based and iconic stages in the next three sections.

7.4.2 Feature-based Matching

Let F^1_i and F^2_j be two sets of features extracted from two images of an outdoor scene, I_1 and I_2. We want to find a transformation $\hat{T}$ and a set of pairs $C_k = (F^1_{i_k}, F^2_{j_k})$ such that $F^2_{j_k} \approx \hat{T}(F^1_{i_k})$, where $T(F)$ denotes the transformed by T of a feature F. The features can be any of those discussed in the previous Sections: points or lines from the local feature extractor, obstacles represented by a ground polygon, or terrain patches represented by their surface equation and their polygonal boundaries. We first investigate the feature matching algorithm independently of any particular feature type so that we can then apply it to any level of terrain representation.

For each feature F_i^1, we can first compute the set of features F_{ij}^2 that could correspond to F_i^1 given an initial estimate T_0 of the displacement. The F_{ij}^2's should lie in a prediction region centered at $T_0(F_i^1)$. The size of the prediction region depends on the confidence we have in T_0 and in the feature extractors. For example, the centers of the polygonal obstacles of Section 7.3.4 are not known accurately, while the curvature points from Section 7.3.5. can be accurately located. The confidence on the displacement T is represented by the maximum distance δ between a point in image 1 and the transformed of its homologue in image 2, $\|Tp^2 - p^1\|$, and by the maximum angle ϵ, between a vector in image 2 and the transformed of its homologue in image 1 by the rotation part of T. The prediction is then defined as the set of features that are at a Cartesian distance lower than δ, and at an angular distance lower than ϵ from $T_0(F_i^2)$. The parameters used to determine if a feature belongs to a prediction region depend on the type of that feature. For example, we use the direction of a line for the test on the angular distance, while the center of an obstacle is used for the test on the Cartesian distance. Some features may be tested only for orientation, such as lines, or only for position, such as point features. The features in each prediction region are sorted according to some feature distance $d(F_i^1, T_0(F_{ij}^2))$ that reflects how well the features are matched. The feature distance depends also on the type of the feature: for points we use the usual distance, for lines we use the angles between the directions, and for polygonal patches (obstacles or terrain patches) we use a linear combination of the distance between the centers, the difference between the areas, the angle between the surface orientations, and the number of neighboring patches. The features in image 1 are also sorted according to an "importance" measure that reflects how important the features are for the matching. Such importance measures include the length of the lines, the strength of the point features (*i.e.* the curvature value) , and the size of the patches. The importance measure also includes the type of the features because some features such as obstacles are more reliably detected than others, such as point features.

Once we have built the prediction regions, we can search for matches between the two images. The search proceeds by matching the features F_i^1 to the features F_{ij}^2 that are in their prediction region starting at the most important feature. We have to control the search in order to avoid a combinatorial explosion by taking advantage of the fact that each time a new match is added both the displacement and the future matches are further constrained. The displacement is constrained by combining the current estimate T with the displacement computed from a new match (F_i^1, F_{ij}^2). Even though the displacement is described by six components, the number of components of the displacement that can be computed from one single match depends on the type of features involved: point matches provide only three components, line matches provide four components (two rotations and two translations), and region matches provide three components. We therefore combine the components of T with those components of the new match that can be computed. A given match prunes the search by constraining the future potential matches in two ways: if connectivity relations between features are available, as in the case of terrain patches, then a match (F_i^1, F_{ij}^2) constrains the possible matches for the neighbors of F_i^1) in that they have to be adjacent to F_{ij}^2. In the case of points or patches, an additional constraint is induced by the relative placement of the features in the scene: two matches, (F_i^1, F_{ij}^2) and $(F_{i'}^1, F_{i'j'}^2)$, are compatible only if the angle between the vectors $w^1 = \overline{F_{i'}^1 F_i^1}$ and $w^2 = \overline{F_{i'j'}^2, F_{ij}^2}$ is lower than π, provided the rotation part of T is no greater than π which is the case in realistic situations. This constraint means that the relative placement of the features remains the same from image to image which is similar to the classical ordering constraint used in stereo matching.

   The result of the search is a set of possible matchings, each of which is a set of pairs $S = (F_{i_k}^1, F_{j_k}^2)_k$ between the two sets of features. Since we evaluated T simply by combining components in the course of the search, we have to evaluate T for each S in order to get an accurate estimate. T is estimated by minimizing an error function of the form:

$$E = \sum_k d(F_{i_k}^1 - T(F_{i_k}^2)) \qquad (7.18)$$

The distance $d(.)$ used in Equation (7.18) depends on the type of the features involved: For point features, it is the usual distance between two points; for lines it is the weighted sum of the angle between the two lines and the distance between the distance vectors of the two lines; for regions it is the weighted sum of the distance between the unit direction vectors and the distance between the two direction vectors. All the components of T can be estimated in general by minimizing E. We have to carefully identify, however, the cases in which insufficient features are present in the scene to fully constrain the transformation. The matching S that realizes the minimum E is reported as the final match between the two maps while the corresponding displacement $\hat{T}$ is reported as the best estimate of the displacement between the two maps. The error $E(\hat{T})$ can then be used to represent the uncertainty in T.

   This approach to feature based matching is quite general so that we can apply it to many different types of features, provided that we can define the distance $d(.)$ in Equation (7.18), the importance measure, and the feature measure. The approach is also fairly efficient as long as δ and ϵ do not become too large, in which case the search space becomes itself large. We describe two implementations of the feature matching algorithm in the next two Sections.

Example: Matching polygonal representations

We have implemented the feature-based matching algorithm on the polygonal descriptions of Section 7.3.4 and 7.3.3. The features are in this case:

- The polygons describing the terrain parametrized by their areas, the equation of the underlying surface, and the center of the region

- The polygons describing the trace of the major obstacles detected (if any).

- The road edges found in the reflectance images if the road detection is reliable enough. The reliability is measured by how much a pair of road edges deviates from the pair found in the previous image.

The obstacle polygons have a higher weight in the search itself because their detection is more reliable than the terrain segmentation, while the terrain regions and the road edges contribute more to the final estimate of the displacement since their localization is better. Once a set of matches and a displacement T are computed, the obstacles and terrain patches that are common between the current map and a new image are combined into new polygons, the new features are added to the map while updating the connectivity between features.

This application of the feature matching has been integrated with the rest of the Navlab system. In the actual system, the estimates of the displacement T_0 are taken from the central database that keeps track of the vehicle's position. The size of prediction region is fixed with $\delta =$ one meter, and $\epsilon = 20°$. This implementation of the feature matching has performed successfully over the course of runs of several hundred meters. The final product of the matching is a map that combines all the observations made during the run, and a list of updated obstacle descriptions that are sent to a map module at regular intervals. Since errors in determining position tend to accumulate during such long runs, we always keep the map centered around the current vehicle position. As a result, the map representation is always accurate close to the current vehicle position. As an example, Figure 7.34 shows the result of the matching on five consecutive images separated by about one meter. The scene in this case is a road bordered by a few trees. Figure 7.32 shows the original sequence of raw range and reflectance images, Figure 7.33 shows perspective views of the corresponding individual maps, and Figure 7.34 is a rendition of the combined maps using the displacement and matches computed from the feature matching algorithm. This last display is a view of the map rotated by 45° about the x axis and shaded by the values from the reflectance image.

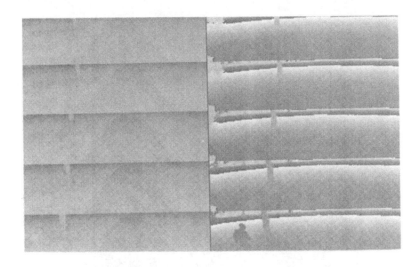

FIGURE 7.32. A sequence of range and reflectance images

Example: Matching local features from high resolution maps

Matching local features from high resolution maps provides the displacement estimate for the iconic matching of high resolution maps. The primitives used for the matching are the high curvature points and lines described in Section 7.3.5. The initial matches are based on the similarity of the length of the lines and the similarity of the curvature strength of the points. The search among candidate matches proceeds as described in Section 7.4.2. Since we have dense elevation at our disposal in this case, we can evaluate a candidate displacement over the entire map by summing up the squared differences between points in one map and points in the transformed map. Figure 7.35 shows the result of the feature matching on a pair of maps. The top image shows the superimposition of the contours and features of the two maps using the estimated displacement (about one meter translation and 4° rotation), while the bottom image shows the correspondences between the point and line features in the two maps. The lower map is transformed by T with respect to the lower right map. Figure 7.36 shows the result of the feature matching in a case in which the maps are separated by a very large displacement. The lower left display shows the area that is common between the two maps after the displacement. Even though the resulting displacement is not accurate enough to reliably merge the maps, it is close enough to the optimum to be used as the starting point of a minimization algorithm.

FIGURE 7.33. Individual maps

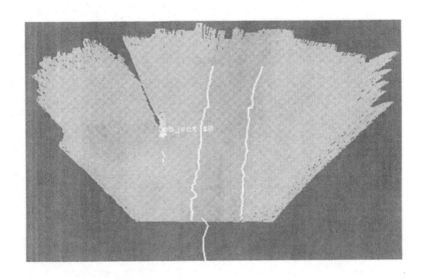

FIGURE 7.34. Perspective view of the combined map

FIGURE 7.35. Matching maps using local features

FIGURE 7.36. Matching maps using local features (large rotation component)

7.4.3   ICONIC MATCHING FROM ELEVATION MAPS

The general idea of the iconic matching algorithm is to find the displacement T between two elevation maps from two different range images that minimizes an error function computed over the entire combined elevation map. The error function E measures how well the first map and the transformed of the second map by T do agree. The easiest formulation for E is the sum of the squared differences between the elevation at a location in the first map and the elevation at the same location computed from the second map using T. To be consistent with the earlier formulation of the locus algorithm, the elevation at any point of the first map is actually the intersection of a line containing this point with the range image. We need some additional notations to formally define E: R and t denote the rotation and translation parts of T respectively, $f_i(u, v)$ is the function that maps a line in space described by a point and a unit vector to a point in by the generalized locus algorithm of Section 7.3.5 applied to image i. We have then:

$$E = \sum \|f_1(u, v) - g(u, v, T)\|^2 \qquad (7.19)$$

where $g(u, v, T)$ is the intersection of the transformed of the line (u, v) by T with image 2 expressed in the coordinate system of image 1 (Figure 7.37). The summation in Equation (7.19) is taken over all the locations (u, v) in the first map where both $f_1(u, v)$ and $g(u, v, T)$ are defined. The lines (u, v) in the first map are parallel to the z-axis. In other words:

$$g(u, v, T) = T^{-1}(f_2(u', v')) = R' f_2(u', v') + t' \qquad (7.20)$$

where $T^{-1} = (R', t') = (R^{-1}, -R^{-1}t)$ is the inverse transformation of T, and $(u', v') = (Ru + t, Rv)$ is the transformed of the line (u, v). This Equation demonstrates one of the reasons why the locus algorithm is powerful: in order to compute $f_2(Ru + t, Rv)$ we can apply directly the locus algorithm, whereas we would have to do some interpolation or resampling if we were using conventional grid-based techniques. We can also at this point fully justify the formulation of the generalized locus algorithm in Section 7.3.5: The transformed line (u', v') can be anywhere in space in the coordinate system of image 2, even though the original line (u, v) is parallel to the z-axis, necessitating the generalized locus algorithm to compute $f_2(u', v')$.

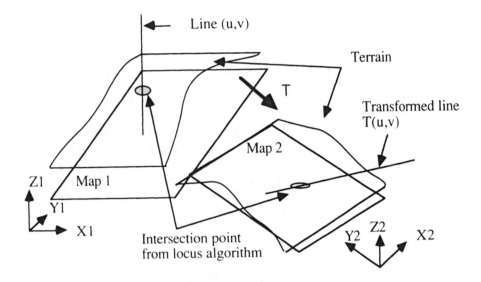

FIGURE 7.37. Principle of the iconic matching algorithm

We now have to find the displacement T for which E is minimum. If $\nu = [\alpha, \beta, \gamma, t_x, t_y, t_z]^t$ is the 6-vector of parameters of T, where the first three components are the rotation angles and the last three are the components of the translation vector, then E reaches a minimum when:

$$\frac{\partial E}{\partial \nu} = 0 \tag{7.21}$$

Assuming an initial estimate T_0, such a minimum can be found by an iterative gradient descent of the form:

$$\nu^{i+1} = \nu^i + k\frac{\partial E}{\partial \nu}(\nu^i) \tag{7.22}$$

where ν^i is the estimate of ν at iteration i. From Equation (7.19), the derivative of E can be computed by:

$$\frac{\partial E}{\partial \nu} = -2 \sum (f_1(u, v) - g(u, v, T)) \frac{\partial g}{\partial \nu}(u, v, T) \tag{7.23}$$

From Equation (7.20), we get the derivative of g:

$$\frac{\partial g}{\partial \nu}(u, v, T) = R' \frac{\partial f_2}{\partial \nu}(u', v') + \frac{\partial R'}{\partial \nu} f_2(u', v') + \frac{\partial t'}{\partial \nu} \tag{7.24}$$

The derivatives appearing in the last two components in Equation (7.24) are the derivatives of the transformation with respect to its parameters which can be computed analytically. The last step to compute the derivative of $g(u, v, T)$ is therefore to compute the derivative of $f_2(u', v')$ with respect to ν. We could write the derivative with respect to each component ν_i of ν by applying the chain rule directly:

$$\frac{\partial f_2}{\partial \nu_i}(u', v') = \frac{\partial f_2}{\partial u} \frac{\partial u'}{\partial \nu_i} + \frac{\partial f_2}{\partial v} \frac{\partial v'}{\partial \nu_i} \tag{7.25}$$

Equation (7.25) leads however to unstabilities in the gradient algorithm because, as we pointed out in Section 7.3.5, the (u, v) representation is an ambiguous representation of lines in space. We need to use a non ambiguous representation in order to correctly compute the derivative. According to equation (7.11), we can use interchangeably the (u, v) representation and the unambiguous (a, b, p, q) representation. Therefore by considering f_2 as a function of the transform by T, $l' = (a', b', p', q')$, of a line $l = (a, b, p, q)$ in image 1, we can transform Equation (7.25) to:

$$\frac{\partial f_2}{\partial \nu_i}(l') = \frac{\partial f_2}{\partial l'} \frac{\partial l'}{\partial \nu_i} \tag{7.26}$$

Since the derivative $\partial f_2 / \partial l'$ depends only on the data in image 2, we cannot compute it analytically and have to estimate it from the image data. We approximate the derivatives of f_2 with respect to $a, b, p,$ and q by differences of the type:

$$\frac{\partial f_2}{\partial a} = \frac{f(a + \Delta a, b, p, q) - f(a, b, p, q)}{\Delta a} \tag{7.27}$$

Approximations such as Equation (7.27) work well because the combination of the locus algorithm and the GNC image smoothing produces smooth variations of the intersection points.

The last derivatives that we have to compute to complete the evaluation of $\partial E / \partial \nu$ are the derivatives of l' with respect to each motion parameter ν_i. We start by observing that if $X = [x, y, z]^t$ is a point on the line of parameter l, and $X' = [x', y', z']^t$ is the transformed of X by T that lies on a line of parameter l', then we have the following relations from Equation (7.11):

$$x = az + p, x' = a'z' + p' \tag{7.28}$$
$$y = bz + q, y' = b'z' + q'$$

By eliminating X and X' between Equation (7.28) and the relation $X' = RX + t$, we have the relation between l and l':

$$a' = \frac{R_x.V}{R_z.V}, \quad p' = R_x.U + t_x - a'(R_z.U + t_z) \tag{7.29}$$

$$b' = \frac{R_y.V}{R_z.V}, \quad q' = R_y.U + t_y - b'(R_z.U + t_z)$$

where R_x, R_y, R_z are the row vectors of the rotation matrix R, $A = [a, b, 1]^t$, $B = [p, q, 0]^t$. We now have l' as a function of l and T, making it easy to compute the derivatives with respect to ν_i from Equation (7.29).

In the actual implementation of the matching algorithm, the points at which the elevation is computed in the first map are distributed on a square grid of ten centimeters resolution. The lines (u, v) are therefore vertical and pass through the centers of the grid cells. E is normalized by the number of points since the since of the overlap region between the two maps is not known in advance. We first compute the $f_1(u, v)$ for the entire grid for image 1, and then apply directly the gradient descent algorithm described above. The iterations stop either when the variation of error ΔE is small enough, or when E itself is small enough. Since the matching is computationally expensive, we compute E over an eight by eight meter window in the first image. The last test ensures that we do not keep iterating if the error is smaller than what can be reasonably achieved given the characteristics of the sensor. Figure 7.38 shows the result of combining three high resolution elevation maps. The displacements between maps are computed using the iconic matching algorithm. The maps are actually combined by replacing the elevation $f_1(u, v)$ by the combination:

$$\frac{\sigma_1 f_1 + \sigma_2 f_2}{\sigma_1 + \sigma_2} \tag{7.30}$$

where σ_1 and σ_2 are the uncertainty values computed as in Section 7.3.5. Equation (7.30) is derived by considering the two elevation values as Gaussian distributions. The resulting mean error in elevation is lower than ten centimeters. We computed the initial T_0 by using the local feature matching of Section 7.4.2. This estimate is sufficient to ensure the convergence to the true value. This is important because the gradient descent algorithm converges towards a local minimum, and it is therefore important to show that T_0 is close to the minimum. Figure 7.39 plots the value of the ν_i's with respect to the number of iterations. These curves show that E converges in a smooth fashion. The coefficient k that controls the rate of convergence is very conservative in this case in order to avoid oscillations about the minimum.

Several variations of the core iconic matching algorithm are possible. First of all, we assumed implicitly that E is a smooth function of ν; this not true in general because the summation in Equation (7.19) is taken only

ltm.seq25-28.gif(view1)

FIGURE 7.38. Combining four maps by the iconic matching algorithm

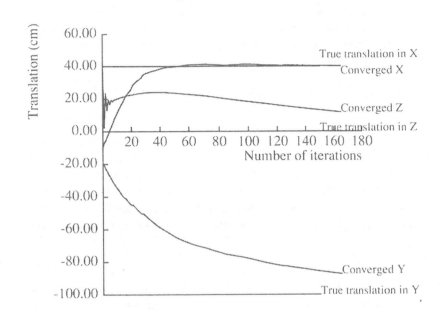

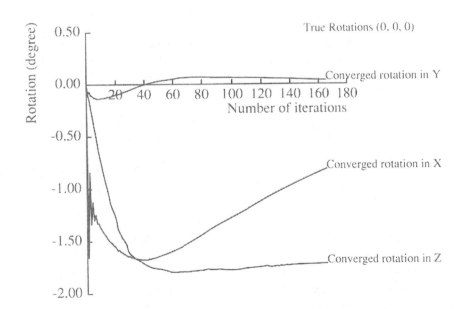

FIGURE 7.39. Convergence rate of the matching algorithm

over the regions in which both f_1 and g are defined, that is the intersection of the regions of map 1 and 2 that is neither range shadows nor outside of the field of view. Such a summation implicitly involves the use of a non-differentiable function that is 1 inside the acceptable region and 0 outside. This does not affect the algorithm significantly because the changes in ν from one iteration to the next are small enough. A differentiable formulation for E would be of the form:

$$E = \sum \mu_1(u, v)\mu_2(T(u, v))\|f_1(u, v) - g(u, v, T)\|^2 \qquad (7.31)$$

where $\mu_i(u, v)$ is a function that is at most 1 when the point is inside a region where $f_i(u, v)$ is defined and vanishes as the point approaches a forbidden region, that is a range shadow or a region outside of the field of view. The summation in Eq. 7.31 is taken over the entire map. In order to avoid a situation in which the minimum is attained when the two maps do not overlap ($E = 0$), we must also normalize E by the number of points in the overlap region. For E to be still smooth, we should therefore normalize by:

$$\sum \mu_1(u, v)\mu_2(u, v) \qquad (7.32)$$

In addition to E being smooth, we also assumed that matching the two maps entirely determines the six parameters of T. This assumption may not be true in all cases. A trivial example is one in which we match two images of a flat plane, where only the vertical translation can be computed from the matching. The gradient algorithm does not converge in those degenerate cases because the minimum $T(\nu)$ may have arbitrarily large values within a surface in parameter space. A modification of the matching algorithm that would ensure that the algorithm does converge to some infinite value changes Equation (7.19) to:

$$E = \sum \|f_1(u, v) - g(u, v, T)\|^2 + \sum_i \lambda_i \nu_i^2 \qquad (7.33)$$

The effect of the weights λ_i is to include the constraint that the ν_i's do not increase to infinity in the minimization algorithm.

7.5   Combining range and intensity data

In the previous Section we have concentrated on the use of 3-D vision as it relates solely to the navigation capabilities of mobile robots. Geometric accuracy was the deciding factor in the choice of representations. This is appropriate when all we need is sufficient information for the vehicle to navigate through its environment. In many cases, however, we need more than geometric descriptions. The most important case is the landmark recognition problem in which we have to identify stored object models in a scene. In that case, geometric information may not be sufficient to unambiguously identify the sought object. Other types of information, such as surface markings, may also be needed. In general, tasks that require some kind of semantic interpretation of an observed scene involve the use of other types of information in addition to the geometric descriptions. Even though this has received relatively little attention in the field of mobile robotics, we anticipate a increasing need for research in this direction as the navigation issues become better understood.

As a first step, we address in this Section the problem of combining 3-D data with data from other sensors. The most interesting problem is the combination of 3-D data with color images since these are the two most common sensors for outdoor robots. Since the sensors have different fields of view and positions, we first present an algorithm for transforming the images into a common frame. As an example of the use of combined range/color images, we describe a simple scene analysis program in Section 7.5.3.

7.5.1 THE GEOMETRY OF VIDEO CAMERAS

The video camera is a standard color vidicon camera equipped with wide-angle lenses. The color images are 480 rows by 512 columns, and each band is coded on eight bits. The wide-angle lens induces a significant geometric distortion in that the relation between a point in space and its projection on the image plane does not obey the laws of the standard perspective transformation. We alleviate this problem by first transforming the actual image into an "ideal" image: if (R, C) is the position in the real image, then the position (r, c) in the ideal image is given by:

$$r = f_r(R, C), c = f_c(R, C) \qquad (7.34)$$

where f_r and f_c are third order polynomials. This correction is cheap since the right-hand side of (7.34) can be put in lookup tables. The actual computation of the polynomial is described in [Mor80] The geometry of the ideal image obeys the laws of the perspective projection in that if $P = [x, y, z]^t$ is a point in space, and (r, c) is its projection in the ideal image plane, then:

$$r = fx/z, c = fy/z \qquad (7.35)$$

where f is the focal length. In the rest of the paper, row and column positions will always refer to the positions in the ideal image, so that perspective geometry is always assumed.

7.5.2 THE REGISTRATION PROBLEM

Range sensor and video cameras have different fields of view, orientations, and positions. In order to be able to merge data from both sensors, we

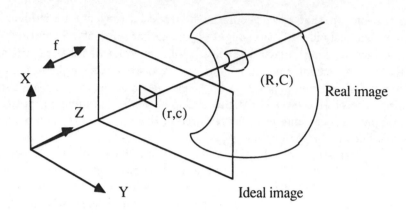

FIGURE 7.40. Geometry of the video camera

first have to estimate their relative positions, known as the calibration or registration problem (Figure 7.41). We approach the problem as a minimization problem in which pairs of pixels are selected in the range and video images. The pairs are selected so that each pair is the image of a single point in space as viewed from the two sensors. The problem is then to find the best calibration parameters given these pairs of points and is further divided into two steps: we first use a simple linear least-squares approach to find a rough initial estimate of the parameters, and then apply a non-linear minimization algorithm to compute an optimal estimate of the parameters.

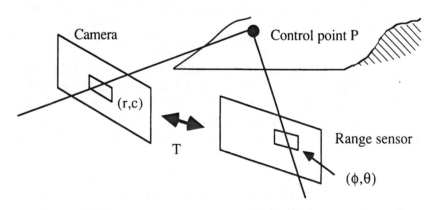

FIGURE 7.41. Geometry of the calibration problem

The calibration problem as a minimization problem

Let P_i be a point in space, with coordinates P_i^e with respect to the range sensor, and coordinates P_i^c with respect to the video camera. The relationship between the two coordinates is:

$$P_i^c = RP_i^e - T \qquad (7.36)$$

where R is a rotation matrix, and T is a translation vector. R is a non-linear function of the orientation angles of the camera: pan (α), tilt (β), and rotation (γ). P_i^e can be computed from a pixel location in the range image. P_i^c is not completely known, it is related to the pixel position in the video image by the perspective transformation:

$$z_i^c r_i = f x_i^c \qquad (7.37)$$
$$z_i^c c_i = f y_i^c \qquad (7.38)$$

where f is the focal length. Substituting (7.36) into (7.37) and (7.38) we get:

$$R_z P_i^e r_i - T_z r_i - f R_x P_i^e + T_x' = 0 \qquad (7.39)$$
$$R_z P_i^e c_i - T_z c_i - f R_y P_i^e + T_y' = 0 \qquad (7.40)$$

where R_x, R_y, and R_z are the row vectors of the rotation matrix R, and $T_y' = fT_y$, $T_x' = fT_x$.

We are now ready to reduce the calibration problem to a least-squares minimization problem. Given n points P_i, we want to find the transformation (R, T) that minimizes the left-hand sides of equations (7.39) and (7.40). We first estimate T by a linear least-squares algorithm, and then compute the optimal estimate of all the parameters.

Initial estimation of camera position

Assuming that we have an estimate of the orientation R, we want to estimate the corresponding T. The initial value of R can be obtained by physical measurements using inclinometers. Under these conditions, the criterion to be minimized is:

$$C = \sum_{i=1}^{n} [(A_i - T_z B_i - f C_i + T_x')^2 + (D_i - T_z E_i - f F_i + T_y')^2] \qquad (7.41)$$

where $A_i = R_z P_i^e r_i$, $B_i = r_i$, $C_i = R_x P_i^e$, $D_i = R_z P_i^e c_i$, $E_i = c_i$, and $F_i = R_y P_i^e$ are known and T_z, T_x', T_y', f are the unknowns.

Equation (7.41) can be put in matrix form:

$$C = \|U - AV\|^2 - \|W - BV\|^2 \qquad (7.42)$$

where $V = [T_x', T_y', T_z, f]^t$, $U = [A_1, .., A_n]^t$, $W = [D_1, .., D_n]^t$, $A = \begin{bmatrix} B_i & 0 & -1 & C_i \\ \cdot & \cdot & & \cdot \\ B_n & 0 & -1 & C_n \end{bmatrix}$, and $B = \begin{bmatrix} E_i & -1 & 0 & F_i \\ \cdot & & \cdot & \cdot \\ E_n & -1 & 0 & F_n \end{bmatrix}$. The minimum for the criterion of Equation (7.42) is attained at the parameter vector:

$$V = (A^t A + B^t B)^{-1}(A^t U + B^t W) \qquad (7.43)$$

Optimal estimation of the calibration parameters

Once we have computed the initial estimate of V, we have to compute a more accurate estimate of (R, T). Since R is a function of (α, β, γ), we can transform the criterion from equation (7.41) into the form:

$$C = \sum_{i=1}^{n} \|I_i - H_i(S)\|^2 \qquad (7.44)$$

where I_i is the 2-vector representing the pixel position in the video image, $I_i = [r_i, c_i]^t$, and S is the full vector of parameters, $S = [T'_x, T'_y, T_z, f, \alpha, \beta, \gamma]^t$. We cannot directly compute C_{min} since the functions H_i are non-linear; instead we linearize C by using the first order approximation of H_i [Low80]:

$$C \approx \sum_{i=1}^{n} \|I_i - H_i(S_0) - J_i \Delta S\|^2 \qquad (7.45)$$

where J_i is the Jacobian of H_i with respect to S, S_0 is the current estimate of the parameter vector, and $\Delta S = S - S_0$. The right-hand side of (7.45) is minimized when its derivative with respect to ΔS vanishes, that is:

$$\sum_{i=1}^{n} J_i^t J_i \Delta S + J_i^t \Delta C_i = 0 \qquad (7.46)$$

where $\Delta C_i = I_i - H_i(S_0)$. Therefore, the best parameter vector for the linearized criterion is:

$$\Delta S = -\sum_{i=1}^{n} (J_i^t J_i)^{-1} J_i^t \Delta C_i \qquad (7.47)$$

Equation (7.47) is iterated until there is no change in S. At each iteration, the estimate S_0 is updated by: $S_0 \leftarrow S_0 + \Delta S$.

Implementation and performance

The implementation of the calibration procedure follows the steps described above. Pairs of corresponding points are selected in a sequence of video and range images. We typically use twenty pairs of points carefully selected at interesting locations in the image (*e.g.* corners). An initial estimate of the camera orientation is $(0, \beta, 0)$, where β is physically measured using an inclinometer. The final estimate of S is usually obtained after less than ten iterations. This calibration procedure has to be applied only once, as long as the sensors are not displaced.

Once we have computed the calibration parameters, we can merge range and video images into a colored-range image. Instead of having one single fusion program, we implemented this as a library of fusion functions that can be divided in two categories:

1. Range $\rightarrow$ video: This set of functions takes a pixel or a set of pixels (r^e, c^e) in the range image and computes the location (r^c, c^c) in the video image. This is implemented by directly applying Equations (7.39) and (7.40).

2. Video $\rightarrow$ range: This set of functions takes a pixel or a set of pixels (r^c, c^c) in the video image and computes the location (r^e, c^e) in the range image. The computed location can be used in turn to compute the location of a intensity pixel in 3-D space by directly applying Equation (7.3). The algorithm for this second set of functions is more involved because a pixel in the video image corresponds to a line in space (Figure 7.40) so that Equations (7.39) and (7.40) cannot be applied directly. More precisely, a pixel (r^c, c^c) corresponds, after transformation by (R, T), to a curve C in the range image. C intersects the image at locations (r^e, c^e), where the algorithm reports the location (r^e, c^e) that is the minimum among all the range image pixels that lie on C of the distance between (r^c, c^c) and the projection of (r^e, c^e) in the video image (using the first set of functions). The algorithm is summarized on Figure 7.42.

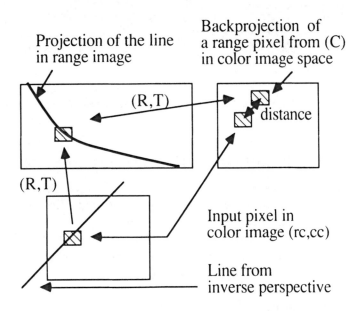

Projection of the line in range image

Backprojection of a range pixel from (C) in color image space

(R, T)

distance

(R, T)

Input pixel in color image (rc,cc)

Line from inverse perspective

FIGURE 7.42. Geometry of the "video $\rightarrow$ range" transformation

Figure 7.43 shows the colored-range image of a scene of stairs and sidewalks, the image is obtained by mapping the intensity values from the color image onto the range image. Figure 7.44 shows a perspective view of the colored-range image. In this example [GMKO86], we first compute the location of each range pixel (r^e, c^e) in the video image, and then assign the color value to the 64 × 256 colored-range image. The final display is obtained by rotating the range pixels, the coordinates of which are computed using Equation (7.3).

FIGURE 7.43. Colored-range image of stairs

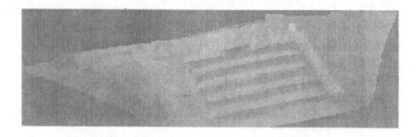

FIGURE 7.44. Perspective view of registered range and color images

7.5.3   APPLICATION TO OUTDOOR SCENE ANALYSIS

An example of the use of the fusion of range and video images is outdoor scene analysis [HK85,KHK88b] in which we want to identify the main components of an outdoor scene, such as trees, roads, grass, etc. The colored-range image concept makes the scene analysis problem easier by providing data pertinent to both geometric information (*e.g.* the shape of the trees) and physical information (*e.g.* the color of the road).

Feature extraction from a colored-range image

The features that we extract from a colored-range image must be related to two types of information: the shapes and the physical properties of the observed surfaces.

The geometric features are used to describe the shape of the objects in the scene. We propose to use two types of features: regions that correspond to smooth patches of surface, and edges that correspond either to transitions between regions, or to transitions between objects (occluding edges). Furthermore, we must be able to describe the features in a compact way. One common approach is to describe the regions as quadric patches, and the edges as sets of tri-dimensional line segments. More sophisticated descriptions are possible [BJ85c], such as bicubic patches or curvature descriptors. We use simpler descriptors since the range data is relatively low resolution, and we do not have the type of accurate geometric model that is suited for using higher order geometric descriptors. The descriptors attached to each geometric feature are:

- The parameters describing the shape of the surface patches. That is the parameters of the quadric surface that approximate each surface patch.

- The shape parameters of the surface patches such as center, area, and elongations.

- The 3-D polygonal description of the edges.

- The 3-D edge types: convex, concave, or occluding.

The surface patches are extracted by fitting a quadric of equation $X^t A X + B^t X + C = 0$ to the observed surfaces, where X is the Cartesian coordinate vector computed from a pixel in the range image. The fitting error,

$$E(A, B, C) = \sum_{X_i \in patch} [X_i^t A X_i + B^t X_i + C]^2 \qquad (7.48)$$

is used to control the growing of regions over the observed surfaces. The parameters A, B, C are computed by minimizing $E(A, B, C)$ as in [FH86].

The features related to physical properties are regions of homogeneous color in the video image, that is regions within which the color values vary smoothly. The choice of these features is motivated by the fact that an homogeneous region is presumably part of a single scene component, although the converse is not true as in the case of the shadows cast by an object on an homogeneous patch on the ground. The color homogeneity criterion we use is the distance $(X - m)^t \Sigma^{-1} (X - m)$ where m is the average mean value on the region, Σ is the covariance matrix of the color distribution over the region, and X is the color value of the current pixel in $(red, green, blue)$ space. This is a standard approach to color image segmentation and pattern recognition. The descriptive parameters that are retained for each region are:

- The color statistics (m, Σ).

- The polygonal representation of the region border.

- Shape parameters such as center or moments.

The range and color features may overlap or disagree. For example, the shadow cast by an object on a flat patch of ground would divide one surface patch into two color regions. It is therefore necessary to have a cross-referencing mechanism between the two groups of features. This mechanism provides a two-way direct access to the geometric features that intersect color features. Extracting the relations between geometric and physical features is straightforward since all the features are registered in the colored-range image.

An additional piece of knowledge that is important for scene interpretation is the spatial relationships between features. For example, the fact that a vertical object is connected to a large flat plane through a concave edge may add evidence to the hypothesis that this object is a tree. As in this example, we use three types of relational data:

- The list of features connected to each geometric or color feature.

- The type of connection between two features (convex / concave / occluding) extracted from the range data.

- The length and strength of the connection. This last item is added to avoid situations in which two very close regions become accidentally connected along a small edge.

Scene interpretation from the colored-range image

Interpreting a scene requires the recognition of the main components of the scene such as trees or roads. Since we are dealing with natural scenes, we cannot use the type of geometric matching that is used in the context of industrial parts recognition [BJ85c]. For example, we cannot assume that a given object has specific quadric parameters. Instead, we have to rely on "fuzzier" evidence such as the verticality of some objects or the flatness of others. We therefore implemented the object models as sets of properties that translate into constraints on the surfaces, edges, and regions found in the image. For example, the description encodes four such properties:

- $P1$: The color of the trunk lies within a specific range $\implies$ constraint on the statistics (m, Σ) of a color region.

- $P2$: The shape of the trunk is roughly cyclindrical $\implies$ constraint on the distribution of the principal values of the matrix A of the quadric approximation.

- $P3$: The trunk is connected to a flat region by a concave edge $\implies$ constraint on the neighbors of the surface, and the type of the connecting edge.

- $P4$: The tree has two parallel vertical occluding edges $\Longrightarrow$ constraint on the 3-D edges description.

Other objects such as roads or grass areas have similar descriptions. The properties P_{ij} of the known object models M_j are evaluated on all the features F_k extracted from the colored-range image. The result of the evaluation is a score S_{ijk} for each pair (P_{ij}, F_k). We cannot rely on individual scores since some may not be satisfied because of other objects, or because of segmentation problems. In the tree trunk example, one of the lateral occluding edges may itself be occluded by some other object, in which case the score for $P4$ would be low while the score for the other properties would still be high. In order to circumvent this problem, we first sort the possible interpretations M_j for a given feature F_k according to all the scores $(S_{ij})_i$. In doing this, we ensure that all the properties contribute to the final interpretation and that no interpretations are discarded at this stage while identifying the most plausible interpretations.

We have so far extracted plausible interpretations only for individual scene features F_k. The final stage in the scene interpretation is to find the interpretations (M_{j_k}, F_k) that are globally consistent. For example, property $P3$ for the tree implies a constraint on a neighboring region, namely that this has to be a flat ground region. Formally, a set of consistency constraints C_{mn} is associated with each pair of objects (M_m, M_n). The C_{mn} constraints are propagated through the individual interpretations (M_{j_k}, F_k) by using the connectivity information stored in the colored-range feature description. The propagation is simple considering the small number of features remaining at this stage.

The final result is a consistent set of interpretations of the scene features, and a grouping of the features into sets that correspond to the same object. The last result is a by-product of the consistency check and the use of connectivity data. Figure 7.45 shows the color and range images of a scene which contains a road, a couple of trees, and a garbage can. Figure 7.46 shows a display of the corresponding colored-range image in which the white pixels are the points in the range image that have been mapped into the video image. This set of points is actually sparse because of the difference in resolutions between the two sensors, and some interpolation was performed to produce the dense regions of Figure 7.46.

Only a portion of the image is registered due to the difference in field of view between the two sensors (60° for the camera versus 30° in the vertical direction for the range sensor). Figure 7.47 shows a portion of the image in which the edge points from the range image are projected on the color image. The edges are interpreted as the side edges of the tree and the connection between the ground and the tree. Figure 7.48 shows the final scene interpretation. The white dots are the main edges found in the range image. The power of the colored-range image approach is demonstrated by the way the road is extracted. The road in this image is separated into many pieces by strong shadows. Even though the shadows do not satisfy the color constraint on road region, they do perform well on the shape criterion (flatness), and on the consistency criteria (both with the other road regions, and with the trees). The shadows are therefore interpreted as road regions and merge with the other regions into one road region. This type of reasoning is in general difficult to apply when only video data is used unless one uses stronger models of the objects such as an explicit model of a shadowed road region. Using the colored-range image also makes the consistency propagation a much easier task than in purely color-based scene interpretation programs [Oht84].

FIGURE 7.45. Color and range images of an outdoor scene

7.6   Conclusion

We have described techniques for building and manipulating 3-D terrain representations from range images. We have demonstrated these techniques on real images of outdoor scenes. Some of them (Sections 7.3.3, 7.3.4, and 7.4.2) were integrated in a large mobile robot system that was suc-

FIGURE 7.46. A view of the corresponding colored-range image

FIGURE 7.47. Edge features from the colored-range image

FIGURE 7.48. Final scene interpretation

cessfully tested in the field. We expect that the module that manipulates and creates these terrain representations will become part of the standard core system of our outdoor mobile robots, just as a local path planner or a low-level vehicle controller are standard modules of a mobile robot system independent of its application. This work will begin by combining the polygonal terrain representation of Section 7.3.4 with the path planner of [Ste88] in order to generate the basic capabilities for an off-road vehicle.

Many issues still remain to be investigated. First of all, we must define a uniform way of representing and combining the uncertainties in the terrain maps. Currently, the uncertainty models depend heavily on the type of sensor used and on the level at which the terrain is represented. Furthermore, the displacements between terrain maps are known only up to a certain level of uncertainty. This level of uncertainty must be evaluated and updated through the matching of maps, whether iconic or feature-based. Regarding the combination of the 3-D representations with representations from other sensors, we need to define an algorithm for sensor registration that is general enough for application to a variety of situations. The algorithms presented in Section 7.5 are still very dependent on the sensors that we used, and on the intended application. Registration schemes such as [GTK88] would enable us to have a more uniform approach to the problem. An added effect of using such a registration algorithm is that we could explicitly represent errors caused by the combination of the sensors, which we did not do in Section 7.5. Another issue concerns our presentation of the three levels of terrain representation, the matching algorithms, and the sensor combination algorithms as separate problems. We should define a common perceptual architecture to integrate these algorithms in a common representation that can be part of the core system of a mobile robot. Finally, we have tackled the terrain representation problems mainly from a geometrical point of view. Except in Section 7.5, we did not attempt to extract semantic interpretations from the representations. A natural extension of this work is to use the 3-D terrain representations to identify known objects in the scene. Another application along these lines is to use the terrain maps to identify objects of interest, such as terrain regions for sampling tasks for a planetary explorer [Kwe88]. Although we have performed some preliminary experiments in that respect [HK88,BW88], extracting semantic information from terrain representations remains a major research area for outdoor mobile robots.

8

Multisensor Fusion for Automatic Scene Interpretation

J. K. Aggarwal
N. Nandhakumar[1]

8.1 Introduction

The area of computer analysis of images for automated detection and classification of objects in a scene has been intensively researched in the recent past. Two kinds of approaches may be noted in current and past research in machine perception - (1) To model the functions of biological vision systems, e.g., edge detection by the human visual system, and (2) To develop a scheme which a machine can use for accomplishing a particular task, e.g. automated detection of faulty placement of components on a printed circuit board. The latter approach produces a scheme that is application specific. In developing a scheme for a particular machine perception task one has a wide choice of sensing modalities and techniques to interpret the sensed signals. One is not limited by characteristics of a biological vision system that one is forced to emulate in the first approach, not even by the restriction that system emulate only the observed behavior of the biological system.

Yet, most reported machine perception research projects in the past have considered only a single sensing modality. This is in spite of the fact that past research has shown it to be very difficult, if at all possible, to extract sufficient information using any single sensing modality to accomplish a given perception task under conditions that are not overly restrictive. Multiple sensors which sense different physical properties of the scene, e.g., visual reflectivity, thermal radiosity, and depth, may be used to overcome this limitation by providing the additional information which is required to minimize the ambiguity in interpretation. Indeed, many biological 'vision' (perception) systems use multiple sensing modalities. Again, the specific modalities and the fusion of information is dictated by the application,

---

[1]Computer and Vision Research Center, The University of Texas at Austin, Austin, TX 78712

i.e., the domain and the manner in which the animal functions. A few of these systems which have been extensively studied include the perceptual mechanism of pit vipers and boid snakes which combine information from thermal and visual imagery, the perceptual system of owls which combine acoustic and visual maps, and those of fish which use electric field sensors and detect the degree of polarization of light. Thus, there are biological precedents as well as practical reasons based on engineering principles for the incorporation of multiple sensing modalities in machine perception.

The use of two or more images obtained from the same sensor has already been used for extracting more information about the imaged scene, and this approach has been intensively researched. For example, two or more visual images have been used to provide depth via stereoscopy, and multiple views using structured lighting have been used to construct more complete models of objects than was possible with a single view. Although additional information regarding the scene is available using multiple images from the same sensor, information is still lacking for meaningful interpretation of images of real, complex scenes.

The use of multiple modalities of imaging is seen as a more promising approach for minimizing the ambiguities in image interpretation. The different types of sensors provide information regarding different physical parameters of scene objects. The simultaneous use of different kinds of sensors thus provides a rich description of the sensed scene and hence is capable of making available highly specific features for classification.

The incorporation of multiple sensors in an automated image analysis system, though ostensibly easy to envision, poses several important and difficult questions. The significant issues are: (i) What do we know about the images generated by each sensor? (ii) How is information derived from one sensor related to information derived from another sensor of perhaps a different type? (iii) What is the best strategy for interpreting multisensory data?

In the following discussion we address these issues, and indicate possible directions for future research aimed at answering the questions which we have just posed. Section 8.2 presents a discussion of Image Models. Section 8.3 delineates methodology for Intersensory Verification of Image Features and Section 8.4 details the evolving ideas on Intersensory Verification from Physical Principles. The ideas presented in these sections are illustrated by presenting the main principles of relevant research which we have conducted in this area. This chapter is not meant to be an exhaustive compendium of such research. We present our perspective on developing computer vision systems which exploit the advantages of multisensor fusion. In Section 8.5 we illustrate some of the ideas presented in sections 8.2 to 8.4 by discussing the salient features of a multisensory machine perception scheme which we have developed for classifying objects in an outdoor scene. This scheme uses information derived from thermal and visual images which are processed concomitantly to derive meaningful features based on intrinsic thermal properties of the imaged objects. Finally, section 8.6 concludes this chapter with a brief summary.

8.2   Image Models

Most image analysis systems process and analyze specific classes of images. It behooves us to design analysis techniques that exploit the knowledge about the specific domain of the given image. However, most low-level and intermediate-level vision algorithms are not domain specific and in applying these algorithms we fail to exploit knowledge about the sensor and the scene. In addition, the knowledge may include information about the scene environment, image acquisition system, the imaging geometry and host of other parameters. In practice, most image analysis techniques are relatively general purpose. They do not adequately exploit the available information regarding their domain of application. This is partly due to our lack of understanding about image models and their relationship with image processing techniques. In particular, given a specific analysis technique, it is rarely known what specific assumptions the image must satisfy in order for the technique to be applicable. Or stated in a different manner, given a set assumption about the domain, can one design an "optimal" analysis technique? The answer to this rhetorical question is obviously "no" in most cases.

Also, vision algorithms have been developed for analyzing images acquired using each of a variety of sensing modalities. Sensors that have been considered include visual monochrome and color, stereoscopic, infrared, laser range (triangulation and time of flight systems), laser radar, millimeter wave radar, and ultraviolet imagers, tactile sensors, acoustic and ultrasonic sensors among others. However, models for images produced by each of these sensors are as yet incomplete and warrant further research.

8.2.1   Classes of Models

Image models may be broadly classified into three categories: (1) Statistical models, (2) Spatial models, and (3) Physical models. Such models have been used in past research in image analysis. However, no coherent theory exists to dictate which model is most suitable for a given application. A formal study of existing image models is required to motivate future research in this area. Each of the aforesaid image models will be briefly discussed. The list of different image models presented below is not meant to be exhaustive. Indeed, new image models are required for specific applications, and the development of more accurate application-specific models is required in future research.

1. **Statistical Models**
   Statistical models describe the pixel population and its spatial distribution. Image texture is particularly describable using statistical methods.

   (a) **First Order Models**
   The simplest description of this type is provided by the image's gray level probability density (GLPD). For a digital image this is a discrete density; it is a probability vector of the form $p = (p_1, p_2, ..., p_k)$ where k is the number of possible gray levels.

   (b) **Higher Order Models**
   The nth-order GLPD of a class of images specifies the probability with which every possible n-tuple of gray level occurs in a given set of relative positions. Each set of displacements is defined by an $(n-1)$-tuple of coordinates pairs $((x_2, y_2), ..., (x_n, y_n))$ which specifies the coordinates of the last $(n-1)$ points relative to the first.

   (c) **Models for Local Property Values**
   An alternative method for describing the spatial relationships among pixels in a class of images is to use the probability density of the values of local image properties. Local distributions which are not unimodal denote clumping of gray levels. Such information is useful for clustering procedures.

2. **Spatial Models**
   Models that specify how an image is broken up into regions generally give more information about the image than models that specify gray-level statistics. Several models may be formulated depending upon interaction between regions, transitions between regions, their sizes and shapes. Spatial models are based on the geometry of objects, object locations, relationships between objects, and the occurrence of objects in an image.

   (a) **Objects On Background**
   Images may be composed of "objects" on a background where objects may be of one or several types. Objects may touch or may be widely spaced so that they rarely touch. Decompositions of an image may be described by:

   i. Statistics of object sizes and shapes, and

   ii. Statistics of object positions and orientations

   (b) **Image Decompositions**
   Mosaic Models: Images may be thought of as being partitioned into regions leading to mosaic images. Image partitions may be generated by various types of Geometrical Processes. Growth

Processes may be used to generate partitions by starting with a regular or a random distribution of points to grow regions.

(c) **Inter-region Transitions**
The boundaries between objects and background or between adjacent pairs of regions may be sharp or gradual.

(d) **Region Shape: Borders**
A region without holes is determined by specifying its border, which is a closed curve. One can model classes of region shapes by defining classes of curves.

3. **Physical Models**
In order to establish accurate image models for each sensor it is important to understand the physical processes that generate the sensed signal. Thus, an accurate model for images sensed by LADAR is not complete without a model of the speckle generation mechanisms, or of atmospheric effects. Expected region sizes and shapes based on size, shape and attitude of imaged objects and the distance from sensor to scene are some possible parameters to be modeled. A priori knowledge of trajectory or other temporal dependence of the image also may be exploited.

Further discussion of physical models is deferred to section 8.4 which raises issues related to modeling the physical phenomena that produce the different images acquired by different imaging modalities. It should be noted that although techniques for the analysis of images acquired by a variety of sensing modalities have been reported, models based on physical phenomena that give rise to these images are at best incomplete.

8.2.2 SOME EXAMPLES OF IMAGE MODELS

In the recent past, we have devoted a great deal of effort to the task of image modeling and analysis. Generalized co-occurrence matrices have been used for modeling and interpreting images based on pixel intensity variation, edge-pixel distribution and extended-edge descriptions [DJA79, DCA81]. Image textures were successfully modeled and detected using nearest-neighbor classifier, linear discriminant classifier and Battacharyya distance figure of merit. Statistical models based on the Fourier spectrum and co-occurrence matrices have also been developed for multiple resolution imagery [RAM87]. Log-Normal distributions were developed for a specific class of photomicrograph images [HSA85]. Geometric Modeling of boundary morphology and modeling of temporal change of boundaries have also been successfully attempted for a class of biomedical imagery [VDA84]. In addition to the above, other approaches to modeling images may be found in recent journal papers and books. For example, various geometrical representations are dealt with in chapter 8 of [BB82] and chapter 10 of [YF86]. Texture models are described in chapter 6 of [BB82] and chapters 11 and 12 of [YF86]. A comprehensive overview of stochastic image modeling techniques is presented in chapter 6 of [Jai86].

The references cited above constitute only a small sample of the available literature on image models. It may be noted that many different approaches are available. It seems unlikely that a general, unified approach is likely to emerge though or is useful or even meaningful given the widely differing requirements that different vision tasks specify. Research in the establishment of accurate and complete models which are application specific needs to be continued and intensified especially from the perspective of using different combinations of sensors for novel applications.

8.3   Intersensory Verification of Image Features

Images derived from the same scene through the use of different sensors, in general, produce different features, which may or may not be caused by the same underlying physical phenomena. For example, edge maps extracted from visual imagery may or may not correspond to jump boundaries extracted from range maps. However, the spatial congruence of features from different images provides increased confidence in the existence of the physical phenomenon causing the features. In the case where edge maps from visual images coincide with jump boundaries extracted from range images, the existence of surface discontinuities is substantiated. Hence, it is important to search for and establish the relationship between features extracted from the different images.

The combination of edges from range and visual imagery is, relatively speaking, a simpler task than the more general tasks of combining information from disparate sensing modalities, e.g., infrared, range, visual, ultraviolet. There are no general principles that address the extraction and combination of information from these different modalities. The extraction of features from each imaging modality depends on the image generation phenomenon which is peculiar to that sensing modality as well as the task being considered. An important class of relationships between features is based on geometric considerations, such as - did these edges arise from the same location in the scene, and is termed feature registration. The issues to be addressed in the registration of features are discussed below.

8.3.1   ISSUES

1. **Spatial Resolution of Images**
   Do the pixels correspond to the same sized surface patch in the scene?
   Are the pixel dimensions of the images of the same size and shape?

2. Co-ordinate Transformations

If the sensors are not co-boresighted or if they are mis-aligned, the transformation that brings the images into alignment needs to be identified. This is a non-trivial task that is complicated by virtue of it being scene-dependent. Appropriate strategies for calibration need to be designed. The strategy would have to be adaptive in nature. For example, the transformation required to spatially register different images of a scene would depend on the distance from the sensors to the scene. Other discrepancies due to the design of the sensors need to be considered. Scanning mechanisms in popular IR cameras used sinusoidal driving signals [Inf], while the visual cameras use linear ramps. Accurate calibration and re-scaling of the coordinates are therefore warranted to register the images produced by these different systems.

3. Search Algorithms

Establishing correspondence between features in different imagery involves computationally intensive search. Appropriate algorithms need to be chosen or designed depending on the task. Several approaches are possible, such as Relaxation Labeling, Heuristic Search, and Dynamic Programming, among others. Past experience in designing and implementing such algorithms [KA87b] has established the severe demands placed on computational power. If the correspondence is to be effected in real-time, the algorithms developed must be "smarter" than those available today. The high degree of parallelism that exists in such algorithms must also be exploited by the design of special architectures dedicated to such search algorithms.

4. Validation

Having established the correspondence between features extracted from differently sensed images it becomes necessary to use the correspondence to assert the existence of the physical phenomena producing the features. A scheme for making such assertions is necessary. Reasoning schemes that assign confidence values to the assertions are also needed. For example, an edge in the visual image that is congruent with a jump boundary in the range image is more supportive of a surface discontinuity, when compared to the situation where these two features do not coincide but are only close to each other. Validation is further complicated by the processing itself. In particular the processing of registered range and visual images may yield edges which are not necessarily accurately registered. This may lead to problems in validation.

5. Architectures for Sensor Fusion

As mentioned above, the process of establishing correspondence between features in different images is computationally intensive. Special purpose architectures are necessary for the different tasks involved in feature registration process if implementation is to produce reasonable performance. The re-scaling and co-ordinate transformation process requires intensive numerical calculations, best performed by "transform-engines" as in the "graphics engines". The correspondence process requires a great deal of parallel search which is best performed by concurrent processors with flexible communication links between them.

8.3.2   Examples of Intersensory Verification of Image Features

Several of the issues raised above have been addressed in our research in multisensor fusion. Research in intersensory verification of image features extracted from visual and range images has in particular produced significant results and has defined useful approaches for future work in this area. The simultaneous use of jump boundaries in range maps and edges from visual intensity images in segmenting images has been investigated by our group [VA86,GMA83,MA82].

The relationship between the features extracted from the two types of images was established. This was used to develop an approach for using both sources of information for segmenting the images. The use of edges extracted from the visual intensity image along with range data has been further investigated in [MBCA85] and [AM86]. The strengths and weaknesses of range and visual imaging modalities has been discussed in [MA85a] with an eye toward combining them into a system that uses the advantages of each domain to offset the disadvantages of the other. A synopsis of information-integration techniques for image segmentation is contained in [MA85b]. An efficient relaxation scheme for establishing feature correspondence for processing stereo images has also been developed [KA87a].

Other researchers have also adopted similar multisensory approaches. The cooperative use of range and color imagery for outdoor navigation is discussed in [SG87,Kan88]. Surfaces extracted from range images are 'colored' using the color camera output and the resulting information is interpreted. Spatial integration of sonar and stereo range data using an occupancy grid has also been reported [ME88]. Surface reconstruction using both stereo and multiple shape-from-texture modules is discussed in [MB88]. The objective of the combined approach is to increase the robustness of the reconstruction process. Spatial integration of microwave radar and visual (optical) imagery for robust surface reconstruction is discussed in [SdK88]. The cooperative use of focus ranging and stereo ranging modules for surface reconstruction using an agile camera system is described in [KK88].

As mentioned earlier in this section there appear to be no general principles that govern the extraction and combination of information from these different modalities. The extraction of features from each imaging modality and establishing relationships between features from different imaging modalities depends largely on the particular image generating mechanisms involved and the application task. Future research in this area must address the mechanisms for extracting appropriate features from the different imaging modalities and also appropriate algorithms for establishing interrelationships so as to synergistically produce new and useful information that would facilitate the task being addressed.

8.4 Intersensory Verification from Physical Principles

The use of multiple sensing modalities helps to alleviate the underconstrained problem of interpreting images sensed by a single sensor. Multiple sensors provide different kinds of information about the scene. In order to make use of the information in an optimal way, and especially to make use of the different types of information available from the different sensors, it is of paramount importance to understand the mechanisms that generate the different images. Such an understanding allows for an analysis of the sensed images with the objective of extracting object dependent parameters which produce the images. Differences in intrinsic object parameters may be then used to identify/classify the sensed objects. Past research has not adequately addressed the importance of accurately modeling the image generating mechanisms. Several issues need to be considered while developing a scheme for analyzing multisensor data based on models of the physical phenomena that generate the images. These issues are discussed briefly below.

8.4.1 ISSUES

1. **Synergism**
   One of the primary objectives of multisensor fusion is to integrate the different kinds of information derived from the outputs of the various sensors so as to provide additional insight to the (sometimes common) mechanisms functioning in the scene that produce the different sensory outputs. Thus, the different signals are to be combined to provide information that is not available by processing the information separately. This property of synergism is one that is a common characteristic of natural biological perceptual systems which employ multiple sensing modalities, and one that needs to be emulated in automated vision systems. The incorporation of synergistic data fusion has heretofore not been considered by other researchers.

2. Models of the Imaging System

(a) **Scene-Sensor Relationship**
Separate, and detailed models of each sensor's imaging system
are required. The analytical models should relate the scene parameters to the digitized pixel gray level in the image. Different
scene conditions require different assumptions. The main consideration is - What is being sensed? This issue is more complex
than it appears. For example, past research in interpreting IR
imagery has rested on the assumption that the gray level is proportional to the scene temperature. Recent research has shown
this to be an inappropriate assumption [NA86]. Surface emissiv-
ities, view factors (imaging geometry), camera gain, etc. need
to be incorporated in the model relating sensed image to the
viewed scene. The dependence of these parameters on weather
conditions, time of day, and season also need to be incorporated.
In the case of LADAR imagery, the dependence of the strength-
of-return signal on the nature of the viewed surface must be
understood. This would be based on a study of surface behavior when illuminated by coherent light. The model relating image to scene would require the incorporation of such parameters
as: carrier frequency, demodulation characteristics, polarization,
surface reflectivity function, etc.

(b) **Algorithms**
Based on such detailed analytical models relating sensed images
to scene parameters, efficient algorithms need to be devised to
evaluate object parameters from each of the sensed signals. For
example, scene temperature may be estimated from IR images,
and relative surface orientation may be computed using visual
intensity images via a shape from shading technique. Suitable
algorithms need to be devised for other imaging modalities including RADAR and LADAR.

3. Scene Models

(a) **Scene Interactions**
Accurate scene models are required. These must incorporate the
various interactions between scene components which affect the
signal received by the sensor. For example, in analyzing IR imagery, scene models used for estimating surface temperature may
not simply assume that the radiation emanating from each object is due to emission but the model must also consider the
radiation arising from various scene objects which is reflected
by the object being viewed. Thus the model should be substantially complete.

(b) **Incorporating Derived Information**

The fusion of several sensors, makes available, in general, information that cannot be directly obtained by processing the sensors separately. IR and visual imagery has been combined to provide surface heat flux estimates. In such situations the scene model must be based on the mechanisms that support this indirectly sensed information. In the case of IR and visual imagery, the scene model is centered around the surface heat balance and comprises the various components by which heat is gained/lost by the surface of the imaged object.

(c) **Discriminatory Intrinsic Object Properties**

The scene models established must relate the information sensed by the different sensors to intrinsic properties of the objects which help distinguish classes of objects from each other. In combining thermal and visual imagery, the intrinsic thermal property identified was the lumped thermal capacitance which varies widely between the established classes of scene objects. The lumped thermal capacitance describes the object's ability to sink/source heat. Such useful intrinsic properties must be identified when integrating other types of imagery.

(d) **Discriminatory Sensor-Derived Features**

The scene model relates the sensor outputs to the useful intrinsic parameters of the sensed objects. Features must be derived based on the sensor outputs so as to provide relative estimates of these intrinsic parameters of objects. The ratio between the conductive and absorbed heat flux estimates which were derived from thermal and visual images was found to provide a relative estimate of the lumped thermal capacitance of the object. The specification of such contextual features allows for a more meaningful interpretation of the imagery.

4. **Interpretation Strategy**

The developed scene models and sensor models provide methods for evaluating meaningful features derived from multiple sensors. Appropriate schemes are needed for classifying objects using the various features derived from the images. Various approaches are possible including: discriminant functions, clustering methods and rule-based strategies. In the past vision systems have been able to interpret scenes in overly constrained worlds. A general scene model for an application is very difficult to specify. Many special conditions arise, e.g. rain and snow in outdoor scenes. Establishing the existence of such special conditions and choosing appropriate algorithms requires the use of an rule-based strategy. Rule-based strategies are especially appropriate in view of the lack of complete models and algorithmic strategies. The rules may be approximate, heuristic rules. Powerful control strategies based on a combination of data-driven and goal-directed processing are required. Information fusion at multiple levels of abstraction is also warranted for robust interpretation [NA87c]. Adequate representation schemes are therefore required for storing information in a convenient manner at the different levels in the hierarchy [NA85]. The design and implementation of an interpretation scheme is thus a major issue that has yet to be addressed with the objective of producing practical solutions.

5. Model Verification

The models developed for the scene and for the sensor-scene relationship need to be qualitatively and quantitatively verified. This may be effected by using the established models to generate synthetic images and comparing these images (both quantitatively and qualitatively) with images acquired from real scenes. In addition to image gray levels, the models should also allow for the prediction of values of features that the multisensory vision system extracts from the imagery. Appropriate error measures need to be established for comparing synthesized images and features with real images. The dependence of the developed models on time-varying parameters can be best verified by such a comparison. The synthesized images may also be useful for goal-directed interpretation by providing images and feature- values of hypothesized situations which would be subject to verification. This area has received very little attention and needs to be intensively investigated in future research.

8.4.2   RECENT WORK IN INTERSENSORY ANALYSIS USING PHYSICAL PRINCIPLES

The Computer and Vision Research Center at The University of Texas at Austin has been intensely involved in the purposive use of physical principles for meaningful interpretation of multisensory data. Thermal and visual imagery has been processed concurrently to provide estimates of surface heat fluxes [NA86,NA87a,NA87b,NA88a,NA88b]. These estimates were used to specify a feature that was shown to relate to the lumped thermal capacitance of the imaged object [NA88b]. An interpretation scheme based on integration of information at the pixel level, as well as at the region level was devised [NA87a,NA87c,NA88b]. The system classified scene objects as being vegetation, building, vehicle, or road. This research, the salient features of which are discussed in the next section, established a useful methodology for multisensor fusion.

The model developed and the processing algorithms discussed in the next section are applicable to a particular combination of sensors, i.e., thermal (85m - 125m band) and monochrome visual cameras. In addition, the model and algorithms are designed for a specific task - that of identifying a specified set of objects in outdoor scenes during clear, daylight conditions. Although the idea of devising a general approach to modeling and interpreting multisensory data is appealing, there however appear to be no general principles to extract and combine information from arbitrary number and arbitrary type of sensors available at this time. The paradigm discussed in the next section is suitable for emulation in other domains including RADAR, LADAR and other imaging modalities.

8.5   Multisensory Vision - An Illustrative Example

We discuss below the salient features of a multisensory machine perception scheme based on the fusion of thermal and visual imagery. Many of the issues identified in the previous sections have been brought to bear in the development of this scheme. We develop a computational model that allows us to derive a map of heat sinks and sources in the imaged scene based on estimates of surface heat fluxes. A feature which quantifies the surface's ability to sink/source heat radiation is derived. Aggregate region features are used in a decision tree based classification scheme to label image regions as vehicle, building, vegetation or road. Real data are used to illustrate the usefulness of the approach.

We assume that the thermal image is segmented into closed regions by a suitable segmentation algorithm and that the thermal and visual images are registered. The thermal image is processed to yield estimates of object surface temperature [NA86,NA87a,NA88a]. The visual image, which is spatially registered with the thermal image, yields information regarding the relative surface orientation of the imaged object [NA86,NA87a,NA88a]. This information is made available at each pixel of the images. Other information such as ambient temperature, wind speed, and the date and time of image acquisition is used in estimating the surface heat fluxes at each pixel of the image. Consider an elemental area on the surface of the imaged object. Assuming one-dimensional heat flow, the heat exchange at the surface of the object is represented by figure 8.1 where, W_i is the incident solar radiation, q_i is the angle between the direction of irradiation and the surface normal, the surface temperature is T_s, and W_{abs} is that portion of the irradiation that is absorbed by the surface. W_{cv} denotes the heat convected from the surface to the air which has temperature T_{amb} and wind speed V, W_{rad} is the heat lost by the surface to the environment via radiation and W_{cd} denotes the heat conducted from the surface into the interior of the object. At any given instant, applying the principle of conservation of energy at the surface, the heat fluxes flowing into the surface of the object must equal those flowing out from the surface. We therefore have,

$$W_{abs} = W_{cv} + W_{cd} + W_{rad} \tag{8.1}$$

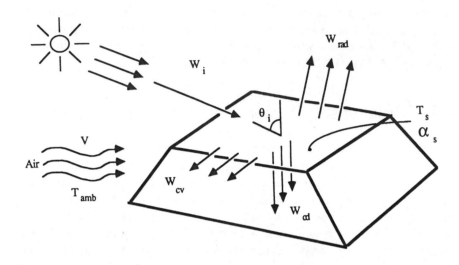

FIGURE 8.1. Heat exchange between the surface of an imaged object and the environment.

W_{abs} is computed at each pixel using surface reflectivity and relative surface orientation information which is estimated from the visual image, along with knowledge of the incident solar radiation. W_{rad} is computed from Stefan-Boltzman's law knowing sky temperature and surface temperature. We use the empirical convection correlations developed for external flow over flat plates for computing W_{cv}. Having estimated W_{abs}, W_{cv} and W_{rad}, W_{cd} is estimated using equation 8.1. The estimation of surface heat fluxes is described in detail in references [NA87a,NA88a].

The surface heat balance described by equation 8.1 and figure 8.1 depends on several time varying parameters. In such a dynamic situation the rate of heat loss / gain at the surface must equal the rate of change of internal energy of the object. Hence, we have:

$$W_{cd} = DV c dTs/dt \qquad (8.2)$$

where, D is the density of the object, V is the volume of the object, c is the specific heat of the object, and t denotes time. Let h denote the convection heat transfer coefficient, e_o the surface emissivity, and s the Stefan-Boltzman constant. Considering a unit surface area, the equivalent thermal circuit for the surface is shown in figure 8.2, where the resistances are given by:

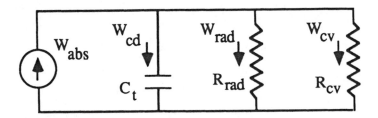

FIGURE 8.2. Equivalent thermal circuit of the imaged surface.

$$R_{cv} = 1/h, \qquad R_{rad} = 1/e_o s(T_s^2 + T_{amb}^2)(T_s + T_{amb}) \qquad (8.3)$$

Note the dependence of the latter on the driving potential i.e., the temperature difference. The lumped thermal capacitance of the object is given by $C_t = DVc$. A relatively high value for C_t implies that the object is able to sink or source relatively large amounts of heat. Note that the conduction heat flux at the surface of the object is the component that affects the internal energy of the object, and is dependent upon both the rate of change of temperature as well as the thermal capacitance. In experiments conducted by us, we have found the rate of change of surface temperature to be very small, except during the short period of time when the surface of the object enters into or exits from a shadow [NA87a]. Hence, in general, the predominant factor in determining the conduction heat flux is the thermal capacitance of the object.

TABLE 8.1. Normalized values of lumped thermal capacitance

Object	Thermal Capacitance ($\times 10^{-6}$ Joules/Kelvin)
Asphalt Pavement	1.95
Concrete Wall	2.03
Brick Wall	1.51
Wood(Oak) Wall	1.91
Granite	2.25
Automobile	0.18

An estimate of W_{cd}, therefore, provides us with a relative estimate of the thermal capacitance of the object, albeit a very approximate one. Table 8.1 lists values of C_t of typical objects imaged in outdoor scenes. The values have been normalized for unit volume of the object. The value shown for automobiles has been computed using the volume of an entire automobile, its weight, and the specific heat value for mild steel.

Note that the thermal capacitance for walls and pavements is signifi-

FIGURE 8.3. Thermal Images

FIGURE 8.4. Visual Image

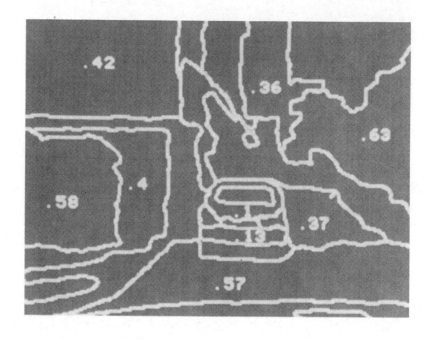

FIGURE 8.5. Region mode of ratio of conducted heat flux to absorbed heat flux.

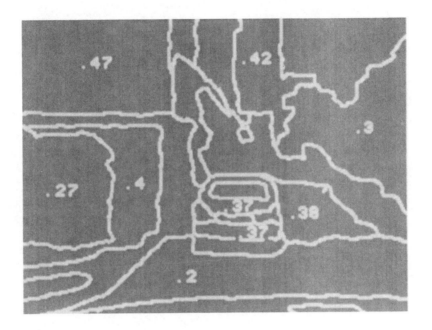

FIGURE 8.6. Surface reflectivity

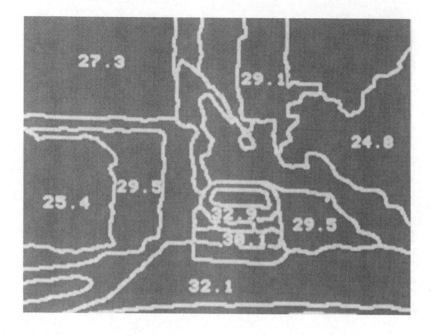

FIGURE 8.7. Average region temperature

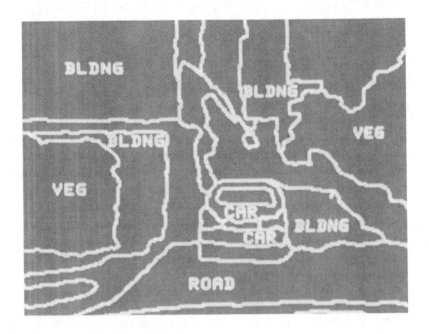

FIGURE 8.8. Classification

cantly greater than that for automobiles and hence W_{cd} may be expected
to be higher for the former regions. Plants absorb a significant percentage
of the incident solar radiation. The energy absorbed is used for photosyn-
thesis and also for transpiration. Only a small amount of the absorbed
radiation is convected into the air. Therefore, if equation 8.1 is used, the
estimate of the W_{cd} will be almost as large (typically 95%) as that of the
absorbed heat flux. Thus W_{cd} is useful in estimating the object's ability to
sink/source heat radiation, a feature shown to be useful in discriminating
between classes of objects. Note that W_{cd} is proportional to the magnitude
of solar irradiation incident on that surface element. In order to minimize
the feature's dependence on differences in absorbed heat flux, a normalized
feature was defined to be the ratio $R = W_{cd}/W_{abs}$.

Although the heat flux ratio W_{cd}/W_{abs} does capture a great deal of
information about the imaged object, it is not discriminatory enough to
unambiguously delineate the identity of the imaged object. The use of other
sources of information is therefore warranted. In the classification scheme
devised, such information includes the surface reflectivity of the region
which is derived from the visual image, and average region temperature
which is derived from the thermal image. Also, a histogram of the values
of W_{cd}/W_{abs} for each region is computed, and the mode of the distribution
is chosen to represent the heat flux ratio for that region. The classification

of regions is based on rules which use the above features. The rules are of the form:

```
IF {VALUE(R) e [0.2,0.9] AND
        VALUE(reflectivity) e [0.35,1.0]}
OR  {VALUE(R) e [-.8,-.3]} THEN INDENTITY = BLDNG
```

Rules of the above form were derived for each class of object to be identified. The intervals were specified heuristically based on observed variations in the values among different regions of the same class.These rules were encoded in a decision tree classifier. The above approach was tested using real data gathered from naturally occurring outdoor scenes. Figure 8.3 shows the visual image of a scene imaged at 1:30 pm in March. Figure 8.4 shows the thermal image. A histogram of values of the ratio W_{cd}/W_{abs} are computed for each region, and the mode of each distribution is obtained (figure 8.5). The surface reflectivity (figure 8.6) of each region and the average region temperature (figure 8.7) are also computed. These features are used by the classification algorithm discussed above which assigns one of the following labels to each region: Vehicle, Building, Vegetation, or Road. Figure 8.8 shows the final labeling produced by the region classifier.

The method described above was tested on similar sets of data other than that presented. These data were obtained at different times of the year. The results were consistent with those presented here. The preliminary results discussed above open several avenues for further research. Significant extensions of this approach to multisensory computer vision are being considered and will be researched in the near future.

8.6   Conclusions

In this paper we have motivated the need for the development of machine perception schemes which use multiple sensing modalities instead of relying only on a single sensing modality. The use of multiple modalities of imaging is argued as a more promising approach for minimizing the ambiguities in scene interpretation. The different types of sensors provide information regarding different physical parameters of scene objects. The simultaneous use of different kinds of sensors thus provides a rich description of the sensed scene and hence is capable of making available highly specific features for classification.

We first identified and then briefly discussed a set of broad considerations involved in developing a multisensory computer vision system. The incorporation of multiple sensing modes introduces many complications into the design of the system. We grouped these design considerations into three broad classes: (1) Image models, (2) Intersensory verification of image features, and (3) Intersensory verification from physical principles. We identified the issues involved in each of these classes, and gave examples of past research where such issues have been addressed. We have also delineated areas where more research is desired.

Finally, we described the salient features of a multisensory scene interpretation system which uses thermal and visual imagery simultaneously to classify imaged objects. The system relied on a model of heat flux exchange between the imaged object and the environment, and classified object based on intrinsic thermal properties of the scene objets. We maintain that such a paradigm for automated machine perception is general and easily extensible to other domains of applications where the choice of sensing modalities may be markedly different from those used for the system outlined here.

Acknowledgements: This work was supported in part by a contract with the Army Research Office (DAAL03-87-K-0089) and by a contract with the National Science Foundation (NSF-DCR 8517583).

Bibliography

[Abd80]   N. N. Abdelmalek. $L1$ solution of overdetermined systems of linear equations. *ACM Trans. Mathematical Software*, 6:220–227, 1980.

[ABM88]   H. L. Anderson, R. Bajcsy, and M. Mintz. Adaptive image segmentation. Technical Report MS-CIS-88-26, Department of Computer and Information Science, University of Pennsylvania, 1988. GRASP Lab 138.

[AFFT85]   N. Ayache, O. D. Faugeras, B. Faverjon, and G. Toscani. Matching depth maps obtained by passive stereo. In *Proc. 3rd Workshop on Computer Vision*, pages 197–204, 1985.

[AH42]   R. L. Anderson and E. E. Houseman. Tables of orthogonal polynomial values extended to n=104. Research Bulletin 297, Iowa State College of Agriculture and Mechanic Arts, Ames, Iowa, 1942.

[All35]   F. E. Allan. The general form of the orthogonal polynomials for simple series with proofs of their simple properties. *Proc. Royal Soc. Edinburgh*, 50:310–320, 1935.

[Alo88]   J. Aloimonos. Visual shape computation. *Proc. IEEE*, 76(8):899–916, 1988.

[AM86]   J. K. Aggarwal and M. J. Magee. Determining motion parameters using intensity guided range sensing. *Pattern Recognition*, 19(2):169–180, 1986.

[Arn74]   R. Arnheim. *Art and visual perception*. University of California Press, Berkeley, 1974.

[Asa88]   M. Asada. Building a 3-D World Model for a Mobile Robot from Sensory Data. In *Proc. IEEE Robotics and Automation*, Philadelphia, 1988.

[Baj85]   R. Bajcsy. Active perception versus passive perception. In *Proceedings Third IEEE Workshop on Vision*, pages 55–59, 1985.

[BAM86]   J. Ben-Arie and A.Z. Meiri. 3-d object recognition by state space search: Optimal geometric matching. In *Proc. IEEE Conf. on Computer Vision and Pattern Recognition*, pages 456–461, Miami Beach, 1986.

[BB81]   H.H. Baker and T. O. Binford. Depth from edge and intensity based stereo. In *Proc. Seventh Int. Joint Conf. Artif. Intell.*, pages 631–636, 1981.

[BB82]   D. H. Ballard and C. M. Brown. *Computer Vision*. Prentice Hall, Englewood Cliffs, N.J., 1982.

[BBW88]   P. J. Besl, J. B. Birch, and L. T. Watson. Robust window operators. In *Proc. 2nd Int'l. Conf. Computer Vision*, Tampa, Fla., 1988. IEEE-CS.

[BC84]   R. M. Bolle and D. B. Cooper. Bayesian recognition of local 3-d shape by approximating image intensity functions with quadric polynomials. *IEEE Trans. Pattern Analysis and Machine Intelligence*, PAMI-6(4):418–429, 1984.

[BC86]   A. Bergman and C. K. Cowan. Noise-Tolerant Range Analysis for Autonomous Navigation. In *Proc. IEEE Conf. on Robotics and Automation*, San Francisco, 1986.

[Bea78]   P. R. Beaudet. Rotationally invariant image operators. In *Proc. 4th Int'l. Conf. on Pattern Recognition*, pages 579–583, Kyoto, Japan, 1978.

[Ben75]   J. Bentley. Multidimensional binary search trees used for associative searching. *Comm. Assoc. Comp. Mach.*, 18(9):509–517, 1975.

[Ber84]   V. Berzins. Accuracy of laplaian edge detectors. *Comp. Vision, Graph. and Image Proc.*, 27:195–210, 1984.

[Bes88a]   P. Besl. Range Imaging Sensors. Technical Report GMR-6090, General Motors Research Lab, Warren, MI, March 1988.

[Bes88b]   P. J. Besl. Active optical range imaging sensors. *Machine Vision Applications*, 1, 1988. see also *Advances in Machine Vision: Architectures and Applications* (J. Sanz, Ed.), Springer-Verlag, New York; (2) Range imaging sensors. Research Report

GMR-6090, General Motors Research Laboratories, Warren, Mich.

[Bes88c]   P. J. Besl. Geometric modeling and computer vision. *Proc. IEEE*, 76(8):936–958, 1988.

[Bes88d]   P. J. Besl. *Surfaces in Range Image Understanding*. Springer-Verlag, New York, 1988.

[BF81]   R. C. Bolles and M. A. Fischler. A RANSAC-based approach to model fitting and its application to finding cylinders in range data. In *Proc. 7th IJCAI*, pages 637–643, Vancouver, B.C., 1981.

[BFH86]   J. M. Beck, R. T. Farouki, and J. Hinds. Surface analysis methods. *IEEE Computer Graphics and Applications*, 12:13–36, 1986.

[BG84]   J. W. Bruce and P. J. Giblin. *Curves and singularities*. Cambridge University Press, Cambridge, UK, 1984.

[BGP83]   R. H. T. Bates, K. L. Garden, and T. M. Peters. Overview of computerized tomography with emphasis on future developments. *Proc. IEEE*, 71(3):356–372, 1983.

[BH77]   M. V. Berry and J. H. Hannay. Umbilic points on gaussian random surfaces. *J. Phys. A.: Math. Gen.*, 10(11):1809–1821, 1977.

[BH86]   R. Bolles and P. Horaud. 3DPO: A three-dimensional part orientation system. *Int. J. Robotics Research*, 5(3):3–26, 1986.

[BH87]   B. Bhanu and C-C. Ho. Cad-based 3d object recognition for robot vision. *IEEE Computer*, pages 19–35, August 1987.

[Bie85]   I. Biederman. Human image understanding: Recent research and theory. *Computer Vision, Graphics, Image Processing*, 32:29–73, 1985.

[Bie87]   I. Biederman. Aspects and extensions of a theory of human image understanding. In *Proc. ICCV-87*, pages 384–392, London, 1987.

[Bin82]   T. O. Binford. Survey of Model-Based Image Analysis Systems. *International Journal of Robotics Research*, 1(1), 1982.

[Bir80]   J. B. Birch. Some convergence properties of interatively reweighted least squares in the location model. *Commun. Stat.*, B9:359–369, 1980.

[BJ85a]   R. H. Bartels and J. J. Jezioranski. Least-squares fitting using orthogonal multinomials. *ACM Trans. Mathematical Software*, 11(3):201–217, 1985.

[BJ85b]   P. J. Besl and R. C. Jain. Three-dimensional Object Recognition. *ACM Comp. Surveys*, 17(1):74–145, March 1985.

[BJ85c]   P. J. Besl and R. C. Jain. Three-dimensional Object Recognition. *ACM Comp. Surveys*, 17(1):74–145, March 1985.

[BJ86]   P. J. Besl and R. C. Jain. Invariant surface characteristics for three dimensional object recognition in range images. *Computer Vision, Graphics, Image Processing*, 33(1):33–88, 1986.

[BJ88]   P. J. Besl and R. C. Jain. Segmentation via variable-order surface fitting. *IEEE Trans. Pattern Analysis and Machine Intelligence*, PAMI-10(2), 1988.

[BK86]   T. Boult and J. R. Kender. Visual surface reconstruction using sparse depth data. In *Proc. Computer Vision Pattern Recognition Conf.*, pages 68–76, Miami, Fla, 1986. IEEE-CS.

[BK88]   K. L. Boyer and A. C. Kak. Structural stereopsis in 3-d vision. *IEEE Trans. Pattern Analysis and Machine Intelligence*, PAMI-10(2):144–166, 1988.

[Bla84]   A. Blake. Reconstructing a visible surface. In *Proc. of Nat'l. Conf. on Artificial Intelligence*, pages 23–26, Austin, TX, 1984. American Association for Artificial Intelligence.

[BM87]   Bir Bhanu and John C. Ming. Recognition of occluded objects: A cluster-structure algorithm. *Pattern Recognition*, 20(2):199–211, 1987.

[BN76]   J. F. Blinn and M. E. Newell. Texture and reflection in computer generated images. *Comm. Assoc. Comp. Mach.*, 19(10):542–547, 1976.

[Bou86]   T. Boult. *Information based complexity in nonlinear equations and computer vision*. PhD thesis, Columbia University, New York, 1986.

[Bou88]   P. Boulanger. Label relaxation technique applied to the stable estimation of a topographic primal sketch. In *Proc. 9th Int'l. Conf. on Pattern Recognition*, 1988.

[Box53]   G. E. P. Box. Non-normality and tests on variance. *Biometrika*, 40:318–335, 1953.

[BP71]   H. G. Barrow and R. J. Popplestone. Relational descriptions in picture processing. In B. Meltzer and D. Michie, editors, *Machine Intelligence*, pages 377–396. Edinburgh University Press, 1971.

[BPT88]   M. Bertero, T. A. Poggio, and V. Torre. Ill-posed problems in early vision. *Proc. IEEE*, 76(8):869–889, 1988.

[BPYA85]   M. Brady, J. Ponce, A. Yuille, and H. Asada. Describing surfaces. *Comp. Vision, Graph. and Image Proc.*, 32:1–28, 1985.

[Bra83]   M. Brady. Criteria for representation of shape. In J. Beck, B. Hope, and A. Rosenfeld, editors, *Human and Machine Vision*. Academic Press, New York, 1983.

[Bro83]   R. A. Brooks. Model-based 3-D interpretations of 2-D images. *IEEE Pattern Analysis and Machine Intelligence*, PAMI-5(2):140–150, 1983.

[Bro85]   R. Brooks. Aspects of Mobile Robot Visual Map Making. In *Second International Robotics Research Symposium*. MIT press, 1985.

[BS81]   Dana H. Ballard and Daniel Sabbah. On shapes. In *Proc. IJCAI 81*, pages 607–612, 1981.

[BS87]   R. Bajcsy and F. Solina. Three dimensional shape representation revisited. In *Proc. First International Conference on Computer Vision*, pages 231–240, 1987.

[BT74]   A. E. Beaton and J. W. Tukey. The fitting of power series, meaning polynomials, illustrated on band-spectroscopic data. *Technometrics*, 16:147–185, 1974.

[Bur81]   D. J. Burr. Elastic matching of line drawings. *IEEE Trans. Pattern Analysis and Machine Intelligence*, PAMI-3:708–713, 1981.

[Bur85]   W. L. Burke. *Applied Differential Geometry*. Cambridge University Press, Cambridge, UK, 1985.

[BW88]   J. Bares and W. Whittaker. Configuration of an autonomous robot for mars exploration. In *Proc. World Conference on Robotics*, 1988.

[BZ87a]   A. Blake and A. Zisserman. *Visual Reconstruction*. MIT Press, 1987.

[BZ87b]   A. Blake and A. Zisserman. *Visual Reconstruction*. MIT Press, Cambridge, MA, 1987.

[CA86]   C. H. Chien and J. K. Aggarwal. Volume/surface octrees for the representation of 3-d objects. *Comp. Vision, Graph. and Image Proc.*, 36:100–113, 1986.

[CA87]   R. T. Chien and J. K. Aggarwal. Shape recognition from single silhouettes. In *Proc. ICCV-87*, pages 1–10, 1987.

[CD86]   Roland T. Chin and Charles R. Dyer. Model-based recognition in robot vision. *Computing Surveys*, 12(4):67–108, 1986.

[Che57]   S. S. Chern. A proof of the uniqueness of Minkowski's problem for convex surfaces. *Am. J. Math*, 79:949–950, 1957.

[Che86]   S-W. Chen. Computing a pose hypothesis from a small set of 3d object features. Computer science technical report, Michigan State University, 1986.

[CHM86]   J. S. Chen, A. Huertas, and G. Medioni. Very fast convolution with laplacian-of-gaussian mask. In *Proc. Computer Vision and Pattern Recognition*, pages 293–298, 1986.

[Cra86]   J. Craig. *Introduction to Robotics*. Addison-Wesley, 1986.

[Dar96]   G. Darboux. *Theorie des surfaces*. Gauthiers-Villars, Paris, 1896. Reprinted Chelsea Publishing, New York.

[Dav63]   P. J. Davis. Orthogonal polynomials. In *Interpolation and Approximation*. Dover, New York, 1963.

[DCA81]   L. S. Davis, M. Clearman, and J. K. Aggarwal. An empirical evaluation of generalized co-occurrence matrices. *IEEE Trans. Pattern Analysis and Machine Intelligence*, PAMI-3(2):214–221, 1981.

[DeB78]   C. DeBoor. *A practical guide to splines*. Springer-Verlag, New York, 1978.

[DH72]   R. O. Duda and P. E. Hart. The use of hough transform to detect lines and curves in pictures. *Comm. Assoc. Comp. Mach.*, 15:11–15, 1972.

[DH73]   O. R. Duda and P. E. Hart. *Pattern classification and scene analysis.* Wiley, New York, 1973.

[DH87]   C. DeBoor and K. Hollig. B-splines without divided differences. In G. Farin, editor, *Geometric Modeling: Algorithms and New Trends*, pages 21–28. SIAM, 1987.

[DHR87]   M. J. Daily, J. G. Harris, and K. Reiser. Detecting Obstacles in Range Imagery. In *Proc. Image Understanding Workshop*, Los Angeles, 1987.

[DHR88]   M.J. Daily, J.G. Harris, and K. Reiser. An Operational Perception System for Cross-Country Navigation. In *Proc. Image Understanding Workshop*, Cambridge, 1988.

[Die77]   P. Dierckx. An algorithm for least-squares fitting of cubic spline surfaces to functions on a rectilinear mesh of a rectangle. *Journal of Computational and Applied Mathematics*, 3(2):113–129, 1977.

[DJA79]   L. S. Davis, S. A. Johns, and J. K. Aggarwal. Texture analysisi using generalized co-occurrence matrices. *IEEE Trans. Pattern Analysis and Machine Intelligence*, PAMI-1(3):251–259, 1979.

[DM86]   R. T. Dunlay and D. G. Morgenthaler. Obstacle Detection and Avoidance from Range Data. In *Proc. SPIE Mobile Robots Conference*, Cambridge, MA, 1986.

[DoC76]   M. P. DoCarmo. *Differential geometry of curves and surfaces.* Prentice-Hall, Englewood Cliffs, NJ, 1976.

[DR78]   L. S. Davis and A. Rozenfeld. Noise cleaning by interated local averaging. *IEEE Trans. Systems, Man, and Cybernetics*, SMC-8(9):705–710, 1978.

[Dre85]   H. Dreyfus. From micro-worlds to knowledge representation: Ai at an impasse. In J. Haugeland, editor, *Mind Design*, pages 161–204. MIT-Bradford, 1985.

[Dun88]   T. Dunlay. Obstacle Avoidance Perception Processing for the Autonomous Land Vehicle. In *Proc. IEEE Robotics and Automation*, Philadelphia, 1988.

370

[Eis09]   L. P. Eisenhart. *An introduction to differential geometry.* Ginn and Co., Boston, 1909. Reprinted Dover, New York 1960.

[Elf87]   A. Elfes. Sonar-Based Real-World Mapping and Navigation. *Journal of Robotics and Automation, Vol. 3,* 1987.

[EW87]   R. D. Eastman and A. M. Waxman. Using disparity function for stereo correspondence. *Comp. Vision, Graph. and Image Proc.,* 39:73–101, 1987.

[FAF86]   O.D. Faugeras, N. Ayache, and B. Faverjon. Building Visual Maps by Combining Noisy Stereo Measurements. In *Proc. IEEE Conf. on Robotics and Automation,* 1986.

[Far86]   R. T. Farouki. The approximation of non-degenerate offset surfaces. *Computer Aided Geometric Design,* 3:15–43, 1986.

[FB81]   M. Fischler and R. Bolles. Random consensus: A paradigm for model-fitting with applications in image analysis and automated cartography. *Comm. Assoc. Comp. Mach.,* 24:381–395, 1981.

[FF87]   M. Fischler and O. Firschein, editors. *Readings in Computer Vision.* Morgan Kaufman Publishers, 1987. Chapter 3.

[FH83]   O. Faugeras and M. Hebert. 3-d recognition and positioning algorithm using geometrical matching between primitive surfaces. In *Proc. 8th Int. Joint Conf. on AI,* pages 996–1002, Karlsruhe, West Germany, 1983.

[FH86]   O.D. Faugeras and M. Hebert. The Representation, Recognition, and Locating of 3-D Objects. *International Journal of Robotics Research,* 5(3), 1986.

[FJ88]   P. Flynn and A. Jain. Surface classification: Hypothesis testing and parameter estimation. In *Proc. IEEE CVPR-88,* pages 261–267, Ann Arbor, 1988.

[FL88]   F. Ferrie and M. Levine. Deriving coarse 3d models of objects. In *Proc. IEEE CVPR-88,* pages 345–353, Ann Arbor, 1988.

[Fol87]   T. A. Foley. Weighted bicubic spline interpolation to rapidly varying data. *ACM Trans. Graphics,* 6(1):1–18, 1987.

[For87]   W. Forstner. Reliability analysis of parameter estimation in linear models with applications to mensuration problems in computer vision. *Comp. Vision, Graph. and Image Proc.,* 40:273–310, 1987.

[FP79]   I. D. Faux and M. J. Pratt. *Computational Geometry for Design and Manufacture*. Ellis Horwood, Chichester, U.K., 1979.

[Fre74]   H. Freeman.   Computer processing of line-drawing images. *Computing Surveys*, 6:57–97, 1974.

[Fuk72]   K. Fukunaga. *Introduction to Statistical Pattern Recognition*. Academic Press, 1972.

[FV82]   J. D. Foley and A. VanDam. *Fundamentals of Interactive Computer Graphics*. Addison-Wesley, Reading, Mass., 1982.

[Gau85]   K. F. Gauss. *Disquistiones generales circa superficies curvas*. Raven Press, New York, 1985. English Translation: General investigations of curved surfaces.

[GCV84]   G. Giralt, R. Chatila, and M. Vaisset. An Integrated Navigation and Motion Control System for Autonomous Multisensory Mobile Robots. In *Proc. 1st International Symposium Robotics Research*, Cambridge, 1984.

[Gen79]   D. Gennery. Object detection and measurement using stereo vision. In *Proc. 6th IJCAI*, pages 320–327, 1979.

[Gib79]   J. Gibson.   *The Ecological Approach to Visual Perception*. Houghton-Mifflin, Boston, 1979.

[GL83]   G. H. Golub and C. F. Van Loan. *Matrix Computations*. Johns Hopkins Univ. Press, Baltimore, Md., 1983.

[GLP84]   W. E. L. Grimson and T. Lozano-Perez. Model-based recognition and localization from sparse range or tactile data. *Int. Journal of Robotics Research*, 3(3):3–35, 1984.

[GMA83]   B. Gil, A. Mitiche, and J. K. Aggarwal. Experiments in combining intensity and range edge maps. *Comp. Vision, Graph. and Image Proc.*, 21:395–411, 1983.

[GMKO86]   Y. Goto, K. Matsuzaki, I. Kweon, and T. Obatake. CMU Sidewalk Navigation System: a Blackboard-Based Outdoor Navigation System Using Sensor Fusion with Colored-Range Images. In *Proc. First Joint Computer Conference*, Dallas, 1986.

[Goa83]   C. Goad.   Special purpose automatic programming for 3d model-based vision. In *Proc. DARPA Image Understanding Workshop*, pages 94–104, Wash. DC, 1983.

[Gol83]   R. Goldman. Two approaches to a quadric model for surfaces. *IEEE Computer Graphics Applic.*, 3(1):21–24, 1983.

[Gom62]   E. II. Gombrich. *Art and Illusion*. Phaidon, Oxford, 1962.

[GP85]   W. E. L. Grimson and T. Pavlidis. Discontinuity detection for visual surface reconstruction. *Comp. Vision, Graph. and Image Proc.*, 30:316–330, 1985.

[Gre83]   J. F. Greenleaf. Computerized tomography with ultrasound. *Proc. IEEE*, 71(3):330–337, 1983.

[Gri81a]   W. E. L. Grimson. A computer implementation of a theory of human stereo vision. *Phil. Trans. R. Soc. Lond.* B, 292:217–253, 1981.

[Gri81b]   W. E. L. Grimson. *From images to surfaces: a study of the human early visual system*. MIT Press, Cambridge, Mass., 1981.

[Gri82]   W. E. L. Grimson. A visual theory of visual surface interpolation. *Proc. R. Soc. Lond.* B, 298:395–427, 1982.

[Gri85]   W. E. L. Grimson. Computational experiments with a feature based stereo algorithm. *IEEE Trans. Pattern Analysis and Machine Intelligence*, PAMI-7(1):17–34, 1985.

[Gri88]   E. Grimson. The combinatorics of object recognition in cluttered environments using constrained search. In *Proc. 2nd. Int. Conf. on Computer Vision*, pages 218–227, Tampa, 1988.

[GT83]   D. Gilbarg and N. Trudinger. *Elliptic Partial Differential Equations of Second Order*. Springer-Verlag, New York, 2 edition, 1983.

[GTK88]   K. Gremban, C.E. Thorpe, and T. Kanade. Geometric Calibration Using Systems of Linear Equations. In *Proc. IEEE Robotics and Automation Conf.*, Philadelphia, 1988.

[Gui78]   E. Guisti. On the equation of surfaces of prescribed mean curvature: existence and uniqueness without boundary conditions. *Inventiones Mathematicae*, 46:111–137, 1978.

[Gup88]   A. Gupta. Range image segmentation for 3-D object recognition. Master's thesis, University of Pennsylvania, 1988.

[GW77]   R. C. Gonzalez and P. Wintz. *Digital Image Processing*. Addison-Wesley, Reading, Mass., 1977.

[HA87]   W. Hoff and N. Ahuja. Extracting surfaces from stereo images: An integrated approach. Technical Report UILU-ENG-87-2204, University of Illinois, 1987.

[Hag88]   G. D. Hager. *Active reduction of uncertainty in multi-sensor systems*. PhD thesis, University of Pennsylvania, 1988.

[Ham68]   F. R. Hampel. *Contributions to the theory of robust estimation*. PhD thesis, Univ. of California, Berkeley, 1968.

[Har82]   L. D. Harmon. Automated tactile sensing. *Int. J. Robotics Research*, 1(2):3–32, 1982.

[Har88a]   R. M Haralick. Pose estimation. In *Machine Vision Workshop*. Center for computer aids to industrial productivity, Rutgers University, New Brunswick, NJ, 1988. (to be published by Academic Press 1989).

[Har88b]   S.Y. Harmon. A Report on the NATO Workshop on Mobile Robot Implementation. In *Proc. IEEE Robotics and Automation*, Philadelphia, 1988.

[HB85]   T. Henderson and B. Bhanu. Intrinsic characteristics as the interface between cad and machine vision systems. *Pattern Recognition Letters*, 3:425–430, 1985.

[Hec86]   P. S. Heckbert. Survey of texture mapping. *IEEE Computer Graphics Applications*, 6(11):56–67, 1986.

[Hic65]   N. J. Hicks. *Notes on differential geometry*. Van Nostrand, Princeton, NJ, 1865.

[HJ87a]   R. Hoffman and A. Jain. Evidence-based 3-d vision system for range images. In *Proc. ICCV-87*, pages 521–525, London, 1987.

[HJ87b]   R. Hoffman and A. K. Jain. Segmentation and classification of range images. *IEEE Trans. Pattern Analysis and Machine Intelligence*, PAMI-9(5):608–620, 1987.

[HJ88]   R. Hoffman and A. Jain. Learning rules for 3d object recognition. In *Proc. IEEE CVPR-88*, pages 885–892, Ann Arbor, 1988.

[HK85]   M. Hebert and T. Kanade. First Results on Outdoor Scene Analysis. In *Proc. IEEE Robotics and Automation*, San Francisco, 1985.

374

[HK86]   M. Herman and T. Kanade. Incremental reconstruction of 3D scenes from multiple, complex images. *Artificial Intelligence*, 30:289–341, 1986.

[HK88]   M. Hebert and T. Kanade. 3-D Vision for Outdoor Navigation by an Autonomous Vehicle. In *Proc. Image Understanding Workshop*, Cambridge, 1988.

[HL83]   W. S. Hinshaw and A. H. Lent. An introduction to NMR imaging: from the bloch equation to the imaging equation. *Proc. IEEE*, 71(3):338–350, 1983.

[Hog79]   R. V. Hogg. Statistical robustness: one view of its use in applications today. *American Statistician*, 33(3):108–115, 1979.

[Hor84]   B. K. P. Horn. Extended gaussian images. *Proc. IEEE*, 72(12):1656–1678, 1984.

[Hor86]   B. K. P. Horn. *Robot Vision*. MIT Press, Cambridge, MA, 1986.

[HR84]   S. L. Hurt and A. Rosenfeld. Noise reduction in three-dimensional digital images. *Pattern Recognition*, 17(4):407–421, 1984.

[HR85]   D. D. Hoffman and W. A. Richards. Parts of recognition. *Cognition*, 18:65–96, 1985.

[HRRS86]   F. R. Hampel, E. M. Ronchetti, P. J. Rousseeuw, and W. A. Stahel. *Robust statistics: the approach based on influence functions*. Wiley, New York, 1986.

[HRW79]   S. Holland, L. Rossal, and M. Ward. ICONSIGHT-I: A vision-controlled robot system for transferring parts from belt conveyors. In G. Dodd and L. Rossal, editors, *Computer Vison and Sensor-based Robotics*, pages 81–100. Plenum, New York, 1979.

[HSA85]   R. D. Hazlett, R. S. Schechter, and J. K. Aggarwal. Image processing techniques for the estimation of drop size distributions. *I&EC Fundamentals*, 24(1):101–105, 1985.

[HSHD87]   D. Harwood, M. Subbarao, H. Hakalahti, and L. Davis. A new class of edge-preserving smoothing filters. *Pattern Recognition Letters*, 6:155–162, 1987.

[Hsi81]   C. C. Hsiung. *A first course in differential geometry*. Wiley-Interscience, New York, 1981.

[HTMS82]   E. Hall, J. Tio, C. McPherson, and F. Sadjadi. Measuring curved surfaces for computer vision. *IEEE Computer*, 15(12):42–54, 1982.

[HU87]   D. Huttenlocher and S. Ullman. Object recognition using alignment. In *Proc. ICCV-87*, pages 102–111, London, 1987.

[Hub64]   P. J. Huber. Robust estimation of a location parameter. *Annals of Mathematical Statistics*, 35:73–101, 1964.

[Hub81]   P. J. Huber. *Robust Statistics*. Wiley, New York, 1981.

[Hue73]   M. Hueckel. A local operator which recognizes edges and lines. *J. Assoc. Comp. Mach*, 20:634–647, 1973.

[HW81]   R. M. Haralick and L. Watson. A facet model for image data. *Comp. Graph. and Image Proc.*, 15:113–129, 1981.

[HWL83]   R. M. Haralick, L. T. Watson, and T. J. Laffey. The topographic primal sketch. *Int. J. Robotics Research*, 2(1):50–72, 1983.

[Ike87]   K. Ikeuchi. Generating an interpretation tree from a cad model for 3d-object recognition in bin-picking tasks. *International Journal of Computer Vision*, 1(2):145–165, 1987.

[Inf]   Inframetrics, Inc., Bedford, MA. *Model 525 - Thermal Imaging Systems, Operations Manual*.

[INH+86]   K. Ikeuchi, H. K. Nishihara, B. K. P. Horn, P. Sobalvarro, and S. Nagata. Determining grasp configurations using photometric stereo. *Int. J. Robotics Research*, 5(1):46–65, 1986.

[Jai86]   A. K. Jain. *Fundamentals of Digital Image Processing*. Prentice Hall, Englewood Cliffs, N.J., 1986.

[Jul60]   B. Julesz. Binocular depth perception of computer-generated patterns. *Bell Syst. Tech J.*, 39:1125–1162, 1960.

[KA87a]   Y. C. Kim and J. K. Aggarwal. Determining object motion in a sequence of stereo images. *IEEE J. Robotics and Automation*, RA-3(6):599–614, 1987.

[KA87b]   Y. C. Kim and J. K. Aggarwal. Positioning 3-d objects using stereo images. *IEEE J. Robotics and Automation*, RA-3(4):361–373, 1987.

[Kak85]   A. C. Kak. Depth perception for robots. In *Handbook of Industrial Robotics*, pages 272–319. John Wiley, New York, 1985.

[Kan88]   T. Kanade. CMU image understanding program. In *Proc. DARPA Image Understanding Workshop*, pages 40–45, 1988.

[KD87]   M. Korn and C. Dyer. 3-D multiview object representations for model-based object recognition. *Pattern Recognition*, 20(1):91–103, 1987.

[KHK88a]   I. Kweon, M. Hebert, and T. Kanade. Perception for Rough Terrain Navigation. In *Proc. SPIE Mobile Robots*, Cambridge, MA, 1988.

[KHK88b]   I. Kweon, M. Hebert, and T. Kanade. Sensor Fusion of Range and Reflectance Data for Outdoor Scene Analysis. In *Proc. Space Operations Automation and Robotics*, Cleveland, 1988.

[KK88]   E. Krotkov and R. Kories. Adaptive control of cooperating sensors: Focus and stereo ranging with an agile camera system. In *Proc. IEEE Conf. on Robotics and Automation*, pages 548–553, 1988.

[KLB85]   J. Kender, K. Lee, and T. Boult. Information-based complexity applied to optimal recovery of 2.5d sketch. In *IEEE Workshop on Computer Vision: Representation and Control*, pages 157–167, 1985.

[KM63]   M.G. Kendall and P.A.P. Moran. *Geometrical Probabilities*. Hafner Publishers, New York, 1963.

[KM76]   K. Kuratorwski and A. Mostowski. *Set Theory*. North-Holland, Amsterdam, 1976.

[Kno83]   G. F. Knoll. Single photon emission computed tomography (spect). *Proc. IEEE*, 71(3):320–329, 1983.

[Koe84]   J. Koenderink. What does the occluding contour tell us about solid shape? *Perception*, 13:321–330, 1984.

[Kre59]   I. Kreyszig. *Differential Geometry*. University of Toronto Press, Toronto, 1959.

[KTB87]   D. Kriegman, E. Triendl, and T.O. Binford. A Mobile Robot: Sensing, Planning and Locomotion. In *Proc. IEEE Conf. on Robotics and Automation*, 1987.

[KvD79]   J. Koenderink and A. van Doorn. The internal representation of solid shape with respect to vision. *Biological Cybernetics*, 32:211–216, 1979.

[KW87]   T. Kanade and J.A. Webb. End of Year Report for Parallel Vision Algorithm Design and Implementation. Technical Report CMU-RI-TR-87-15, The Robotics Institute, Carnegie-Mellon University, 1987.

[Kwe88]   I. Kweon. Modeling Rugged 3-D Terrain from Multiple Range Images for Use by Mobile Robots. PhD thesis proposal, 1988.

[Lee85]   D. Lee. Optimal algorithms for image understanding: current status and future plans. *J. Complexity*, 1(1):138–146, 1985.

[Lee88]   D. Lee. Some computational aspects of low-level computer vision. *Proc. IEEE*, 76(8):890–898, 1988.

[LH74]   C. L. Lawson and R. J. Hanson. *Solving least squares problems*. Prentice-Hall, Englewood Cliffs, NJ, 1974.

[LH87]   M. Livingstone and D. Hubel. Psychophysical evidence for separate channels for the perception of form, color, movement, and depth. *The Journal of Neuroscience*, 7(11):3415–3468, 1987.

[LHB87]   S. A. Lloyd, E. R. Haddow, and J. F. Boyce. A parallel binocular stereo algorithm utilizing dynamic programming. *Comp. Vision, Graph. and Image Proc.*, 39:202–225, 1987.

[Lip69]   M. M. Lipschutz. *Differential Geometry*. McGraw-Hill, New York, 1969.

[Liv88]   M. Livingstone. Art, illusion, and the visual system. *Scientific American*, pages 78–85, January 1988.

[Low80]   D.G. Lowe. Solving for the Parameters of Object Models from Image Descriptions. In *DARPA Image Understanding Workshop*, 1980.

[Low85]   D. Lowe. *Perceptual Organization and Visual Recognition*. Kluwer, Boston, 1985.

[LP79]   T. Lozano-Perez. An Algorithm for Planning Collision Free Paths among Polyhedral Obstacles. *Communications of the ACM*, October 1979.

[LSW88]   Y. Lamden, J. Schwartz, and H. Wolfson. On recognition of 3-d objects from 2-d images. In *Proc. 1988 IEEE Int. Conf. on Robotics and Automation*, pages 1407–1413, Philadelphia, 1988.

[Luc85]   B.D. Lucas. Generalized Image Matching by the Method of Differences. Technical Report CMU-CS-85-160, Carnegie-Mellon University, 1985.

[MA82]   A. Mitiche and J. K. Aggarwal. Detection of edges using range information. In *Proc. 1982 IEEE Int'l. Conf. on Acoustics, Speech and Signal Processing*, pages 1906–1911, Paris, France, 1982.

[MA85a]   M. J. Magee and J. K. Aggarwal. Using multisensory image to derive the structure of three-dimensional objects - a review. *Comp. Vision, Graph. and Image Proc.*, 32:145–157, 1985.

[MA85b]   A. Mitiche and J. K. Aggarwal. Image segmentation by conventional and information-integrating techniques: A synopsis. *Image and Vision Computing*, 3(2):49–61, 1985.

[Mal88]   S. G. Mallat. *Multiresolution representation and wavelets*. PhD thesis, University of Pennsylvania, 1988.

[Mar82]   R. R. Martin. *Principal patches for computational geometry*. PhD thesis, Cambridge University, UK, 1982.

[MB88]   M. L. Moerdler and T. E. Boult. The integration of information from stereo and multiple shape-from-texture cues. In *Proc. DARPA Image Understanding Workshop*, pages 786–793, Cambridge, MA, 1988.

[MBCA85]   M. J. Magee, B. A. Boyter, C. H. Chien, and J. K. Aggarwal. Experiments in intensity guided range sensing recognition of three-dimensional objects. *IEEE Trans. Pattern Analysis and Machine Intelligence*, PAMI-7(6):629–637, 1985.

[ME88]   L. Matthies and A. Elfes. Integration of sonar and stereo range data using a grid-based representation. In *Proc. IEEE Int'l. Conf. on Robotics and Automation*, pages 727–733, Philadelphia, PA, 1988.

[MF81]   J. E. W. Mayhew and J. P. Frisby. Psychophysical and computational studies towards a theory of human stereopsis. *Artificial Intelligence*, 17:349–385, 1981.

[Min97]   H. Minkowski. Allgemeine lehrsatze uber die konvexen poly-
            eder.   Nachrichten von der Koniglichen Gesellschaft der
            Wissenschaften, Mathematisch-Physikalische Klasse, Gottin-
            gen,, 1897. pp. 198-219.

[MN85]   G. Medioni and R. Nevatia. Segment-based stereo matching.
            Comp. Vision, Graph. and Image Proc., 31:2–18, 1985.

[Mor80]   H.P. Moravec. Obstacle Avoidance and Navigation in the Real
            World by a Seeing Robot Rover. Technical Report CMU-RI-
            TR-3, Carnegie-Mellon University, 1980.

[Mor83]   H. P. Moravec. The Stanford cart and the CMU rover. *Proc.
            IEEE*, 71(7):872–884, 1983.

[MP79]   D. Marr and T. Poggio. A computational theory of human
            stereo vision. *Proc. R. Soc. Lond.* B, 204:3201–328, 1979.

[MP80]   Montgomery and Peck. *Introduction to Linear Regression
            Analysis*. Wiley, 1980. See Chapter 9.

[MS87]   L. Matthies and S.A. Shafer. Error Modeling in Stereo Navi-
            gation. *Journal of Robotics and Automation, Vol. 3*, 1987.

[MT82]   R. D. Martin and D. J. Thomson. Robust-resistant spectrum
            estimation. *Proc. IEEE*, 70(9):1097–1115, 1982.

[NA85]   N. Nandhakumar and J. K. Aggarwal. The artificial intelli-
            gence approach to pattern recognition - a perspective and an
            overview. *Pattern Recognition*, 18(6):383–389, 1985.

[NA86]   N. Nandhakumar and J. K. Aggarwal. Integrating information
            from thermal and visual images for scene analysis. In *Proc.
            SPIE Conf. on Applications of Artificial Intelligence III*, pages
            132–142, Orlando, FL, 1986.

[NA87a]   N. Nandhakumar and J. K. Aggarwal. Multisensor fusion
            for scene perception - integrating thermal and visual imagery.
            Computer and Vision Research Center Technical Report TR-
            87-9-41, The University of Texas at Austin, Austin, TX, 1987.

[NA87b]   N. Nandhakumar and J. K. Aggarwal. Multisensor integra-
            tion - experiments in integrating thermal and visual sensors.
            In *Proc. First Int'l. Conf. on Computer Vision*, pages 83–92,
            London, UK, 1987.

[NA87c]   N. Nandhakumar and J. K. Aggarwal. Synergetic integration of thermal and visual images for computer vision. In *Proc. SPIE Conf. on Infrared Sensors and Sensor Fusion*, Orlando, FL, 1987.

[NA88a]   N. Nandhakumar and J. K. Aggarwal. Integrated analysis of therman and visual images for scene interpretation. *IEEE Trans. Pattern Analysis and Machine Intelligence*, PAMI-10(4):469–481, 1988.

[NA88b]   N. Nandhakumar and J. K. Aggarwal. Thermal and visual information fusion for outdoor scene perception. In *Proc. IEEE Int'l. Conf. Robotics and Automation*, pages 1306–1308, Philadelphia, PA, 1988.

[NB77]   R. Nevatia and T. O. Binford. Description and recognition of curved objects. *Artificial Intelligence*, 8:77–98, 1977.

[NB80]   R. Nevatia and K. R. Babu. Linear feature extraction and description. *Comp. Graph. and Image Proc.*, 13:257–269, 1980.

[Nev76]   R. Nevatia. Depth measurement by motion stereo. *Comp. Graph. and Image Proc.*, 5:203–214, 1976.

[Nis84]   II. K. Nishihara. PRISM: A practical real-time imaging stereo matcher. *Optical Engineering*, 23:536–545, 1984.

[NJ88]   S. M. Naik and R. C. Jain. Spline-based surface fitting on range images for cad applications. In *Proc. CVPR-88*, pages 249–253, Ann Arbor, MI, 1988.

[Oht84]   Y. Ohta. *Knowledge-based Interpretation of Outdoor Natural Color Scenes*. Pittman Publishing, Inc., 1984.

[OK85]   Y. Ohta and T. Kanade. Stereo by intra- and inter-scanline search using dynamic programming. *IEEE Trans. Pattern Analysis and Machine Intelligence*, PAMI-7(2):139–154, 1985.

[O'N66]   B. O'Neill. *Elementary Differential Geometry*. Academic Press, New York, 1966.

[OR87]   D.J. Orser and M. Roche. The Extraction of Topographic Features in Support of Autonomous Underwater Vehicle Navigation. In *Proc. Fifth International Symposium on Unmanned Untethered Submersible*, University of New Hampshire, 1987.

[OS75]   A. V. Oppenheim and R. W. Shafer. *Digital Signal Processing*. Prentice-Hall, Englewood Cliffs, NJ, 1975.

[PA79]   T. Pavlidis and F. Ali. A hierarchical syntactic shape ana-
           lyzer. *IEEE Trans. Pattern Analysis and Machine Intelligence*,
           PAMI-1(1):2–9, 1979.

[Pav77]   T. Pavlidis. *Structural pattern recognition*. Springer, New
           York, 1977.

[Pav79]   T. Pavlidis. The use of a syntactic shape analyzer for con-
           tour matching. *IEEE Trans. Pattern Analysis and Machine
           Intelligence*, PAMI-1(3):307–310, 1979.

[PB85]   J. Ponce and M. Brady. Toward a Surface Primal Sketch.
           In *Proc. IEEE International Conference on Robotics and Au-
           tomation*, St Louis, 1985.

[Pen86]   Alex P. Pentland. Perceptual organization and the representa-
           tion of natural form. *Artificial Intelligence*, 28:293–331, 1986.

[Pen87]   A. Pentland. Recognition by parts. In *Proc. ICCV-87*, pages
           612–620, London, 1987.

[Pog58]   A. V. Pogorelov. *Differential Geometry*. Noordhoff, Gronigen,
           Netherlands, 1958.

[Por83]   I. R. Porteous. The normal singularities of surfaces in $\Re^3$.
           Proc. Symposia in Pure Mathematics, 40, 1983. Part 2.

[Pot83]   M. Potmesil. Generating models of solid objects by matching
           3d surface segments. In *8th Int'l. Joint Conf. on A. I.*, pages
           1089–1093, Karlsruhe, West Germany, 1983.

[Pot87]   M. Potmesil. Generating octree models of 3d objects from their
           silhouettes. *Comp. Vision, Graph. and Image Proc.*, 40(1):1–
           29, 1987.

[Pow81]   M. J. D. Powell. *Approximation theory and methods*. Cam-
           bridge University Press, Cambridge, UK, 1981.

[Pra78]   W. K. Pratt. *Digital Image Processing*. Wiley, New York, 1978.

[Pre70]   J. Prewitt. Object enhancement and extraction. In B. Lipkin
           and A. Rosenfeld, editors, *Picture Processing and Psychopic-
           torics*, pages 75–149. Academic Press, New York, 1970.

[Pro83]   J. G. Proakis. *Digital Communications*. McGraw-Hill, New
           York, 1983.

382

[RAM87] S. J. Roan, J. K. Aggarwal, and W. N. Martin. Multiple resolution imagery and texture analysis. *Pattern Recognition*, 21(1):17–31, 1987.

[Ram88] V. S. Ramachandran. Perception of shape from shading. *Nature*, 331(6152):133–166, 1988.

[Req77] A. A. G. Requicha. Mathematical models of rigid solid objects. Production Automation Project Report TM-28, University of Rochester, 1977.

[Req80] A. Requicha. Representations for rigid solids: Theory, methods and systems. *Computing Surveys*, 12(4):437–464, 1980.

[RG75] L. R. Rabiner and B. Gold. *Theory and Applications of Digital Signal Processing*. Prentice-Hall, Englewood Cliffs, NJ, 1975.

[RHK87] J. G. Rogers, R. Harrop, and P. E. Kinahan. The theory of three-dimensional image reconstruction for pet (positron emission tomography). *IEEE Trans. Medical Imaging*, MI-6(3):239–243, 1987.

[RHS+83] R. A. Robb, E. A. Hoffman, L. J. Sinak, L. D. Harris, and E. L. Ritman. High speed three-dimensional x-ray computed tomography. *Proc. IEEE*, 71(3):308–319, 1983.

[RK82] A. Rosenfeld and A. Kak. *Digital Picture Processing, 2nd Ed.* Academic Press, New York, 1982.

[RL87] P. J. Rousseuw and A. M. Leroy. *Robust Regression and Outlier Detection*. Wiley, New York, 1987.

[Rob88] K.S. Roberts. A New Representation for a Line. In *Proc. Computer Vision and Patter Recognition*, Ann Arbor, MI, 1988.

[Ros74] A. Rosenfeld. Digital straight line segments. *IEEE Trans. on Computers*, c-23(12):1264–1269, 1974.

[Ros78] E. Rosch. Principles of categorization. In E. Rosch and B. Lloyd, editors, *Cognition and categorization*. Erlbaum, Hellsdale, NJ, 1978.

[Rou84] P. J. Rousseuw. Least median of squares regression. *J. Am. Statistical Assoc.*, 79(388):871–880, 1984.

[RT78] A.A. G. Requicha and R. B. Tilove. Mathematical foundations of constructive solid geometry: general topology of closed regular sets. Production Automation Project Report TM-27, University of Rochester, 1978.

[San88]   P. T. Sander. *On reliably inferring differential structure from threee-dimensional images.* PhD thesis, McGill University, Montreal, Canada, 1988.

[SC86]   R.C. Smith and P. Cheeseman. On the Representation and Estimation of Spatial Uncertainty. *International Journal of Robotics Research*, 1986.

[SdK88]   S. W. Shaw, R. J. P. deFigueiredo, and K. Kumar. Fusion of radar and optical sensors for space robotic vision. In *Proc. IEEE Conf. on Robotics and Automation*, pages 1842–1846, 1988.

[SE85]   G. Stockman and J. C. Esteva. 3d object pose from clustering with multiple views. *Pattern Recognition Letters*, 3:279–286, 1985.

[SG87]   A. Stentz and Y. Goto. The CMU navigational architecture. In *Proc. DARPA Image Understanding Workshop*, pages 440–446, Los Angeles, CA, 1987.

[Sin88]   S. Sinha. Ph.d prospectus, 1988. Univ. of Michigan, Ann Arbor.

[SK83]   S. A. Shafer and T. Kanade. The theory of straight homogeneous generalized cylinders and taxonomy of generalized cylinders. Technical Report CMU-CS-83-105, Carnegie-Mellon Univ., Pittsburgh, Pa., 1983.

[SK84]   M. Suk and H. Kang. New measures of similarity between two contours based on optimal bivariate transforms. *Comp. Vision, Graph. and Image Proc.*, 26:168–182, 1984.

[SKB82]   G. Stockman, S. Kopstein, and S. Benett. Matching images to models for registration and object recognition using clustering. *IEEE Trans. Pattern Analysis and Machine Intelligence*, 4(3):229–241, 1982.

[SMHM84] L. Shapiro, J. Moriarity, R. Haralick, and P. Mulgaonkar. Matching three-dimensional objects using a relational paradigm. *Pattern Recognition*, 17(4):385–405, 1984.

[Sol87]   F. Solina. *Shape recovery and segmentation with deformable part models.* PhD thesis, University of Pennsylvania, 1987.

[Spi79]   M. Spivak. *A Comprehensive Introduction to Differential Geometry.* Publish or Perish Press, 2nd edition, 1979.

384

[Ste88]   T. Stenz. *The NAVLAB System for Mobile Robot Navigation.* PhD thesis, Carnegie-mellon University, Fall 1988.

[Sti73]   S. M. Stigler. Simon newcomb, percy daniell, and the history of robust estimation. *J. Amer. Statist. Assoc.*, 68:872–879, 1973.

[Sto69]   J. Stoker. *Differential Geometry.* Wiley-Interscience, New York, 1969.

[Sto87]   George Stockman. Object recognition and localization via pose clustering. *Comp. Vision, Graph. and Image Proc.*, 40:361–387, 1987.

[Str61]   D. J. Struik. *Lectures on Classical Differential Geometry.* Addison-Wesley, Reading, Mass, 1961.

[SW88]   S. Shafer and W. Whittaker. June 1987 Annual Report: Development of an Integrated Mobile Robot System at Carnegie Mellon. Technical Report CMU-RI-TR-88-10, The Robotics Institute, Carnegie-Mellon University, 1988.

[SY81]   T. W. Sze and Y. H. Yang. A simple contour matching algorithm. *IEEE Trans. Pattern Analysis and Machine Intelligence*, PAMI-3:676–678, 1981.

[SZ88a]   P. T. Sander and S. W. Zucker. Inferring differential structure from 3-d images: smooth cross sections of fibre bundles. Technical Report CIM-88-6, McGill Research Center for Intelligent Machines, McGill University, Montreal, Canada, 1988.

[SZ88b]   P. T. Sander and S. W. Zucker. Singularities of principal direction fields from 3-d images. In *Proc 2nd Int'l. Conf. Computer Vision*, Tampa, Florida, 1988. IEEE.

[Sze88a]   R. Szeliski. *Bayesian Modeling of Uncertainty in Low-Level Vision.* PhD thesis, Carnegie-mellon University, Computer Science Department, July 1988.

[Sze88b]   R. Szeliski. Estimating Motion from Sparse Range Data without Correspondence. In *Proc. International Conf. on Computer Vision*, Tarpon Springs, Florida, December 1988.

[Ter83]   D. Terzopoulos. Multilevel computational processes for visual surface reconstruction. *Comp. Vision, Graph. and Image Proc.*, 24:52–96, 1983.

[Ter84]   D. Terzopoulos. *Multiresolution computation of visual surface representations.* PhD thesis, MIT, Cambridge, 1984.

[Ter86]   D. Terzopoulos. Regularization of inverse visual problems involving discontinuities. *IEEE Trans. Pattern Analysis and Machine Intelligence*, 8(4):413–424, 1986.

[TH84]   B. Tversky and K. Hemenway. Objects, Parts, and Categories. *Journal of Experimental Psychology: General*, 113(2):169–193, 1984.

[THKS88]   C.E. Thorpe, M. Hebert, T. Kanade, and S.A. Shafer. Vision and Navigation for the Carnegie-Mellon Navlab. *PAMI*, 10(3), 1988.

[Tho79]   J.A. Thorpe. *Elementary topics in differential geometry.* Springer-Verlag, New York, 1979.

[Tho84]   C.E. Thorpe. *The CMU Rover and the FIDO Vision and Navigation System.* PhD thesis, Carnegie-mellon University, 1984.

[TK88]   S. Tanaka and A. C. Kak. A rule-based approach to binocular stereopsis. Technical Report TR-EE-88-33, School of Electrical Engineering, Purdue University, 1988.

[TMGM88]   M.A. Turk, D.G. Morgenthaler, K.D. Gremban, and M. Marra. VITS- A Vision System for Autonomous Land Vehicle Navigation. *PAMI*, 10(3), may 1988.

[TPBF87]   D. Terzopoulos, J. Platt, A. Barr, and K. Fleischer. Elastically deformable models. *Computer Graphics*, 21:205–214, 1987.

[Tsa83]   R. Tsai. Multifram image point matching and 3-D surface reconstruction. *IEEE Trans. Pattern Analysis and Machine Intelligence*, PAMI-5(2):159–173, 1983.

[Tsi87]   G. Tsikos. *Segmentation of 3-D scenes using multi-modal interaction between machine vision and programmable mechanical scene manipulation.* PhD thesis, University of Pennsylvania, 1987.

[Tuk60]   J. W. Tukey. A survey of sampling from contaminated distributions. In I. Olkin, editor, *Contributions to Probability and Statistics.* Stanford University Press, 1960.

[Tuk62]   J. W. Tukey. The future of data analysis. *Annals of Mathematical Statistics*, 33:1–67, 1962.

[VA86]   B. C. Vemuri and J. K. Aggarwal. 3-d model construction from multiple views using range and intensity data. In *Proc.*

IEEE Computer Society Conf. Computer Vision and Pattern Recognition, pages 435–437, Miami Beach, FL, 1986.

[VA87]   B. C. Vemuri and J. K. Aggarwal. Representation and recognition of objects from dense range maps. *IEEE Trans. Circuits and Systems*, CAS-34(11):1351–1363, 1987.

[VA88]   B. Vemuri and J. Aggarwal. Localization of objects from range data. In *Proc. IEEE CVPR-88*, pages 893–898, Ann Arbor, 1988.

[VDA84] B. C. Vemuri, K. R. Diller, and J. K. Aggarwal. A model for characterizing the motion of the solid-liquid interface in freezing solutions. *Pattern Recognition*, 17(3):313–319, 1984.

[VMA86] B. C. Vemuri, A. Mitiche, and J. K. Aggarwal. Curvature-based representation of objects from range data. *Image and Vision Computing*, 4(2):107–114, 1986.

[Wea27] C.E. Weatherburn. *Differential Geometry of three dimensions.* Cambridge Univ. Press, Cambridge, UK, 1927.

[Wil59] T. J. Willmore. *An introduction to differential geometry.* Oxford University Press, Oxford, UK, 1959.

[Win84] P. Winston. *Artificial Intelligence.* Addison Wesley, 1984.

[Wit83] A. P. Witkin. Scale-space filtering. In *Proc. 8th Int. Joint. Conf. Artif. Intell.*, pages 1019–1022, Karlsruhe, West Germany, 1983.

[Wit84] A. P. Witkin. Scale-space filtering: a new approach to multi-scale description. In S. Ullmand and W. Richards, editors, *Image Understanding*. Ablex, Norwood, NJ, 1984.

[WK86]   J.A. Webb and T. Kanade. Vision on a Systolic Array Machine. In L. Uhr, editor, *Evaluation of multicomputers for image processing*. Academic Press, 1986.

[WPZ87] R. Watts, F. Pont, and D. Zuk. Characterization of the ERIM/ALV Sensor - Range and Reflectance. Technical report, Environmental Research Institute of Michigan, Ann Arbor, MI, 1987.

[XT87]   G. Xu and S. Tsuji. Inferring surfaces from boundaries. In *Proc. ICCV-87*, pages 716–720, London, 1987.

[YF86]   T. Y. Young and K. S. Fu. *Handbook of Pattern Recognition and Image Processing.* Academic Press, London, 1986.

[ZH81]   S. W. Zucker and R. M. Hummel. A three-dimensional edge operator. *IEEE Trans. Pattern Analysis and Machine Intelligence*, 3(3):324–331, 1981.

[ZPFL85]   D. Zuk, F. Pont, R. Franklin, and V. Larrowe. A System for Autonomous Land Navigation. Technical Report IR-85-540, Environmental Research Institute of Michigan, Ann Arbor MI, 1985.